Inside Out Outside In

EXPLORING AMERICAN LITERATURE

Victoria Holder
San Francisco State University

Dorothy Lindsay
San Francisco State University

Lyn Motai
San Francisco State University

Deborah vanDommelen
San Francisco State University

Karen Wiederholt
San Francisco State University

D0207146

HOUGHTON MIFFLIN COMPANY   BOSTON   NEW YORK

Director, World Languages: Marketing and ESL Publishing   Susan Maguire
Senior Associate Editor   Kathy Sands Boehmer
Editorial Assistant   Manuel Muñoz
Senior Project Editor   Kathryn Dinovo
Senior Cover Design Coordinator   Deborah Azerrad Savona
Senior Manufacturing Coordinator   Marie Barnes
Marketing Manager   Jay Hu
Marketing Associate   Claudia Martínez

Cover design   Rebecca Fagan
Cover image   Lawrence, Jacob (b. 1917). *The Library,* 1960. National Museum of
             American Art, Smithsonian Institution, Washington, D.C., U.S.A.

Drawings on page 200 by Judith Jacobson

For permission to use copyrighted materials, grateful acknowledgment is made to the
copyright holders listed on pages 331–332, which is hereby considered an extension of this
copyright page.

http://college.hmco.com

Printed in the U.S.A.

Library of Congress Catalog Card Number 00-133917

ISBN-13: 978-0-395-98605-9
ISBN-10: 0-395-98605-2

9-FFG-10 09 08 07

To Helen Hinze-Pocher
and Our Students

Contents

Table of Contents by Literary Elements
Note: all chapters include a section on characterization

STORY/POEM	FIGURATIVE LANGUAGE*	FORE-SHADOWING	IRONY	MOOD	PERSONIFICATION	POINT OF VIEW	SETTING	LANGUAGE/ STYLE†	THEME	TONE
Gaston	•				•	•				
At Home in the World	•							•		
Raymond's Run							•	•		
Bluebirdbluebirdthrumywindow			•			•		•		
Two Kinds									•	
The Waltz	•							•	•	•
Silent Snow, Secret Snow	•					•		•	•	
A Blessing	•			•	•		•			
Aunt Moon's Young Man	•					•	•			
D.P.	•				•	•			•	
Mass of the Moon Eclipse	•							•	•	•
Hills Like White Elephants	•						•	•	•	
On the Road	•		•							
The Local Production of Cinderella	•					•			•	•
One Human Hand	•					•		•		
The Magic Barrel		•				•			•	
Romero's Shirt	•			•		•	•			
Sunday in the Park	•		•							
Black Boy	•						•			
Gravity	•		•							•
The Confounding	•							•	•	

*Includes imagery, simile, metaphor, symbolism and personification.   †Includes language, rhythm, rhyme, line breaks, and/or placement of words on page.

Preface

The guiding philosophy in the development of *Inside Out/Outside In* is that, through literature, students are able to develop skills essential to their academic, professional, and personal success. Through reading and analysis, critical thinking, and analytical writing about a literary text, students develop the ability to see, understand, and appreciate more than one perspective.

The teaching materials for *Inside Out/Outside In* support the literature teacher as a guide, a facilitator who assists students through step-by-step analysis of a literary text. The activities invite interaction and engage students in the story or poem and its language. Because students are encouraged to formulate and support their own interpretations of the readings, they learn that exploring the world inside a literary text can be a rewarding experience.

FEATURES

Inside Out/Outside In is a literary reader with strong comprehension and literary analysis components. The intended audience is all college composition students, both native speakers of English and nonnative speakers. The activities are especially appropriate for students who have had limited experience in analyzing and writing about literature.

Features of *Inside Out/Outside In* include the following:

- Individual, partner, and group activities that engage students in a thorough analysis of a literary work
- Varied writing tasks that encourage students to explore literature, formally and informally, in relation to their own ideas, values, and experience

- Interactive work that teaches advanced language and critical thinking skills and exposes students to new cultural perspectives
- Charts, sketches, diagrams, and role plays that tap into students' different learning styles
- A varied collection of short stories and poems that allows flexibility in sequencing chapters and in choosing themes
- Comprehensive activities that eliminate the need for additional materials

THE STORIES AND POEMS

The stories and poems in *Inside Out/Outside In* represent diverse perspectives on the American experience, with works from established writers such as Ernest Hemingway, contemporary writers such as Toni Cade Bambara, and emerging writers such as Li-Young Lee. Selections lend themselves to several pedagogical goals, such as teaching a specific literary element or showing the universal relevance of a single character's dilemma.

The stories and poems include varied lengths, complexities, moods, subject matters, themes, and genres. Although teachers may find thematic links as they become familiar with the literary texts, the stories and poems have not been organized in a particular sequence and may be taught in whatever order fits a teacher's syllabus. However, the "Suggested Teaching Sequences" on page xvii may give teachers ideas for different ways to organize a course.

Poems appear in separate chapters and are not meant to be taught in conjunction with specific stories. However, teachers may discover that poems and stories often complement each other in content, theme, or style.

HOW TO USE *INSIDE OUT/OUTSIDE IN*

Planning a Syllabus

The chapters may be used in any order. In choosing an order, teachers may want to consider the length and complexity of the story or poem and the order in which they want to introduce different literary elements. Generally, shorter or more accessible pieces—such as "Gaston," "Two Kinds," "Sunday in the Park," or "A Blessing"—work well at the beginning of a course. On the other hand, these selections may also be used toward the end of a course to provide variation in mood or theme, especially after more challenging literary texts, such as "Mass of the Moon Eclipse," "Hills Like White Elephants," or "Silent Snow, Secret Snow." Teachers can refer to the "Table of Contents by Literary Elements" (and the main table of contents) when planning a syllabus.

Organization of the Chapters, with Suggestions for Teaching

Preparation

Prereading activities provide important cultural, historical, or geographical background and help students connect their own knowledge and experience to what they are about to read. Questions are designed to activate schema for reading without leading students to one predetermined interpretation of the story or poem.

Suggestions for Teaching

Some instructors may want to use prereading activities extensively, whereas others may prefer to skip over this step entirely, allowing students to use other reading strategies.

Analyzing the Story or Poem

Activities in this section are designed to move students inductively through different levels of complexity of a story or poem by first establishing essential background, such as the characters, setting, or point of view, and then allowing students to uncover less obvious details from the literary text.

The questions ask that students support their ideas with evidence, including specific line numbers, from the story or poem. The process of finding evidence allows students to interact closely with the literary piece and to gather support for ideas that they can use later when developing responses to writing topics.

Suggestions for Teaching

For all questions, students can work alone or write or discuss answers with partners or in groups. Alternatively, assigning questions for homework often leads to more productive and articulate in-class discussions by allowing more time for students to formulate their ideas.

Elements of Literature

Because different stories and poems lend themselves to the teaching of different literary elements, teachers will find a variation in the number of activities devoted to the literary elements in each chapter. All chapters contain a section on characterization. Beyond that, the reading itself determines the particular literary elements included or the amount of teaching material provided for the exploration of the different elements. Some chapters may include activities on setting, foreshadowing, or point of view, whereas others may focus on irony, tone, or figurative language. Each activity in this section is designed to help students to focus in a systematic way on one literary element and to find and analyze its use in the story or poem.

> ### *Suggestions for Teaching*
>
> Teachers can choose the activities they think will most engage the students and/or enhance their understanding of a literary element and how it works within a reading. Literary terms are presented in boldface type throughout the book and signal that the meaning of the term, with examples of its use, appears in Appendix A, "Literary Terms." (See the description of this section, page xiv.)

Exploring Further

Activities in this section encourage students, through careful critical analysis, to arrive at a deeper understanding of a story or poem, such as figuring out a character's motivation for an action or formulating a more complex interpretation of a theme. The purpose of the "Exploring Further" section is to provide new angles, propose new ideas, or further probe a literary element to help students discover deeper levels of meaning.

> ### *Suggestions for Teaching*
>
> Teachers will find that "Exploring Further" questions cover a range of topics. Like other sections, teachers can select from the list of questions, depending on their teaching goals for that chapter and/or the depth of discussion reached in previous class activities.

Writing in Response

Short, informal writing topics allow students to explore their ideas about the story or poem in an unstructured way, encouraging them to react, make associations, and discover connections. This section appears after many activities throughout the chapters.

> ### *Suggestions for Teaching*
>
> Teachers will find these short writing topics useful for getting students to generate and synthesize ideas and for helping students prepare to respond to longer and more formal essay writing tasks. (See "Essay Topics" described on page xiii.)

Creative Writing

"Creative Writing" topics invite students to explore a story or poem from the perspective of a poet, storyteller, or writer of fiction and to experiment with different styles of writing and/or different elements of literature.

> ### *Suggestions for Teaching*
>
> "Creative Writing" activities can offer new insights into a reading and an enjoyable complement to analysis and discussion. These topics can also give students confidence and practice that provide a foundation for working through Appendix C, "Creative Writing: Writing a Story or Poem." (See description on page xv.)

Essay Topics

These writing topics are for longer academic essays. The topics encourage students to draw on analytical work from different sections of a chapter and to synthesize ideas from class discussion and/or their informal writing. Each topic provides a focus for responding to a story or poem while allowing students to develop their own interpretation of a literary text.

> ### *Suggestions for Teaching*
>
> All activities in a chapter help prepare students for the "Essay Topics." If teachers want to help students further formulate their ideas and opinions about a story or poem, they may use many of the essay topics as a basis for prewriting activities such as discussions, debates, or freewriting. Items in "Essay Topics" are offered as suggestions. Students may also want to develop their own topics in response to the readings. (See the description of "Writing about Literature: A Guide for Students" (on page xiv) for information and ideas for writing about literature.)

Author Profile

These short biographical sketches complement the readings by giving background about the authors' life, education, and literary achievements. The "Author Profile," which appears at the end of the chapter, does not provide information that leads students to one single interpretation of the story or poem.

> ### *Suggestions for Teaching*
>
> Students may find reading the "Author Profile" useful at some point in their work on a story or poem. Because some profiles discuss the style of the writer, reading the profile may be particularly appropriate as a final activity for in-class discussions or preparation for a writing assignment. Students can use the information in the "Author Profile" to make connections between ideas or to generate new ones before they begin a final writing task.

SUPPLEMENTAL SECTIONS

Glossary

Vocabulary words that students may need help understanding are defined in the "Glossary" according to their use in the story or poem. Words that appear in the glossary have not been marked or highlighted in the story or poem so that students are not distracted as they read. Readers will find specific cultural, geographical, or historical terms defined in footnotes with the stories and poems in the chapters.

> ### Suggestions for Teaching
>
> Instructors who work with developmental learners and nonnative speakers of English will find it useful to introduce this glossary at the beginning of a course. Making students aware of this companion reference, with its easily accessible and contextualized definitions, will facilitate students' reading of the stories and poems.

Author Profile Bibliography

A list of sources has been included for reference purposes.

Appendix A: Literary Terms

Literary terms appear in **boldface type** in *Inside Out/Outside In*. This appendix includes definitions of the terms and contextualized examples from the stories and poems. Some chapters contain additional explanation in the teaching materials about a literary term or element as it is used in a specific story or poem.

> ### Suggestions for Teaching
>
> Teachers can use this appendix to augment prereading activities—for example, if they want students to review a literary element introduced in an earlier chapter. Glossary entries can also be assigned for reading homework to prepare students for in-class work, which might include working in pairs or groups to generate examples of the literary element for a particular story or poem.

Appendix B:
Writing about Literature: A Guide for Students

Written for the student, this appendix is a reference that can help students as they annotate and gather evidence, read and interpret literature, and work through the different stages of the writing process. The prewriting section assists students in developing their own topics and responses to a reading. In addition, this appendix offers information on citing, quoting, and paraphrasing with examples using a reading selection, "Gaston," from *Inside Out/Outside In*.

Suggestions for Teaching

The design of this chapter allows teachers to choose only those sections on which they want to focus. Teachers may ask students to read specific sections for homework to prepare them for in-class activities devoted to writing. Instructors may also draw on examples from this chapter as they develop lesson plans for teaching critical reading, writing about literature, or citing sources.

Appendix C:
Creative Writing: Writing a Story or Poem

This appendix offers students the opportunity to write an original poem or story. As preparation for their writing, students first review the stories and poems they have read in the course, looking closely at the use of such literary elements as setting, theme, and point of view. Students then move through activities designed to help them generate ideas, clarify tasks, write, and revise their work.

Suggestions for Teaching

If teachers choose to incorporate this appendix into their syllabi, they will find useful activities for not only helping students discover their own creative processes but also for encouraging students to take a deeper look at the complexities of the readings in *Inside Out/Outside In* from the perspective of the writer as artist or craftsperson. This appendix can help students gain a better understanding of the role literary elements play in a work.

ACKNOWLEDGMENTS

Many people helped us with this book. We are especially grateful to the following for their contributions and support: Nathalie Destandau, Nick Driver, Linda Gajdusek, Judith Jacobson, Laura Jensen, Joe Lindsay, Nina Lindsay, Susan Maguire, Izumi Motai, Manuel Muñoz, Suzanne Munro, Bernadette O'Brien, Patricia Porter, Rudi Richardson, Kathy Sands-Boehmer, Kathleen Smith, David van-Dommelen, and Caio and Senta.

Suggested Teaching Sequences

The stories and poems in each of the following suggested teaching sequences are tied together by a common element. The selections in each sequence were chosen to alternate mood, style, theme, genre, and author while retaining the common element.

WRITING ABOUT ONE'S OWN

8: "A Blessing," 3: "Raymond's Run," 9: "Aunt Moon's Young Man," 15: "One Human Hand," 5: "Two Kinds," 20: "Gravity," 16: "The Magic Barrel," 17: "Romero's Shirt"

WHO WE ARE AND WHO WE WERE:
HOW THE PAST INFLUENCES THE PRESENT

9: "Aunt Moon's Young Man," 5: "Two Kinds," 21: "The Confounding," 4: "Bluebirdbluebirdthrumywindow," 15: "One Human Hand," 8: "A Blessing," 2: "At Home in the World," 17: "Romero's Shirt"

LOVE AND COMMUNICATION

18: "Sunday in the Park," 12: "Hills Like White Elephants," 1: "Gaston," 10: "D.P.," 14: "The Local Production of Cinderella," 5: "Two Kinds," 7: "Silent Snow, Secret Snow"

STRUGGLE TO COMMUNICATE

1: "Gaston," 18: "Sunday in the Park," 5: "Two Kinds," 6: "The Waltz," 12: "Hills Like White Elephants," 11: "Mass of the Moon Eclipse," 7: "Silent Snow, Secret Snow"

ALIENATION

Childhood: 10: "D.P.," 5: "Two Kinds," 3: "Raymond's Run," 7: "Silent Snow, Secret Snow"

Adulthood: 1: "Gaston," 13: "On the Road," 18: "Sunday in the Park," 20: "Gravity," 14: "The Local Production of Cinderella," 9: "Aunt Moon's Young Man," 4: "Bluebirdbluebirdthrumywindow"

FULL CIRCLE (TRAVELING WEST)

3: "Raymond's Run," 20: "Gravity," 8: "A Blessing," 9: "Aunt Moon's Young Man," 17: "Romero's Shirt," 5: "Two Kinds," 14: "The Local Production of Cinderella," 1: "Gaston," 16: "The Magic Barrel"

CHILDREN

1: "Gaston," 9: "Aunt Moon's Young Man," 10: "D.P.," 15: "One Human Hand," 3: "Raymond's Run," 5: "Two Kinds," 20: "Gravity," 19: "Black Boy," 7: "Silent Snow, Secret Snow"

CHRONOLOGICAL ACCORDING TO WHEN THE STORY TAKES PLACE

21: "The Confounding," 19: "Black Boy," 6: "The Waltz," 12: "Hills Like White Elephants," 13: "On the Road," 10: "D.P.," 2: "At Home in the World," 4: "Bluebirdbluebirdthrumywindow," 11: "Mass of the Moon Eclipse"

DREAMS AND DREAMERS

8: "A Blessing," 10: "D.P.," 3: "Raymond's Run," 2: "At Home in the World," 9: "Aunt Moon's Young Man," 17: "Romero's Shirt," 13: "On the Road"

TWO BY TWO

18: "Sunday in the Park" and 6: "The Waltz" (irony); 9: "Aunt Moon's Young Man" and 13: "On the Road" (religion and hypocrisy); 4: "Bluebirdbluebirdthrumywindow" and 11: "Mass of the Moon Eclipse" (bearing witness and absence); 10: "D.P." and 19: "Black Boy" (racism); 16: "The Magic Barrel" and 14: "The Local Production of Cinderella" (alter egos)

OPPOSITES ATTRACT

8: "A Blessing," 6: "The Waltz," 12: "Hills Like White Elephants," 5: "Two Kinds,"
16: "The Magic Barrel," 14: "The Local Production of Cinderella"

RELIGION, MYTH, AND MAGIC

21: "The Confounding," 13: "On the Road," 8: "A Blessing," 17: "Romero's Shirt,"
16: "The Magic Barrel," 11: "Mass of the Moon Eclipse"

CHAPTER 1

Gaston

WILLIAM SAROYAN

PREPARATION

ACTIVITY 1

Do this activity with a partner or in small groups. Work quickly and answer spontaneously.

1. Make a list of specific things that in some way represent you. They could be things you use or see every day or things that you use or see rarely but are very important to you. A friend would recognize you from this list but might also be surprised by some of the items. Here are some examples: sunglasses, the color green, horses, novels, bike, dogs and cats, fountain pens, cell phones.

2. What does it mean to say "ugh" about something? What things do you say "ugh" about?

WRITING IN RESPONSE

Choose one of the items on your list in Activity 1 and write briefly about it. Tell why you chose that item to represent you.

Gaston

WILLIAM SAROYAN

They were to eat peaches, as planned, after her nap, and now she sat across from the man who would have been a total stranger except that he was in fact her father. They had been together again (although she couldn't quite remember when they had been together before) for almost a hundred years now, or was it only since the day before yesterday? Anyhow, they were together again, and he was kind of funny. First, he had the biggest mustache she had ever seen on anybody, although to her it was not a mustache at all; it was a lot of red and brown hair under his nose and around the ends of his mouth. Second, he wore a blue-and-white striped jersey instead of a shirt and tie, and no coat. His arms were covered with the same hair, only it was a little lighter and thinner. He wore blue slacks, but no shoes and socks. He was barefoot, and so was she, of course.

He was at home. She was with him in his home in Paris, if you could call it a home. He was very old, especially for a young man—thirty-six, he had told her; and she was just six, just up from sleep on a very hot afternoon in August.

That morning, on a little walk in the neighborhood, she had seen peaches in a box outside a small store and she had stopped to look at them, so he had bought a kilo.

Now, the peaches were on a large plate on the card table at which they sat.

There were seven of them, but one of them was flawed. It *looked* as good as the others, almost the size of a tennis ball, nice red fading to light green, but where the stem had been there was now a break that went straight down into the heart of the seed.

He placed the biggest and best-looking peach on the small plate in front of the girl, and then took the flawed peach and began to remove the skin. When he had half the skin off the peach he ate that side, neither of them talking, both of them just being there, and not being excited or anything—no plans, that is.

The man held the half-eaten peach in his fingers and looked down into the cavity, into the open seed. The girl looked, too.

While they were looking, two feelers poked out from the cavity. They were attached to a kind of brown knob-head, which followed the feelers, and then two large legs took a strong grip on the edge of the cavity and hoisted some of the rest of whatever it was out of the seed, and stopped there a moment, as if to look around.

The man studied the seed dweller, and so, of course, did the girl.

The creature paused only a fraction of a second, and then continued to come out of the seed, to walk down the eaten side of the peach to wherever it was going.

The girl had never seen anything like it—a whole big thing made out of brown color, a knob-head, feelers, and a great many legs. It was very active, too. Almost businesslike, you might say. The man placed the peach back on the plate. The creature moved off the peach onto the surface of the white plate. There it came to a thoughtful stop.

"Who is it?" the girl said.

"Gaston."

"Where does he live?"

"Well, he *used* to live in this peach seed, but now that the peach has been harvested and sold, and I have eaten half of it, it looks as if he's out of house and home."

"Aren't you going to squash him?"

"No, of course not, why should I?"   50

"He's a bug. He's *ugh*."

"Not at all. He's Gaston the grand boulevardier."°

"Everybody hollers when a bug comes out of an apple, but you don't holler or *anything*."

"Of course not. How would we like it if somebody hollered every time we came out of our house?"

"Why *would* they?"

"Precisely. So why should we holler at Gaston?"

"He's not the same as us."

"Well, not exactly, but he's the same as a lot of other occupants of peach   60
seeds. Now, the poor fellow hasn't got a home, and there he is with all that pure design and handsome form, and nowhere to go."

"Handsome?"

"Gaston is just about the handsomest of his kind I've ever seen."

"What's he saying?"

"Well, he's a little confused. Now, inside that house of his he had everything in order. Bed here, porch there, and so forth."

"Show me."

The man picked up the peach, leaving Gaston entirely alone on the white plate. He removed the peeling and ate the rest of the peach.   70

"Nobody else I know would do that," the girl said. "They'd throw it away."

"I can't imagine why. It's a perfectly good peach."

He opened the seed and placed the two sides not far from Gaston. The girl studied the open halves.

"Is *that* where he lives?"

"It's where he used to live. Gaston is out in the world and on his own now. You can see for yourself how comfortable he was in there. He had everything."

"Now what has he got?"

"Not very much, I'm afraid."

"What's he going to do?"   80

"What are we going to do?"

"Well, we're not going to squash him, that's one thing we're *not* going to do," the girl said.

"What *are* we going to do, then?"

"Put him back?"

"Oh, *that* house is finished."

"Well, he can't live in our house, can he?"

°*grand boulevardier* a sophisticated, sociable Parisian man

"Not happily."

"Can he live in our house *at all?*"

90 "Well, he could *try,* I suppose. Don't you want to eat a peach?"

"Only if it's a peach with somebody in the seed."

"Well, see if you can find a peach that has an opening at the top, because if you can, that'll be a peach in which you're likeliest to find somebody."

The girl examined each of the peaches on the big plate.

"They're all shut," she said.

"Well, eat one, then."

"No. I want the same kind that you ate, with somebody in the seed."

"Well, to tell you the truth, the peach I ate would be considered a bad peach, so of course stores don't like to sell them. I was sold that one by mistake, most

100 likely. And so now Gaston is without a home, and we've got six perfect peaches to eat."

"I don't want a perfect peach. I want a peach with people."

"Well, I'll go out and see if I can find one."

"Where will I go?"

"You'll go with me, unless you'd rather stay. I'll only be five minutes."

"If the phone rings, what shall I say?"

"I don't think it'll ring, but if it does, say hello and see who it is."

"If it's my mother, what shall I say?"

"Tell her I've gone to get you a bad peach, and anything else you want to tell

110 her."

"If she wants me to go back, what shall I say?"

"Say yes if you want to go back."

"Do you want me to?"

"Of course not, but the important thing is what you want, not what I want."

"Why is *that* the important thing?"

"Because I want you to be where you want to be."

"I want to be here."

"I'll be right back."

He put on socks and shoes, and a jacket, and went out. She watched Gaston

120 trying to find out what to do next. Gaston wandered around the plate, but everything seemed wrong and he didn't know what to do or where to go.

The telephone rang and her mother said she was sending the chauffeur to pick her up because there was a little party for somebody's daughter who was also six, and then tomorrow they would fly back to New York.

"Let me speak to your father," she said.

"He's gone to get a peach."

"*One* peach?"

"One with people."

"You haven't been with your father two days and already you *sound* like him."

130 "There *are* peaches with people in them. I know. I saw one of them come out."

"A *bug?*"

"Not a bug. Gaston."

"*Who?*"

"Gaston the grand something."

"Somebody else gets a peach with a bug in it, and throws it away, but not him. He makes up a lot of foolishness about it."

"It's not foolishness."

"All right, all right, don't get angry at me about a horrible peach bug of some kind."   140

"Gaston is right here, just outside his broken house, and I'm not angry at you."

"You'll have a lot of fun at the party."

"OK."

"We'll have fun flying back to New York, too."

"OK."

"Are you glad you saw your father?"

"Of course I am."

"Is he funny?"

"Yes."

"Is he crazy?"   150

"Yes. I mean, no. He just doesn't holler when he sees a bug crawling out of a peach seed or anything. He just looks at it carefully. But it *is* just a bug, isn't it, *really*?"

"That's all it is."

"And we'll *have* to squash it?"

"That's right. I can't wait to see you, darling. These two days have been like two years to me. Good-bye."

The girl watched Gaston on the plate, and she actually didn't like him. He was all *ugh*, as he had been in the first place. He didn't have a home anymore and he was wandering around on the white plate and he was silly and wrong and ridicu-   160 lous and useless and all sorts of other things. She cried a little, but only inside, because long ago she had decided she didn't like crying because if you ever started to cry it seemed as if there was so much to cry about you almost couldn't stop, and she didn't like that at all. The open halves of the peach seed were wrong, too. They were ugly or something. They weren't clean.

The man bought a kilo of peaches but found no flawed peaches among them, so he bought another kilo at another store, and this time his luck was better, and there were *two* that were flawed. He hurried back to his flat and let himself in.

His daughter was in her room, in her best dress.

"My mother phoned," she said, "and she's sending the chauffeur for me be-   170 cause there's another birthday party."

"Another?"

"I mean, there's *always* a lot of them in New York."

"Will the chauffeur bring you back?"

"No. We're flying back to New York tomorrow."

"Oh."

"I liked being in your house."

"I liked having you here."

"Why do you live here?"

180 "This is my home."

"It's nice, but it's a lot different from our home."

"Yes, I suppose it is."

"It's kind of like Gaston's house."

"Where *is* Gaston?"

"I squashed him."

"Really? Why?"

"Everybody squashes bugs and worms."

"Oh. Well. I found you a peach."

"I don't want a peach anymore."

190 "OK."

He got her dressed, and he was packing her stuff when the chauffeur arrived. He went down the three flights of stairs with his daughter and the chauffeur, and in the street he was about to hug the girl when he decided he had better not. They shook hands instead, as if they were strangers.

He watched the huge car drive off, and then he went around the corner where he took his coffee every morning, feeling a little, he thought, like Gaston on the white plate.

ANALYZING THE STORY

ACTIVITY 2

Divide these questions among a few small groups. Each group reports its answers to the class.

1. For each of the three human characters in "Gaston," write a list in the following chart of specific things that represent that character. Base your choices on evidence from the story and give line numbers for each item. An example has been done for you.

FATHER	DAUGHTER	MOTHER
striped jersey (line 9)		

2. Describe the **setting** of the story (see Appendix A for more information about words in boldface type). Give specific details.

3. Describe the physical appearance of the father. How old is the father? How old does he seem to the girl?

4. How old is the girl? What does she do or say that seems typical of a child of that age? How do you imagine the little girl looks? How might the mother look? Why do you think so?

5. Do the girl and father know each other well?

    a. What makes you think so?

    b. How often do they see each other?

    c. How long do you think this current visit is supposed to last?

    d. How long does it actually last?

6. Where is the girl's mother during this visit? Where do the mother and daughter live?

7. Describe what the father and daughter saw when they "looked down into the cavity, into the open seed." (lines 27–28)

8. What is the girl's reaction to Gaston? How does the girl describe the bug and its behavior?

9. What does it mean to say that Gaston is "out of house and home"? (lines 47–48) What things does he no longer have?

10. Before the father goes out to get her more peaches, does the girl want to stay with him? How do you know?

11. Who calls the girl while the father is out? What does the girl talk about? How does this phone call influence the girl's plans?

12. How do the girl's feelings change about Gaston? Why do you think this happens?

WRITING IN RESPONSE

Respond briefly to these questions in writing.

How do you feel after reading "Gaston"? What details of the characters and the story make you feel that way?

Elements of Literature

Point of View

ACTIVITY 3

The **point of view,** or the perspective we see the story through, usually stays the same, but the writer can also change the point of view within the story.

Read the following excerpts from "Gaston" and determine which character's point of view is expressed. Underline the words that tell you whose viewpoint it is.

    Example: The daughter's point of view:

      "They had been together again (<u>although she couldn't quite remember</u> when they had been together before) for almost a hundred years now, or was it only since the day before yesterday?" (lines 3–5)

1. "She was with him in his home in Paris, if you could call it a home." (lines 12–13)
2. "He was very old, especially for a young man—thirty-six, he had told her. . . ." (line 13)
3. "The girl had never seen anything like it. . . ." (line 38)
4. ". . . he was silly and wrong and ridiculous. . . . " (lines 160–161)
5. "'You haven't been with your father two days and already you *sound* like him.'" (line 129)
6. ". . . he was about to hug the girl when he decided he had better not." (lines 193–194)
7. ". . . feeling a little . . . like Gaston on the white plate." (lines 196–197)

WRITING IN RESPONSE

Write briefly on this topic.

Explain why you think the author begins the story with one point of view and shifts to another. What effect does this have?

Characterization

ACTIVITY 4

Divide into three groups, one for each character. Then do the following:

1. Study the lines (in the charts that follow) that are said by, to, or about your character.
2. Answer these questions:
   a. What specifically does each quotation show about the character?
   b. What do the quotations taken together tell you about the character?
   c. How would you describe this character's manner, attitude, and feelings?
3. Next, find two more quotations from the story to support your conclusions about the character.

Father

LINES	QUOTATION
43–44	"'Who is it?' the girl said." "'Gaston.'"
61–62	"'Now, the poor fellow hasn't got a home, and there he is with all that pure design and handsome form, and nowhere to go.'"
103	"'Well, I'll go out and see if I can find one.'"
114	"'Of course not, but the important thing is what you want, not what I want.'"
166–167	"The man bought a kilo of peaches but found no flawed peaches among them, so be bought another kilo at another store . . . "
189–190	"'I don't want a peach anymore.'" "'OK.'"
193–194	". . . he was about to hug the girl when he decided he had better not."

Mother

LINES	QUOTATION
122–123	"The telephone rang and the mother said she was sending the chauffeur to pick her up because there was a little party . . . "
129	"'You haven't been with your father two days, and already you sound like him.'"
139–140	"'All right, all right, don't get angry with me about a horrible peach bug of some kind.'"
156–157	"'I can't wait to see you, darling. These two days have been like two years to me.'"

Daughter

LINES	QUOTATION
71	"'Nobody else I know would do that,' the girl said. 'They'd throw it away.'"
82	"'Well, we're not going to squash him, that's one thing we're *not* going to do.'"
91	"'Only if it's a peach with somebody in the seed.'"
138	"'It's not foolishness.'"
151	"'Yes. I mean, no.'"
179	"'Why do you live here?'"

WRITING IN RESPONSE

Respond briefly to these questions in writing. Compare your responses with those of two or three classmates.

How are the characters like each other? How are they different? Do any characters change in the story?

Figurative Language

Simile

ACTIVITY 5

Some of Saroyan's descriptions of Gaston could also be applied to the father. In this **simile** at the end of the story, Saroyan compares the father and the bug directly: The father was "feeling a little . . . like Gaston on the white plate." (lines 196–197) To understand what this simile means, we have to analyze other parts of the story.

Complete this chart with your ideas about how the father might be like Gaston. Then discuss the comparisons. The first one has been done for you.

GASTON	HOW IS THE FATHER SIMILAR?
1. "'. . . he *used* to live in this peach seed, but now . . . it looks as if he's out of house and home.'" (lines 46–48)	*He used to make his home with his family, but he no longer has a family and is alone.*
2. "'He's not the same as us.'" (line 59)	
3. "'Well, he's a little confused.'" (line 66)	
4. "'Now, inside that house of his he had everything in order.'" (lines 66–67)	
5. "'Gaston is out in the world and on his own now.'" (line 76)	
6. "Gaston wandered around the plate, but everything seemed wrong and he didn't know what to do or where to go." (lines 120–121)	

7. "'. . . he was silly and wrong and ridiculous and useless . . . '" (lines 160–161)	
8. "[The father's house is] kind of like Gaston's house." (line 183)	
9. ". . . feeling a little . . . like Gaston on the white plate." (lines 196–197)	

Exploring Further

An important element in understanding a story is context, or the place and time of the story, as well as information we learn from what precedes or follows a particular event, conversation, gesture, or other detail. Context can give us further insight into the characters and their motivations.

In answering the following questions about the characters in "Gaston," consider the contexts of the passages indicated.

1. Lines 109–118: In these lines the father reveals a lot about his attitudes and values about life and relationships. Describe what you think these are.

2. Lines 158–165: What does this passage tell us about the girl's experience and feelings? What do you think she cried about before? How does the girl's description of the "open halves of the peach seed" relate to her life?

3. Lines 177–187: What is the daughter trying to communicate to her father in this dialogue?

4. Line 194: What is significant about the fact that the father and daughter "shook hands instead, as if they were strangers"? What does this act tell us about their relationship?

WRITING IN RESPONSE

Respond briefly to these questions in writing.

1. Later in her life, what do you think the girl will remember about this visit with her father? What has she learned from her experience with Gaston and the peach?

2. In this story, Saroyan gives the bug a name but not the people. Why do you think he made these choices?

3. The father does not hug the girl at the end of the story. Write about why you think this is significant. What does it tell you about the father and daughter's relationship?

ESSAY TOPICS

1. Choose one of the three characters from "Gaston" and write an essay in which you describe what kind of person that character is. Consider the following:
   - Physical descriptions
   - Examples of thoughts, opinions, and perceptions of the character
   - Dialogue between the characters
   - Reference to the material things that are associated with the character

2. On one level, "Gaston" is a simple and sometimes humorous story about three characters with no names and a bug named Gaston. On a deeper level, the story presents a picture of a father and daughter who attempt to love and understand each other after a long separation and ultimately fail.

   Write an essay, using references from the text, to explain why the father's and daughter's attempts at love and understanding do not seem to succeed. Be sure to consider the following:
   - Characterizations of the father and daughter
   - The father's apparent beliefs and values
   - The daughter's habits and attitudes

3. At the end of the story, the father goes "around the corner where he took his coffee every morning." He feels a little "like Gaston on the white plate." (lines 195–197) Write an essay in which you discuss how the father and Gaston are alike.

4. One theme of "Gaston" is individuality and how this is perceived by others. Write a two-part essay in which you examine this theme.

   Part 1: Consider the father and how he is unique and different in the eyes of the daughter and the mother.

   a. Does his individual style cause the mother to perceive him negatively or positively?
   b. How does the mother's attitude about the father affect the daughter's perception of him?
   c. How does the girl perceive her father?

   Part 2: Consider yourself and your own circumstances.

   a. What effect does your individual style have on the way you are perceived by family and friends?
   b. Is it positive or negative, and why?

   Be sure to connect your own experience in some way with the story "Gaston."

William Saroyan

William Saroyan (1908–1981) was born in Fresno, California, the son of Armenian immigrants. Coming from a relatively poor background, with only limited education, Saroyan went on to write short stories, plays, novels, and autobiographical pieces.

Saroyan published eight volumes of short stories from 1934 to 1939. He has said that he wrote about 100 stories a year during that period. His stories have been described as portraying a fragile and unstable universe full of strange, lonely, confused, and gentle people. In his short stories and most notably in his novels, Saroyan also explored his troubled marriage and his concern with his role as a father.

He was profoundly influenced by aspects of his Armenian heritage, specifically the Turkish massacres of 1894, which left many Armenians homeless and forced to flee to other countries. Besides being symbolically homeless, Saroyan was literally homeless from the age of three, when he was placed in an orphanage by his poverty-stricken mother. The alienation, rootlessness, and melancholy that characterize much of his work can be traced to these early experiences. At the same time, his writings reflect his impulse toward joy and self-realization.

Saroyan received the Pulitzer Prize for literature in 1940 but refused it, saying that he did not believe in literary prizes.

CHAPTER 2

At Home in the World

ROSEMARY CATACALOS

PREPARATION

ACTIVITY 1

Discuss these questions in groups. Be prepared to summarize your discussion for the class.

1. What are the similarities and differences between dreams you have when you're asleep and dreams you have when you're awake? Do either of these kinds of dreams have poetic qualities? If so, which kind of dream? How are they similar?

2. Do you remember your dreams? If so, tell your group a sleep dream that you have had. Ask each person in the group to tell what she or he thinks the dream might reveal about you—your fears, your hopes, your relationships. What did you discover?

3. If we examine our dreams for clues about our inner selves, how might that be similar to examining and interpreting poetry? How might it be different?

At Home in the World
for Beverly Lowry
1988

ROSEMARY CATACALOS

The dream is of something coming. Growing
as the heart does in love, inevitably
bent on its own motion, a sunflower turning
a ripe face toward its source.
The dream is of something possible and regular,   5
the silence of an old man husking pinenuts
in a whitewashed courtyard at sunset, the fading
light: memory become dream again.

The dream is pure necessity. For what
are the givens if not that we give everything,   10
whatever it takes? There are bombs
in innocent places. Old friends grow tired
and want to die. The night-blooming
cereus° is doused in its one moment
of fire. A storm carries away   15
trucks full of children mouthing questions.
It can strike anywhere, this life.

Which is why we are hard on its heels, saying
always, *If these things are true, then so
is the dream.* Why we hold the dream out   20
like some mismatched gift, but a gift
even so. For a grandmother who remembers
its name, for a little boy straining
on tiptoe to see into a snow-filled park.

ANALYZING THE POEM

ACTIVITY 2

Answer the following questions. Give evidence from the poem to support your
answers, where appropriate, and include line numbers for each piece of evidence.

1. Rewrite the following lines in your own words. Describe what is happening,
   literally.

   a. "the silence of an old man husking pinenuts/in a whitewashed court-
      yard . . ." (lines 6–7)
   b. "Growing/as the heart does in love . . ." (lines 1–2)
   c. ". . . a sunflower turning/a ripe face toward its source." (lines 3–4)

°*cereus* a kind of cactus that blooms at night

2. What is the memory the **narrator** (see Appendix A for more information about terms in boldface type) is referring to in "memory become dream again"? (line 8) How does a memory become a dream?

3. In the first stanza of the poem, the narrator answers the question "What is the dream?" What is the narrator's answer?

4. In the second stanza, the narrator refers to "the givens," things that are assumed or taken for granted. Explain what is meant by "the givens" in lines 10–11.

5. What are the four examples in the second stanza, and what do they have in common?

6. What does "it" refer to in line 17? Why does the poet use the word *strike*? How does the word *strike* relate to the four examples in this stanza?

7. In the second stanza and the beginning of the third, the narrator answers the question "Why do we need the dream?" What is the narrator's answer?

8. The third stanza begins with "Which is why we are hard on its heels . . ." (line 18) What does it mean to be hard on the heels of something? What does "its" refer to in this line?

9. What does "these" refer to in line 19?

10. In the third stanza, the narrator answers the question "What do we do with the dream?" What is the narrator's answer?

11. The poem "At Home in the World" is not a narrative poem in which a story is told. Explain what the poem does instead of telling a story.

12. Is this poem more abstract or more concrete? Explain.

WRITING IN RESPONSE

Respond briefly to these questions in writing.

1. What do you like about this poem? Consider the language and style as well as the content.

2. What do you find in the poem that is related to or connected to your life or your dreams?

Elements of Literature

Language and Style

ACTIVITY 3

In each stanza, the poet repeats certain words, phrases, or grammatical structures. Work in groups to analyze the poet's use of repetition.

1. Choose one of the three stanzas and do the following:
   a. List all the repeated words, phrases, and grammatical structures.
   b. Discuss the effect of these repetitions on the reader. In what other kinds of writing or speaking do we often find repetition? Is the effect similar or different?
   c. Present your findings to your classmates.

2. Reread the poem aloud. Why might the poet be using repetition throughout the poem?

Figurative Language

Metaphor

ACTIVITY 4

Catacalos uses **metaphors** in "At Home in the World," comparing the dream to many things.

With a partner or in small groups, answer these questions about the figures of speech in the poem.

1. What do we discover about the dream, which the **narrator** describes, from the images listed in the chart? For each image, write the qualities associated with it and how these qualities could be connected to the dream. The first one has been done for you.

IMAGE	CONNECTION TO THE DREAM
a. "something coming" (line 1)	*Something in the future; something positive and hopeful; a possibility. Dreams are often about positive things in the future.*
b. "Growing/as the heart does in love" (lines 1–2)	
c. "inevitably/bent on its own motion" (lines 2–3)	
d. "a sunflower turning/a ripe face toward its source" (lines 3–4)	
e. "something possible and regular" (line 5)	

2. In the third stanza, the narrator compares the dream to a "mismatched gift." (line 21) Think of several examples of mismatched gifts. Why might someone give a gift that is mismatched? What possible connections are there between the dream and a mismatched gift?

Exploring Further

Write or discuss the answers to these questions. Give evidence from the poem to support your answers and include line numbers for each piece of evidence.

1. Is Catacalos writing about a sleep dream, a daydream, both, or neither? Explain.

2. What does it mean to be "at home" somewhere? What is the meaning of the title, and how does it connect to the poem?

3. The poem has strong imagery, both negative and positive. How do these opposites work together? What effect does this have on the reader?

4. Why do you think the narrator uses "we" in lines 10, 18, and 20? Who does the narrator include?

5. *"If these things are true, then so/is the dream."* (lines 19–20) Why is this sentence italicized?

6. What associations do you make with a grandmother remembering the name of something? (lines 22–23) To what does "its" refer? (line 23)

7. Why does a little boy strain "on tiptoe" to see something? (lines 23–24)

8. What is the connection between "the gift" of the dream and the pairing of the two images in the last three lines of the poem?

9. Catacalos could have written a poem in which she describes her own dream. Why do you think she chose, instead, to use figurative language and a series of images to make her point about the dream?

CREATIVE WRITING

Write a poem that incorporates a few key, partial lines (listed below) from "At Home in the World." Connect the ways you finish the lines with each other, as Catacalos does. Give your poem a title.

The dream is of something . . .
The dream is of something . . .
The dream is . . .
Which is why . . .

If you want, share your poem with the class. Do your readers see the connections you made?

ESSAY TOPICS

1. In "At Home in the World," Catacalos both defines the dream and gives reasons that we need it. How does she do this and why?

2. Why does the author choose "At Home in the World" as a title for this poem?

AUTHOR PROFILE

Rosemary Catacalos

Of Mexican and Greek ancestry, Rosemary Catacalos was born in San Antonio, Texas, and has worked and taught primarily in the southwestern and western United States. In addition to working as a newspaper reporter and columnist, she has been active in many aspects of the field of poetry. She has written two books of poems, *As Long as It Takes* and *Again for the First Time,* and has received a variety of prizes and fellowships. She worked with poets-in-school projects for more than ten years. Catacalos has been involved in grant review and policy development panels for the National Endowment for the Arts. From 1991 to 1996, she was executive director of the Poetry Center and American Poetry Archives at San Francisco State University. Catacalos now holds a position as an affiliated scholar of the Stanford Institute for Research on Women and Gender and is at work on a new collection of poems and a memoir.

CHAPTER 3

Raymond's Run

TONI CADE BAMBARA

PREPARATION

ACTIVITY 1

With a partner or in small groups, discuss the following questions and do the activities.

1. What are some responsibilities in the home or community that you or people you know had as children?
   a. Which responsibilities were more difficult than others? Why?
   b. What are the short- and long-term effects of giving children serious responsibilities?

2. What do you feel may be some differences between the expectations people have about the personalities and behavior of boys versus those of girls?

3. Read the first paragraph of the story.
   a. How old do you think the **narrator** (see Appendix A for more information on terms in boldface type) "I" is?
   b. Do you think "I" is a girl or boy?
   c. Why do you think "I" has to "mind" his or her brother?
   d. What might the narrator mean by "which is enough" at the end of the paragraph?

Raymond's Run

TONI CADE BAMBARA

I don't have much work to do around the house like some girls. My mother does that. And I don't have to earn my pocket money by hustling; George runs errands for the big boys and sells Christmas cards. And anything else that's got to get done, my father does. All I have to do in life is mind my brother Raymond, which is enough.

Sometimes I slip and say my little brother Raymond. But as any fool can see he's much bigger and he's older too. But a lot of people call him my little brother cause he needs looking after cause he's not quite right. And a lot of smart mouths got lots to say about that too, especially when George was minding him. But now, if anybody has anything to say to Raymond, anything to say   10
about his big head, they have to come by me. And I don't play the dozens° or believe in standing around with somebody in my face doing a lot of talking. I much rather just knock you down and take my chances even if I am a little girl with skinny arms and a squeaky voice, which is how I got the name Squeaky. And if things get too rough, I run. And as anybody can tell you, I'm the fastest thing on two feet.

There is no track meet that I don't win the first place medal. I used to win the twenty-yard dash when I was a little kid in kindergarten. Nowadays, it's the fifty-yard dash. And tomorrow I'm subject to run the quarter-meter relay all by myself and come in first, second, and third. The big kids call me Mercury cause   20
I'm the swiftest thing in the neighborhood. Everybody knows that—except two people who know better, my father and me. He can beat me to Amsterdam Avenue with me having a two fire-hydrant headstart and him running with his hands in his pockets and whistling. But that's private information. Cause can you imagine some thirty-five-year-old man stuffing himself into PAL shorts° to race little kids? So far as everyone's concerned, I'm the fastest and that goes for Gretchen, too, who has put out the tale that she is going to win the first-place medal this year. Ridiculous. In the second place, she's got short legs. In the third place, she's got freckles. In the first place, no one can beat me and that's all there is to it.   30

I'm standing on the corner admiring the weather and about to take a stroll down Broadway so I can practice my breathing exercises, and I've got Raymond walking on the inside close to the buildings, cause he's subject to fits of fantasy and starts thinking he's a circus performer and that the curb is a tightrope strung high in the air. And sometimes after a rain he likes to step down off his tightrope right into the gutter and slosh around getting his shoes and cuffs wet. Then I get hit when I get home. Or sometimes if you don't watch him he'll dash across traffic to the island in the middle of Broadway and give the pigeons a fit.

°*play the dozens* from African-American oral tradition, a verbal game of power that children play; includes references to "your mama," and "someone's mother"

°*PAL shorts* athletic shorts with the logo for the "Police Athletic League," a youth organization sponsored by the police department

Then I have to go behind him apologizing to all the old people sitting around
trying to get some sun and getting all upset with the pigeons fluttering around
them, scattering their newspapers and upsetting the waxpaper lunches in their
laps. So I keep Raymond on the inside of me, and he plays like he's driving a
stage coach which is O.K. by me so long as he doesn't run me over or interrupt
my breathing exercises, which I have to do on account of I'm serious about my
running, and I don't care who knows it.

Now some people like to act like things come easy to them, won't let on
that they practice. Not me. I'll high-prance down 34th Street like a rodeo pony
to keep my knees strong even if it does get my mother uptight so that she
walks ahead like she's not with me, don't know me, is all by herself on a shopping trip, and I am somebody else's crazy child. Now you take Cynthia Procter
for instance. She's just the opposite. If there's a test tomorrow, she'll say something like, "Oh, I guess I'll play handball this afternoon and watch television
tonight," just to let you know she ain't thinking about the test. Or like last week
when she won the spelling bee for the millionth time, "A good thing you got
'receive,' Squeaky, cause I would have got it wrong. I completely forgot about
the spelling bee." And she'll clutch the lace on her blouse like it was a narrow
escape. Oh, brother. But of course when I pass her house on my early morning
trots around the block, she is practicing the scales on the piano over and over
and over and over. Then in music class she always lets herself get bumped
around so she falls accidently on purpose onto the piano stool and is so surprised to find herself sitting there that she decides just for fun to try out the ole
keys. And what do you know—Chopin's waltzes just spring out of her fingertips
and she's the most surprised thing in the world. A regular prodigy. I could kill
people like that. I stay up all night studying the words for the spelling bee. And
you can see me any time of day practicing running. I never walk if I can trot,
and shame on Raymond if he can't keep up. But of course he does, cause if he
hangs back someone's liable to walk up to him and get smart, or take his
allowance from him, or ask him where he got that great big pumpkin head.
People are so stupid sometimes.

So I'm strolling down Broadway breathing out and breathing in on counts of
seven, which is my lucky number, and here comes Gretchen and her sidekicks:
Mary Louise, who used to be a friend of mine when she first moved to Harlem
from Baltimore and got beat up by everybody till I took up for her on account of
her mother and my mother used to sing in the same choir when they were
young girls, but people ain't grateful, so now she hangs out with the new girl
Gretchen and talks about me like a dog; and Rosie, who is as fat as I am skinny
and has a big mouth where Raymond is concerned and is too stupid to know
that there is not a big deal of difference between herself and Raymond and that
she can't afford to throw stones. So they are steady coming up Broadway and I
see right away that it's going to be one of those Dodge City scenes° cause the
street ain't that big and they're close to the buildings just as we are. First I think

°*Dodge City scene* a hostile confrontation on the street; the reference is to a famous cowboy
shootout in a Kansas town in western movies

I'll step into the candy store and look over the new comics and let them pass.
But that's chicken and I've got a reputation to consider. So then I think I'll just
walk straight on through them or even over them if necessary. But as they get to
me, they slow down. I'm ready to fight, cause like I said I don't feature a whole
lot of chit-chat, I much prefer to just knock you down right from the jump and
save everybody a lotta precious time.

"You signing up for the May Day races?" smiles Mary Louise, only it's not a
smile at all. A dumb question like that doesn't deserve an answer. Besides, there's
just me and Gretchen standing there really, so no use wasting my breath talking
to shadows.   90

"I don't think you're going to win this time," says Rosie, trying to signify with
her hands on her hips all salty, completely forgetting that I have whupped her
behind many times for less salt than that.

"I always win cause I'm the best," I say straight at Gretchen who is, as far as
I'm concerned, the only one talking in this ventriloquist–dummy routine.
Gretchen smiles, but it's not a smile, and I'm thinking that girls never really smile
at each other because they don't know how and don't want to know how and
there's probably no one to teach us how, cause grown-up girls don't know either. Then they all look at Raymond who has just brought his mule team to a
standstill. And they're about to see what trouble they can get into through him.   100

"What grade you in now, Raymond?"

"You got anything to say to my brother, you say it to me, Mary Louise Williams
of Raggedy Town, Baltimore."

"What are you, his mother?" sasses Rosie.

"That's right, Fatso. And the next word out of anybody and I'll be *their*
mother too." So they just stand there and Gretchen shifts from one leg to the
other and so do they. Then Gretchen puts her hands on her hips and is about to
say something with her freckle-face self but doesn't. Then she walks around me
looking me up and down but keeps walking up Broadway, and her sidekicks follow her. So me and Raymond smile at each other and he says, "Gidyap" to his   110
team and I continue with my breathing exercises, strolling down Broadway toward the ice man on 145th with not a care in the world cause I am Miss Quicksilver herself.

I take my time getting to the park on May Day because the track meet is the
last thing on the program. The biggest thing on the program is the May Pole
dancing, which I can do without, thank you, even if my mother thinks it's a
shame I don't take part and act like a girl for a change. You'd think my mother'd
be grateful not to have to make me a white organdy dress with a big satin sash
and buy me new white baby-doll shoes that can't be taken out of the box till the
big day. You'd think she'd be glad her daughter ain't out there prancing around a   120
May Pole getting the new clothes all dirty and sweaty and trying to act like a
fairy or a flower or whatever you're supposed to be when you should be trying
to be yourself, whatever that is, which is, as far as I am concerned, a poor Black
girl who really can't afford to buy shoes and a new dress you only wear once a
lifetime cause it won't fit next year.

I was once a strawberry in a Hansel and Gretel pageant when I was in nursery school and didn't have no better sense than to dance on tiptoe with my arms in a circle over my head doing umbrella steps° and being a perfect fool just
130   so my mother and father could come dressed up and clap. You'd think they'd know better than to encourage that kind of nonsense. I am not a strawberry. I do not dance on my toes. I run. That is what I am all about. So I always come late to the May Day program, just in time to get my number pinned on and lay in the grass till they announce the fifty-yard dash.

I put Raymond in the little swings, which is a tight squeeze this year and will be impossible next year. Then I look around for Mr. Pearson, who pins the numbers on. I'm really looking for Gretchen if you want to know the truth, but she's not around. The park is jam-packed. Parents in hats and corsages and breast-pocket handkerchiefs peeking up. Kids in white dresses and light-blue suits. The
140   parkees unfolding chairs and chasing the rowdy kids from Lenox as if they had no right to be there. The big guys with their caps on backwards, leaning against the fence swirling the basketballs on the tips of their fingers, waiting for all these crazy people to clear out the park so they can play. Most of the kids in my class are carrying bass drums and glockenspiels and flutes. You'd think they'd put in a few bongos or something for real like that.

Then here comes Mr. Pearson with his clipboard and his cards and pencils and whistles and safety pins and fifty million other things he's always dropping all over the place with his clumsy self. He sticks out in a crowd because he's on stilts. We used to call him Jack and the Beanstalk to get him mad. But I'm the only one that
150   can outrun him and get away, and I'm too grown for that silliness now.

"Well, Squeaky," he says, checking my name off the list and handing me number seven and two pins. And I'm thinking he's got no right to call me Squeaky, if I can't call him Beanstalk.

"Hazel Elizabeth Deborah Parker," I correct him and tell him to write it down on his board.

"Well, Hazel Elizabeth Deborah Parker, going to give someone else a break this year?" I squint at him real hard to see if he is seriously thinking I should lose the race on purpose just to give someone else a break. "Only six girls running this time," he continues, shaking his head sadly like it's my fault all of New York didn't
160   turn out in sneakers. "That new girl should give you a run for your money." He looks around the park for Gretchen like a periscope in a submarine movie. "Wouldn't it be a nice gesture if you were . . . to ahhh . . ."

I give him such a look he couldn't finish putting that idea into words. Grownups got a lot of nerve sometimes. I pin number seven to myself and stomp away, I'm so burnt. And I go straight for the track and stretch out on the grass while the band winds up with "Oh, the Monkey Wrapped His Tail Around the Flag Pole," which my teacher calls by some other name. The man on the loudspeaker is calling everyone over to the track and I'm on my back looking at the sky, trying to pretend I'm in the country, but I can't, because even grass in the

---

°*umbrella steps* special way of stepping, used in children's games; arms are outstretched and child turns 360 degrees to form an umbrella-like shape in the air

city feels hard as sidewalk, and there's just no pretending you are anywhere but in a "concrete jungle" as my grandfather says.   170

The twenty-yard dash takes all of two minutes cause most of the little kids don't know no better than to run off the track or run the wrong way or run smack into the fence and fall down and cry. One little kid, though, has got the good sense to run straight for the white ribbon up ahead so he wins. Then the second-graders line up for the thirty-yard dash and I don't even bother to turn my head to watch cause Raphael Perez always wins. He wins before he even begins by psyching the runners, telling them they're going to trip on their shoelaces and fall on their faces or lose their shorts or something, which he doesn't really have to do since he is very fast, almost as fast as I am. After that is the forty-yard dash which I use to run when I was in the first grade. Raymond is hollering from the swings cause he   180 knows I'm about to do my thing cause the man on the loudspeaker has just announced the fifty-yard dash, although he might just as well be giving a recipe for angel food cake cause you can hardly make out what he's sayin for the static. I get up and slip off my sweat pants and then I see Gretchen standing at the starting line, kicking her legs out like a pro. Then as I get into place I see that ole Raymond is on line on the other side of the fence, bending down with his fingers on the ground just like he knew what he was doing. I was going to yell at him but then I didn't. It burns up your energy to holler.

Every time, just before I take off in a race, I always feel like I'm in a dream, the kind of dream you have when you're sick with fever and feel all hot and weight-   190 less. I dream I'm flying over a sandy beach in the early morning sun, kissing the leaves of the trees as I fly by. And there's always the smell of apples, just like in the country when I was little and used to think I was a choo-choo train, running through the fields of corn and chugging up the hill to the orchard. And all the time I'm dreaming this, I get lighter and lighter until I'm flying over the beach again, getting blown through the sky like a feather that weighs nothing at all. But once I spread my fingers in the dirt and crouch over the Get on Your Mark, the dream goes and I am solid again and am telling myself, Squeaky you must win, you must win, you are the fastest thing in the world, you can even beat your fa-ther up Amsterdam if you really try. And then I feel my weight coming back just   200 behind my knees then down to my feet then into the earth and the pistol shot explodes in my blood and I am off and weightless again, flying past the other runners, my arms pumping up and down and the whole world is quiet except for the crunch as I zoom over the gravel in the track. I glance to my left and there is no one. To the right, a blurred Gretchen, who's got her chin jutting out as if it would win the race all by itself. And on the other side of the fence is Ray-mond with his arms down to his side and the palms tucked up behind him, run-ning in his very own style, and it's the first time I ever saw that and I almost stop to watch my brother Raymond on his first run. But the white ribbon is bouncing toward me and I tear past it, racing into the distance till my feet with a mind of   210 their own start digging up footfuls of dirt and brake me short. Then all the kids standing on the side pile on me, banging me on the back and slapping my head with their May Day programs, for I have won again and everybody on 151st Street can walk tall for another year.

"In first place . . ." the man on the loudspeaker is clear as a bell now. But then he pauses and the loudspeaker starts to whine. Then static. And I lean down to catch my breath and here comes Gretchen walking back, for she's overshot the finish line too, huffing and puffing with her hands on her hips taking it slow, breathing in steady time like a real pro and I sort of like her a little for the first

220   time. "In first place . . ." and then three or four voices get all mixed up on the loudspeaker and I dig my sneaker into the grass and stare at Gretchen who's staring back, we both wondering just who did win. I can hear old Beanstalk arguing with the man on the loudspeaker and then a few others running their mouths about what the stopwatches say. Then I hear Raymond yanking at the fence to call me and I wave to shush him, but he keeps rattling the fence like a gorilla in a cage like in them gorilla movies, but then like a dancer or something he starts climbing up nice and easy but very fast. And it occurs to me, watching how smoothly he climbs hand over hand and remembering how he looked running with his arms down to his side and with the wind pulling his mouth back and

230   his teeth showing and all, it occurred to me that Raymond would make a very fine runner. Doesn't he always keep up with me on my trots? And he surely knows how to breathe in counts of seven cause he's always doing it at the dinner table, which drives my brother George up the wall. And I'm smiling to beat the band cause if I've lost this race, or if me and Gretchen tied, or even if I've won, I can always retire as a runner and begin a whole new career as a coach with Raymond as my champion. After all, with a little more study I can beat Cynthia and her phony self at the spelling bee. And if I bugged my mother, I could get piano lessons and become a star. And I have a big rep as the baddest thing around. And I've got a roomful of ribbons and medals and awards. But what has

240   Raymond got to call his own?

So I stand there with my new plans, laughing out loud by this time as Raymond jumps down from the fence and runs over with his teeth showing and his arms down to the side, which no one before him has quite mastered as a running style. And by the time he comes over I'm jumping up and down so glad to see him—my brother Raymond, a great runner in the family tradition. But of course everyone thinks I'm jumping up and down because the men on the loudspeaker have finally gotten themselves together and compared notes and are announcing "In first place—Miss Hazel Elizabeth Deborah Parker." (Dig that.) "In second place—Miss Gretchen P. Lewis." And I look over at Gretchen wondering

250   what the "P" stands for. And I smile. Cause she's good, no doubt about it. Maybe she'd like to help me coach Raymond; she obviously is serious about running, as any fool can see. And she nods to congratulate me and then she smiles. And I smile. We stand there with this big smile of respect between us. It's about as real a smile as girls can do for each other, considering we don't practice real smiling every day, you know, cause maybe we too busy being flowers or fairies or strawberries instead of something honest and worthy of respect . . . you know . . . like being people.

ANALYZING THE STORY

ACTIVITY 2

Answer the following questions. Give evidence from the story to support your answers and include line numbers for each piece of evidence.

1. Who is the narrator? Why is she called Squeaky? How old is she?
2. Squeaky lives in a section of Manhattan called Harlem. What do you know about this neighborhood?
3. What is "not quite right" (line 8) about Raymond?
4. How old do you think George and Raymond are? How do you know?
5. Who is the fastest runner in the neighborhood, and why is it a secret?
6. With whom does Squeaky go most places? With whom does Gretchen go most places? How might this difference affect Squeaky's feelings and behavior toward other children?
7. What does Squeaky think of Maypole dancing? Why?
8. Why are only six girls running in Squeaky's race this year?
9. Why does Squeaky jump up and down at the end of the race?
10. What kind of smiling goes on after the race is over? Why is this important for Squeaky?

ACTIVITY 3

Match the information on the left with the character(s) on the right. For some items, you will need to infer information from the story. Letter "a" has been done for you.

a. Studies and practices hard but won't admit it	___ Mary Louise
b. A gorilla and a dancer in the same sentence	___ Squeaky
c. Typically concentrate more on being decorative than accomplished	___ Gretchen
d. Betrayed a protective friend	___ Raymond
e. Has been beaten up by Squeaky	___ girls
f. Lived in the country	___ mother
g. Likes to be called by her real name, not her nickname	___ Rosie
h. Feel proud of Squeaky for the honor she brings them	_a_ Cynthia
i. Is embarrassed to walk down 34th Street with her own daughter	___ baby Squeaky
j. Might be able to beat Squeaky in a race	___ people on 151st St.

A C T I V I T Y   4

The following questions are in three sections. Divide the class into three groups, one for each section, and answer the questions.

1. Brainstorm a few possible answers to these questions.
    a. What might be some examples of "hustling"? (line 2)
    b. What kinds of things do you think the "smart mouths" said to Raymond? (line 9)
    c. Based on what happens immediately afterward, what could some of Raymond's "fits of fantasy" (line 33) be?
    d. What kind of circus tricks might Raymond do on his "tightrope"? (line 34)

2. Prepare an explanation for each of the following actions.
    a. Raymond "brought his mule team to a standstill." (lines 99–100) What was he doing?
    b. Squeaky "squints" at Mr. Pearson as an answer to his question about letting someone else win the race. (line 157) What does her "squint" mean?
    c. What is the "nice gesture" that Mr. Pearson wants from Squeaky? (line 162)
    d. "Grownups got a lot of nerve. . . . I . . . stomp away. . . . " (lines 164–165) What is Squeaky's point?

3. Discuss answers to the following questions.
    a. Raymond's breathing "drives . . . George up the wall." (line 233) How does George feel about Raymond's breathing? What else do you know about George and Raymond together?
    b. "I'm smiling to beat the band." (lines 233–234) Why is Squeaky so happy? What does it tell us about her feelings toward Raymond?
    c. Squeaky's father gives her a "two fire-hydrant headstart." (line 23) How far do you think that is? How does her father seem to feel about her running? How does this compare with her mother's apparent feelings?

Elements of Literature

Characterization

A C T I V I T Y   5

Identify the characters to whom the following nicknames and expressions refer. Then answer the questions that follow.

Squeaky _____   *periscope* _____

Mercury _____   *Miss Quicksilver* _____

pumpkin head _____   *old Beanstalk* _____

prodigy _____   a real pro _____

sidekicks _____   *a gorilla* _____

ventriloquist _____   a dancer _____

dummy _____	*her phony self* _____
Fatso _____	my champion _____
freckle-face _____	flowers, fairies, and strawberries _____

- What do the names in italics in the list reveal about the personality and attitude of both that character and the character who "invented" the nickname?
- Which of the characters are runners, and which are not? Is any difference in Squeaky's attitude toward runners and nonrunners revealed through the narrator's descriptions?

ACTIVITY 6

With a partner or in small groups, discuss the following questions and do the activity.

1. Examine the following quotations from the story. What do they reveal about Squeaky's attitude and feelings toward Raymond? Are these attitudes and feelings consistent or inconsistent?

	a. "Then I have to go behind him apologizing to all the old people sitting around. . . ." (line 39)
	b. "Then as I get into place I see that ole Raymond is on line on the other side of the fence. . . ." (lines 185–186)
	c. ". . . getting his shoes and cuffs wet. Then I get hit when I get home." (lines 36–37)
	d. ". . . I almost stop to watch my brother Raymond on his first run." (lines 208–209)
	e. ". . . ask him where he got that great big pumpkin head. People are so stupid sometimes." (lines 68–69)
	f. ". . . then like a dancer or something he starts climbing up nice and easy but very fast." (lines 226–227)
	g. "And a lot of smart mouths got lots to say about that too, especially when George was minding him. But now, if anybody has anything to say to Raymond, anything to say about his big head, they have to come by me." (lines 8–11)
	h. ". . . I'm jumping up and down so glad to see him—my brother Raymond, a great runner in the family tradition." (lines 244–245)
	i. ". . . a whole new career as a coach with Raymond as my champion." (lines 235–236)

2. In the left column, number the quotations in the order in which they occur in the story.

3. At which point does a change occur in Squeaky's view of Raymond? What is this change? Why is it important?

WRITING IN RESPONSE

Respond briefly to this question in writing. Compare your response with those of two or three classmates.

How do you think Squeaky will be different after the end of the story now that she knows Raymond is an excellent runner?

Language and Style

ACTIVITY 7

Prepare answers to the following questions. Then work in groups to compare your ideas.

1. The narrator, Squeaky, begins many of her sentences with "And," "But," "Or," "So," and "Then." Find all examples of these sentence starters in the story and circle or underline them so that they stand out.

   a. What effect does the writer achieve by having the narrator tell her story this way?

   b. During the track meet, these conjunctions appear less often at the beginning of sentences. Why? What is the effect, if any, of this change in **style?**

2. In what tense is the story written?

   a. Why is it written in this tense?

   b. Read the first paragraph aloud and change all the present tense verbs to past tense as you read. What effect does this have?

   c. Do the same for the last paragraph, starting with lines 252–253, "And I smile." Does reading it in the past tense change your feeling about the passage? How?

3. Squeaky tells the story in a rather childlike, irreverent, informal dialect. This may be a result not only of her youth but also of the tough urban environment in which she is growing up. Another factor that may have helped form her language is the defensive attitude she has developed while taking care of and protecting Raymond.

   Find examples of this type of language in the story and write them in a chart similar to the one on page 31. Include what the examples tell us about Squeaky's attitude. The first few have been done for you.

LINE	WHAT SQUEAKY SAYS	WHAT THE LANGUAGE REVEALS
6	"... any fool can see ..."	Irreverent, cynical attitude
11	"... they have to come by me ..."	Childlike city toughness
12–13	"I much rather ..."	Informal dialect

WRITING IN RESPONSE

Write briefly on this topic.

When people say cruel things to Raymond, Squeaky declares her feelings in her usual irreverent manner, saying that she doesn't like to stand "around with somebody in [her] face doing a lot of talking." (line 12) She would "much rather just knock you down. . . ." (lines 13–14) "And if things get too rough, [she] run[s]." (lines 14–15) If you had children (or if you already do), would you want them to play with a child like Squeaky? Why or why not?

Setting

ACTIVITY 8

Answer the following questions about the **setting.**

1. What is Squeaky's environment like? Find examples from the story of her urban surroundings, such as fire hydrants or grass as "hard as sidewalk." (line 169) What are the advantages and disadvantages of this environment for a child?

2. Who makes up Squeaky's community? What kind of people are they? (Include friends, family, neighbors, school relationships, and strangers.)

3. How might Squeaky's attitudes and behavior be different if she were living in a more affluent or less urban community? What aspects of the story would be different?

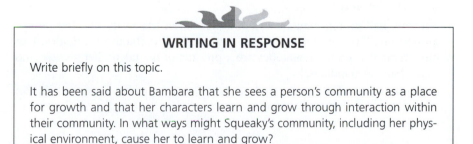

WRITING IN RESPONSE

Write briefly on this topic.

It has been said about Bambara that she sees a person's community as a place for growth and that her characters learn and grow through interaction within their community. In what ways might Squeaky's community, including her physical environment, cause her to learn and grow?

Exploring Further

In groups, discuss the following questions. When you have finished, decide whether you think "Raymond's Run" is the best title for the story. If so, why? If not, suggest a different title. Explain your decision to the class.

1. What "little girl" things does Squeaky despise so much, and why does she have such negative feelings about them? How might these feelings be connected to her commitment to running?

   a. How does Squeaky's lack of respect for things traditionally connected with girls affect her friendships?
   b. Squeaky claims that girls do not seem to know how to smile at each other no matter how old they are. (lines 96–99) What does she mean, and why does she think so?
   c. What is the significance of the "real smiling" that goes on at the end of the story between Squeaky and Gretchen? Why would a sincere smile between girls be so important?

2. Most of "Raymond's Run" seems to be about Squeaky, little girls, and running. Yet toward the end, the focus moves to Raymond's ability as a runner. What connections are there between Raymond's newly discovered talent and the narrator's smiles? What important change is taking place inside Squeaky?

ESSAY TOPICS

1. Write an essay in which you explain how taking care of Raymond has affected Squeaky's life and her relationships with other children. Include a discussion of how you think Squeaky would like other children to feel about her. Does she want them to be afraid of her? To respect her? To like her? Does she know what she wants? How is her feeling about Raymond at the end of the story related to these questions?

2. What does Squeaky learn in "Raymond's Run"? How will her life be different as a result of her experiences in the story? Write an essay that answers these questions.

3. Give the story "Raymond's Run" a new title and write an essay in which you explain why your title is appropriate, based on the ideas or theme(s) you have found in the story.

4. Squeaky has strong opinions and attitudes about the world and the people around her. Write an essay in which you briefly describe these attitudes. Discuss in what ways these attitudes are a product of her talent, her gender, and her urban surroundings.

AUTHOR PROFILE

Toni Cade Bambara

Toni Cade Bambara (1939–1995), born Toni Cade, added the name Bambara herself as an adult. She received her B.A. in theater from Queens College in 1959, studied with the Commedia del'Arte in Milan, and received her M.A. at City College of New York in 1964. Subsequently, she became involved in theater and social work, taught college English and Afro-American Studies, went to Cuba and Vietnam, and helped found the Southern Collective of African-American Writers.

In addition to writing two collections of short stories—*Gorilla, My Love* (1972), from which "Raymond's Run" is taken, and *The Sea Birds Are Still Alive* (1977)—Bambara has also written a novel, *The Salt Eaters* (1981), and several screenplays. She has also edited two collections: *The Black Woman* (1970), about the double hardship of being both black and female, and *Tales and Stories for Black Folks* (1971), an anthology designed for young African Americans.

Bambara feels that African Americans have unique problems and that gender and political conflicts are felt more deeply within the African-American community than in the country at large. Especially intertwined with their community is African-American women's sense of individuality, and in Bambara's stories, these women learn and grow through hardship and through interaction within that community.

CHAPTER 4

Bluebirdbluebird thrumywindow

SONIA SANCHEZ

PREPARATION

ACTIVITY 1

Bertolt Brecht (1898–1956) was a German playwright whose work has political content. In addition to being entertaining, he intended to make people think and perhaps even change their minds about contemporary issues in society.

Read the lines by Brecht at the top of page 36. Then, with a partner or in small groups, discuss the following questions.

1. Which groups in society might Brecht mean by those who "live in darkness" and those who "live in light"?

2. When Brecht ends with "those in darkness out of sight," what do you think he is saying about human nature? What might his political message be?

3. What can you predict about the content of "Bluebirdbluebirdthrumywindow," based on the lines by Brecht?

ACTIVITY 2

In America, we think of ourselves as a civilized people living in a democratic society. What do *civilized* and *democratic society* mean? How do our associations with these two terms contrast with our associations with the word *uncivilized*?

In the following chart, brainstorm a list or a cluster of as many associations as you can make for each of the three words. What is different about your groups of words? What is the same? Which words in each group describe American society today? Explain.

CIVILIZED	UNCIVILIZED	DEMOCRATIC SOCIETY

ACTIVITY 3

Read the first twelve lines of "Bluebirdbluebirdthrumywindow" and answer the following questions.

1. What is the Supreme Court? What is its function?

2. Which rights are not considered fundamental by the Supreme Court, according to the text? Which rights are considered fundamental?

3. Explain your understanding of the phrase "only those rights essential to our concept of ordered liberty." (line 4)

4. According to the text, which rights should people have for society to be considered civilized? Review the ideas you came up with in Activity 2 when you brainstormed associations with the words *civilized* and *democratic society*. How do those ideas compare with the notions about the Supreme Court in "Bluebirdbluebirdthrumywindow"? (lines 1–8)

5. Think of other countries or systems of government with which you're familiar. Do they consider other rights, different from those given in the text, to be fundamental? Explain.

6. Sanchez's piece is about homelessness. How are fundamental and nonfundamental rights related to this issue? (lines 1–8)

7. Review the ideas you came up with in Activity 2 when you brainstormed associations with the word *uncivilized*. Do your ideas connect with the **verbal irony** in the question, "Isn't it lovely to be civilized?" (line 8) How? (See Appendix A for more information about terms in boldface type.)

8. Whose minds do you think Sanchez may be trying to change with her piece?

Bluebirdbluebirdthrumywindow

SONIA SANCHEZ

denn die einen sind im Dunkeln
(some there are who live in darkness)
und die andern sind im Licht
(while the others live in light)
und man siehet die im Lichte
(we see those who live in daylight)
die im Dunkeln sieht man nicht
(those in darkness out of sight)
—Bertolt Brecht

And the Supreme Court said housing and welfare are not fundamental rights.
The right to vote, marry and procreate are the only fundamental rights.
Question: What rights are considered fundamental?
Answer: Only those rights essential to our concept of ordered liberty.
Question: What do you mean? Make it plain, girl. Make it plain.
Answer: In other words, a democratic society without these rights would not
be considered civilized. If you don't have 'em, you ain't civilized.
Isn't it lovely to be civilized?
You've seen her. You know you have. She sits on cardboard at Broad and Co-
10   lumbia in front of Zavelle's. Four coats layer her body. Towels are wrapped with a
rope around her feet to keep them warm. A plastic bag full of her belongings
stands in formation next to her. She's anywhere between 40 and 70 years-old. A
grey Black woman of North Philadelphia. Sitting sharply. Watching the whirl of
people pass by, she sits through winter, spring, summer, fall and law students
keeping time to memory.
You've seen her. You know you have. The old woman walking her ulcerated
legs down Market street; the old harridan mumbling pieces of a dead dream as
she examines garbage can after garbage can.
"Hey there, girlie. Can you spare me a quarter? I ain't eaten in four days.
20   C'mon now, honey. Just one little quarter."
So you give her a quarter and keep on walking to your apartment. So you hand
her the money that relieves you of her past present and future. Onward Christian°
country marching off as to war, with your cross behind you, going as before.
She was turning the corner of the rest room at Pennsylvania Station as I came
out of the stall. It was 10:59 p.m., and I was waiting for the 11:59 p.m. to
Philadelphia. She entered the bathroom, walking her swollen black feet, dragging
her polkadot feet in blue house slippers. Her cape surrounded her like a shroud.
She grunted herself down underneath one of the hand dryers.
I watched her out of the corner of my eyes as I washed and dried my hands.
30   What did she remind me of? This cracked body full of ghosts. This beached black
whale. This multilayered body gathering dust.

°*Onward Christian* reference to the Christian hymn "Onward Christian Soldiers"

Whose mother are you? Whose daughter were you for so many years? What grandchild is standing still in your eyes? What is your name, old black woman of bathrooms and streets?

She opened her dirty sheet of belongings and brought out an old plastic bowl. She looked up and signaled to me.

"Hey you. There. Yeah. You. Miss. Could you put some water in this there bowl for me please? It's kinda hard for me to climb back up once I sits down here for the night."

I took the bowl and filled it with water. There was no hot water, only cold. I   40
handed it to her, and she turned the bowl up to her mouth and drank some of the water. Then she began the slow act of taking off her slippers and socks. The socks numbered six. They were all old and dirty. But her feet. A leper's feet. Cracked. Ulcerated. Peeling with dirt and age.

She baptized one foot and then the other with water. Yes. Wash the "souls"° of your feet, my sister. Baptize them in bathroom water. We're all holy here.

You've seen her. You know you have. Sitting in the lower chambers of the garage. Guarding the entering and exiting cars. Old black goddess of our American civilization at its peak.

She sits still as a Siamese. Two shopping bags surround her like constant   50
lovers. She sits on two blankets. A heavy quilt is wrapped around her body.

"Good morning, sister." I scream against the quiet. Her eyes. Closed. Open into narrow slits. Yellow sleep oozes out of her eyes. Then a smile of near-recognition. A smile of gratitude perhaps. Here I am, her smile announces, in the upper sanctum° of Manhattan. A black Siamese for these modern monuments. Let those who would worship at my shrine come now or forever hold their peace. Hee. Hee. Hee.

She leans toward me and says, "Glorious morning, ain't it? You has something for yo' ole sister today? For yo' old mother?"

The blue and white morning stretches her wings across the dying city. I lean   60
forward and give her five dollars. The money disappears under her blanket as she smiles a lightning smile. Her eyes open and for the first time I see the brown in her eyes. Brown-eyed woman. She looks me in the eye and says, "Don't never go to sleep on the world, girl. Whiles you sleeping the world scrambles on. Keep yo' eyes open all the time."

Then she closes her eyes and settles back into a sinister stillness. I stand waiting for more. After all, we have smiled at each other for years. I have placed five dollars regularly into her hand. I wait. She does not move, and I finally walk on down the street. What were you waiting for girl? What more could she possibly say to you that you don't already know? Didn't you already know who and what   70
she was from her voice, from her clothes? Hadn't you seen her for years on the streets and in the doorways of America? Didn't you recognize her?

I walk the long block to my apartment. It will be a long day. I feel exhausted already. Is it the New York air? My legs become uncoordinated. Is it the rhythm of

---

° *"souls"* a play on the word "soles"
°*sanctum* a sacred or holy place

the city that tires me so this morning? I must find a chair, or curb, a doorway to rest on. My legs are going every which way but up.

I find a doorway on Broadway. I lean. Close my eyes to catch my morning breath. Close my mouth to silence the screams moving upward like vomit.

80   She was once somebody's mama. I ain't playing the dozens.° She was once someone's child toddling through the playgrounds of America in tune to bluebirdbluebird thru my window, bluebirdbluebird thru my window.

Where do the bluebirds go when they're all used up?

ANALYZING THE POEM

ACTIVITY 4

Answer the following questions with a partner or in small groups. Give evidence from the poem to support your answers and include line numbers for each piece of evidence.

1. What is your initial reaction to "Bluebirdbluebirdthrumywindow"? What words or images cause you to feel the way you do?

2. Is this a short story or a poem? How do you know?

3. The literary term for this type of poem is **prose poem.** Explain in your own words what this means.

4. Who is the **narrator?** Is the narrator a man or a woman? Is the narrator a character in the piece?

5. Who are the other characters? Do they have names?

6. How are lines 1–8 different from the rest of the piece? Who do you think is asking the questions? Who is giving the answers? Discuss different possibilities.

7. Who do you think the "you" refers to in line 7?

8. Of whom do you think the narrator asks the question "Isn't it lovely to be civilized?" (line 8) What are the different possibilities?

9. Lines 9–10 contain a specific reference to Broad and Columbia. This is a street corner in what city? Find other references to specific places and cities in the text. Are these references positive or negative for you? Explain.

10. What ethnic group is represented in the way language is used in the following examples? Explain.
    a. "Make it plain, girl. Make it plain." (line 5)
    b. "'Hey there, girlie. Can you spare me a quarter? I ain't eaten in four days. C'mon now, honey. Just one little quarter.'" (lines 19–20)
    c. "Yes. Wash the 'souls' of your feet, my sister." (lines 45–46)

11. Where does the title "Bluebirdbluebirdthrumywindow" come from?

°*playing the dozens* from African-American oral tradition, a children's verbal game of power; includes references to "your mama" and "someone's mother"

WRITING IN RESPONSE

Read "Bluebirdbluebirdthrumywindow" aloud. Then respond briefly to these questions in writing.

1. How does this reading affect your understanding of the words and images?

2. How does reading aloud affect the way you understand the form of the prose poem?

3. Explain what you discovered as you read the prose poem aloud.

Elements of Literature

Characterization

ACTIVITY 5

1. How many characters does the author refer to in lines 9–81? Follow these steps to find out.

   a. Circle all the first-person references *(I, me, my)* that refer to the narrator.
   b. Draw boxes around all the second-person references *(you)*.
   c. Underline all the third-person references to women *(she, her)*.
   d. Make a mark or notation in your text for each time there is a change in place or time. (*Hint:* Shifts in tense can help you determine a change of place or time.) These marks will help you know when the description of each character begins and ends. Look at these examples:

   "You've seen her. You know you have. She sits on cardboard at
   place
   Broad and Columbia in front of Zavelle's." (lines 9–10)
   time
   ". . . she sits through winter, spring, summer, fall . . . " (line 14)

   "You've seen her. You know you have. The old woman
   change in time and place
   walking . . . down Market street . . . " (lines 16–17)

   How many characters are in the prose poem from lines 9–81?

2. How many women besides the narrator are there? What do all the women have in common? How are they different?

3. Can you identify the race of the homeless women? Of the narrator? How do you know?

4. In lines 9–72, identify all the occurrences of "you" that refer to the narrator. Then identify all the occurrences of "you" that refer to a homeless woman. To what do the other occurrences of "you" refer? How do you know?

Point of View

ACTIVITY 6

Sanchez writes "Bluebirdbluebirdthrumywindow" using the rare **second-person point of view,** addressing the reader directly as "you."

1. How many times does the narrator say, "You've seen her. You know you have"?

2. Why does the narrator say not only "You've seen her" but also "You know you have"? In what situations might you say to someone, "You know you have"?

3. What do you think Sanchez's purpose is in using the second person in the lines described above? What is the effect of the second-person point of view?

4. Notice that after each time the narrator gives money to the women, she shifts the pronoun reference to "you." What meaning does the narrator imply in the following lines?

"So you give her a quarter and keep on walking to your apartment." (line 21)
   "What were you waiting for girl? What more could she possibly say to you that you don't already know? Didn't you already know who and what she was from her voice, from her clothes?" (lines 69–71)

5. What effect does using second person in the lines above have on the reader? Why?

6. In what ways might Sanchez's choice of second-person point of view be related to the fact that she is writing about homelessness? Explain.

CREATIVE WRITING

Write a few paragraphs or lines of poetry that have political content, such as tenants' rights, environmental issues, or discrimination against a group of people. Use second-person point of view and repetition in a style that is similar to Sanchez's. When you are finished writing, share your work with the class and discuss the effect the second-person point of view has on the reader or listener.

Language and Style

A C T I V I T Y   7

The language that Sanchez uses in "Bluebirdbluebirdthrumywindow" creates vivid pictures in our minds so that we can see, hear, smell, taste, and feel what the characters are experiencing. One way Sanchez creates these images is by making direct or indirect comparisons between two unlike things.

For example, the narrator describes the second homeless woman as "mumbling pieces of a dead dream." (line 17) Usually we use the word *mumbling* when someone is speaking words, not pieces of something, especially something as abstract as a dead dream. Sanchez's comparison is unusual, draws our attention, and creates an evocative image.

Using lines 9–72, find references that contain descriptive language or comparisons that fit the categories in the following chart. Refer to the examples to help you.

DEATH	PAIN/DISEASE
"mumbling pieces of a dead dream" (line 17)	*"walking her swollen black feet" (line 26)*

HEAVINESS/LACK OF MOVEMENT	TIMELESSNESS/LACK OF CHANGE
"sits still as a siamese" (line 50)	*"through winter, spring, summer, fall" (line 14)*

A C T I V I T Y   8

Answer the following questions with a partner or in small groups. If appropriate, give evidence from the prose poem to support your answers and include line numbers for each piece of evidence.

1. What is your reaction to the way the narrator uses many references to death, pain, and disease to describe the women?

2. Discuss why the poet might have chosen so many references to heaviness and timelessness. How do the references to lack of movement and lack of change help us understand the homeless women and the situations they find themselves in? Explain.

3. How does the poet's use of such descriptive language make you feel as you read the piece? Why?

WRITING IN RESPONSE

Write briefly on this topic. Compare your response with those of two or three classmates.

How is the experience of the narrator similar to or different from your experience with homeless people? Think about what she sees, how she reacts, and how she interacts with the homeless women she encounters.

Exploring Further

Continue analyzing "Bluebirdbluebirdthrumywindow" with these questions.

1. Put a check mark (✓) above all references to family in the prose poem. Look for words that refer to family members, such as *mother, sister, grandchild*. Then answer the following questions:

   a. In the bathroom, the narrator refers to the homeless woman as "my sister." (line 46) In the garage, the homeless woman refers to the narrator as "sister" when she greets her (line 52) and then to herself as "yo' ole sister" and "yo' old mother." (line 59) What are possible reasons for these family references? What do you think Sanchez wants to imply?

   b. Why do you think the narrator asks, "Whose mother are you? Whose daughter were you for so many years? What grandchild is standing still in your eyes?" (lines 32–33) Where are the answers to these questions?

   c. In lines 79–80, the narrator says, "She was once somebody's mama. . . . She was once someone's child . . . ." What do you think the significance of the word *once* is in these lines? What point might Sanchez be making?

2. While the "blue and white morning stretches her wings across the dying city," the narrator "lean[s] forward and give[s] [the woman] five dollars." (lines 60–61) Why does the narrator give the woman money? How does the narrator feel after she does?

3. The narrator explains how she feels after an encounter with the woman who sits "in the lower chambers of the garage." (lines 47–48)

   a. Why does the narrator feel "exhausted" (line 73) even though it is still morning?

   b. Why does she "close [her] eyes" and "close [her] mouth to silence the screams moving upward like vomit"? (lines 77–78)

   c. What effect do these lines have on the reader?

   d. What message do you think Sanchez wants to convey? Explain.

4. Each of the first four homeless women can be associated with a specific place in a specific city: Broad and Columbia or Market Street in Philadelphia and Pennsylvania Station in Manhattan. Toward the end of the piece, the narrator

refers to seeing the fourth homeless woman "for years on the streets and in the doorways of America," (lines 71–72) with the fifth homeless woman described as "once . . . toddling through the playgrounds of America." (lines 79–80) Why do you think Sanchez shifts from references to specific places in cities to the broader references to America?

5. Writers often use irony to illustrate their points, using words that contrast what is said with what is meant. For example, when the narrator says "Isn't it lovely to be civilized?" (line 8) we understand that the author's underlying message is actually the opposite, that she questions how civilized our society is. Why does the author question how civilized our society is? Why does the narrator refer to the fourth homeless woman as the "Old black goddess of our American civilization at its peak"? (lines 48–49) Explain the irony in these statements.

6. Discuss the title "Bluebirdbluebirdthrumywindow."

   a. Why do you think Sanchez chose this title?
   b. Why do you think she ended the piece with "She was once someone's child toddling through the playgrounds of America in tune to bluebirdbluebird thru my window, bluebirdbluebird thru my window"? (lines 79–81)
   c. What do you think the significance might be of the final line, "Where do the bluebirds go when they're all used up"? (line 82)

7. Discuss the possible connections between the lines by Bertolt Brecht at the beginning of the piece and the narrator's descriptions of and reactions to the homeless women.

   a. Who are the people "who live in darkness" and those who "live in light"?
   b. Why do we see "those who live in daylight" and "[keep] those in darkness out of sight"?
   c. Why do you think Sanchez includes these lines as part of her piece on homelessness?

8. How did you react to homeless people before reading "Bluebirdbluebirdthrumywindow"? How did the piece make you feel? Now that you have read and discussed the prose poem, do you think you might look at homeless people differently when you encounter them?

ESSAY TOPICS

1. Write an essay that illustrates your interpretation of Sanchez's message in "Bluebirdbluebirdthrumywindow." Support your ideas with examples from the text and explain how Sanchez is successful in making her point about homelessness.

2. Discuss Sanchez's style of writing and the effect it has on the reader. Consider the following as you develop your ideas: Sanchez's use of descriptive language, point of view, shifts in time and place, irony, and prose poem style.

3. Explain how "Bluebirdbluebirdthrumywindow" has affected you. Discuss how the piece makes you feel and why. Show how your perceptions of homeless people have changed (or why they have not changed) as a result of reading and studying this prose poem.

AUTHOR PROFILE

Sonia Sanchez

Sonia Sanchez, author of sixteen books of poems, essays, and dramas, was born in 1934 in Birmingham, Alabama, and grew up in Harlem in New York City. In her words, "If you write, you have to have a love for language," and her poetry reflects a style that is "free [and] conversational" with the influence of the jazz and blues of black music. One of the foremost voices of the Black Arts Movement (1960–1970), Sanchez has been committed to creating poetry that serves as a political "call to arms" to show that "it is possible to be human" and to "turn people away from [feelings of] racial superiority." Well known for her fresh and energetic performance style, Sanchez reads her poetry with the vocal intonations of Africans and African Americans and inspires emotional responses from the audiences who listen to her work.

Sanchez received the American Book Award in 1985 for *homegirls and handgrenades,* the volume of poetry in which "Bluebirdbluebirdthrumywindow" appears. In 1998 she was nominated for both the National Book Critics Circle and the National Association for the Advancement of Colored People (NAACP) Image Awards. Currently, Sanchez is Laura Carnell Professor of English and Women's Studies at Temple University in Philadelphia.

CHAPTER 5

Two Kinds

AMY TAN

PREPARATION

ACTIVITY 1

With a partner or in small groups, discuss the following questions.

1. How did your parents' expectations of you influence your decisions during your adolescent years?

2. How do your parents' expectations influence your decisions now?

3. What do you know about your parents' pasts and about what influenced their decisions and choices in life?

4. What do you know about the political situation in China in 1949, who it affected, and why?

WRITING IN RESPONSE

Write briefly on this topic.

Were you a conforming or rebellious child or adolescent? Why do you think you were that way?

JING-MEI WOO

Two Kinds

AMY TAN

My mother believed you could be anything you wanted to be in America. You could open a restaurant. You could work for the government and get good retirement. You could buy a house with almost no money down. You could become rich. You could become instantly famous.

"Of course you can be prodigy, too," my mother told me when I was nine. "You can be best anything. What does Auntie Lindo know? Her daughter, she is only best tricky."

America was where all my mother's hopes lay. She had come here in 1949 after losing everything in China: her mother and father, her family home, her first husband, and two daughters, twin baby girls. But she never looked back with regret. There were so many ways for things to get better.

We didn't immediately pick the right kind of prodigy. At first my mother thought I could be a Chinese Shirley Temple.° We'd watch Shirley's old movies on TV as though they were training films. My mother would poke my arm and say, "*Ni kan*"—You watch. And I would see Shirley tapping her feet, or singing a sailor song, or pursing her lips into a very round O while saying, "Oh my goodness."

"*Ni kan*," said my mother as Shirley's eyes flooded with tears. "You already know how. Don't need talent for crying!"

Soon after my mother got this idea about Shirley Temple, she took me to a beauty training school in the Mission district° and put me in the hands of a student who could barely hold the scissors without shaking. Instead of getting big fat curls, I emerged with an uneven mass of crinkly black fuzz. My mother dragged me off to the bathroom and tried to wet down my hair.

"You look like Negro Chinese," she lamented, as if I had done this on purpose.

The instructor of the beauty training school had to lop off these soggy clumps to make my hair even again. "Peter Pan is very popular these days," the instructor assured my mother. I now had hair the length of a boy's, with straight-across bangs that hung at a slant two inches above my eyebrows. I liked the haircut and it made me actually look forward to my future fame.

In fact, in the beginning, I was just as excited as my mother, maybe even more so. I pictured this prodigy part of me as many different images, trying each one on for size. I was a dainty ballerina girl standing by the curtains, waiting to hear the right music that would send me floating on my tiptoes. I was like the Christ child lifted out of the straw manger, crying with holy indignity. I was Cinderella stepping from her pumpkin carriage with sparkly cartoon music filling the air.

°*Shirley Temple* an American child actress, popular in the 1930s
°*Mission district* a San Francisco neighborhood

In all of my imaginings, I was filled with a sense that I would soon become *perfect*. My mother and father would adore me. I would be beyond reproach. I would never feel the need to sulk for anything.

But sometimes the prodigy in me became impatient. "If you don't hurry up and get me out of here, I'm disappearing for good," it warned. "And then you'll always be nothing."

Every night after dinner, my mother and I would sit at the Formica kitchen table. She would present new tests, taking her examples from stories of amazing children she had read in *Ripley's Believe It or Not,°* or *Good Housekeeping, Reader's Digest,* and a dozen other magazines she kept in a pile in our bathroom. My mother got these magazines from people whose houses she cleaned. And since she cleaned many houses each week, we had a great assortment. She would look through them all, searching for stories about remarkable children.

The first night she brought out a story about a three-year-old boy who knew the capitals of all the states and even most of the European countries. A teacher was quoted as saying the little boy could also pronounce the names of the foreign cities correctly.

"What's the capital of Finland?" my mother asked me, looking at the magazine story.

All I knew was the capital of California, because Sacramento was the name of the street we lived on in Chinatown. "Nairobi!" I guessed, saying the most foreign word I could think of. She checked to see if that was possibly one way to pronounce "Helsinki" before showing me the answer.

The tests got harder—multiplying numbers in my head, finding the queen of hearts in a deck of cards, trying to stand on my head without using my hands, predicting the daily temperatures in Los Angeles, New York, and London.

One night I had to look at a page from the Bible for three minutes and then report everything I could remember. "Now Jehoshaphat had riches and honor in abundance and . . . that's all I remember, Ma," I said.

And after seeing my mother's disappointed face once again, something inside of me began to die. I hated the tests, the raised hopes and failed expectations. Before going to bed that night, I looked in the mirror above the bathroom sink and when I saw only my face staring back—and that it would always be this ordinary face—I began to cry. Such a sad, ugly girl! I made high-pitched noises like a crazed animal, trying to scratch out the face in the mirror.

And then I saw what seemed to be the prodigy side of me—because I had never seen that face before. I looked at my reflection, blinking so I could see more clearly. The girl staring back at me was angry, powerful. This girl and I were the same. I had new thoughts, willful thoughts, or rather thoughts filled with lots of won'ts. I won't let her change me, I promised myself. I won't be what I'm not.

So now on nights when my mother presented her tests, I performed listlessly, my head propped on one arm. I pretended to be bored. And I was. I got so bored

40

50

60

70

°*Ripley's Believe It or Not* a newspaper column about amazing facts and events; popular since 1918

80   I started counting the bellows of the foghorns out on the bay while my mother drilled me in other areas. The sound was comforting and reminded me of the cow jumping over the moon. And the next day, I played a game with myself, seeing if my mother would give up on me before eight bellows. After a while I usually counted only one, maybe two bellows at most. At last she was beginning to give up hope.

Two or three months had gone by without any mention of my being a prodigy again. And then one day my mother was watching *The Ed Sullivan Show*° on TV. The TV was old and the sound kept shorting out. Every time my mother got halfway up from the sofa to adjust the set, the sound would go back on and Ed 90   would be talking. As soon as she sat down, Ed would go silent again. She got up, the TV broke into loud piano music. She sat down. Silence. Up and down, back and forth, quiet and loud. It was like a stiff embraceless dance between her and the TV set. Finally she stood by the set with her hand on the sound dial.

She seemed entranced by the music, a little frenzied piano piece with this mesmerizing quality, sort of quick passages and then teasing lilting ones before it returned to the quick playful parts.

"*Ni kan*," my mother said, calling me over with hurried hand gestures. "Look here."

I could see why my mother was fascinated by the music. It was being 100   pounded out by a little Chinese girl, about nine years old, with a Peter Pan haircut. The girl had the sauciness of a Shirley Temple. She was proudly modest like a proper Chinese child. And she also did this fancy sweep of a curtsy, so that the fluffy skirt of her white dress cascaded slowly to the floor like the petals of a large carnation.

In spite of these warning signs, I wasn't worried. Our family had no piano and we couldn't afford to buy one, let alone reams of sheet music and piano lessons. So I could be generous in my comments when my mother bad-mouthed the little girl on TV.

"Play note right, but doesn't sound good! No singing sound," complained my 110   mother.

"What are you picking on her for?" I said carelessly. "She's pretty good. Maybe she's not the best, but she's trying hard." I knew almost immediately I would be sorry I said that.

"Just like you," she said. "Not the best. Because you not trying." She gave a little huff as she let go of the sound dial and sat down on the sofa.

The little Chinese girl sat down also to play an encore of "Anitra's Dance" by Grieg. I remember the song, because later on I had to learn how to play it.

Three days after watching *The Ed Sullivan Show,*° my mother told me what my schedule would be for piano lessons and piano practice. She had talked to Mr. 120   Chong, who lived on the first floor of our apartment building. Mr. Chong was a retired piano teacher and my mother had traded housecleaning services for weekly

°*Ed Sullivan Show* a TV variety show, popular in the 1950s

lessons and a piano for me to practice on every day, two hours a day, from four until six.

When my mother told me this, I felt as though I had been sent to hell. I whined and then kicked my foot a little when I couldn't stand it anymore.

"Why don't you like me the way I am? I'm *not* a genius! I can't play the piano. And even if I could, I wouldn't go on TV if you paid me a million dollars!" I cried.

My mother slapped me. "Who ask you be genius?" she shouted. "Only ask you be your best. For you sake. You think I want you be genius? Hnnh! What for! Who ask you!"

"So ungrateful," I heard her mutter in Chinese. "If she had as much talent as she has temper, she would be famous now."

Mr. Chong, whom I secretly nicknamed Old Chong, was very strange, always tapping his fingers to the silent music of an invisible orchestra. He looked ancient in my eyes. He had lost most of the hair on top of his head and he wore thick glasses and had eyes that always looked tired and sleepy. But he must have been younger than I thought, since he lived with his mother and was not yet married.

I met Old Lady Chong once and that was enough. She had this peculiar smell like a baby that had done something in its pants. And her fingers felt like a dead person's, like an old peach I once found in the back of the refrigerator; the skin just slid off the meat when I picked it up.

I soon found out why Old Chong had retired from teaching piano. He was deaf. "Like Beethoven!" he shouted to me. "We're both listening only in our head!" And he would start to conduct his frantic silent sonatas.

Our lessons went like this. He would open the book and point to different things, explaining their purpose: "Key! Treble! Bass! No sharps or flats! So this is C major! Listen now and play after me!"

And then he would play the C scale a few times, a simple chord, and then, as if inspired by an old, unreachable itch, he gradually added more notes and running trills and a pounding bass until the music was really something quite grand.

I would play after him, the simple scale, the simple chord, and then I just played some nonsense that sounded like a cat running up and down on top of garbage cans. Old Chong smiled and applauded and then said, "Very good! But now you must learn to keep time!"

So that's how I discovered that Old Chong's eyes were too slow to keep up with the wrong notes I was playing. He went through the motions in half-time. To help me keep rhythm, he stood behind me, pushing down on my right shoulder for every beat. He balanced pennies on top of my wrists so I would keep them still as I slowly played scales and arpeggios.° He had me curve my hand around an apple and keep that shape when playing chords. He marched stiffly to show me how to make each finger dance up and down, staccato° like an obedient little soldier.

°*arpeggios* the rapid playing of a musical chord, from the lowest note to the highest
°*staccato* the playing of musical notes so that each note is short, distinct, and separated from each other note

He taught me all these things, and that was how I also learned I could be lazy and get away with mistakes, lots of mistakes. If I hit the wrong notes because I hadn't practiced enough, I never corrected myself. I just kept playing in rhythm. And Old Chong kept conducting his own private reverie.

So maybe I never really gave myself a fair chance. I did pick up the basics pretty quickly, and I might have become a good pianist at that young age. But I
170   was so determined not to try, not to be anybody different that I learned to play only the most ear-splitting preludes, the most discordant hymns.

Over the next year, I practiced like this, dutifully in my own way. And then one day I heard my mother and her friend Lindo Jong both talking in a loud bragging tone of voice so others could hear. It was after church, and I was leaning against the brick wall wearing a dress with stiff white petticoats. Auntie Lindo's daughter, Waverly, who was about my age, was standing farther down the wall about five feet away. We had grown up together and shared all the closeness of two sisters squabbling over crayons and dolls. In other words, for the most part, we hated each other. I thought she was snotty. Waverly Jong had gained a
180   certain amount of fame as "Chinatown's Littlest Chinese Chess Champion."

"She bring home too many trophy," lamented Auntie Lindo that Sunday. "All day she play chess. All day I have no time do nothing but dust off her winnings." She threw a scolding look at Waverly, who pretended not to see her.

"You lucky you don't have this problem," said Auntie Lindo with a sigh to my mother.

And my mother squared her shoulders and bragged: "Our problem worser than yours. If we ask Jing-mei wash dish, she hear nothing but music. It's like you can't stop this natural talent."

And right then, I was determined to put a stop to her foolish pride.

190   A few weeks later, Old Chong and my mother conspired to have me play in a talent show which would be held in the church hall. By then, my parents had saved up enough to buy me a secondhand piano, a black Wurlitzer spinet with a scarred bench. It was the showpiece of our living room.

For the talent show, I was to play a piece called "Pleading Child" from Schumann's *Scenes from Childhood*. It was a simple, moody piece that sounded more difficult than it was. I was supposed to memorize the whole thing, playing the repeat parts twice to make the piece sound longer. But I dawdled over it, playing a few bars and then cheating, looking up to see what notes followed. I never really listened to what I was playing. I daydreamed about being somewhere else,
200   about being someone else.

The part I liked to practice best was the fancy curtsy: right foot out, touch the rose on the carpet with a pointed foot, sweep to the side, left leg bends, look up and smile.

My parents invited all the couples from the Joy Luck Club to witness my debut. Auntie Lindo and Uncle Tin were there. Waverly and her two older brothers had also come. The first two rows were filled with children both younger and older than I was. The littlest ones got to go first. They recited simple nursery rhymes, squawked out tunes on miniature violins, twirled Hula Hoops, pranced in pink ballet tutus, and when they bowed or curtsied, the audience would sigh in unison, "Awww," and then clap enthusiastically.

When my turn came, I was very confident. I remember my childish excitement. It was as if I knew, without a doubt, that the prodigy side of me really did exist. I had no fear whatsoever, no nervousness. I remember thinking to myself, This is it! This is it! I looked out over the audience, at my mother's blank face, my father's yawn, Auntie Lindo's stiff-lipped smile, Waverly's sulky expression. I had on a white dress layered with sheets of lace, and a pink bow in my Peter Pan haircut. As I sat down I envisioned people jumping to their feet and Ed Sullivan rushing up to introduce me to everyone on TV.

And I started to play. It was so beautiful. I was so caught up in how lovely I looked that at first I didn't worry how I would sound. So it was a surprise to me when I hit the first wrong note and I realized something didn't sound quite right. And then I hit another and another followed that. A chill started at the top of my head and began to trickle down. Yet I couldn't stop playing, as though my hands were bewitched. I kept thinking my fingers would adjust themselves back, like a train switching to the right track. I played this strange jumble through two repeats, the sour notes staying with me all the way to the end.

When I stood up, I discovered my legs were shaking. Maybe I had just been nervous and the audience, like Old Chong, had seen me go through the right motions and had not heard anything wrong at all. I swept my right foot out, went down on my knee, looked up and smiled. The room was quiet, except for Old Chong, who was beaming and shouting, "Bravo! Bravo! Well done!" But then I saw my mother's face, her stricken face. The audience clapped weakly, and as I walked back to my chair, with my whole face quivering as I tried not to cry, I heard a little boy whisper to his mother, "That was awful," and the mother whispered back, "Well, she certainly tried."

And now I realized how many people were in the audience, the whole world it seemed. I was aware of eyes burning into my back. I felt the shame of my mother and father as they sat stiffly throughout the rest of the show.

We could have escaped during intermission. Pride and some strange sense of honor must have anchored my parents to their chairs. And so we watched it all: the eighteen-year-old boy with a fake mustache who did a magic show and juggled flaming hoops while riding a unicycle. The breasted girl with white makeup who sang from *Madama Butterfly* and got honorable mention. And the eleven-year-old boy who won first prize playing a tricky violin song that sounded like a busy bee.

After the show, the Hsus, the Jongs, and the St. Clairs from the Joy Luck Club came up to my mother and father.

"Lots of talented kids," Auntie Lindo said vaguely, smiling broadly.

"That was somethin' else," said my father, and I wondered if he was referring to me in a humorous way, or whether he even remembered what I had done.

Waverly looked at me and shrugged her shoulders. "You aren't a genius like me," she said matter-of-factly. And if I hadn't felt so bad, I would have pulled her braids and punched her stomach.

But my mother's expression was what devastated me: a quiet, blank look that said she had lost everything. I felt the same way, and it seemed as if everybody were now coming up, like gawkers at the scene of an accident, to see what parts were actually missing. When we got on the bus to go home, my father was humming the busy-bee tune and my mother was silent. I kept thinking she wanted to wait until we got home before shouting at me. But when my father unlocked the
260   door to our apartment, my mother walked in and then went to the back, into the bedroom. No accusations. No blame. And in a way, I felt disappointed. I had been waiting for her to start shouting, so I could shout back and cry and blame her for all my misery.

I assumed my talent-show fiasco meant I never had to play the piano again. But two days later, after school, my mother came out of the kitchen and saw me watching TV.

"Four clock," she reminded me as if it were any other day. I was stunned, as though she were asking me to go through the talent-show torture again. I wedged myself more tightly in front of the TV.
270   "Turn off TV," she called from the kitchen five minutes later.

I didn't budge. And then I decided. I didn't have to do what my mother said anymore. I wasn't her slave. This wasn't China. I had listened to her before and look what happened. She was the stupid one.

She came out from the kitchen and stood in the arched entryway of the living room. "Four clock," she said once again, louder.

"I'm not going to play anymore," I said nonchalantly. "Why should I? I'm not a genius."

She walked over and stood in front of the TV. I saw her chest was heaving up and down in an angry way.
280   "No!" I said, and I now felt stronger, as if my true self had finally emerged. So this was what had been inside me all along.

"No! I won't!" I screamed.

She yanked me by the arm, pulled me off the floor, snapped off the TV. She was frighteningly strong, half pulling, half carrying me toward the piano as I kicked the throw rugs under my feet. She lifted me up and onto the hard bench. I was sobbing by now, looking at her bitterly. Her chest was heaving even more and her mouth was open, smiling crazily as if she were pleased I was crying.

"You want me to be someone that I'm not!" I sobbed. "I'll never be the kind of daughter you want me to be!"
290   "Only two kinds of daughters," she shouted in Chinese. "Those who are obedient and those who follow their own mind! Only one kind of daughter can live in this house. Obedient daughter!"

"Then I wish I wasn't your daughter. I wish you weren't my mother," I shouted. As I said these things I got scared. It felt like worms and toads and slimy things crawling out of my chest, but it also felt good, as if this awful side of me had surfaced, at last.

"Too late change this," said my mother shrilly.

And I could sense her anger rising to its breaking point. I wanted to see it spill over. And that's when I remembered the babies she had lost in China, the ones we never talked about. "Then I wish I'd never been born!" I shouted. "I wish 300 I were dead! Like them."

It was as if I had said the magic words. Alakazam!—and her face went blank, her mouth closed, her arms went slack, and she backed out of the room, stunned, as if she were blowing away like a small brown leaf, thin, brittle, lifeless.

It was not the only disappointment my mother felt in me. In the years that followed, I failed her so many times, each time asserting my own will, my right to fall short of expectations. I didn't get straight As. I didn't become class president. I didn't get into Stanford. I dropped out of college.

For unlike my mother, I did not believe I could be anything I wanted to be. I could only be me. 310

And for all those years, we never talked about the disaster at the recital or my terrible accusations afterward at the piano bench. All that remained unchecked, like a betrayal that was now unspeakable. So I never found a way to ask her why she had hoped for something so large that failure was inevitable.

And even worse, I never asked her what frightened me the most: Why had she given up hope?

For after our struggle at the piano, she never mentioned my playing again. The lessons stopped. The lid to the piano was closed, shutting out the dust, my misery, and her dreams.

So she surprised me. A few years ago, she offered to give me the piano, for my 320 thirtieth birthday. I had not played in all those years. I saw the offer as a sign of forgiveness, a tremendous burden removed.

"Are you sure?" I asked shyly. "I mean, won't you and Dad miss it?"

"No, this your piano," she said firmly. "Always your piano. You only one can play."

"Well, I probably can't play anymore," I said. "It's been years."

"You pick up fast," said my mother, as if she knew this was certain. "You have natural talent. You could been genius if you want to."

"No I couldn't."

"You just not trying," said my mother. And she was neither angry nor sad. She 330 said it as if to announce a fact that could never be disproved. "Take it," she said.

But I didn't at first. It was enough that she had offered it to me. And after that, every time I saw it in my parents' living room, standing in front of the bay windows, it made me feel proud, as if it were a shiny trophy I had won back.

Last week I sent a tuner over to my parents' apartment and had the piano reconditioned, for purely sentimental reasons. My mother had died a few months before and I had been getting things in order for my father, a little bit at a time. I put the jewelry in special silk pouches. The sweaters she had knitted in yellow, pink, bright orange—all the colors I hated—I put those in moth-proof boxes. I found some old Chinese silk dresses, the kind with little slits up the sides. I 340 rubbed the old silk against my skin, then wrapped them in tissue and decided to take them home with me.

After I had the piano tuned, I opened the lid and touched the keys. It sounded even richer than I remembered. Really, it was a very good piano. Inside the bench were the same exercise notes with handwritten scales, the same second-hand music books with their covers held together with yellow tape.

I opened up the Schumann book to the dark little piece I had played at the recital. It was on the left-hand side of the page, "Pleading Child." It looked more difficult than I remembered. I played a few bars, surprised at how easily the notes came back to me.

350

And for the first time, or so it seemed, I noticed the piece on the right-hand side. It was called "Perfectly Contented." I tried to play this one as well. It had a lighter melody but the same flowing rhythm and turned out to be quite easy. "Pleading Child" was shorter but slower; "Perfectly Contented" was longer, but faster. And after I played them both a few times, I realized they were two halves of the same song.

ANALYZING THE STORY

ACTIVITY 2

Answer the following questions. Give evidence from the story to support your answers and include line numbers for each piece of evidence.

1. Who is the **narrator?** (See Appendix A for more information about words in boldface type.) When is the narrator first described? When do we learn her name?

2. How old is Jing-mei at the beginning of the story? At the end? How old is the narrator?

3. Line breaks (spaces) follow lines 304 and 334. What do these breaks in the text indicate?

4. What do we know about the background of Jing-mei's mother?

   a. What does the mother do for a living?
   b. How does she pay for the piano lessons? What does this imply?

5. Jing-mei's mother said that there are "'only two kinds of daughters.'" (line 290) What are the two kinds? Which kind does Jing-mei start out as? Does this change?

6. What do we know about Old Chong, the piano teacher?

7. Where in the story does the conflict reach a climax? (See **plot** in Appendix A.)

WRITING IN RESPONSE

Respond briefly to these questions in writing. Compare your responses with those of two or three classmates.

Although it has serious and sad moments, "Two Kinds" is also humorous. For example, after a serious argument between Jing-mei and her mother, (lines 124–133) the author inserts a humorous description of Old Chong and his mother. What effect do you think humor has at this point? What else do you find humorous in the story?

Elements of Literature

Characterization

ACTIVITY 3

In "Two Kinds," the mother and daughter are vividly portrayed, both through the details Tan employs and through her use of **point of view.**

Form three groups, one for each section below. In each group, follow these steps:

- Discuss what the following lines from the story mean and what they reveal about the character.
- Find other lines that depict the character and discuss them.
- Circle the adjectives from the list in the chart that best describe the character. You may also provide adjectives of your own. Next to each word that you choose, write the number of the line(s) that support it.

Jing-mei as a Young Girl

1. ". . . in the beginning, I was just as excited as my mother, maybe even more so. I pictured this prodigy part of me as many different images . . . ." (lines 31–32)

2. "I was filled with a sense that I would soon become *perfect*. My mother and father would adore me. I would be beyond reproach." (lines 38–39)

3. "After seeing my mother's disappointed face once again, something inside of me began to die. I hated the tests, the raised hopes and failed expectations." (lines 67–68)

4. "The girl staring back at me was angry, powerful. This girl and I were the same. I had new thoughts, willful thoughts, or rather thoughts filled with lots of won'ts." (lines 75–77)

5. "'Why don't you like me the way I am? I'm *not* a genius! I can't play the piano! And even if I could . . . .'" (lines 126–127)

6. ". . . I also learned that I could be lazy and get away with mistakes, lots of mistakes." (lines 164–165)
7. ". . . I might have become a good pianist at that young age. But I was so determined not to try, not to be anybody different. . . ." (lines 169–170)
8. Additional lines:

ADJECTIVES THAT DESCRIBE JING-MEI AS A CHILD	LINE(S) THAT SUPPORT THE CHOICE OF ADJECTIVES
Unrealistic	
Confused	
Proud	
Resentful	
Frightened	
Vain	
Lazy	
Stubborn	

- Based on your discussion, answer these questions.
  a. Where does a shift in Jing-mei's self-image and attitude occur? What causes it?
  b. What new image and attitude does Jing-mei appear to adopt?

Jing-mei as an Adult Looking Back

1. ". . . I failed her so many times, each time asserting my own will, my right to fall short of expectations." (lines 306–307)

2. "For unlike my mother, I did not believe I could be anything I wanted to be. I could only be me." (lines 309–310)
3. "I never asked her what frightened me the most: Why had she given up hope?" (lines 315–316)
4. "And after that . . . it made me feel proud, as if it were a shiny trophy I had won back." (lines 332–334)
5. Additional lines:

ADJECTIVES THAT DESCRIBE JING–MEI AS AN ADULT	LINE(S) THAT SUPPORT THE CHOICE OF ADJECTIVES
Guilty	
Self-defeating	
Insecure	
Regretful	
Independent	
Realistic	
Confused	

- Based on your discussion, answer the following questions.
    a. How does the adult Jing-mei understand the conflict between her mother and herself?
    b. Why did her mother's loss of hope frighten her? Is she still frightened about it? Why or why not?
    c. Jing-mei says that she "never found a way to ask why [her mother] had hoped for something so large that failure was inevitable." (lines 313–314) Do you agree that Jing-mei's failure was inevitable? Why or why not?
    d. At the end of the story, why is she proud of being given the piano?

Jing-mei's Mother

1. The first two paragraphs (lines 1–7)

2. "My mother slapped me. . . . 'Only ask you be your best. For you sake . . . .'" (lines 129–130)

3. "But my mother's expression was what devastated me: a quiet, blank look that said that she had lost everything." (lines 254–255)

4. "I assumed my talent-show fiasco meant I never had to play the piano again. But two days later . . . my mother came out of the kitchen . . . . 'Four clock,' she reminded me as if it were any other day." (lines 264–267)

5. "'Only two kinds of daughters . . . those who are obedient and those who follow their own mind! Only one kind of daughter can live in this house. Obedient daughter!'" (lines 290–292)

6. ". . . She backed out of the room, stunned, as if she were blowing away like a small brown leaf, thin, brittle, lifeless." (lines 303–304)

7. "You pick up fast. . . . You could been genius if you want to." (line 327–328)

8. Additional lines:

ADJECTIVES THAT DESCRIBE JING-MEI'S MOTHER	LINE(S) THAT SUPPORT THE CHOICE OF ADJECTIVES
Proud	
Determined	
Stubborn	
Domineering	
Optimistic	
Unrealistic	
Devoted	
Demanding	

- Based on your discussion, answer the following questions.

  a. Look at the adjectives you chose for the adult Jing-mei and the adjectives you chose for her mother. Are any of these the same or somewhat similar? How might these similarities affect their relationship?

  b. What significant differences can you find in the adjectives that describe the adult Jing-mei and her mother? How might these differences affect their relationship?

WRITING IN RESPONSE

Write briefly on these topics.

1. As a child, Jing-mei "was filled with a sense that [she] would soon become *perfect*." (lines 38–39) But she also feared that the "prodigy" in her would disappear for good, "and then [she would] always be nothing." (lines 42–43) From her perspective as a child, what would it take to make Jing-mei "something"? Where does she get these ideas?

2. At the end, do you think Jing-mei considers herself a failure? (lines 309–322) Provide evidence for your opinion.

CREATIVE WRITING

1. Examine the following passages, all perceived and told from Jing-mei's point of view. Then rewrite one of the passages from the point of view of Jing-mei's mother.

   Before you rewrite the passage, determine the following:

   a. What do we know at this point in the story about the mother's personality and motivations?

   b. What would therefore change in the scene and dialogue?
      Passage 1: Lines 78–85
      Passage 2: Lines 94–104
      Passage 3: Lines 124–133
      Passage 4: Lines 227–235
      Passage 5: Lines 254–263
      Passage 6: Lines 298–304

2. After you finish the rewrite, discuss or write about this question: How does your understanding of the situation, the mother–daughter relationship, and the conflict change by rewriting the passage?

Theme

ACTIVITY 4

In "Two Kinds," the author examines in-depth **themes** about parent–child and generational issues.

Using the following lines and passages, create thematic statements based on these specific situations in the story. First, write out the lines indicated from the story. Then briefly paraphrase or quote other passages in the story that support this theme. Compare your theme statements with those of other students. An example has been done for you.

> *Example:* Lines 129–133
>   "My mother slapped me. 'Who ask you be genius?' she shouted. 'Only ask you be your best. For you sake. You think I want you be genius? Hnnh? What for! Who ask you?'"
>   "'So ungrateful,' I heard her mutter in Chinese. 'If she had as much talent as she has temper, she would be famous now.'"
>
> *Theme statement:*
>   Parents sometimes have high—and unrealistic—expectations of a child that may eventually confuse or hurt that child.
>
> *Other supporting evidence:*
>   Lines 5–7; lines 44–50; lines 86–101; lines 264–283; lines 196–200; lines 324–325; lines 327–331

1. Line 77

    Theme statement:

    Other supporting evidence:

    _____

2. Lines 1–11

    Theme statement:

    Other supporting evidence:

    _____

3. Lines 317–322

   Theme statement:

   Other supporting evidence:

   _____

4. Lines 351–356

   Theme statement:

   Other supporting evidence:

   _____

5. Lines of your choice that show another theme

   Theme statement:

   Other supporting evidence:

WRITING IN RESPONSE

Write briefly on this topic.

Choose one of the themes of the story and relate it to your own experience.

Exploring Further

As you answer the following questions about conflict in "Two Kinds," give evidence to support your answers and line numbers for each piece of evidence, where appropriate.

1. In lines 311–313, Jing-mei says that "for all those years, we never talked about the disaster at the recital or my terrible accusations afterward at the piano bench. All that remained unchecked, like a betrayal that was now unspeakable." What betrayal is she speaking of? Do you think Jing-mei means that she

betrayed her mother or that her mother betrayed her? Or both? Explain your answer.

2. Jing-mei says that what frightened her the most was that her mother had "given up hope." (line 316) Since Jing-mei is so determined not to play the piano, why is she so frightened when her mother finally stops pushing her to play?

3. Do you think Jing-mei's mother gave up hope?

4. What does the title "Two Kinds" mean? Find all the references you can to "two kinds" in the story. What does the idea of "two kinds" have to do with the conflict in the story?

ESSAY TOPICS

1. Write an essay in which you explain what you think the title "Two Kinds" means. In order to answer fully, analyze all possible references to "two kinds"—including the two piano pieces—and determine how they are connected.

2. Throughout "Two Kinds" there is conflict between Jing-mei and her mother. Despite their opposing wishes, Jing-mei and her mother share many characteristics. Choose two adjectives that each describe both Jing-mei and her mother. Write an essay in which you explain how each adjective relates to both Jing-mei and her mother. Discuss how the shared characteristics affect their relationship.

3. By remembering the conflicts she has had with her mother, what do you think Jing-mei has learned about herself? Write an essay in which you explain in detail what conflicts she has faced and what (if any) self-knowledge she has gained.

AUTHOR PROFILE

Amy Tan

Amy Tan was born in Oakland, California, in 1952, and grew up in various San Francisco Bay Area cities. Following the deaths of her brother and father in 1967–68, she moved with her family to Switzerland. She received a B.A. in English and linguistics and an M.A. in linguistics from San Jose State University, and began doctoral studies in linguistics at the University of California, Berkeley. Tan went on to work as a language development consultant and project director for programs serving disabled children, and as a freelance writer specializing in corporate communications.

A self-described workaholic, Tan left the corporate world to focus on writing and has written stories, essays, and three best-selling works: *The Joy Luck Club* (1989), from which the story "Two Kinds" is taken, *The Kitchen God's Wife* (1991), and *The Hundred Secret Senses,* (1995). She also co-wrote (with Ron Bass) the screenplay for the movie version of *The Joy Luck Club* in 1994.

Tan's books and stories are often included in the multicultural curriculums of high schools and colleges, an honor she feels ambivalent about, as evidenced in a speech she has delivered at universities across the country, "Required Reading and Other Dangerous Subjects." In addition to writing, she performs in a "literary garage band" with novelist Stephen King and columnist Dave Barry; proceeds from performances benefit literacy and first amendment rights groups.

CHAPTER 6

The Waltz

DOROTHY PARKER

PREPARATION

ACTIVITY 1

With a partner or in small groups, discuss the following questions.

1. Think of a time when you said yes to a request even though you didn't want to do it. Why did you agree to do something that you did not want to do?

2. Do you know how to waltz? What associations do you have with waltzing?

3. If a person were described to you as a "cannonball" on the dance floor, what might it imply about the way that person dances? Would you want to dance with him or her? Why or why not?

4. Of whom might you ask the following questions: Did you go to the circus this year? What's your favorite ice cream? How do you spell cat?

5. Read the first three sentences of "The Waltz" aloud.

   a. What is the effect of the use of the **first-person point of view** on your sympathy toward the **narrator?** (See Appendix A for more information about terms in boldface type.)

   b. In the first sentence "Why," the speaker does not use "Why" to ask for a reason. Instead, it expresses a feeling of surprise and pleasure. Do you think the narrator is being insincere? Why or why not?

   c. What is the contradiction between the first sentence and the next two?

   d. What might be a reason for the italics?

6. Based on your responses to questions 1 through 5, what do you think is going to happen in this story?

The Waltz

DOROTHY PARKER

Why, thank you so much, I'd adore to.

I don't want to dance with him. I don't want to dance with anybody. And even if I did, it wouldn't be him. He'd be well down among the last ten. I've seen the way he dances; it looks like something you do on Saint Walpurgis Night.° Just think, not a quarter of an hour ago, here I was sitting, feeling so sorry for the poor girl he was dancing with. And now *I'm* going to be the poor girl. Well, well. Isn't it a small world?

And a peach of a world, too. A true little corker. Its events are so fascinatingly unpredictable, are not they? Here I was, minding my own business, not doing a stitch of harm to any living soul. And then he comes into my life, all smiles and city manners, to sue me for the favor of one memorable mazurka.° Why, he scarcely knows my name, let alone what it stands for. It stands for Despair, Bewilderment, Futility, Degradation, and Premeditated Murder, but little does he wot.° I don't wot his name, either; I haven't any idea what it is. Jukes,° would be my guess from the look in this eyes. How do you do Mr. Jukes? And how is that dear little brother of yours, with the two heads? 10

Ah, now why did he have to come around me, with his low requests? Why can't he let me lead my own life? I ask so little—just to be left alone in my quiet corner of the table, to do my evening brooding over all my sorrows. And he must come, with his bows and his scrapes and his may-I-have-this-ones. And I had to go and tell him that I'd adore to dance with him. I cannot understand why I wasn't struck right down dead. Yes, and being struck dead would look like a day in the country, compared to struggling out a dance with this boy. But what could I do? Everyone else at the table had got up to dance, except him and me. There was I, trapped. Trapped like a trap in a trap. 20

What can you say, when a man asks you to dance with him? I most certainly will *not* dance with you, I'll see you in hell first. Why, thank you, I'd like to awfully, but I'm having labor pains. Oh, yes, *do* let's dance together—it's so nice to meet a man who isn't a scaredy-cat about catching my beri-beri. No. There was nothing for me to do, but say I'd adore to. Well, we might as well get it over with. All right, Cannonball, let's run out on the field. You won the toss; you can lead. 30

Why, I think it's more of a waltz, really. Isn't it? We might just listen to the music a second. Shall we? Oh, yes, it's a waltz. Mind? Why, I'm simply thrilled. I'd love to waltz with you.

I'd love to waltz with you. I'd love to waltz with you. I'd love to have my tonsils out, I'd love to be in a midnight fire at sea. Well, it's too late now. We're

°*Saint Walpurgis Night* the night before May 1 (May Day) when the feast of St. Walpurgis was traditionally celebrated among Germanic peoples. According to legend, witches from all over the countryside convened to perform wild dances and evil rituals to honor the devil.

°*mazurka* a fast Polish dance (rhythmically different from a waltz)

°*wot* know

°*Jukes* a fictitious name used to refer to a feebleminded family that was the object of a genetic/sociological study during the nineteenth century

getting under way. *Oh.* Oh, dear. Oh, dear, dear, dear. Oh, this is even worse than I thought it would be. I suppose that's the one dependable law of life—everything is always worse than you thought it was going to be. Oh, if I had any real grasp of what this dance would be like, I'd have held out for sitting it out. Well, it will probably amount to the same thing in the end. We'll be sitting it out on the floor in a minute, if he keeps this up.

I'm so glad I brought it to his attention that this is a waltz they're playing. Heaven knows what might have happened, if he had thought it was something fast; we'd have blown the sides right out of the building. Why does he always want to be somewhere that he isn't? Why can't we stay in one place long enough to get acclimated? It's this constant rush, rush, rush, that's the curse of American life. That's the reason that we're all of us so—*Ow!* For God's sake, don't *kick,* you idiot; this is only second down. Oh, my shin. My poor, poor shin, that I've had ever since I was a little girl!

Oh, no, no, no. Goodness, no. It didn't hurt the least little bit. And anyway it was my fault. Really it was. Truly. Well, you're just being sweet, to say that. It really was all my fault.

I wonder what I'd better do—kill him this instant, with my naked hands, or wait and let him drop in his traces. Maybe it's best not to make a scene. I guess I'll just lie low, and watch the pace get him. He can't keep this up indefinitely— he's only flesh and blood. Die he must, and die he shall, for what he did to me. I don't want to be of the oversensitive type, but you can't tell me that kick was unpremeditated. Freud says there are no accidents. I've led no cloistered life, I've known dancing partners who have spoiled my slippers and torn my dress; but when it comes to kicking, I am Outraged Womanhood. When you kick me in the shin, *smile*.

Maybe he didn't do it maliciously. Maybe it's just his way of showing his high spirits. I suppose I ought to be glad that one of us is having such a good time. I suppose I ought to think myself lucky if he brings me back alive. Maybe it's captious to demand of a practically strange man that he leave your shins as he found them. After all, the poor boy's doing the best he can. Probably he grew up in the hill country, and never had no larnin'.° I bet they had to throw him on his back to get shoes on him.

Yes, it's lovely, isn't it? It's simply lovely. It's the loveliest waltz. Isn't it? Oh, I think it's lovely, too.

Why, I'm getting positively drawn to the Triple Threat here. He's my hero. He has the heart of a lion, and the sinews of a buffalo. Look at him—never a thought of the consequences, never afraid of his face, hurling himself into every scrimmage, eyes shining, cheeks ablaze. And shall it be said that I hung back? No, a thousand times no. What's it to me if I have to spend the next couple of years in a plaster cast? Come on, Butch,° right through them! Who wants to live forever?

Oh. Oh, dear. Oh, he's all right, thank goodness. For a while I thought they'd have to carry him off the field. Ah, I couldn't bear to have anything happen to

°*larnin'* learning (formal education)
°*Butch* a nickname sometimes given to a man who is rough or unfriendly

him. I love him. I love him better than anybody in the world. Look at the spirit   80
he gets into a dreary, commonplace waltz; how effete the other dancers seem,
beside him. He is youth and vigor and courage, he is strength and gaiety and—
Ow! Get off my instep, you hulking peasant! What do you think I am, anyway—a
gangplank? *Ow!*

No, of course it didn't hurt. Why, it didn't a bit. Honestly. And it was all my
fault. You see, that little step of yours—well, it's perfectly lovely, but it's just a
tiny bit tricky to follow at first. Oh, did you work it up yourself? You really
did? Well, aren't you amazing! Oh, now I think I've got it. Oh, I think it's lovely.
I was watching you do it when you were dancing before. It's awfully effective
when you look at it.   90

It's awfully effective when you look at it. I bet I'm awfully effective when you
look at me. My hair is hanging along my cheeks, my skirt is swaddled about me, I
can feel the cold damp of my brow. I must look like something out of "The Fall of
the House of Usher." This sort of thing takes a fearful toll of a woman my age. And
he worked up his little step himself, he with his degenerate cunning. And it was
just a tiny bit tricky at first, but now I think I've got it. Two stumbles, slip, and a
twenty-yard dash; yes. I've got it. I've got several other things, too, including a split
shin and a bitter heart. I hate this creature I'm chained to. I hated him the moment
I saw his leering, bestial face. And here I've been locked in his noxious embrace
for the thirty-five years this waltz has lasted. Is that orchestra never going to stop   100
playing? Or must this obscene travesty of a dance go on until hell burns out?

Oh, they're going to play another encore. Oh, goody. Oh, that's lovely. Tired? I
should say I'm not tired. I'd like to go on like this forever.

I should say I'm not tired. I'm dead, that's all I am. Dead, and in what a cause!
And the music is never going to stop playing, and we're going on like this, Dou-
ble-Time° Charlie and I, throughout eternity. I suppose I won't care any more,
after the first hundred thousand years. I suppose nothing will matter then, not
heat nor pain nor broken heart nor cruel, aching weariness. Well. It can't come
too soon for me.

I wonder why I didn't tell him I was tired. I wonder why I didn't suggest   110
going back to the table. I could have said let's just listen to the music. Yes, and if
he would, that would be the first bit of attention he has given it all evening.
George Jean Nathan° said that the lovely rhythms of the waltz should be listened
to in stillness and not be accompanied by strange gyrations of the human body. I
think that's what he said. I think it was George Jean Nathan. Anyhow, whatever
he said and whoever he was and whatever he's doing now, he's better off than I
am. That's safe. Anybody who isn't waltzing with this Mrs. O'Leary's cow° I've
got here is having a good time.

Still if we were back at the table, I'd probably have to talk to him. Look at
him—what could you say to a thing like that! Did you go to the circus this year,   120

°*Double-Time* twice as fast as normal

°*George Jean Nathan* a U.S. drama critic, author, and editor (1882–1958)

°*Mrs. O'Leary's cow* the cow that, according to legend, caused the Great Chicago Fire of 1871
by knocking over a lighted lantern and setting the O'Leary barn on fire

what's your favorite kind of ice cream, how do you spell cat? I guess I'm as well off here. As well off as if I were in a cement mixer in full action.

I'm past all feeling now. The only way I can tell when he steps on me is that I can hear the splintering of bones. And all the events of my life are passing before my eyes. There was the time I was in a hurricane in the West Indies, there was the day I got my head cut open in the taxi smash, there was the night the drunken lady threw a bronze ash-tray at her own true love and got me instead, there was that summer that the sailboat kept capsizing. Ah, what an easy, peaceful time was mine, until I fell in with Swifty, here. I didn't know what trouble
130   was, before I got drawn into this *danse macabre.*° I think my mind is beginning to wander. It almost seems to me as if the orchestra were stopping. It couldn't be, of course; it could never, never be. And yet in my ears there is a silence like the sound of angel voices. . . .

Oh, they've stopped, the mean things. They're not going to play any more. Oh, darn. Oh, do you think they would? Do you really think so, if you gave them fifty dollars? Oh, that would be lovely. And look, do tell them to play this same thing. I'd simply adore to go on waltzing.

ANALYZING THE STORY

ACTIVITY 2

Answer the following questions. Give evidence from the story to support your answers and include line numbers for each piece of evidence.

1. What is the narrator doing at the beginning of the story? Who interrupts her and what does he ask her to do? Where do you think they are?

2. What does the narrator mean when she says, "Isn't it a small world"? (line 7) Is she pleased that this man has asked her to dance? How do you know?

3. Read the statements in italics, which begin as indicated in the chart, and record what you think was said immediately before each one.

ITALIC STATEMENTS	WHAT WAS SAID IMMEDIATELY BEFORE
a. *"Oh, no, no, no. Goodness, no."* (line 51)	
b. *"Yes, it's lovely . . . "* (line 70)	
c. *"No, of course it didn't hurt."* (line 85)	
d. *"Oh, they're going to play another encore."* (line 102)	

°*danse macabre* a dance that leads to death

4. What does the narrator mean when she says "I cannot understand why I was not struck right down dead"? (lines 21–22)

5. To what does she compare waltzing with this man in lines 35–36? What does she mean?

6. What is the meaning of "Why does he always want to be somewhere that he isn't"? (lines 45–46) What is she saying about the speed of his dancing?

7. The narrator tells her dance partner that his dance step is "perfectly lovely, but . . . a tiny bit tricky to follow . . . ." (lines 86–87) Is she being honest? Explain.

8. What do "two stumbles, slip, and a twenty-yard dash" (lines 96–97) imply about the man's dance step?

9. What does "it" refer to when the narrator says "that would be the first bit of attention he has given it all evening"? (line 112) What is the narrator's point?

10. What happens at the end of the story? Does this surprise you? Why or why not?

11. "The Waltz" is a **satire** of human behavior. What aspect of behavior is it satirizing?

Elements of Literature

Characterization

A C T I V I T Y 3

Answer the following questions. Give evidence from the story to support your answers and include line numbers for each piece of evidence.

1. Does the narrator notice the young man before he asks her to dance? Explain.

2. Does the young man know the difference between a waltz and a mazurka? How might this affect his dancing?

3. Is the young man a good dancer in the opinion of the narrator?

4. Look at the repetition of "why" questions. (lines 17–18 and lines 45–47) Based on these lines, do you feel the narrator is dancing with the man because she is *polite* or because she *does not know how to refuse*? Find evidence from other parts of the story that supports your decision.

WRITING IN RESPONSE

Write briefly on these topics.

1. Form groups of three and do the following:
   a. Freewrite about Statement 1 for ten minutes.
   b. Pass the paper to the next person in the group. That person reads what the first group member wrote and responds to it for five to ten minutes.
   c. Repeat with the third group member.
   d. Read the two responses to the original freewriting and discuss similarities and differences.
   e. Compare your ideas with those of other groups in the class.
   f. Repeat steps a–e for Statement 2, with a different group of three.

   Statement 1: The narrator does/does not like to dance. (Choose one.)
   Statement 2: The young man does/does not know how the narrator feels about him. (Choose one.)

2. In the beginning of the story, the narrator describes life as "fascinatingly un-predictable." (lines 8–9) Find three other generalizations she makes about life. Based on what you find, would you describe her as an optimistic, posi-tive person or as negative and cynical? Explain and support your ideas with specific information from the story.

3. The narrator gives a detailed description of her experience dancing with the man, yet there is no information given about his physical appearance or the setting. We don't know what he looks like, whether they are in a restaurant or at a party, or anything else about the physical environment or the people involved. What else would you like to know about them? Why do you think the author leaves out such information?

Figurative Language

ACTIVITY 4

Throughout "The Waltz," the narrator uses **figurative language** to compare her partner to something else, something unrelated to him or to the situation. For ex-ample, "second down," (line 49) "kicking," (line 61) "scrimmage," (lines 74–75) and "carry him off the field" (line 79) are expressions related to football. They imply that her partner dances like a football player. What does it mean to dance like someone playing football?

Work with a partner to find other examples of figurative language and discuss what each comparison reveals about the narrator's feelings toward the young man and the situation. List your examples on the board and explain your inter-pretation to the class.

Language and Style

ACTIVITY 5

Repetition is a key feature in Dorothy Parker's **style.** Examine any paragraph and you will find repeated words, phrases, and whole sentences—sometimes word for word, sometimes with a slight alteration or synonym. You will also find repeated grammatical forms, called *parallel structure,* in her writing.

1. Choose three to five consecutive sentences in the story and rewrite them so that the repetition is made clear visually. Put the repeated words, phrases, or grammatical structures directly under each other, as in these examples (repeated items are also italicized).

    a. "Just think, *not a quarter of an hour ago,*
        here I was sitting,
                feeling so sorry for *the poor girl*
            he was dancing with. And
            now I'm going to be *the poor girl.*" (lines 4–6)
    b. "*Well,*
        well. Isn't it *a small*   *world?* ¶ And
                a peach of a world, too.
                a true little   *corker.*" (lines 6–8)
    c. "*Here I was, minding* my own business, not
                doing a stitch of harm to any living soul." (lines 9–10)

2. Share your results with the class. Write your examples on the board, if possible.

3. Choose a different passage of three to five sentences in which the repetition is especially noticeable and read it aloud to the class. As a class, discuss the effect of these repetitions on the tone—that is, the voice of the narrator—on pace and continuity, and on humor.

ACTIVITY 6

1. Divide the class into five groups. Each group works on a different section of the story.

    Group 1: Lines 1–31   Group 4: Lines 91–118
    Group 2: Lines 32–62   Group 5: Lines 119–the end
    Group 3: Lines 63–90

2. In your group, complete the following chart of paired opposites with appropriate words from your assigned section of the story. For example, under the category "Sadness/Happiness," "sorrows" (line 19) would be appropriate for Group 1, and "thrilled" (line 33) would be appropriate for Group 2.

    a. If the word or words are being used sarcastically, put an "S" next to the example to indicate that it means the opposite.
    b. Circle any words that come from the italicized sections of the story. Some examples have been filled in for you.

SADNESS/HAPPINESS	DEATH/LIFE	DAMAGE/GOOD CONDITION
sorrows (line 19)		
(*thrilled*)*s (line 33)*		
HOPELESSNESS/HOPE	FEAR OR ANGER/CALM	DANGER/SAFETY
HUMILIATION/DIGNITY	HOSTILITY/FRIENDSHIP	FATIGUE/ENERGY
PAIN/COMFORT	STUPIDITY/INTELLIGENCE	

3. When each group has finished, put all the examples on the board under the correct headings.

4. As a class, examine all the words on the board.

   a. Do you see any patterns?
   b. Do the words seem primarily positive or negative?
   c. How might they affect the mood of the story as a whole?
   d. What difference is there between words used in the italicized and in the nonitalicized sections of the story?
   e. What does this difference tell us about the narrator?
   f. Are the sarcastic words positive or negative? Explain.

Exploring Further

Continue your analysis of "The Waltz" with these questions for discussion or writing.

1. The narrator in "The Waltz" makes several general statements about life. Read a few of the narrator's generalizations below. Then do or answer the following:

   a. Discuss what each one means and what has happened in the story that has caused her to make this generalization.
   b. Is she being serious or sarcastic?

  c. Do you feel the story supports the generalization or that it contradicts it? Explain.

Generalization 1: "[The world's] events are so fascinatingly unpredictable . . . ." (lines 8–9)
Generalization 2: "I suppose that's the one dependable law of life—everything is always worse than you thought it was going to be." (lines 38–39)
Generalization 3: "Freud says there are no accidents." (line 59)
Generalization 4: "Who wants to live forever?" (line 77)

2. The narrator seems to agree with Freud that there are no accidents. If she really does agree, how would that fact undermine the truth of or show her confusion about the following other statements she makes?

  a. "I ask so little—just to be left alone in my quiet corner of the table, to do my evening brooding over all my sorrows." (lines 18–19) Is the narrator being honest with herself? Explain.
  b. "There I was, trapped. Trapped like a trap in a trap." (line 25) Can you think of some legitimate excuses the narrator could have given?
  c. "Why, I'm getting positively drawn to the Triple Threat here. He's my hero" (line 72) *and* "I hate this creature I'm chained to." (line 98) Is it possible that the narrator is unconsciously attracted to the excitement of the situation? If so, how?
  d. "I wonder why I didn't tell him I was tired." (line 110) Why *didn't* she tell him she was tired, after all?
  e. "Still, if we were back at the table, I'd probably have to talk to him." (line 119) Based on what you know about the two characters, is it possible that talking to the man might have been more unpleasant for the narrator than dancing with him? Explain.

3. *Role Play.* Work with a partner. One of you will role-play the narrator, and the other will role-play a close friend. It is the next day after the story. The friend asks the narrator this question:

  Why did you agree to let the man give the musicians fifty dollars so you could continue waltzing with him?

Follow these steps:

  a. Continue the conversation.
  b. After two minutes, reverse roles and repeat.
  c. After two more minutes, find a new partner and repeat. Continue with new partners until you have several satisfactory answers to the question.
  d. Share your conclusions with the class.

WRITING IN RESPONSE

Respond briefly to these questions in writing.

1. Why does the narrator agree to dance with the young man in the first place?

2. "The Waltz" is written as an inner monologue with a small amount of outer monologue (her comments to the man) interspersed throughout the story. How does this technique of inner and outer monologue affect our under-standing of the characters?

ESSAY TOPICS

1. Write an essay in which you explain how Parker uses figurative language and humor in "The Waltz" to show what a bad dancer the narrator thinks the young man is.

2. Use evidence from "The Waltz" to support or to contradict *one* of the following statements. Keep in mind the narrator's feelings, attitudes, and confusion about what she really wants and why she behaves as she does.

    Anyone can "just say no."
    Lonely people do desperate things.
    Opposites attract.
    Bad situations only get worse.
    A negative attitude yields a negative experience.
    Things are always worse than you expect them to be.
    Some people do not know what they want.
    We do not always learn from our mistakes.
    There are no accidents.
    Perfect manners can cause perfect misery.

AUTHOR PROFILE
Dorothy Parker

Dorothy Parker was born Dorothy Rothschild on August 22, 1893, into a wealthy New York family. By age twenty she was able to support herself comfortably with writing. At first, she wrote captions for advertisements, reviews for magazines, and poems, but she soon became well known for her witty play and book reviews, her articles, her weekly columns, and her short stories. In 1917 she married a man named Edwin Parker but divorced him in 1928, keeping only his last name, which she felt was a much better professional name than Rothschild.

Dorothy Parker's famous wit was often too strong: she was able to see through people's falseness, and she made fun of them, especially in reviews. As a result she was fired at least once from a good position and often made enemies. Nevertheless, the fact that she could also make fun of herself made it easier for readers to accept her criticism of others. In 1934 she married again and moved to Hollywood to write for the movies. She continued to write screenplays, articles, plays, poems, and stories for the rest of her life, although her concern over the growing seriousness of world events undermined her humorous spirit and weakened her ability to write satire. She moved back and forth between the East and West Coasts, divorced and remarried, and finally settled back in New York where she died on June 7, 1967.

CHAPTER 7

Silent Snow, Secret Snow

CONRAD AIKEN

PREPARATION

ACTIVITY 1

With a partner or in small groups, discuss the following questions.

1. Write a sentence that describes your feelings about snow. Discuss with a partner.

2. After a heavy snowfall, sound is absorbed and seems to disappear as quickly as it is produced. Can you think of any other instances when sound is immediately absorbed? What sort of mood does this create?

3. In "Silent Snow, Secret Snow," there is no real snow. Discuss with your partner what the title might refer to in a figurative sense.

ACTIVITY 2

Read the first part of the story in small sections as indicated below; then answer the questions as a class before you read the rest of the story.

1. Read the first five lines of the story.

   a. What might "it" be?
   b. Why does the writer use "Mother and Father" instead of Mom and Dad or mother and father?

2. Read the next sentence. (lines 5–10)

   a. What is a trinket, and how is this word related to the list of things that follows?

b. What is the trinket that the boy carries?

c. How old do you think the boy is? What makes you think so?

3. Read the next two sentences. (lines 10–13)

a. What is "it" compared to?

b. Does "it" seem positive or negative? Explain.

4. Finish reading the first paragraph. (lines 13–21)

a. Where is the boy? What's happening? Who else is there?

b. How well is the boy paying attention to the lesson? What is he paying attention to?

c. What mood does the first paragraph create? Find evidence in the writer's use of language to support your view.

5. Read to the end of the fifth paragraph. (lines 22–37)

a. Describe Miss Buell.

b. Why does the class laugh? Does the boy laugh? Why or why not? How is he feeling? What is he thinking about while Miss Buell is discussing the tropics?

c. What does "of that morning, the first one, and then of all the others" mean? (lines 36–37)

d. What do you think is going to happen in this story?

Silent Snow, Secret Snow

CONRAD AIKEN

Just why it should have happened, or why it should have happened just when it did, he could not, of course, possibly have said; nor perhaps would it even have occurred to him to ask. The thing was above all a secret, something to be preciously concealed from Mother and Father; and to that very fact it owed an enormous part of its deliciousness. It was like a peculiarly beautiful trinket to be carried unmentioned in one's trouser pocket—a rare stamp, an old coin, a few tiny gold links found trodden out of shape on the path in the park, a pebble of carnelian, a seashell distinguishable from all others by an unusual spot or stripe—and, as if it were any one of these, he carried around with him everywhere a warm
10   and persistent and increasingly beautiful sense of possession. Nor was it only a sense of possession—it was also a sense of protection. It was as if, in some delightful way, his secret gave him a fortress, a wall behind which he could retreat into heavenly seclusion. This was almost the first thing he had noticed about it—apart from the oddness of the thing itself—and it was this that now again, for the fiftieth time, occurred to him, as he sat in the little schoolroom. It was the half-hour for geography. Miss Buell was revolving with one finger, slowly, a huge terrestrial globe which had been placed on her desk. The green and yellow continents passed and repassed, questions were asked and answered, and now the little girl in front of him, Deirdre, who had a funny little constellation of freckles on the back
20   of her neck, exactly like the Big Dipper, was standing up and telling Miss Buell that the equator was the line that ran round the middle.

Miss Buell's face, which was old and grayish and kindly, with gray stiff curls beside the cheeks, and eyes that swam very brightly, like little minnows, behind thick glasses, wrinkled itself into a complication of amusements.

"Ah! I see. The earth is wearing a belt, or a sash. Or someone drew a line round it!"

"Oh no—not that—I mean——"

In the general laughter, he did not share, or only a very little. He was thinking about the Arctic and Antarctic regions, which of course, on the globe, were
30   white. Miss Buell was now telling them about the tropics, the jungles, the steamy heat of equatorial swamps, where the birds and butterflies, and even the snakes, were like living jewels. As he listened to these things, he was already, with a pleasant sense of half-effort, putting his secret between himself and the words. Was it really an effort at all? For effort implied something voluntary, and perhaps even something one did not especially want; whereas this was distinctly pleasant, and came almost of its own accord. All he needed to do was to think of that morning, the first one, and then of all the others——

But it was all so absurdly simple! It had amounted to so little. It was nothing, just an idea—and just why it should have become so wonderful, so permanent,
40   was a mystery—a very pleasant one, to be sure, but also, in an amusing way, foolish. However, without ceasing to listen to Miss Buell, who had now moved up to the north temperate zones, he deliberately invited his memory of the first morning. It was only a moment or two after he had waked up—or perhaps the

moment itself. But was there, to be exact, an exact moment? Was one awake all at once? or was it gradual? Anyway, it was after he had stretched a lazy hand up toward the headrail, and yawned, and then relaxed again among his warm covers, all the more grateful on a December morning, that the thing had happened. Suddenly, for no reason, he had thought of the postman, he remembered the postman. Perhaps there was nothing so odd in that. After all, he heard the postman almost every morning in his life—his heavy boots could be heard clumping round the corner at the top of the little cobbled hill-street, and then, progressively nearer, progressively louder, the double knock at each door, the crossings and re-crossings of the street, till finally the clumsy steps came stumbling across to the very door, and the tremendous knock came which shook the house itself.

(Miss Buell was saying, "Vast wheat-growing areas in North America and Siberia."

Deirdre had for the moment placed her left hand across the back of her neck.)

But on this particular morning, the first morning, as he lay there with his eyes closed, he had for some reason *waited* for the postman. He wanted to hear him come round the corner. And that was precisely the joke—he never did. He never came. He never had come—*round the corner*—again. For when at last the steps *were* heard, they had already, he was quite sure, come a little down the hill, to the first house; and even so, the steps were curiously different—they were softer, they had a new secrecy about them, they were muffled and indistinct; and while the rhythm of them was the same, it now said a new thing—it said peace, it said remoteness, it said cold, it said sleep. And he had understood the situation at once—nothing could have seemed simpler—there had been snow in the night, such as all winter he had been longing for; and it was this which had rendered the postman's first footsteps inaudible, and the later ones faint. Of course! How lovely! And even now it must be snowing—it was going to be a snowy day—the long white ragged lines were drifting and sifting across the street, across the faces of the old houses, whispering and hushing, making little triangles of white in the corners between cobblestones, seething a little when the wind blew them over the ground to a drifted corner; and so it would be all day, getting deeper and deeper and silenter and silenter.

(Miss Buell was saying, "Land of perpetual snow.")

All this time, of course (while he lay in bed), he had kept his eyes closed, listening to the nearer progress of the postman, the muffled footsteps thumping and slipping on the snow-sheathed cobbles; and all the other sounds—the double knocks, a frosty far-off voice or two, a bell ringing thinly and softly as if under a sheet of ice—had the same slightly abstracted quality, as if removed by one degree from actuality—as if everything in the world had been insulated by snow. But when at last, pleased, he opened his eyes, and turned them toward the window, to see for himself this long-desired and now so clearly imagined miracle— what he saw instead was brilliant sunlight on a roof; and when, astonished, he jumped out of bed and stared down into the street, expecting to see the cobbles obliterated by the snow, he saw nothing but the bare bright cobbles themselves.

Queer, the effect this extraordinary surprise had had upon him—all the following morning he had kept with him a sense as of snow falling about him, a

90   secret screen of new snow between himself and the world. If he had not
dreamed such a thing—and how could he have dreamed it while awake?—how
else could one explain it? In any case, the delusion had been so vivid as to affect
his entire behavior. He could not now remember whether it was on the first or
the second morning—or was it even the third?—that his mother had drawn attention to some oddness in his manner.

"But my darling"—she had said at the breakfast table—"what has come over
you? You don't seem to be listening. . . ."

And how often that very thing had happened since!

(Miss Buell was now asking if anyone knew the difference between the North
100   Pole and the Magnetic Pole. Deirdre was holding up her flickering brown hand,
and he could see the four white dimples that marked the knuckles.)

Perhaps it hadn't been either the second or third morning—or even the
fourth or fifth. How could he be sure? How could he be sure just when the delicious *progress* had become clear? Just when it had really *begun?* The intervals
weren't very precise. . . . All he now knew was, that at some point or other—
perhaps the second day, perhaps the sixth—he had noticed that the presence of
the snow was a little more insistent, the sound of it clearer; and, conversely, the
sound of the postman's footsteps more indistinct. Not only could he not hear
the steps come round the corner, he could not even hear them at the first
110   house. It was below the first house that he heard them; and then, a few days
later, it was below the second house that he heard them; and a few days later
again, below the third. Gradually, gradually, the snow was becoming heavier, the
sound of its seething louder, the cobblestones more and more muffled. When he
found, each morning, on going to the window, after the ritual of listening, that
the roofs and cobbles were as bare as ever, it made no difference. This was,
after all, only what he had expected. It was even what pleased him, what re-
warded him: the thing was his own, belonged to no one else. No one else knew
about it, not even his mother and father. There, outside, were the bare cobbles;
and here, inside, was the snow. Snow growing heavier each day, muffling the
120   world, hiding the ugly, and deadening increasingly—above all—the steps of the
postman.

"But, my darling"—she had said at the luncheon table—"what has come over
you? You don't seem to listen when people speak to you. That's the third time
I've asked you to pass your plate. . . ."

How was one to explain this to Mother? or to Father? There was, of course,
nothing to be done about it: nothing. All one could do was to laugh embarrassedly, pretend to be a little ashamed, apologize, and take a sudden and somewhat
disingenuous interest in what was being done or said. The cat had stayed out all
night. He had a curious swelling on his left cheek—perhaps somebody had
130   kicked him, or a stone had struck him. Mrs. Kempton was or was not coming to
tea. The house was going to be housecleaned, or "turned out," on Wednesday instead of Friday. A new lamp was provided for his evening work—perhaps it was
eyestrain which accounted for this new and so peculiar vagueness of his—
Mother was looking at him with amusement as she said this, but with something
else as well. A new lamp? A new lamp. Yes, Mother, No, Mother, Yes, Mother.

School is going very well. The geometry is very easy. The history is very dull. The geography is very interesting—particularly when it takes one to the North Pole. Why the North Pole? Oh, well, it would be fun to be an explorer. Another Peary or Scott or Shackleton.° And then abruptly he found his interest in the talk at an end, stared at the pudding on his plate, listened, waited, and began once more—   140
ah, how heavenly, too, the first beginnings—to hear or feel—for could he actually hear it?—the silent snow, the secret snow.

   (Miss Buell was telling them about the search for the Northwest Passage, about Hendrik Hudson, the *Half Moon*.)°

   This had been, indeed, the only distressing feature of the new experience; the fact that it so increasingly had brought him into a kind of mute misunderstanding, or even conflict, with his father and mother. It was as if he were trying to lead a double life. On the one hand, he had to be Paul Hasleman, and keep up the appearance of being that person—dress, wash, and answer intelligently when spoken to—; on the other, he had to explore this new world which had been   150
opened to him. Nor could there be the slightest doubt—not the slightest—that the new world was the profounder and more wonderful of the two. It was irresistible. It was miraculous. Its beauty was simply beyond anything—beyond speech as beyond thought—utterly incommunicable. But how then, between the two worlds, of which he was thus constantly aware, was he to keep a balance? One must get up, one must go to breakfast, one must talk with Mother, go to school, do one's lessons—and, in all this, try not to appear too much of a fool. But if all the while one was also trying to extract the full deliciousness of another and quite separate existence, one which could not easily (if at all) be spoken of—how was one to manage? How was one to explain? Would it be safe to   160
explain? Would it be absurd? Would it merely mean that he would get into some obscure kind of trouble?

   These thoughts came and went, came and went, as softly and secretly as the snow; they were not precisely a disturbance, perhaps they were even a pleasure; he liked to have them; their presence was something almost palpable, something he could stroke with his hand, without closing his eyes, and without ceasing to see Miss Buell and the schoolroom and the globe and the freckles on Deirdre's neck; nevertheless he did in a sense cease to see, or to see the obvious external world, and substituted for this vision the vision of snow, the sound of snow, and the slow, almost soundless, approach of the postman. Yesterday, it had been only   170
at the sixth house that the postman had become audible; the snow was much deeper now, it was falling more swiftly and heavily, the sound of its seething was more distinct, more soothing, more persistent. And this morning, it had been—as nearly as he could figure—just above the seventh house—perhaps only a step or two above; at most, he had heard two or three footsteps before the knock had sounded. . . . And with each such narrowing of the sphere, each nearer approach of the limit at which the postman was first audible, it was odd how sharply was increased the amount of illusion which had to be carried into the ordinary

°*Peary or Scott or Shackleton* three North Pole explorers
°*Half Moon* name of Henry Hudson's ship

business of daily life. Each day, it was harder to get out of bed, to go to the win-
180   dow, to look out at the—as always—perfectly empty and snowless street. Each
day it was more difficult to go through the perfunctory motions of greeting
Mother and Father at breakfast, to reply to their questions, to put his books together and go to school. And at school, how extraordinarily hard to conduct
with success simultaneously the public life and the life that was secret! There
were times when he longed—positively ached—to tell everyone about it—to
burst out with it—only to be checked almost at once by a far-off feeling as of
some faint absurdity which was inherent in it—but *was* it absurd?—and more
importantly by a sense of mysterious power in his very secrecy. Yes; it must be
kept secret. That, more and more, became clear. At whatever cost to himself,
190   whatever pain to others——

(Miss Buell looked straight at him, smiling, and said, "Perhaps we'll ask Paul.
I'm sure Paul will come out of his daydream long enough to be able to tell us.
Won't you, Paul?" He rose slowly from his chair, resting one hand on the brightly
varnished desk, and deliberately stared through the snow toward the blackboard.
It was an effort, but it was amusing to make it. "Yes," he said slowly, "it was what
we now call the Hudson River. This he thought to be the Northwest Passage. He
was disappointed." He sat down again, and as he did so Deirdre half turned in
her chair and gave him a shy smile, of approval and admiration.)

At whatever pain to others.

200   This part of it was very puzzling, very puzzling. Mother was very nice, and so
was Father. Yes, that was all true enough. He wanted to be nice to them, to tell
them everything—and yet, was it really wrong of him to want to have a secret
place of his own?

At bed-time, the night before, Mother had said, "If this goes on, my lad, we'll
have to see a doctor, we will! We can't have our boy—" But what was it she had
said? "Live in another world"? "Live so far away"? The word "far" had been in it,
he was sure, and then Mother had taken up a magazine again and laughed a little, but with an expression which wasn't mirthful. He had felt sorry for her. . . .

The bell rang for dismissal. The sound came to him through long curved par-
210   allels of falling snow. He saw Deirdre rise, and had himself risen almost as soon—
but not quite as soon—as she.

II.   On the walk homeward, which was timeless, it pleased him to see
through the accompaniment, or counterpoint, of snow, the items of mere exter-
nality on his way. There were many kinds of brick in the sidewalks, and laid in
many kinds of pattern. The garden walls, too, were various, some of wooden pal-
ings, some of plaster, some of stone. Twigs of bushes leaned over the walls: the
little hard green winter-buds of lilac, on gray stems, sheathed and fat; other
branches very thin and fine and black and desiccated. Dirty sparrows huddled in
the bushes, as dull in color as dead fruit left in leafless trees. A single starling
220   creaked on a weather vane. In the gutter, beside a drain, was a scrap of torn and
dirty newspaper, caught in a little delta of filth; the word ECZEMA appeared in
large capitals, and below it was a letter from Mrs. Amelia D. Cravath, 2100 Pine
Street, Fort Worth, Texas, to the effect that after being a sufferer for years she had

been cured by Caley's Ointment. In the little delta, beside the fan-shaped and deeply runneled continent of brown mud, were lost twigs, descended from their parent trees, dead matches, a rusty horse-chestnut burr, a small concentration of eggshell, a streak of yellow sawdust which had been wet and now was dry and congealed, a brown pebble, and a broken feather. Farther on was a cement sidewalk, ruled into geometrical parallelograms, with a brass inlay at one end commemorating the contractors who had laid it, and, halfway across, an irregular and random series of dog-tracks, immortalized in synthetic stone. He knew these well, and always stepped on them; to cover the little hollows with his own foot had always been a queer pleasure; today he did it once more, but perfunctorily and detachedly, all the while thinking of something else. That was a dog, a long time ago, who had made a mistake and walked on the cement while it was still wet. He had probably wagged his tail, but that hadn't been recorded. Now, Paul Hasleman, aged twelve, on his way home from school, crossed the same river, which in the meantime had frozen into rock. Homeward through the snow, the snow falling in bright sunshine. Homeward?

Then came the gateway with the two posts surmounted by egg-shaped stones which had been cunningly balanced on their ends, as if by Columbus, and mortared in the very act of balance; a source of perpetual wonder. On the brick wall just beyond, the letter H had been stenciled, presumably for some purpose. H? H.

The green hydrant, with a little green-painted chain attached to the brass screw-cap.

The elm tree, with the great gray wound in the bark, kidney-shaped, into which he always put his hand—to feel the cold but living wood. The injury, he had been sure, was due to the gnawings of a tethered horse. But now it deserved only a passing palm, a merely tolerant eye. There were more important things. Miracles. Beyond the thoughts of trees, mere elms. Beyond the thoughts of sidewalks, mere stone, mere brick, mere cement. Beyond the thoughts even of his own shoes, which trod these sidewalks obediently, bearing a burden—far above—of elaborate mystery. He watched them. They were not very well polished; he had neglected them, for a very good reason: they were one of the many parts of the increasing difficulty of the daily return to daily life, the morning struggle. To get up, having at last opened one's eyes, to go to the window, and discover no snow, to wash, to dress, to descend the curving stairs to breakfast——

At whatever pain to others, nevertheless, one must persevere in severance, since the incommunicability of the experience demanded it. It was desirable, of course, to be kind to Mother and Father, especially as they seemed to be worried, but it was also desirable to be resolute. If they should decide—as appeared likely—to consult the doctor, Doctor Howells, and have Paul inspected, his heart listened to through a kind of dictaphone, his lungs, his stomach—well, that was all right. He would go through with it. He would give them answer for question, too—perhaps such answers as they hadn't expected? No. That would never do. For the secret world must, at all costs, be preserved.

The bird-house in the apple tree was empty—it was the wrong time of year for wrens. The little round black door had lost its pleasure. The wrens were

230

240

250

260

270   enjoying other houses, other nests, remoter trees. But this too was a notion
       which he only vaguely and grazingly entertained—as if, for the moment, he
       merely touched an edge of it; there was something further on, which was already
       assuming a sharper importance; something which already teased at the corners
       of his eyes, teasing also at the corner of his mind. It was funny to think that he
       so wanted this, so awaited it—and yet found himself enjoying this momentary
       dalliance with the bird-house, as if for a quite deliberate postponement and en-
       hancement of the approaching pleasure. He was aware of his delay, of his smiling
       and detached and now almost uncomprehending gaze at the little bird-house; he
       knew what he was going to look at next: it was his own little cobbled hill-street,
280   his own house, the little river at the bottom of the hill, the grocer's shop with
       the cardboard man in the window—and now, thinking of all this, he turned his
       head, still smiling, and looking quickly right and left through the snow-laden
       sunlight.

       And the mist of snow, as he had foreseen, was still on it—a ghost of snow
       falling in the bright sunlight, softly and steadily floating and turning and paus-
       ing, soundlessly meeting the snow that covered, as with a transparent mirage,
       the bare bright cobbles. He loved it—he stood still and loved it. Its beauty was
       paralyzing—beyond all words, all experience, all dream. No fairy story he had
       ever read could be compared with it—none had ever given him this extraordi-
290   nary combination of ethereal loveliness with a something else, unnameable,
       which was just faintly and deliciously terrifying. What was this thing? As he
       thought of it, he looked upward toward his own bedroom window, which was
       open—and it was as if he looked straight into the room and saw himself lying
       half awake in his bed. There he was—at this very instant he was still perhaps
       actually there—more truly there than standing here at the edge of the cobbled
       hill-street, with one hand lifted to shade his eyes against the snow-sun. Had he
       indeed ever left his room, in all this time? since that very first morning? Was the
       whole progress still being enacted there, was it still the same morning, and him-
       self not yet wholly awake? And even now, had the postman not yet come round
300   the corner? . . .

       This idea amused him, and automatically, as he thought of it, he turned his
       head and looked toward the top of the hill. There was, of course, nothing
       there—nothing and no one. The street was empty and quiet. And all the more
       because of its emptiness it occurred to him to count the houses—a thing which,
       oddly enough, he hadn't before thought of doing. Of course, he had known there
       weren't many—many, that is, on his own side of the street, which were the ones
       that figured in the postman's progress—but nevertheless it came as something of
       a shock to find that there were precisely *six*, above his own house—his own
       house was the seventh.

310   Six!

       Astonished, he looked at his own house—looked at the door, on which was
       the number thirteen—and then realized that the whole thing was exactly and
       logically and absurdly what he ought to have known. Just the same, the realiza-
       tion gave him abruptly, and even a little frighteningly, a sense of hurry. He was
       being hurried—he was being rushed. For—he knit his brow—he couldn't be

mistaken—it was just above the *seventh* house, his *own* house, that the postman had first been audible this very morning. But in that case—in that case—did it mean that tomorrow he would hear nothing? The knock he had heard must have been the knock of their own door. Did it mean—and this was an idea which gave him a really extraordinary feeling of surprise—that he would never hear the   320
postman again?—that tomorrow morning the postman would already have passed the house, in a snow so deep as to render his footsteps completely inaudible? That he would have made his approach down the snow-filled street so soundlessly, so secretly, that he, Paul Hasleman, there lying in bed, would not have waked in time, or waking, would have heard nothing?

But how could that be? Unless even the knocker should be muffled in the snow—frozen tight, perhaps? . . . But in that case——

A vague feeling of disappointment came over him; a vague sadness as if he felt himself deprived of something which he had long looked forward to, something much prized. After all this, all this beautiful progress, the slow delicious ad-   330
vance of the postman through the silent and secret snow, the knock creeping closer each day, and the footsteps nearer, the audible compass of the world thus daily narrowed, narrowed, narrowed, as the snow soothingly and beautifully encroached and deepened, after all this, was he to be defrauded of the one thing he had so wanted—to be able to count, as it were, the last two or three solemn footsteps, as they finally approached his own door? Was it all going to happen, at the end, so suddenly? or indeed, had it already happened? with no slow and subtle gradations of menace, in which he could luxuriate?

He gazed upward again, toward his own window which flashed in the sun; and this time almost with a feeling that it would be better if he *were* still in bed,   340
in that room; for in that case this must still be the first morning, and there would be six more mornings to come—or, for that matter, seven or eight or nine—how could he be sure?—or even more.

III.   After supper, the inquisition began. He stood before the doctor, under the lamp, and submitted silently to the usual thumpings and tappings.

"Now will you please say 'Ah!'?"

"Ah!"

"Now again, please, if you don't mind."

"Ah!"

"Say it slowly, and hold it if you can——"   350

"Ah-h-h-h-h——"

"Good."

How silly all this was. As if it had anything to do with his throat! Or his heart, or lungs!

Relaxing his mouth, of which the corners, after all this absurd stretching, felt uncomfortable, he avoided the doctor's eyes, and stared toward the fireplace, past his mother's feet (in gray slippers) which projected from the green chair, and his father's feet (in brown slippers) which stood neatly side by side on the hearth rug.

"Hm. There is certainly nothing wrong there . . . ?"   360

He felt the doctor's eyes fixed upon him, and, as if merely to be polite, returned the look, but with a feeling of justifiable evasiveness.

"Now, young man, tell me—do you feel all right?"

"Yes, sir, quite all right."

"No headaches? no dizziness?"

"No, I don't think so."

"Let me see. Let's get a book, if you don't mind—yes, thank you, that will do
splendidly—and now, Paul, if you'll just read it, holding it as you would normally
hold it——"

370   He took the book and read:

"And another praise have I to tell for this the city our mother, the gift of a
great god, a glory of the land most high; the might of horses, the might of young
horses, the might of the sea. . . . For thou, son of Cronus, our lord Poseidon, hath
throned herein this pride, since in these roads first thou didst show forth the
curb that cures the rage of steeds. And the shapely oar, apt to men's hands, hath
a wondrous speed on the brine, following the hundred-footed Nereids. . . . O land
that art praised above all lands, now is it for thee to make those bright praises
seen in deeds."°

He stopped, tentatively, and lowered the heavy book.

380   "No—as I thought—there is certainly no superficial sign of eyestrain."

Silence thronged the room, and he was aware of the focused scrutiny of the
three people who confronted him. . . .

"We could have his eyes examined—but I believe it is something else."

"What could it be?" That was his father's voice.

"It's only this curious absent-mindedness—" This was his mother's voice.

In the presence of the doctor, they both seemed irritatingly apologetic.

"I believe it is something else. Now Paul—I would like very much to ask you
a question or two. You will answer them, won't you—you know I'm an old, old
friend of yours, eh? That's right! . . ."

390   His back was thumped twice by the doctor's fat fist—then the doctor was
grinning at him with false amiability, while with one fingernail he was scratching
the top button of his waistcoat. Beyond the doctor's shoulder was the fire, the
fingers of flame making light prestidigitation against the sooty fireback, the soft
sound of their random flutter the only sound.

"I would like to know—is there anything that worries you?"

The doctor was again smiling, his eyelids low against the little black pupils, in
each of which was a tiny white bead of light. Why answer him? why answer him
at all? "At whatever pain to others"—but it was all a nuisance, this necessity for
resistance, this necessity for attention; it was as if one had been stood up on a

400   brilliantly lighted stage, under a great round blaze of spotlight; as if one were
merely a trained seal, or a performing dog, or a fish, dipped out of an aquarium
and held up by the tail. It would serve them right if he were merely to bark or
growl. And meanwhile, to miss these last few precious hours, these hours of

°Lines 371–378 are from *Oedipus at Colonus* by Sophocles, in which the banished Oedipus is
able to go beyond pain through darkness and death.

which each minute was more beautiful than the last, more menacing—! He still
looked, as if from a great distance, at the beads of light in the doctor's eyes, at
the fixed false smile, and then, beyond, once more at his mother's slippers, his father's slippers, the soft flutter of the fire. Even here, even amongst these hostile
presences, and in this arranged light, he could see the snow, he could hear it—it
was in the corners of the room, where the shadow was deepest, under the sofa,
behind the half-opened door which led to the dining room. It was gentler here,   410
softer, its seethe the quietest of whispers, as if, in deference to a drawing room, it
had quite deliberately put on its "manners"; it kept itself out of sight, obliterated
itself, but distinctly with an air of saying, "Ah, but just wait! Wait till we are alone
together! Then I will begin to tell you something new! Something white! something cold! something sleepy! something of cease, and peace, and the long
bright curve of space! Tell them to go away. Banish them. Refuse to speak. Leave
them, go upstairs to your room, turn out the light and get into bed—I will go
with you, I will be waiting for you, I will tell you a better story than Little Kay of
the Skates, or The Snow Ghost—I will surround your bed, I will close the windows, pile a deep drift against the door, so that none will ever again be able to   420
enter. Speak to them! . . ." It seemed as if the little hissing voice came from a slow
white spiral of falling flakes in the corner by the front window—but he could
not be sure. He felt himself smiling, then, and said to the doctor, but without
looking at him, looking beyond him still——

"Oh no, I think not——"

"But are you quite sure, my boy?"

His father's voice came softly and coldly then—the familiar voice of silken
warning.

"You needn't answer at once, Paul—remember we're trying to help you—
think it over and be quite sure, won't you?"   430

He felt himself smiling again, at the notion of being quite sure. What a joke! As
if he weren't so sure that reassurance was no longer necessary, and all this cross-
examination a ridiculous farce, a grotesque parody! What could they know about
it? these gross intelligences, these humdrum minds so bound to the usual, the ordinary? Impossible to tell them about it! Why, even now, even now, with the
proof so abundant, so formidable, so imminent, so appallingly present here in
this very room, could they believe it?—could even his mother believe it? No—it
was only too plain that if anything were said about it, the merest hint given, they
would be incredulous—they would laugh—they would say "Absurd!"—think
things about him which weren't true. . . .   440

"Why no, I'm not worried—why should I be?"

He looked then straight at the doctor's low-lidded eyes, looked from one of
them to the other, from one bead of light to the other, and gave a little laugh.

The doctor seemed to be disconcerted by this. He drew back in his chair, resting a fat white hand on either knee. The smile faded slowly from his face.

"Well, Paul!" he said, and paused gravely, "I'm afraid you don't take this quite
seriously enough. I think you perhaps don't quite realize—don't quite realize—"
He took a deep quick breath and turned, as if helplessly, at a loss for words, to
the others. But Mother and Father were both silent—no help was forthcoming.

450   "You must surely know, be aware, that you have not been quite yourself, of late? Don't you know that? . . ."

    It was amusing to watch the doctor's renewed attempt at a smile, a queer disorganized look, as of confidential embarrassment.

    "I feel all right, sir," he said, and again gave the little laugh.

    "And we're trying to help you." The doctor's tone sharpened.

    "Yes, sir, I know. But why? I'm all right. I'm just *thinking,* that's all."

    His mother made a quick movement forward, resting a hand on the back of the doctor's chair.

    "Thinking?" she said. "But my dear, about what?"

460   This was a direct challenge—and would have to be directly met. But before he met it, he looked again into the corner by the door, as if for reassurance. He smiled again at what he saw, at what he heard. The little spiral was still there, still softly whirling, like a ghost of a white kitten chasing the ghost of a white tail, and making as it did so the faintest of whispers. It was all right! If only he could remain firm, everything was going to be all right.

    "Oh, about anything, about nothing—*you* know the way you do!"

    "You mean—daydreaming?"

    "Oh, no—thinking!"

    "But thinking about *what?*"

470   "Anything."

    He laughed a third time—but this time, happening to glance upward toward his mother's face, he was appalled at the effect his laughter seemed to have upon her. Her mouth had opened in an expression of horror. . . . This was too bad! Unfortunate! He had known it would cause pain, of course—but he hadn't expected it to be quite so bad as this. Perhaps—perhaps if he just gave them a tiny gleaming hint——?

    "About the snow," he said.

    "What on earth?" This was his father's voice. The brown slippers came a step nearer on the hearth-rug.

480   "But my dear, what do you mean?" This was his mother's voice.

    The doctor merely stared.

    "Just *snow,* that's all. I like to think about it."

    "Tell us about it, my boy."

    "But that's all it is. There's nothing to tell. *You* know what snow is?"

    This he said almost angrily, for he felt that they were trying to corner him. He turned sideways so as no longer to face the doctor, and the better to see the inch of blackness between the window-sill and the lowered curtain—the cold inch of beckoning and delicious night. At once he felt better, more assured.

    "Mother—can I go to bed, now, please? I've got a headache."

490   "But I thought you said——"

    "It's just come. It's all these questions—! Can I, mother?"

    "You can go as soon as the doctor has finished."

    "Don't you think this thing ought to be gone into thoroughly, and *now?*" This was Father's voice. The brown slippers again came a step nearer, the voice was the well-known "punishment" voice, resonant and cruel.

"Oh, what's the use, Norman——"

Quite suddenly, everyone was silent. And without precisely facing them, nevertheless he was aware that all three of them were watching him with an extraordinary intensity—staring hard at him—as if he had done something monstrous, or was himself some kind of monster. He could hear the soft irregular flutter of the flames; the cluck-click-cluck-click of the clock; far and faint, two sudden spurts of laughter from the kitchen, as quickly cut off as begun; a murmur of water in the pipes; and then, the silence seemed to deepen, to spread out, to become world-long and world-wide, to become timeless and shapeless, and to center inevitably and rightly, with a slow and sleepy but enormous concentration of all power, on the beginning of a new sound. What this new sound was going to be, he knew perfectly well. It might begin with a hiss, but it would end with a roar—there was no time to lose—he must escape. It mustn't happen here——

Without another word, he turned and ran up the stairs.

IV. Not a moment too soon. The darkness was coming in long white waves. A prolonged sibilance filled the night—a great seamless seethe of wild influence went abruptly across it—a cold low humming shook the windows. He shut the door and flung off his clothes in the dark. The bare black floor was like a little raft tossed in waves of snow, almost overwhelmed, washed under whitely, up again, smothered in curled billows of feather. The snow was laughing; it spoke from all sides at once; it pressed closer to him as he ran and jumped exulting into his bed.

"Listen to us!" it said. "Listen! We have come to tell you the story we told you about. You remember? Lie down. Shut your eyes, now—you will no longer see much—in this white darkness who could see, or want to see? We will take the place of everything. . . . Listen——"

A beautiful varying dance of snow began at the front of the room, came forward and then retreated, flattened out toward the floor, then rose fountain-like to the ceiling, swayed, recruited itself from a new stream of flakes which poured laughing in through the humming window, advanced again, lifted long white arms. It said peace, it said remoteness, it said cold—it said——

But then a gash of horrible light fell brutally across the room from the opening door—the snow drew back hissing—something alien had come into the room—something hostile. This thing rushed at him, clutched at him, shook him—and he was not merely horrified, he was filled with such a loathing as he had never known. What was this? this cruel disturbance? this act of anger and hate? It was as if he had to reach up a hand toward another world for any understanding of it—an effort of which he was only barely capable. But of that other world he still remembered just enough to know the exorcising words. They tore themselves from his other life suddenly——

"Mother! Mother! Go away! I hate you!"

And with that effort, everything was solved, everything became all right: the seamless hiss advanced once more, the long white wavering lines rose and fell like enormous whispering sea-waves, the whisper becoming louder, the laughter more numerous.

500

510

520

530

540

"Listen!" it said. "We'll tell you the last, the most beautiful and secret story—shut your eyes—it is a very small story—a story that gets smaller and smaller—it comes inward instead of opening like a flower—it is a flower becoming a seed—a little cold seed—do you hear? we are leaning closer to you——"

The hiss was now becoming a roar—the whole world was a vast moving screen of snow—but even now it said peace, it said remoteness, it said cold, it said sleep.

ANALYZING THE STORY

ACTIVITY 3

The following questions are divided into Parts I–IV, according to the story. You may want to divide the class into four groups to answer these questions, one section per group. Be prepared to report your answers to the class.

Part I (lines 38–211)

1. What month is it?
2. How is the postman described in lines 59–69? Be specific.
3. What is different about "this particular morning, the first morning"? (line 58) List all the differences.
4. How does the boy explain the differences to himself? What does he assume has happened? Is he correct in his explanation? How do you know?
5. Why is the narration about Miss Buell now in parentheses? When do the parentheses start? Why?
6. What happens on "the second day, perhaps the sixth"? (line 106)
7. What does the boy discover each morning when he goes to the window? How does he feel about it?
8. How does the boy respond to his parents' concern? (lines 122–142) Give a word or phrase to describe his response.
9. Paul lives in two worlds. What are they? (See lines 145–160.)
10. What does Miss Buell call what Paul is doing? (line 192) What does Paul's mother call it? (line 206) In your view, what is happening to Paul, and why might this be happening to him?

Part II (lines 212–343)

1. How does Paul refer to what he sees on his walk home, (lines 213–214) and how does he feel about what he sees?
2. Are the things that Paul sees appealing or not appealing? Why do you think so? Find specific language in the story as support.

3. What two things does Paul want simultaneously? (lines 260–267)

4. In lines 284–291, the writer describes the snow and how Paul feels about it. Make a list of words describing snow in this section. How many of the words on your list are positive, and how many are negative? What does this tell you about how Paul is feeling?

5. Why does Paul react with astonishment when he realizes that his house is the seventh house?

6. What does Paul feel he will be deprived of, and why does this disappoint him? (line 329)

7. Which of the following phrases show contradiction? Explain the contradiction.

   "beautiful progress" (330)
   "soothingly and beautifully encroached and deepened" (333–334)
   "slow and subtle gradations of menace, in which he could luxuriate" (337–338)

8. Do you think that whatever is happening to Paul seems positive or negative to him? Explain.

Part III (lines 344–509)

1. Describe Paul's parents' physical position while the doctor is examining him.

2. What is the doctor first looking for when he examines Paul? (line 383) Later, he says, " 'I believe it is something else.' " (387–389) What does the doctor believe it is?

3. In lines 395–424, Paul reacts to the doctor's question, " 'Is there anything that worries you?' " His reaction has several phases. What are they?

4. How does Paul finally answer the doctor's question?

5. Why is the doctor "disconcerted" by both Paul's answer and the way he gives it? (444) How does the doctor's manner change as he continues?

6. What must Paul have looked like to the doctor and his parents in lines 442–470?

7. The mother, the father, and the doctor all respond differently when Paul tells them that he is thinking about the snow. How does each respond? Be specific.

8. Is everyone really silent "quite . . . suddenly"? (line 497) What makes you think so? What is happening?

9. What is "this new sound"? (line 506) Why does Paul run upstairs?

Part IV (lines 510–547)

1. In lines 510–521, Paul describes the snow. Make a list of the images and actions. How many of these are positive, and how many are negative?

2. What is the "gash of horrible light"? (line 527) What is the alien thing that comes into his room? What does it do, and how does Paul respond?

3. Sketch "a flower becoming a seed." (lines 543–544) How is this image related to what is happening to Paul?

WRITING IN RESPONSE

Write briefly on this topic.

Do you think the story ends happily or unhappily? Explain.

Elements of Literature

Figurative Language

ACTIVITY 4

Discuss the following questions in groups.

1. What two extreme geographic locations and climates are mentioned in Part I of the story? Are they mentioned before or after we hear about Paul's imaginary snow? What colors and feelings do you associate with each of these extremes? How does the contrast between these two locations parallel Paul's two worlds?

2. We know Paul has these interests: He likes geography. (line 137) He is especially interested in the North Pole (line 137) and the Antarctic. (line 29) He expresses interest in being a polar explorer. (lines 138–139) Find other words related to explorers or adventure in the story. Write your findings on the board. As a class, review the examples of explorer/adventurer images on the board; then answer these questions.

   a. Why do people become explorers? What are their goals?
   b. In what ways is Paul himself like an explorer?
   c. Why might Paul want to be an explorer? What might he be searching for?

3. The voice Paul hears tells him he will hear a story that "gets smaller and smaller" (line 542) and rather than being a seed opening into a flower, the flower turns into a seed, "a little cold seed." (lines 543–544) Has Paul found what an explorer wants to find? Has he found what he wants? Explain.

Characterization

A C T I V I T Y 5

In "Silent Snow, Secret Snow" Paul lives in two worlds, one external and the other secret. Work in groups to answer the following questions about his two worlds.

1. Compare Paul's external and secret worlds. Find representative elements of each world in different parts of the story. Why is Paul's secret world more fascinating to him than the real world?

2. How well does Paul balance his two worlds? How does he hold on to the external world? Is he able to focus on it when necessary? Give examples.

3. What conclusions can you reach about what is happening to Paul? Compare your ideas with the other groups in the class.

Language and Style

A C T I V I T Y 6

Conrad Aiken was a poet as well as a writer of prose. As a result, his prose has many poetic qualities: he uses **rhythm** and repetition; he makes careful lexical (vocabulary) and syntactical (grammatical form) connections between sentences; he uses **imagery,** not explanation, to present much of his story. (See Appendix A for more information about terms in boldface type.) With these poetic qualities, Aiken pushes the reader to examine, interpret, and interact with the words in order to better understand the story's complexities.

1. As an example, read lines 135–139 in "Silent Snow, Secret Snow." Then read the same lines written below in poetry form. Notice that this format emphasizes repetition.

A new lamp?
A new lamp.
Yes, Mother.
No, Mother.
Yes, Mother.

School is going very well.
The geometry is very easy.
The history is very dull.
The geography is very interesting—
Particularly when it takes one to
The North Pole.
Why the North Pole?
Oh, well, it would be fun to be an explorer.
Another Peary,
Or Scott,
Or Shackleton.

2. Now answer these questions.

   a. What do you notice about lexical repetition and syntactic repetition in the poetic format?
   b. What effect does this have?
   c. What do the repeated references to geography tell us about the way Paul might feel about his new experience with snow?

3. Look through the story for another passage that contains repetitions of words and structures, as well as some images of cold and snow.

   a. Write that passage in poetry form, putting repetitions of words, phrases, and syntactic structures under, rather than next to, one another.
   b. Show your poem to a partner and discuss the similarities between your two poems. In each one, what does your visual representation of repetition and imagery reveal about what is happening to Paul?

Theme

ACTIVITY 7

Discuss the following questions about **theme** in groups. Write down any new questions you may have during your discussion or any questions you cannot answer. Discuss these later with the whole class.

1. We all have escapes: daydreams, hobbies, reading, sports, music. These escapes often relax us and pull us away from the worries of day-to-day life. Does Paul's mental escape seem natural and normal? Does he fight against it? Should he? Explain. Should people fight against mental escape? Why or why not?

2. Could Paul pull himself back into the real world if he wanted to, or is he helpless against this vision of snow? Why do you think so? Are we all helpless against our escapes, or can we control them if we want to? Explain.

3. Paul feels safe, secure, and protected in his mental world of beautiful snow. In fact, he does not know that this escape is an imaginary barrier between himself and reality. In what situations might people feel happier and safer in their imagination than in their day-to-day life? What might cause some people to go beyond normal daydreaming into a fantasy that takes abnormal control of their minds?

4. Do you think Aiken in "Silent Snow, Secret Snow" presents an objective view of a retreat into isolation? Does he make any judgments? Is he sympathetic? Explain.

WRITING IN RESPONSE

The following should be done as a series of consecutive freewrites. Write for about ten minutes on one topic. Then go immediately to the next one and do the same.

1. Although Paul seems to be thinking about other things, he is able to answer Miss Buell and the doctor clearly and appropriately. He seems to be balancing his mental world and the outside world quite successfully. Do you think he might still be able to do this at the end of the story? Why or why not?

2. Do you think Paul's last words to his mother indicate that he is in touch with reality when he says them, or do they show that he is no longer aware of what he is saying or its consequences? What makes you think so?

3. Aiken noted that a true artist should make his or her public comprehend the artist's inner vision, but should at the same time allow the audience to be aware of surrounding reality. What did he mean by this? In the story, how is Paul able to do this for himself?

4. Some artists become artists partly because of their alienation and withdrawal from the world around them. This alienation gives them a unique perspective on life. At the same time, they are often criticized for their "abnormality" and are considered by some to be "ill" and in need of a cure. How is Paul like an artist in this sense?

5. If you were an artist (or if you are), would you choose to live primarily in the real world or in an isolated aesthetic reality? Why?

6. In your opinion, is an ideal, imaginary world of snow more beautiful, more "artistic," than the real world of snow? Explain.

7. Aiken was interested in Freud, schizophrenia, and other psychological problems. Clinically speaking, Paul is retreating into the painless, unreal world of the schizophrenic. Does a person's retreat into a painless isolation help or hurt that person? In other words, does the story have a happy ending or a sad one? Explain.

Exploring Further

Paul hears the postman later and later each day. Finally, he realizes his house is the seventh house, which means he will not hear the postman anymore. What might be the **symbolic** meaning of the postman and this silence?

1. To find your answer, freewrite on one of the following topics for ten minutes.

   • The postman symbolizes the real world.
   • The postman symbolizes sanity/insanity.
   • The postman symbolizes life/death.

- The postman symbolizes communication.
- The postman symbolizes innocence.

2. Exchange your paper with someone who has chosen a different topic, read that paper, and write a brief response to it (five to ten minutes).

3. Repeat steps 1 and 2 with a different topic and a different partner.

4. Discuss your discoveries with the class.

CREATIVE WRITING

Imagine that you are a psychologist in training and Paul has come to you to seek help. He has slowly and reluctantly told you about what he thinks and feels. Write a report to your supervisor in which you explain what you think is happening to Paul and why. Your supervisor needs to know how you came to your conclusions, so use evidence from the story to support your view. End with a prognosis: Tell what you think will happen to Paul.

ESSAY TOPIC

Aiken witnessed the death of his parents when he was eleven years old. His father shot his mother and then killed himself. The event devastated Aiken. His profound grief led him to the study of psychological trauma and the teachings of Sigmund Freud, where he found some relief and guidance. He became especially interested in schizophrenia, notably feelings of alienation and separation, visions, voices and hallucinations, and other abnormal sensory escapes caused by a horrifying experience.

Write an essay in which you explain how Paul could be an example of a psychological withdrawal from the world as a result of a reality too painful to bear. In your essay, describe in detail how he is losing his normal attachment to reality and sanity. What else might we need to know about Paul's life in order to understand why he is unable to tolerate reality?

AUTHOR PROFILE

Conrad Aiken

Conrad Aiken was born in 1889 in Savannah, Georgia, a city that would always be home to him, no matter where he went. His father was a successful doctor and literary man, but his parents fought a great deal and Aiken frequently had to mediate between the two of them or between them and his three younger siblings. When Aiken was eleven, he heard the usual angry shouting in the house, but it was accompanied by an unfamiliar sound of gunshots. Aiken discovered both his parents dead. His father had shot his mother, then himself.

Aiken spent the rest of his life trying to recover from this moment when the world came to a complete stop for him. He was separated from his brothers and sisters, sent to New England, and shunted from relative to relative for the duration of his childhood. Eventually, he went to Harvard and became a writer. He published novels, poems, short stories, and an autobiography, *Ushant*, all of which were artistic expressions of his painful search for peace of mind after his traumatic childhood experience. The study of Freud and psychoanalysis and the release of suppressed consciousness had such an influence on Aiken that they became a natural part of all his literary work. He treated the conscious and the unconscious as if they operated nearly simultaneously, resulting in his trademark poetic prose.

Although Aiken's memories of Savannah were painful, he eventually returned there. He died in Savannah in 1973.

CHAPTER 8

A Blessing

JAMES WRIGHT

PREPARATION

ACTIVITY 1

With a partner or in small groups discuss the following questions and do the activities.

1. What does *blessing* mean?

2. The expression "Count your blessings" means "Remember all the good things in your life and appreciate them." What are some of your blessings? Which ones do you consider most important? Freewrite to answer these questions and share what you wrote with a partner.

3. You are about to read the poem "A Blessing" by James Wright. How do you expect this poem might be different in style from your freewrite?

A Blessing

JAMES WRIGHT

Just off the highway to Rochester, Minnesota,
Twilight bounds softly forth on the grass.
And the eyes of those two Indian ponies
Darken with kindness.
They have come gladly out of the willows   5
To welcome my friend and me.
We step over the barbed wire into the pasture
Where they have been grazing all day, alone.
They ripple tensely, they can hardly contain their happiness
That we have come.   10
They bow shyly as wet swans. They love each other.
There is no loneliness like theirs.
At home once more,
They begin munching the young tufts of spring in the darkness.
I would like to hold the slenderer one in my arms,   15
For she has walked over to me
And nuzzled my left hand.
She is black and white,
Her mane falls wild on her forehead,
And the light breeze moves me to caress her long ear   20
That is delicate as the skin over a girl's wrist.
Suddenly I realize
That if I stepped out of my body I would break
Into blossom.

ANALYZING THE POEM

ACTIVITY 2

Answer the following questions. Give evidence from the poem to support your answers and include line numbers for each piece of evidence.

1. Where does the poem take place? Find Rochester, Minnesota, on a map. What kind of climate do you think this area has?

2. Who is the narrator of the poem? In which line do you first become aware of this?

3. Who are the characters in the poem (both human and animal)? Make a list of the details used to describe each character. Include the character's gender, if you know it.

4. Reread lines 22–24: "Suddenly I realize/That if I stepped out of my body I would break/Into blossom." What does to "break into blossom" mean? What usually blossoms?

WRITING IN RESPONSE

Respond briefly to this question in writing. Compare your response with those of two or three of your classmates.

What feeling did you get from the poem, and why?

Elements of Literature

Setting

ACTIVITY 3

In groups, discuss the following questions about **setting.** (See Appendix A for more information about terms in boldface type.) Choose one member of your group to summarize your ideas for the rest of the class.

1. Why do you think Wright specifically mentions Rochester, Minnesota, instead of simply saying, "near a city in the northern Midwest"? Consider that Rochester is a small city far from highly developed, large metropolitan areas in a state known for its long, cold winters.

2. Why do you think the poet uses the word *highway* instead of *road*, which is a more general term? Discuss associations we have with the word *highway*. How does this word choice affect what we know about the people, the horses, and the situation in the poem?

3. A barbed-wire fence is normally difficult to climb over because it is sharply pointed. Yet, in the poem, they simply "step over" it. (line 7) What conclusion can you draw about the fence and the setting from this detail?

4. What are the different meanings of "twilight," (line 2) and which of these meanings could be related to the poem?

5. Describe what you think the weather feels and looks like in the Rochester area at the time of year the poem takes place.

6. Although there are no specific colors mentioned in the poem, with the exception of "black and white," (line 18) there are a few words that are associated with color. Find these words and discuss the color(s) associated with them. What is the effect of this nonspecific presentation of color in the poem?

Characterization

A C T I V I T Y 4

Answer the following questions with a partner.

1. About the ponies:

   a. For each of the following lines, tell what happens and what it shows about the feelings of the ponies. The first one is done for you.

LINE(S)	WHAT HAPPENS	PONIES' FEELINGS
3–4	*The ponies' eyes become dark "with kindness."*	*The ponies appear to be happy that the humans are coming.*
5–6		
8		
9		
11		
12		
14		
16		
17		

   b. According to the narrator, which of the feelings and actions in the preceding chart happen because of the humans? Put an asterisk (*) next to those lines.

   c. Which of the feelings and actions in the chart above do not happen because of the humans? Put an X next to those lines.

2. About the humans:

    a. For each of the following lines, tell what happens and what it shows about the feelings of the humans. The first one is done for you.

LINE(S)	WHAT HAPPENS	HUMANS' FEELINGS
7	The narrator and his friend cross over the fence to the place where the ponies have been grazing.	The humans want to get closer to the ponies.
15		
20		
22–24		

    b. According to the narrator of the poem, which of the feelings and actions in the preceding chart happen because of the ponies? Put an asterisk (*) next to those lines.

    c. Which of the feelings and actions do not happen because of the ponies? Put an X next to those lines.

3. About the human and animal interaction:

    a. Why do you think the poem focuses on one female horse?

    b. Why does the poet include the "friend" (line 6) who plays no significant role in the poem? How would the poem be different if the narrator were alone?

    c. Does the narrator seem to be a man or a woman? Is this important? Explain.

    d. Based on your answers to parts 1, 2, and 3, what do you think the poet is saying about the interaction between the ponies and the humans? Be prepared to summarize your conclusions to the class, providing evidence from the poem where necessary.

Figurative Language

Personification

ACTIVITY 5

Make a list here of all the places in the poem where Wright uses **personification.** Write the reason that he uses this figure of speech and what effect it has. The first one is done for you.

LINE NUMBER(S)	QUOTATION	REASON AND EFFECT
2	"Twilight bounds softly forth . . ."	The poet wants to make twilight leap like a person so that the coming night feels alive, familiar, and personal.

CREATIVE WRITING

Choose a nonhuman thing in your life and personify it. First, make a list of at least ten human qualities that you feel this thing could have. Then, write a paragraph or two in which you describe the thing you chose, using personification.

Simile

ACTIVITY 6

1. Find the two **similes** in the poem. Answer these questions about each one:
    a. What is the actual object?
    b. What is the object being compared to?
    c. What associations do you have with what the first object is compared to?
    d. What dimension is added to the original object through the comparison?

2. How does the poet's use of similes contribute to the conclusions you reached about the interaction between humans and animals in Activity 4, item 3?

WRITING IN RESPONSE

Write briefly on this topic.

How does the writer's use of personification and simile contribute to the overall mood of the poem? Explain.

Exploring Further

Write or discuss the answers to these questions. Give evidence from the poem to support your answers and include line numbers for each piece of evidence.

1. The sentence "They love each other" (line 11) is followed immediately by "There is no loneliness like theirs." (line 12) How do you explain the pairing of these sentences? "At home once more" (line 13) follows the lines about love and loneliness. Why are the ponies "at home" again?

2. It is not until the last three lines of the poem that we really know what the narrator is feeling. Why does the narrator reveal his or her feelings at the end?

3. What causes plants to blossom? What causes the narrator to feel as if he or she might blossom?

4. What would it look like if a person "[broke] / into blossom"? (lines 23–24) Do a sketch of how you imagine this would look.

5. In writing that the narrator "would break / into blossom," (lines 23–24) is the poet still using the technique of personification? Explain.

6. Consider the title again. What is the blessing in the poem? Why does it occur? Why is the title "A Blessing" instead of "The Blessing"?

ESSAY TOPICS

1. What mood does Wright create in the poem "A Blessing"? How does he create it, and why do you think he chooses this mood? Explain with details from the poem.

2. Why is the poem called "A Blessing"?

3. Discuss the interactions between humans, animals, and nature in the poem. How does Wright show this interaction, and why do you think he does it? Explain with details from the poem.

AUTHOR PROFILE

James Wright

James Wright (1928–1980) was born in Martins Ferry, Ohio. During his career, he taught at several universities, among them two universities in Minnesota: the University of Minnesota and Macalester College. In addition to writing poetry, Wright translated poems from Spanish and Czech and wrote essays. He won the Pulitzer Prize for Poetry in 1972 for his *Collected Poems*.

Wright is well known for both his poems about the midwestern United States and his poems about Italy, where he traveled and lived. In a rare interview with Dave Smith in 1979, Wright said that a sense of place is very important to a writer: "There is such a genius in place, a presence, and because there is, people's feelings accumulate about it." He went on to say that he cared very much about nature, the living world. He felt that "in the poetry of nature there is the willingness to approach living creatures with the kind of attentiveness that is almost a reverence," that the poet is paying attention to nature both physically and spiritually. When asked what makes a good poem, Wright answered that "a poem is good because of the pleasure that it provides us," but added that pleasure is not enough; we can find an even deeper pleasure in trying to see the truth.

CHAPTER 9

Aunt Moon's Young Man

LINDA HOGAN

PREPARATION

ACTIVITY 1

With a partner or in small groups, discuss the following questions.

1. Read the first paragraph of "Aunt Moon's Young Man." In what ways is the description of autumn similar to or different from your image of autumn? What associations do you have with autumn?

2. Based on this first paragraph, where do you think the story might take place?

3. This story begins at a country fair. What kinds of activities take place there?

WRITING IN RESPONSE

Write for ten minutes in response to both of these questions. Share your ideas with your classmates.

1. When you were fifteen or sixteen years old, what rules of behavior were "good" young men or women expected to follow? What values did your family and community expect you to accept and live by? Consider how these rules and values were affected by your gender, class, and ethnic background.

   Write a list of those rules of behavior and be prepared to share them with the class. Use the following format:

   "Good" (*name your ethnicity here*) men/women are supposed to:
   "Good" (*name your ethnicity here*) men/women are *not* supposed to:

2. When you were in your teens, did you mostly try to fit in to your community by following these rules, or did you mostly break the rules? Did you do both? Explain.

ACTIVITY 2

Answer the questions in each section after you finish the corresponding part of "Aunt Moon's Young Man."

Section 1 (Lines 1–270)

1. Who is the **narrator?** (See Appendix A for more information about terms in boldface type.) About how old do you think she is at the beginning of the story? Consider the following evidence and then find two more pieces of evidence that hint at the narrator's age in this part of the story:

   "I looked at [my mother's] face, looked out the window at the dark man, and looked back at my mother again. I had never thought about her from inside the skin." (lines 109–111)

2. At the opening of the story, a young man comes to town. What other main events mark the passage of time in this section of the story?

3. At what point in her life do you think the narrator tells this story, at the time it occurs, or later? Explain.

4. Begin to fill out the character chart in Activity 3, page 125. Add to the chart as you answer the questions for the remaining two sections of the story.

5. Imagine that "Aunt Moon's Young Man" will be made into a film. You are a member of the film crew, assigned to find a location, animals, and properties for the film. Read the opening scene (lines 1–78) carefully and then fill out this chart.

ANIMALS: INCLUDE COLORS AND SOUNDS	WEATHER/ATMOSPHERE: INCLUDE COLOR, QUALITY OF LIGHT AND AIR	LANDSCAPE: INCLUDE COLOR, MOUNTAINS, VEGETATION

Next, write a short paragraph describing the opening scene. Consider these questions as you write:

- How big is the town?
- How would you describe the surrounding landscape?
- What colors are dominant in this scene?
- How would you describe the weather and the air?

6. What kind of relationship is developing between Isaac and Aunt Moon in this section of the story? How do you feel about this relationship? Explain.

Section 2 (Lines 271–477)

1. What events take place in this section of the story? Note that the narrator moves backward and forward through time rather than narrating the story chronologically. You may want to mark in brackets the parts of the story that move backward in time.

2. Have you changed your mind about the age of the narrator? If so, why? As an observer of the events, did the narrator understand everything she saw? Explain your answer and provide examples.

3. In lines 364–372, we learn how Bess Evening's similarity with the changing phases of the moon inspires the narrator to nickname her "Aunt Moon." Read lines 364–434 and lines 500–502. Next to each moon phase, write any words or phrases that are associated with Aunt Moon's "phases" or moods.

   "Full and happy" moon:

   "Small and weak" moon:

4. At the end of this section, the narrator's mother tells her not to "'go over to Bessie's house anymore.'" (line 470) Why? Explain your answer.

5. What is the relationship between Isaac and Aunt Moon at the end of this section of the story? Has your feeling about Aunt Moon and Isaac's relationship changed in any way?

Section 3 (Lines 478–647)

1. Who and what appears at both the story's beginning and toward the ending? How much time passes in the story? Give specific evidence.

2. Describe the weather and the air on the day that Aunt Moon's dog, Mister, died.
   a. How does the weather change after the dog is shot?
   b. What other references to killing and death are made in lines 509–549?
   c. What do these references reveal about Aunt Moon?

3. How old do you think the narrator is at the end of the story?

4. In the last line of the story, the narrator leaves town with "a small, beautiful woman in [her] eye." (line 647) Scan the whole story and mark other references to woman or women "in the eye."

Aunt Moon's Young Man

Linda Hogan

That autumn when the young man came to town, there was a deep blue sky. On their way to the fair, the wagons creaked into town. One buckboard,° driven by cloudy white horses, carried a grunting pig inside its wooden slats. Another had cages of chickens. In the heat, the chickens did not flap their wings. They sounded tired and old, and their shoulders drooped like old men.

There was tension in the air. Those people who still believed in omens would turn to go home, I thought, white chicken feathers caught on the wire cages they brought, reminding us all that the cotton was poor that year and that very little of it would line the big trailers outside the gins.

A storm was brewing over the plains,° and beneath its clouds a few people from   10
the city drove dusty black motorcars through town, angling around the statue of General Pickens on Main Street. They refrained from honking at the wagons and the white, pink-eyed horses. The cars contained no animal life, just neatly folded stacks of quilts, jellies, and tomato relish, large yellow gourds, and pumpkins that looked like the round faces of children through half-closed windows.

"The biting flies aren't swarming today," my mother said. She had her hair done up in rollers. It was almost dry. She was leaning against the window frame, looking at the ink-blue trees outside. I could see Bess Evening's house through the glass, appearing to sit like a small, hand-built model upon my mother's shoulder. My mother was a dreamer, standing at the window with her green dress   20
curved over her hip.

Her dress was hemmed slightly shorter on one side than on the other. I de-cided not to mention it. The way she leaned, with her abdomen tilted out, was her natural way of standing. She still had good legs, despite the spidery blue veins she said came from carrying the weight of us kids inside her for nine months each. She also blamed us for her few gray hairs.

She mumbled something about "the silence before the storm" as I joined her at the window.

She must have been looking at the young man for a long time, pretending to watch the sky. He was standing by the bushes and the cockscombs. There was a   30
flour sack on the ground beside him. I thought at first it might be filled with something he brought for the fair, but the way his hat sat on it and a pair of black boots stood beside it, I could tell it held his clothing, and that he was pass-ing through Pickens on his way to or from some city.

"It's mighty quiet for the first day of fair," my mother said. She sounded far away. Her eyes were on the young stranger. She unrolled a curler and checked a strand of hair.

We talked about the weather and the sky, but we both watched the young man. In the deep blue of sky his white shirt stood out like a light. The low hills were fire-gold and leaden.   40

°*buckboard* a four-wheel open carriage pulled by a horse
°*plains* long expanses of fairly flat land with little vegetation

One of my mother's hands was limp against her thigh. The other moved down from the rollers and touched the green cloth at her chest, playing with a flaw in the fabric.

"Maybe it was the tornado,"° I said about the stillness in the air. The tornado had passed through a few days ago, touching down here and there. It exploded my cousin's house trailer, but it left his motorcycle standing beside it, untouched. "Tornadoes have no sense of value," my mother had said. "They are always taking away the saints and leaving behind the devils."

50 The young man stood in that semi-slumped, half-straight manner of fullblood Indians. Our blood was mixed like Heinz 57, and I always thought of purebloods as better than us. While my mother eyed his plain moccasins,° she patted her rolled hair as if to put it in order. I was counting the small brown flowers in the blistered wallpaper, the way I counted ceiling tiles in the new school, and counted each step when I walked.

I pictured Aunt Moon inside her house up on my mother's shoulder. I imagined her dark face above the yellow oilcloth, her hands reflecting the yellow as they separated dried plants. She would rise slowly, as I'd seen her do, take a good long time to brush out her hair, and braid it once again. She would pet her dog, Mister, with long slow strokes while she prepared herself for the fair.

60 My mother moved aside, leaving the house suspended in the middle of the window, where it rested on a mound of land. My mother followed my gaze. She always wanted to know what I was thinking or doing. "I wonder," she said, "why in tarnation Bess's father built that house up there. It gets all the heat and wind."

I stuck up for Aunt Moon. "She can see everything from there, the whole town and everything."

"Sure, and everything can see her. A wonder she doesn't have ghosts."

I wondered what she meant by that, everything seeing Aunt Moon. I guessed by her lazy voice that she meant nothing. There was no cutting edge to her words.

70 "And don't call her Aunt Moon." My mother was reading my mind again, one of her many tricks. "I know what you're thinking," she would say when I thought I looked expressionless. "You are thinking about finding Mrs. Mark's ring and holding it for a reward."

I would look horrified and tell her that she wasn't even lukewarm, but the truth was that I'd been thinking exactly those thoughts. I resented my mother for guessing my innermost secrets. She was like God, everywhere at once knowing everything. I tried to concentrate on something innocent. I thought about pickles. I was safe; she didn't say a word about dills or sweets.

Bess, Aunt Moon, wasn't really my aunt. She was a woman who lived alone
80 and had befriended me. I liked Aunt Moon and the way she moved, slowly, taking up as much space as she wanted and doing it with ease. She had wide lips and straight eyelashes.

°*tornado* a destructive, funnel-shaped wind that moves across miles of land, particularly in the midwestern United States

°*moccasins* soft leather shoes traditionally worn by some Native Americans

Aunt Moon dried medicine herbs in the manner of her parents. She knew about plants, both the helpful ones and the ones that were poisonous in all but the smallest of doses. And she knew how to cut wood and how to read the planets. She told me why I was stubborn. It had to do with my being born in May. I believed her because my father was born a few days after me, and he was stubborn as all get out, even compared to me.

Aunt Moon was special. She had life in her. The rest of the women in town were cold in the eye and fretted over their husbands. I didn't want to be like them. They condemned the men for drinking and gambling, but even after the loudest quarrels, ones we'd overhear, they never failed to cook for their men. They'd cook platters of lard-fried chicken, bowls of mashed potatoes, and pitchers of creamy flour gravy.

Bess called those meals "sure death by murder."

Our town was full of large and nervous women with red spots on their thin-skinned necks, and we had single women who lived with brothers and sisters or took care of an elderly parent. Bess had comments on all of these: "They have eaten their anger and grown large," she would say. And there were the sullen ones who took care of men broken by the war, women who were hurt by the men's stories of death and glory but never told them to get on with living, like I would have done.

Bessie's own brother, J.D., had gone to the war and returned with softened, weepy eyes. He lived at the veterans hospital and he did office work there on his good days. I met him once and knew by the sweetness of his eyes that he had never killed anyone, but something about him reminded me of the lonely old shacks out on cotton farming land. His eyes were broken windows.

"Where do you think that young man is headed?" my mother asked.

Something in her voice was wistful and lonely. I looked at her face, looked out the window at the dark man, and looked back at my mother again. I had never thought about her from inside the skin. She was the mind reader in the family, but suddenly I knew how she did it. The inner workings of the mind were clear in her face, like words in a book. I could even feel her thoughts in the pit of my stomach. I was feeling embarrassed at what my mother was thinking when the stranger crossed the street. In front of him an open truck full of prisoners passed by. They wore large white shirts and pants, like immigrants from Mexico. I began to count the flowers in the wallpaper again, and the truckful of prisoners passed by, and when it was gone, the young man had also vanished into thin air.

Besides the young man, another thing I remember about the fair that year was the man in the bathroom. On the first day of the fair, the prisoners were bending over like great white sails, their black and brown hands stuffing trash in canvas bags. Around them the children washed and brushed their cows and raked fresh straw about their pigs. My friend Elaine and I escaped the dust-laden air and went into the women's public toilets, where we shared a stolen cigarette. We heard someone open the door, and we fanned the smoke. Elaine stood on the toilet seat so her sisters wouldn't recognize her shoes. Then it was silent, so we opened the stall and stepped out. At first the round dark man, standing by the door, looked like a woman, but then I noticed the day's growth of beard at his

130   jawline. He wore a blue work shirt and a little straw hat. He leaned against the
wall, his hand moving inside his pants. I grabbed Elaine, who was putting lipstick
on her cheeks like rouge, and pulled her outside the door, the tube of red lipstick in her hand.

Outside, we nearly collapsed by a trash can, laughing. "Did you see that? It was
a man! A man! In the women's bathroom." She smacked me on the back.

We knew nothing of men's hands inside their pants, so we began to follow
him like store detectives, but as we rounded a corner behind his shadow, I saw
Aunt Moon walking away from the pigeon cages. She was moving slowly with
her cane, through the path's sawdust, feathers, and sand.

140   "Aunt Moon, there was a man in the bathroom," I said, and then remembered
the chickens I wanted to tell her about. Elaine ran off. I didn't know if she was
still following the man or not, but I'd lost interest when I saw Aunt Moon.

"Did you see those chickens that lay the green eggs?" I asked Aunt Moon.

She wagged her head no, so I grabbed her free elbow and guided her past the
pigeons with curly feathers and the turkeys with red wattles,° right up to the
chickens.

"They came all the way from South America. They sell for five dollars, can you
imagine?" Five dollars was a lot for chickens when we were still recovering from
the Great Depression, men were still talking about what they'd done with the
CCC, and children still got summer complaint and had to be carried around crip-

150   pled for months.

She peered into the cage. The eggs were smooth and resting in the straw. "I'll
be" was all she said.

I studied her face for a clue as to why she was so quiet, thinking she was mad
or something. I wanted to read her thoughts as easily as I'd read my mother's. In
the strange light of the sky, her eyes slanted a bit more than usual. I watched her
carefully. I looked at the downward curve of her nose and saw the young man
reflected in her eyes. I turned around.

On the other side of the cage that held the chickens from Araucania was the
man my mother had watched. Bess pretended to be looking at the little Jersey

160   cattle in the distance, but I could tell she was seeing that man. He had a calm
look on his face and his dark chest was smooth as oil where his shirt was
opened. His eyes were large and black. They were fixed on Bess like he was a
hypnotist or something magnetic that tried to pull Bess Evening toward it, even
though her body stepped back. She did step back, I remember that, but even so,
everything in her went forward, right up to him.

I didn't know if it was just me or if his presence charged the air, but suddenly
the oxygen was gone. It was like the fire at the Fisher Hardware when all the air
was drawn into the flame. Even the chickens clucked softly, as if suffocating, and
the cattle were more silent in the straw. The pulse in everything changed.

170   I don't know what would have happened if the rooster hadn't crowed just
then, but he did, and everything returned to normal. The rooster strutted and we
turned to watch him.

°*wattles* the red flesh growing from the throat of male turkeys

Bessie started walking away and I went with her. We walked past the men and boys who were shooting craps° in a cleared circle. One of them rubbed the dice between his hands as we were leaving, his eyes closed, his body's tight muscles willing a winning throw. He called me Lady Luck as we walked by. He said, "There goes Lady Luck," and he tossed the dice.

At dinner that evening we could hear the dance band tuning up in the makeshift beer garden, playing a few practice songs to the empty tables with their red cloths. They played "The Tennessee Waltz." For a while, my mother sang along with it. She had brushed her hair one hundred strokes and now she was talking and regretting talking all at the same time. "He was such a handsome man," she said. My father wiped his face with a handkerchief and rested his elbows on the table. He chewed and looked at nothing in particular. "For the longest time he stood there by the juniper bushes." 180

My father drank some coffee and picked up the newspaper. Mother cleared the table, one dish at a time and not in stacks like usual. "His clothes were neat. He must not have come from very far away." She moved the salt shaker from the end of the table to the center, then back again.

"I'll wash," I volunteered. 190

Mother said, "Bless you," and touched herself absently near the waist, as if to remove an apron. "I'll go get ready for the dance," she said.

My father turned a page of the paper.

The truth was, my mother was already fixed up for the dance. Her hair looked soft and beautiful. She had slipped into her new dress early in the day, "to break it in," she said. She wore nylons and she was barefoot and likely to get a runner. I would have warned her, but it seemed out of place, my warning. Her face was softer than usual, her lips painted to look full, and her eyebrows were much darker than usual.

"Do you reckon that young man came here for the rodeo?" She hollered in from the living room, where she powdered her nose. Normally she made up in front of the bathroom mirror, but the cabinet had been slammed and broken mysteriously one night during an argument so we had all taken to grooming ourselves in the small framed mirror in the living room. 200

I could not put my finger on it, but all the women at the dance that night were looking at the young man. It wasn't exactly that he was handsome. There was something else. He was alive in his whole body while the other men walked with great effort and stiffness, even those who did little work and were still young. Their male bodies had no language of their own in the way that his did. The women themselves seemed confused and lonely in the presence of the young man, and they were ridiculous in their behavior, laughing too loud, blushing like schoolgirls, or casting him a flirting eye. Even the older women were brighter than usual. Mrs. Tubby, whose face was usually as grim as the statue of General Pickens, the Cherokee hater, played with her necklace until her neck had red lines from the chain. Mrs. Tens twisted a strand of her hair over and over. Her sister tripped over a chair because she'd forgotten to watch where she was going. 210

°*craps* a gambling game played with dice

The men, sneaking drinks from bottles in paper bags, did not notice any of the fuss.

Maybe it was his hands. His hands were strong and dark.

220   I stayed late, even after wives pulled their husbands away from their ball game talk and insisted they dance.

My mother and father were dancing. My mother smiled up into my father's face as he turned her this way and that. Her uneven skirt swirled a little around her legs. She had a run in her nylons, as I predicted. My father, who was called Peso by the townspeople, wore his old clothes. He had his usual look about him, and I noticed that faraway, unfocused gaze on the other men too. They were either distant or they were present but rowdy, embarrassing the women around them with the loud talk of male things: work and hunting, fights, this or that pretty girl. Occasionally they told a joke, like, "Did you hear the one about the traveling salesman?"

230   The dancers whirled around the floor, some tapping their feet, some shuffling, the women in new dresses and dark hair all curled up like in movie magazines, the men with new leather boots and crew cuts. My dad's rear stuck out in back, the way he danced. His hand clutched my mother's waist.

That night, Bessie arrived late. She was wearing a white dress with a full gathered skirt. The print was faded and I could just make out the little blue stars on the cloth. She carried a yellow shawl over her arm. Her long hair was braided as usual in the manner of the older Chickasaw° women, like a wreath on her head. She was different from the others with her bright shawls. Sometimes she wore a heavy shell necklace or a collection of bracelets on her arm. They jangled when she 240   talked with me, waving her hands to make a point. Like the time she told me that the soul is a small woman inside the eye who leaves at night to wander new places.

No one had ever known her to dance before, but that night the young man and Aunt Moon danced together among the artificial geraniums and plastic carnations. They held each other gently like two breakable vases. They didn't look at each other or smile the way the other dancers did; that's how I knew they liked each other. His large dark hand was on the small of her back. Her hand rested tenderly on his shoulder. The other dancers moved away from them and there was empty space all around them.

250   My father went out into the dark to smoke and to play a hand or two of poker. My mother went to sit with some of the other women, all of them pulling their damp hair away from their necks and letting it fall back again, or furtively putting on lipstick, fanning themselves, and sipping their beers.

"He puts me in the mind of a man I once knew," said Mrs. Tubby.

"Look at them," said Mrs. Tens. "Don't you think he's young enough to be her son?"

With my elbows on my knees and my chin in my hands, I watched Aunt Moon step and square when my mother loomed up like a shadow over the bleachers where I sat.

°*Chickasaw* Native American peoples who originally lived in what is now the states of Mississippi and Alabama and who were forcibly moved to Oklahoma

"Young lady," she said in a scolding voice. "You were supposed to go home   260
and put the children to bed."

I looked from her stern face to my sister Susan, who was like a chubby angel
sleeping beside me. Peso Junior had run off to the gambling game, where he was
pushing another little boy around. My mother followed my gaze and looked at
Junior. She put her hands on her hips and said, "Boys!"

My sister Roberta, who was twelve, had stayed close to the women all night,
listening to their talk about the fullblood who had come to town for a rodeo or
something and who danced so far away from Bessie that they didn't look
friendly at all except for the fact that the music had stopped and they were still
waltzing.   270

Margaret Tubby won the prize money that year for the biggest pumpkin. It was
220.4 centimeters in circumference and weighed 190 pounds and had to be
carried on a stretcher by the volunteer firemen. Mrs. Tubby was the town's chief
social justice. She sat most days on the bench outside the grocery store. Sitting
there like a full-chested hawk on a fence, she held court. She had watched Bess
Evening for years with her sharp gold eyes. "This is the year I saw it coming," she
told my mother, as if she'd just been dying for Bess to go wrong. It showed up in
the way Bess walked, she said, that the woman was coming to a no good end just
like the rest of her family had done.

"When do you think she had time to grow that pumpkin?" Mother asked as   280
we escaped Margaret Tubby's court on our way to the store. I knew what she
meant, that Mrs. Tubby did more time with gossip than with her garden.

Margaret was even more pious than usual at that time of year when the green
tent revival followed on the heels of the fair, when the pink-faced men in white
shirts arrived and, really, every single one of them was a preacher. Still, Margaret
Tubby kept her prize money to herself and didn't give a tithe° to any church.

With Bess Evening carrying on with a stranger young enough to be her
son, Mrs. Tubby succeeded in turning the church women against her once and
for all. When Bessie walked down the busy street, one of the oldest dances of
women took place, for women in those days turned against each other easily,   290
never thinking they might have other enemies. When Bess appeared, the women
stepped away. They vanished from the very face of earth that was named
Comanche Street. They disappeared into the Oklahoma redstone shops like swal-
lows swooping into their small clay nests. The women would look at the new
bolts of red cloth in Terwilligers with feigned interest, although they would
never have worn red, even to a dog fight. They'd purchase another box of face
powder in the five and dime, or drink cherry phosphates° at the pharmacy without so much as tasting the flavor.

But Bessie was unruffled. She walked on in the empty mirage of heat, the
sound of her cane blending in with horse hooves and the rhythmic pumping of   300
oil wells out east.

°*tithe* a voluntary contribution, usually one-tenth of one's income, given to support a church
°*phosphate* an old-fashioned soda fountain drink

At the store, my mother bought corn meal, molasses, and milk. I bought penny candy for my younger sisters and for Peso Junior with the money I earned by helping Aunt Moon with her remedies. When we passed Margaret Tubby on the way out, my mother nodded at her, but said to me, "That pumpkin grew fat on gossip. I'll bet she fed it with nothing but all-night rumors." I thought about the twenty-five-dollar prize money and decided to grow pumpkins next year.

My mother said, "Now, don't you get any ideas about growing pumpkins, young lady. We don't have room enough. They'd crowd out the cucumbers and tomatoes."

310   My mother and father won a prize that year, too. For dancing. They won a horse lamp for the living room. "We didn't even know it was a contest," my mother said, free from the sin of competition. Her face was rosy with pleasure and pride. She had the life snapping out of her like hot grease, though sometimes I saw that life turn to a slow and restless longing, like when she daydreamed out the window where the young man had stood that day.

Passing Margaret's post and giving up on growing a two-hundred-pound pumpkin, I remembered all the things good Indian women were not supposed to do. We were not supposed to look into the faces of men. Or laugh too loud. We were not supposed to learn too much from books because that kind of knowledge was a
320   burden to the soul. Not only that, it always took us away from our loved ones. I was jealous of the white girls who laughed as loud as they wanted and never had rules. Also, my mother wanted me to go to college no matter what anyone else said or thought. She said I was too smart to stay home and live a life like hers, even if the other people thought book learning would ruin my life.

Aunt Moon with her second sight and heavy breasts managed to break all the rules. She threw back her head and laughed out loud, showing off the worn edges of her teeth. She didn't go to church. She did a man's work, cared for animals, and chopped her own wood. The gossiping women said it was a wonder Bessie Evening was healthy at all and didn't have female problems—meaning
330   with her body, I figured.

The small woman inside her eye was full and lonely at the same time.

Bess made tonics, remedies,° and cures. The church women, even those who gossiped, slipped over to buy Bessie's potions° at night and in secret. They'd never admit they swallowed the "snake medicine," as they called it. They'd say to Bess, "What have you got to put the life back in a man? My sister has that trouble, you know." Or they'd say, "I have a friend who needs a cure for the sadness." They bought remedies for fever and for coughing fits, for sore muscles and for sleepless nights.

Aunt Moon had learned the cures from her parents, who were said to have
340   visited their own sins upon their children, both of whom were born out of wedlock from the love of an old Chickasaw man and a young woman from one of those tribes up north. Maybe a Navajo° or something, the people thought.

°*remedies* medicines, often prepared at home, to relieve pain or to cure

°*potions* liquid medicine, often associated with magical qualities

°*Navajo* Native American peoples inhabiting parts of Arizona, New Mexico, and Utah, in the southwestern United States

But Aunt Moon had numerous talents and I respected them. She could pull cotton, pull watermelons, and pull babies with equal grace. She even delivered those scrub cattle, bred with Holsteins too big for them, caesarean. In addition to that, she told me the ways of the world and not just about the zodiac or fortune cards. "The United States is in love with death," she would say. "They sleep with it better than with lovers. They celebrate it on holidays, the Fourth of July, even in spring when they praise the loss of a good man's body."

She would tend her garden while I'd ask questions. What do you think about heaven? I wanted to know. She'd look up and then get back to pulling the weeds. "You and I both would just grump around up there with all those right-eous people. Women like us weren't meant to live on golden streets. We're Indi-ans," she'd say as she cleared out the space around a bean plant. "We're like these beans. We grew up from mud." And then she'd tell me how the people emerged right along with the crawdads from the muddy female swamps of the land. "And what is gold anyway? Just something else that comes from mud. Look at the con-quistadors."° She pulled a squash by accident. "And look at the sad women of this town, old already and all because of gold." She poked a hole in the ground and replanted the roots of the squash. "Their men make money, but not love. They give the women gold rings, gold-rimmed glasses, gold teeth, but their skin dries up for lack of love. Their hearts are little withered raisins." I was embarrassed by the mention of making love, but I listened to her words.

This is how I came to call Bessie Evening by the name of Aunt Moon: She'd been teaching me that animals and all life should be greeted properly as our kinfolk. "Good day, Uncle," I learned to say to the longhorn° as I passed by on the road. "Good morning, cousins. Is there something you need?" I'd say to the sparrows. And one night when the moon was passing over Bessie's house, I said, "Hello, Aunt Moon. I see you are full of silver again tonight." It was so much like Bess Evening, I began to think, that I named her after the moon. She was sometimes full and happy, sometimes small and weak. I began saying it right to her ears: "Auntie Moon, do you need some help today?"

She seemed both older and younger than thirty-nine to me. For one thing, she walked with a cane. She had developed some secret ailment after her young daughter died. My mother said she needed the cane because she had no mortal human to hold her up in life, like the rest of us did.

But the other thing was that she was full of mystery and she laughed right out loud, like a Gypsy, my mother said, pointing out Bessie's blue-painted walls, bright clothes and necklaces, and all the things she kept hanging from her ceiling. She decorated outside her house, too, with bits of blue glass hanging from the trees, and little polished quartz crystals that reflected rainbows across the dry hills.

Aunt Moon had solid feet, a light step, and a face that clouded over with emo-tion and despair one moment and brightened up like light the next. She'd beam

°*conquistadors* a reference to Spanish conquerors who came to what is now the American Southwest in search of gold during the seventeenth and eighteenth centuries

°*longhorn* a breed of cattle with long horns

and say to me, "Sassafras° will turn your hair red," and throw back her head to laugh, knowing full well that I would rinse my dull hair with sassafras that very night, ruining my mother's pans.

I sat in Aunt Moon's kitchen while she brewed herbals in white enamel pans on the woodstove. The insides of the pans were black from sassafras and burdock° and other plants she picked. The kitchen smelled rich and earthy. Some days it was hard to breathe from the combination of woodstove heat and pollen from the plants, but she kept at it and her medicine for cramps was popular with the women in town.

Aunt Moon made me proud of my womanhood, giving me bags of herbs and an old eagle feather that had been doctored by her father back when people used to pray instead of going to church. "The body divines everything," she told me, and sometimes when I was with her, I knew the older Indian world was still here and I'd feel it in my skin and hear the night sounds speak to me, hear the voice of water tell stories about people who lived here before, and the deep songs came out from the hills.

One day I found Aunt Moon sitting at her table in front of a plate of untouched toast and wild plum jam. She was weeping. I was young and didn't know what to say, but she told me more than I could ever understand. "Ever since my daughter died," she told me, "my body aches to touch her. All the mourning has gone into my bones." Her long hair was loose that day and it fell down her back like a waterfall, almost to the floor.

After that I had excuses on the days I saw her hair loose. "I'm putting up new wallpaper today," I'd say, or "I have to help Mom can peaches," which was the truth.

"Sure," she said, and I saw the tinge of sorrow around her eyes even though she smiled and nodded at me.

Canning the peaches, I asked my mother what it was that happened to Aunt Moon's daughter.

"First of all," my mother set me straight, "her name is Bess, not Aunt Moon." Then she'd tell the story of Willow Evening. "That pretty child was the light of that woman's eye," my mother said. "It was all so fast. She was playing one minute and the next she was gone. She was hanging on to that wooden planter and pulled it right down onto her little chest."

My mother touched her chest. "I saw Bessie lift it like it weighed less than a pound—did I already tell you that part?"

All I had seen that day was Aunt Moon holding Willow's thin body. The little girl's face was already gone to ashes and Aunt Moon blew gently on her daughter's skin, even though she was dead, as if she could breathe life back into her one more time. She blew on her skin the way I later knew that women blow sweat from lovers' faces, cooling them. But I knew nothing of any kind of passion then.

°*sassafras* either an herb, or the bark, or the roots of a tree used for cooking, medicinal purposes, or to add coloring
°*burdock* a plant whose leaves, flowers, and fruit are used for medicinal purposes or for cooking

The planter remained on the dry grassy mound of Aunt Moon's yard, and even though she had lifted it, no one else, not even my father, could move it. It was still full of earth and dead geraniums, like a monument to the child.

"That girl was all she had," my mother said through the steam of boiling water. "Hand me the ladle, will you?"   430

The peaches were suspended in sweet juice in their clear jars. I thought of our lives—so short, the skin so soft around us that we could be gone any second from our living—thought I saw Willow's golden brown face suspended behind glass in one of the jars.

The men first noticed the stranger, Isaac, when he cleaned them out in the poker game that night at the fair. My father, who had been drinking, handed over the money he'd saved for the new bathroom mirror and took a drunken swing at the young man, missing him by a foot and falling on his bad knee. Mr. Tubby told his wife he lost all he'd saved for the barber shop business, even though everyone in town knew he drank it up long before the week of the fair. Mr. Tens lost his Mex-   440
ican silver ring. It showed up later on Aunt Moon's hand.

Losing to one another was one thing. Losing to Isaac Cade meant the dark young man was a card sharp and an outlaw. Even the women who had watched the stranger all that night were sure he was full of demons.

The next time I saw Aunt Moon, it was the fallow season of autumn, but she seemed new and fresh as spring. Her skin had new light. Gathering plants, she smiled at me. Her cane moved aside the long dry grasses to reveal what grew underneath. Mullein was still growing, and holly.

I sat at the table while Aunt Moon ground yellow ochre in a mortar. Isaac came in from fixing the roof. He touched her arm so softly I wasn't sure she felt   450
it. I had never seen a man touch a woman that way.

He said hello to me and he said, "You know those fairgrounds? That's where the three tribes used to hold sings." He drummed on the table, looking at me, and sang one of the songs. I said I recognized it, a song I sometimes dreamed I heard from the hill.

A red handprint appeared on his face, like one of those birthmarks that only show up in the heat or under the strain of work or feeling.

"How'd you know about the fairgrounds?" I asked him.

"My father was from here." He sat still, as if thinking himself into another time. He stared out the window at the distances that were in between the blue curtains.   460

I went back to Aunt Moon's the next day. Isaac wasn't there, so Aunt Moon and I tied sage in bundles with twine. I asked her about love.

"It comes up from the ground just like corn," she said. She pulled a knot tighter with her teeth.

Later, when I left, I was still thinking about love. Outside where Bess had been planting, black beetles were digging themselves under the turned soil, and red ants had grown wings and were starting to fly.

When I returned home, my mother was sitting outside the house on a chair. She pointed at Bess Evening's house. "With the man there," she said, "I think it best you don't go over to Bessie's house anymore."   470

I started to protest, but she interrupted. "There are no ands, ifs, or buts about it."

I knew it was my father who made the decision. My mother had probably argued my point and lost to him again, and lost some of her life as well. She was slowed down to a slumberous pace. Later that night as I stood by my window looking toward Aunt Moon's house, I heard my mother say, "God damn them all and this whole damned town."

"There now," my father said. "There now."

"She's as dark and stained as those old black pans she uses," Margaret Tubby said about Bess Evening one day. She had come to pick up a cake from Mother for
480   the church bake sale. I was angered by her words. I gave her one of those "looks could kill" faces, but I said nothing. We all looked out the window at Aunt Moon. She was standing near Isaac, looking at a tree. It leapt into my mind suddenly, like lightning, that Mrs. Tubby knew about the blackened pans. That would mean she had bought cures from Aunt Moon. I was smug about this discovery.

Across the way, Aunt Moon stood with her hand outstretched, palm up. It was filled with roots or leaves. She was probably teaching Isaac about the remedies. I knew Isaac would teach her things also, older things, like squirrel sickness and porcupine disease that I'd heard about from grandparents.

Listening to Mrs. Tubby, I began to understand why, right after the fair, Aunt
490   Moon had told me I would have to fight hard to keep my life in this town. Mrs. Tubby said, "Living out of wedlock! Just like her parents." She went on, "History repeats itself."

I wanted to tell Mrs. Tubby a thing or two myself. "History, my eye," I wanted to say. "You're just jealous about the young man." But Margaret Tubby was still angry that her husband had lost his money to the stranger, and also because she probably still felt bad about playing with her necklace like a young girl that night at the fair. My mother said nothing, just covered the big caramel cake and handed it over to Mrs. Tubby. My mother looked like she was tired of fools and that included me. She looked like the woman inside her eye had just wandered off.

500   I began to see the women in Pickens as ghosts. I'd see them in the library looking at the stereopticons,° and in the ice cream parlor. The more full Aunt Moon grew, the more drawn and pinched they became.

The church women echoed Margaret. "She's as stained as her pans," they'd say, and they began buying their medicines at the pharmacy. It didn't matter that their coughs returned and that their children developed more fevers. It didn't matter that some of them could not get pregnant when they wanted to or that Mrs. Tens grew thin and pale and bent. They wouldn't dream of lowering themselves to buy Bessie's medicines.

My mother ran hot water into the tub and emptied one of her packages of bub-
510   ble powder in it. "Take a bath," she told me. "It will steady your nerves."

I was still crying, standing at the window, looking out at Aunt Moon's house through the rain.

°*stereopticons* "magic" lanterns with two projectors that produce disappearing images

The heavy air had been broken by an electrical storm earlier that day. In a sudden crash, the leaves flew off their trees, the sky exploded with lightning, and thunder rumbled the earth. People went to their doors to watch. It scared me. The clouds turned green and it began to hail and clatter.

That was when Aunt Moon's old dog, Mister, ran off, went running like crazy through the town. Some of the older men saw him on the street. They thought he was hurt and dying because of the way he ran and twitched. He butted right into a tree and the men thought maybe he had rabies or something. They meant   520 to put him out of his pain. One of them took aim with a gun and shot him, and when the storm died down and the streets misted over, everything returned to heavy stillness and old Mister was lying on the edge of the Smiths' lawn. I picked him up and carried his heavy body up to Aunt Moon's porch. I covered him with sage, like she would have done.

Bess and Isaac had gone over to Alexander that day to sell remedies. They missed the rain, and when they returned, they were happy about bringing home bags of beans, ground corn, and flour.

I guess it was my mother who told Aunt Moon about her dog.

That evening I heard her wailing. I could hear her from my window and I   530 looked out and saw her with her hair all down around her shoulders like a black shawl. Isaac smoothed back her hair and held her. I guessed that all the mourning was back in her bones again, even for her little girl, Willow.

That night my mother sat by my bed. "Sometimes the world is a sad place," she said and kissed my hot forehead. I began to cry again.

"Well, she still has the burro," my mother said, neglecting to mention Isaac.

I began to worry about the burro and to look after it. I went over to Aunt Moon's against my mother's wishes, and took carrots and sugar to the gray burro. I scratched his big ears.

By this time, most of the younger and healthier men had signed up to go to   540 Korea° and fight for their country. Most of the residents of Pickens were mixed-blood Indians and they were even more patriotic than white men. I guess they wanted to prove that they were good Americans. My father left and we saw him off at the depot. I admit I missed him saying to me, "The trouble with you is you think too much." Old Peso, always telling people what their problems were. Margaret Tubby's lazy son had enlisted because, as his mother had said, "It would make a man of him," and when he was killed in action, the townspeople resented Isaac, Bess Evening's young man, even more since he did not have his heart set on fighting the war.

Aunt Moon was pregnant the next year when the fair came around again, and   550 she was just beginning to show. Margaret Tubby had remarked that Bess was visiting all those family sins on another poor child.

This time I was older. I fixed Mrs. Tubby in my eyes and I said, "Miss Tubby, you are just like history, always repeating yourself."

°*Korea* a reference to the Korean War (1950–1953)

She pulled her head back into her neck like a turtle. My mother said, "Hush, Sis. Get inside the house." She put her hands on her hips. "I'll deal with you later." She almost added, "Just wait till your father gets home."

Later, I felt bad, talking that way to Margaret Tubby so soon after she lost her son.

560 Shortly after the fair, we heard that the young man inside Aunt Moon's eye was gone. A week passed and he didn't return. I watched her house from the window and I knew, if anyone stood behind me, the little house was resting up on my shoulder.

Mother took a nap and I grabbed the biscuits off the table and snuck out.

"I didn't hear you come in," Aunt Moon said to me.

"I didn't knock," I told her. "My mom just fell asleep. I thought it'd wake her up."

Aunt Moon's hair was down. Her hands were on her lap. A breeze came in the window. She must not have been sleeping and her eyes looked tired. I gave her the biscuits I had taken off the table. I lied and told her my mother had sent them over. We ate one.

570 Shortly after Isaac was gone, Bess Evening again became the focus of the town's women. Mrs. Tubby said, "Bessie would give you the shirt off her back. She never deserved a no good man who would treat her like dirt and then run off." Mrs. Tubby went over to Bess Evening's and bought enough cramp remedy from the pregnant woman to last her and her daughters for the next two years.

Mrs. Tens lost her pallor. She went to Bessie's with a basket of jellies and fruits, hoping in secret that Bess would return Mr. Tens's Mexican silver ring now that the young man was gone.

The women were going to stick by her; you could see it in their squared shoulders. They no longer hid their purchases of herbs. They forgot how they'd

580 looked at Isaac's black eyes and lively body with longing that night of the dance. If they'd had dowsing rods, the spilt willow branches would have flown up to the sky, so much had they twisted around the truth of things and even their own natures. Isaac was the worst of men. Their husbands, who were absent, were saints who loved them. Every morning when my mother said her prayers and forgot she'd damned the town and everybody in it, I heard her ask for peace for Bessie Evening, but she never joined in with the other women who seemed happy over Bessie's tragedy.

Isaac was doubly condemned in his absence. Mrs. Tubby said, "What kind of fool goes off to leave a woman who knows about tea leaves and cures for diseases of

590 the body and the mind alike? I'll tell you what kind, a card shark, that's what."

Someone corrected her. "Card *sharp*, dearie, not *shark*."

Who goes off and leaves a woman whose trees are hung with charming stones, relics, and broken glass, a woman who hangs sage and herbs to dry on her walls and whose front porch is full of fresh-cut wood? Those women, how they wanted to comfort her, but Bess Evening would only go to the door, leave them standing outside on the steps, and hand their herbs to them through the screen.

My cousins from Denver° came for the fair. I was going to leave with them and get a job in the city for a year or so, then go on to school. My mother in-

°*Denver* the capital city of Colorado

sisted she could handle the little ones alone now that they were bigger, and that I ought to go. It was best I made some money and learned what I could, she   600 said.

"Are you sure?" I asked while my mother washed her hair in the kitchen sink.

"I'm sure as the night's going to fall." She sounded lighthearted, but her hands stopped moving and rested on her head until the soap lather began to disappear. "Besides, your dad will probably be home any day now."

I said, "Okay then, I'll go. I'll write you all the time." I was all full of emotion, but I didn't cry.

"Don't make promises you can't keep," my mother said, wrapping a towel around her head.

I went to the dance that night with my cousins, and out in the trees I let Jim   610 Tens kiss me and promised him that I would be back. "I'll wait for you," he said. "And keep away from those city boys."

I meant it when I said, "I will."

He walked me home, holding my hand. My cousins were still at the dance. Mom would complain about their late city hours. Once she even told us that city people eat supper as late as eight o'clock P.M. We didn't believe her.

After Jim kissed me at the door, I watched him walk down the street. I was surprised that I didn't feel sad.

I decided to go to see Aunt Moon one last time. I was leaving at six in the morning and was already packed and I had taken one of each herb sample I'd   620 learned from Aunt Moon, just in case I ever needed them.

I scratched the burro's gray face at the lot and walked up toward the house. The window was gold and filled with lamplight. I heard an owl hooting in the distance and stopped to listen.

I glanced in the window and stopped in my tracks. The young man, Isaac, was there. He was speaking close to Bessie's face. He put his finger under her chin and lifted her face up to his. He was looking at her with soft eyes and I could tell there were many men and women living inside their eyes that moment. He held her cane across the back of her hips. With it, he pulled her close to him and held her tight, his hands on the cane pressing her body against his.   630 And he kissed her. Her hair was down around her back and shoulders and she put her arms around his neck. I turned to go. I felt dishonest and guilty for looking in at them. I began to run.

I ran into the bathroom and bent over the sink to wash my face. I wiped Jim Tens's cold kiss from my lips. I glanced up to look at myself in the mirror, but my face was nothing, just shelves of medicine bottles and aspirin. I had forgotten the mirror was broken.

From the bathroom door I heard my mother saying her prayers, fervently, and louder than usual. She said, "Bless Sis's Aunt Moon and bless Isaac, who got arrested for trading illegal medicine for corn, and forgive him for escaping from jail."   640

She said this so loud, I thought she was talking to me. Maybe she was. Now how did she read my mind again? It made me smile, and I guessed I was reading hers.

All the next morning, driving through the deep blue sky, I thought how all the women had gold teeth and hearts like withered raisins. I hoped Jim Tens would marry one of the Tubby girls. I didn't know if I'd ever go home or not. I had Aunt Moon's herbs in my bag, and the eagle feather wrapped safe in a scarf. And I had a small, beautiful woman in my eye.

ANALYZING THE STORY

Elements of Literature

Characterization

ACTIVITY 3

Hogan sometimes reveals a character's personality directly in the story, as, for example, when the narrator tells us in the beginning of the story that her "mother was a dreamer." (line 20) More often, we have to infer something about the character from appearance, actions, thoughts, speech, or even possessions. An example is lines 68–69 when the narrator says that her mother had "no cutting edge to her words" when she spoke of Aunt Moon. From this remark we might infer that the mother does not gossip about or criticize others.

Fill out the chart at right as specifically as you can. Give line references. You do not have to include information that you infer.

ACTIVITY 4

Using the character chart in Activity 3, work with a group to help the class come to a better understanding of a single character or group of characters. Your group should be prepared to present answers to the questions that follow. Give line references and explain the context in which the lines occur.

1. What, if anything, is revealed *directly* about the character's or group's personality? From whose **point of view** is the character or group being described, and how does this influence our knowledge of or feelings about the character or group?

2. What do this character's or group's appearance, age, possessions, actions, and thoughts reveal about personality, motivations, or needs? Choose three or four details to share with the class. For each one, explain how these details help you understand the character's or group's personality.

3. How is this character or group of characters different from other individuals or groups of characters? Would you characterize this person or group of people as insiders or outsiders in the community? Or as both?

	NARRATOR	AUNT MOON	NARRATOR'S MOTHER	ISAAC CADE	TOWN WOMEN	TOWN MEN
Adjectives or phrases that directly reveal personality	*"stubborn"* (line 86)					
Appearance, age, possessions						
Actions, thoughts, or speech that reveal personality, motivations, or needs	*"I stuck up for Aunt Moon"* (line 64)					

CREATIVE WRITING

The story's point of view affects our understanding of the characters. To better understand how this happens, rewrite the scene at the dance (lines 205–270) in the voice of Margaret Tubby.

- Before you begin, decide how you want your readers to feel about Tubby. Do you want them to like or dislike her, feel annoyed with her, feel sympathy for her?

- Use the first-person, or Margaret's, voice.

- Keeping Margaret Tubby's perspective in mind, add or omit details from the scene about the appearance, possessions, actions, and speech of the other characters at the dance.

How does this changed point of view help you see the characters differently than you do through the narrator's eyes?

Figurative Language

Simile and Symbolism

ACTIVITY 5

In groups, answer the following questions and be prepared to report your conclusions to the class. Use specific line references where appropriate and explain the context in which they appear.

1. The narrator frequently uses **similes** to describe other characters. For example, when the town women turn against Aunt Moon, the narrator says that she "began to see the women in Pickens as ghosts." (line 500) By comparing the women to ghosts, the narrator implies that the women have no life left in them and that they have become withered. Find similes in the story that describe Aunt Moon. Discuss what two things are being compared in the simile and what qualities they illustrate.

2. Toward the end of the story, the narrator uses a simile when she tells Margaret Tubby off. The narrator says: "'Miss Tubby, you are just like history, always repeating yourself.'" (lines 553–554) Find and explain other similes to describe the town women. Discuss what two things are being compared in the simile and what qualities they illustrate.

3. Find specific references to Aunt Moon's house, including its location and the colors, objects, and weather associated with it. Discuss the associations you have with each of these physical or natural elements. How is the house a **symbol** of Aunt Moon's character and of her position in the town?

4. Read the description of the town's people at the dance in lines 230–242. Note how the dress and hairstyle of the town women contrast with those of Aunt Moon.

   a. Choose from this or another passage two objects of Aunt Moon's clothing, jewelry, or hairstyle that set her apart from "the artificial geraniums and plastic carnations" at the dance. (lines 244–245). Discuss the associations you have with each of these objects or styles.

   b. What do they reveal about Aunt Moon's character?

   c. Discuss whether these objects or her hairstyle are symbolic.

5. Compare the paragraphs you wrote describing the opening scene of the story (Activity 2, Section 1, item 5, page 107).

   a. Choose two elements of the **setting** (objects, weather, atmosphere, land-scape, color) that you think might be symbolic.

   b. Skim the story to determine whether these elements reappear in the story and, if so, where and when.

   c. Discuss what associations you have with each of these elements and what each one may be symbolic of.

WRITING IN RESPONSE

Write briefly on these topics.

1. An eagle feather has particular symbolic meanings for many Native American cultures in the United States. Choose an object, element of nature, or other tangible item that has symbolic value in your culture, in your community, or among your friends. What associations do you have with it, and what is it symbolic of?

2. Think back to the questions regarding the nickname "Aunt Moon" (Activity 2, Section 2, item 3, page 108) and explain what a full moon symbolizes to you.

Exploring Further

Write or discuss the answers to these questions. Give evidence from the story to support your answers and include line numbers for each piece of evidence.

1. Why do you think Hogan chooses to move backward and forward through time rather than narrating the story chronologically? Why, for instance, doesn't she begin with Aunt Moon as a young woman, learning cures and remedies from her parents? What is the significance of how the story begins and ends for the narrator?

2. Consider the title of the story. Do you think Aunt Moon would call Isaac Cade her "young man"? Whose point of view is expressed in this title? Along with

the passage of time mentioned in question 1, what does the title reveal about one possible theme in this story?

3. Create a few similes of your own to describe Aunt Moon and other characters in the story. Use story references to justify your comparisons.

4. This story takes place during what people in the United States call the Korean War (1950–1953). There are many references to death in the story. In fact, Aunt Moon says that "'the United States is in love with death . . . . They sleep with it better than with lovers. They celebrate it on holidays, the Fourth of July, even in spring when they praise the loss of a good man's body.'" (lines 347–349)

   a. What and whom do you think she is referring to when she says "in spring" and "the loss of a good man's body"?
   b. What does Aunt Moon's comment reveal about her, particularly in relation to her community?
   c. What is your reaction to her assertion?

5. Find other references to death in the story. Who dies and who is associated with death? Who lives and who is associated with life? How does death help us understand one or more of the story's central conflicts? As you answer these questions, consider how death in this story relates to the struggles between or within various characters or groups of characters, between characters and society, or between characters and nature.

6. How has the narrator changed during the course of the story? In what ways has Aunt Moon influenced these changes? In what ways has the mother influenced these changes?

7. Why do you think Hogan begins and ends the story in autumn? How does her choice of season help us to better understand the story?

WRITING IN RESPONSE

Respond briefly to this question in writing.

Knowing what you do now about the narrator and the people of Pickens, do you think the narrator will ever return to Pickens to live?

ESSAY TOPICS

1. Imagine that five years have passed since the end of the story. As the narrator has matured, she has looked back at her years growing up in Pickens in order to figure out how those experiences helped to make her the person she is now.

   Write a letter in the voice of the narrator (use "I") to Aunt Moon, the narrator's mother, or the town women. Explain what you (the narrator) learned about life from the people of Pickens and especially from the person to whom you are writing. Support your assessment of what you've learned by focusing on specific scenes, moments, or descriptions from the story.

2. In discussing the inspiration for this story, Hogan said that she remembered "the sky and the land" of Oklahoma where her grandparents lived in the 1950s and 1960s. Throughout the story, Hogan uses elements of nature, such as the sky and land, to create a particular mood, to contribute to a characterization, or to suggest a particular conflict or theme. For example, after the narrator asks Aunt Moon "about love," (line 462) she notes that Bess had been planting outside and that "red ants had grown wings and were starting to fly." (lines 466–467) The image of the ants sprouting wings and flying away suggests the metamorphosis that the narrator undergoes in the course of the story.

Write an essay in which you analyze Hogan's use of elements of nature to help us better understand the story.

3. Write an essay in which you analyze Hogan's use of figurative language, explaining how such language helps us to better understand any of the following: characters, events, or themes.

AUTHOR PROFILE

Linda Hogan

Linda Hogan (1947–   ) was born in Denver, Colorado, and raised on a reservation in Oklahoma. A member of the Chickasaw tribe, Hogan has been greatly influenced in her work by tribal life, her family's storytelling and values, and, as she refers to it, "the spirit of place." Commenting on "Aunt Moon's Young Man," Hogan writes, "I remember the sky and the land, and all of my work is a part of that early landscape and the influence it worked deep inside me. This story . . . brings together the colors of the sky, the people, and the history." The natural world in Hogan's work is inseparable from the lives of her characters, especially the women. Paula Gunn Allen, Laguna Pueblo Indian, poet and essayist, comments that Hogan's women are good at "grieving . . . . They are also good at making connections, at seeing the tragic relationships that are piling up around us in this particular phase of world history . . . ." Hogan herself says, "I love Aunt Moon. For me, she is one of the courageous female heroes and adventurers I have seldom seen in stories." Hogan has written aggressively in opposition to all the forces in the modern world that threaten to destroy the natural world and the spirit of people who relate closely to the land. "Having a money economy," Hogan says, "leads to the exploitation of people and land [and] to people who have false needs."

Hogan's poetry collections include *Savings: Poems* (1988) and *Book of Medicines: Poems* (1993). She has also published collections of short stories, including *That Horse* (1985) and *The Big Woman* (1987), and a novel, *Mean Spirits* (1990).

CHAPTER 10

D.P.

KURT VONNEGUT, JR.

PREPARATION

ACTIVITY 1

With a partner or in small groups, answer the following questions.

1. What do you imagine life was like in villages in Europe before World War II? Do you think visitors from other countries and cultures would have been common? Explain.

2. "Displaced Person" (D.P.) is a term that originated during wartime. What do you think it means?

3. What do you know about the effects of World War II on the German cities, villages, and economy?

4. After its defeat in World War II, Germany was, for a period of time, occupied and governed by Allied forces from the United States, the Soviet Union, Britain, and France. This was called the Occupation. What effect do you think the Occupation had on the German people at that time?

5. At the time of World War II (1939–45), African-American (then called colored or Negro) soldiers and white American soldiers were segregated into troops by race. Which other aspects of life in parts of America were segregated at that time? Do you think racial segregation existed in Germany at that time? Why or why not?

WRITING IN RESPONSE

Write briefly on these topics.

1. What words and images do you associate with war? Explain your associations.
2. How might African Americans have felt serving in segregated troops in World War II? Why?

D.P.

KURT VONNEGUT, JR.

Eighty-one small sparks of human life were kept in an orphanage set up by
Catholic nuns in what had been the gamekeeper's house on a large estate overlooking the Rhine. This was in the German village of Karlswald, in the American
Zone of Occupation.° Had the children not been kept there, not been given the
warmth and food and clothes that could be begged for them, they might have
wandered off the edges of the earth, searching for parents who had long ago
stopped searching for them.

Every mild afternoon the nuns marched the children, two by two, through the
woods, into the village and back, for their ration of fresh air. The village carpen-
10   ter, an old man who was given to thoughtful rests between strokes of his tools,
always came out of his shop to watch the bobbing, chattering, cheerful, ragged
parade, and to speculate, with idlers his shop attracted, as to the nationalities of
the passing children's parents.

"See the little French girl," he said one afternoon. "Look at the flash of those
eyes!"

"And look at that little Pole swing his arms. They love to march, the Poles,"
said a young mechanic.

"Pole? Where do you see any Pole?" said the carpenter.

"There—the thin, sober-looking one in front," the other replied.

20   "Aaaaah. He's too tall for a Pole," said the carpenter. "And what Pole has flaxen
hair like that? He's a German."

The mechanic shrugged. "They're all German now, so what difference does it
make?" he said. "Who can prove what their parents were? If you had fought in
Poland, you would know he was a very common type."

"Look—look who's coming now," said the carpenter, grinning. "Full of arguments as you are, you won't argue with me about *him*. There we have an American!" He called out to the child. "Joe—when you going to win the championship
back?"

"Joe!" called the mechanic. "How is the Brown Bomber° today?"

30   At the very end of the parade, a lone, blue-eyed colored° boy, six years old,
turned and smiled with sweet uneasiness at those who called out to him every
day. He nodded politely, murmuring a greeting in German, the only language he
knew.

His name, chosen arbitrarily by the nuns, was Karl Heinz. But the carpenter
had given him a name that stuck, the name of the only colored man who had
ever made an impression on the villagers' minds, the former heavyweight champion of the world, Joe Louis.

"Joe!" called the carpenter. "Cheer up! Let's see those white teeth sparkle, Joe."

°*Zone of Occupation* sector of Germany governed by one of the Allied countries who won World
War II
°*the Brown Bomber* boxer Joe Louis
°*colored* dark skinned, sometimes used to refer to African Americans (not current usage)

Joe obliged shyly.

The carpenter clapped the mechanic on the back. "And if *he* isn't a German 40
too! Maybe it's the only way we can get another heavyweight champion."

Joe turned a corner, shooed° out of the carpenter's sight by a nun bringing up
the rear. She and Joe spent a great deal of time together, since Joe, no matter
where he was placed in the parade, always drifted to the end.

"Joe," she said, "you are such a dreamer. Are all your people such dreamers?"

"I'm sorry, sister," said Joe. "I was thinking."

"Dreaming."

"Sister, am I the son of an American soldier?"

"Who told you that?"

"Peter. Peter said my mother was a German, and my father was an American 50
soldier who went away. He said she left me with you, and then went away too."
There was no sadness in his voice—only puzzlement.

Peter was the oldest boy in the orphanage, an embittered old man of fourteen, a German boy who could remember his parents and brothers and sisters
and home, and the war, and all sorts of food that Joe found impossible to imagine. Peter seemed superhuman to Joe, like a man who had been to heaven and
hell and back many times, and knew exactly why they were where they were,
how they had come there, and where they might have been.

"You mustn't worry about it, Joe," said the nun. "No one knows who your
mother and father were. But they must have been very good people, because 60
you are so good."

"What is an American?" said Joe.

"It's a person from another country."

"Near here?"

"There are some near here, but their homes are far, far away—across a great
deal of water."

"Like the river."

"More water than that, Joe. More water than you have ever seen. You can't
even see the other side. You could get on a boat and go for days and days and
still not get to the other side. I'll show you a map sometime. But don't pay any at- 70
tention to Peter, Joe. He makes things up. He doesn't really know anything about
you. Now, catch up."

Joe hurried, and overtook the end of the line, where he marched purposefully
and alertly for a few minutes. But then he began to dawdle again, chasing ghost-
like words in his small mind: . . . soldier . . . German . . . American . . . your
people . . . champion . . . Brown Bomber . . . more water than you've ever seen.

"Sister," said Joe, "are Americans like me? Are they brown?"

"Some are, some aren't, Joe."

"Are there many people like me?"

"Yes. Many, many people." 80

"Why haven't I seen them?"

°*shooed* requested or forced to leave

"None of them have come to the village. They have places of their own."

"I want to go there."

"Aren't you happy here, Joe?"

"Yes. But Peter says I don't belong here, that I'm not a German and never can be."

"Peter! Pay no attention to him."

"Why do people smile when they see me, and try to make me sing and talk, and then laugh when I do?"

90   "Joe, Joe! Look quickly," said the nun. "See—up there, in the tree. See the little sparrow with the broken leg. Oh poor, brave little thing—he still gets around quite well. See him, Joe? Hop, hop, hippity-hop."

One hot summer day, as the parade passed the carpenter's shop, the carpenter came out to call something new to Joe, something that thrilled and terrified him.

"Joe! Hey, Joe! Your father is in town. Have you seen him yet?"

"No, sir—no, I haven't," said Joe. "Where is he?"

"He's teasing," said the nun sharply.

"You see if I'm teasing, Joe," said the carpenter. "Just keep your eyes open

100   when you go past the school. You have to look sharp, up the slope and into the woods. You'll see, Joe."

"I wonder where our little friend the sparrow is today," said the nun brightly. "Goodness, I hope his leg is getting better, don't you, Joe?"

"Yes, yes I do, sister."

She chattered on about the sparrow and the clouds and the flowers as they approached the school, and Joe gave up answering her.

The woods above the school seemed still and empty.

But then Joe saw a massive brown man, naked to the waist and wearing a pistol, step from the trees. The man drank from a canteen, wiped his lips with the

110   back of his hand, grinned down on the world with handsome disdain, and disappeared again into the twilight of the woods.

"Sister!" gasped Joe. "My father—I just saw my father!"

"No, Joe—no you didn't."

"He's up there in the woods. I saw him. I want to go up there, sister."

"He isn't your father, Joe. He doesn't know you. He doesn't want to see you."

"He's one of my people, sister!"

"You can't go up there, Joe, and you can't stay here." She took him by the arm to make him move. "Joe—you're being a bad boy, Joe."

Joe obeyed numbly. He didn't speak again for the remainder of the walk,

120   which brought them home by another route, far from the school. No one else had seen his wonderful father, or believed that Joe had.

Not until prayers that night did he burst into tears.

At ten o'clock, the young nun found his cot empty.

Under a great spread net that was laced with rags, an artillery piece squatted in the woods, black and oily, its muzzle thrust at the night sky. Trucks and the rest of the battery were hidden higher on the slope.

Joe watched and listened tremblingly through a thin screen of shrubs as the soldiers, indistinct in the darkness, dug in around their gun. The words he over-heard made no sense to him.

"Sergeant, why we gotta dig in, when we're movin' out in the mornin', and it's   130
just maneuvers anyhow? Seems like we could kind of conserve our strength, and just scratch around a little to show where we'd of dug if there was any sense to it."

"For all you know, boy, there may *be* sense to it before mornin'," said the sergeant. "You got ten minutes to get to China and bring me back a pigtail. Hear?"

The sergeant stepped into a patch of moonlight, his hands on his hips, his big shoulders back, the image of an emperor. Joe saw that it was the same man he'd marveled at in the afternoon. The sergeant listened with satisfaction to the sounds of digging, and then, to Joe's alarm, strode toward Joe's hiding place.

Joe didn't move a muscle until the big boot struck his side. *"Ach!"*°

"Who's that?" The sergeant snatched Joe from the ground, and set him on his   140
feet hard. "My golly, boy, what you doin' here? Scoot!° Go on home! This ain't no place for kids to be playin'." He shined a flashlight in Joe's face. "Doggone,"° he muttered. "Where you come from?" He held Joe at arm's length, and shook him gently, like a rag doll. "Boy, how you get here—swim?"

Joe stammered in German that he was looking for his father.

"Come on—how you get here? What you doin'? Where's your mammy?"

"What you got there, sergeant?" said a voice in the dark.

"Don't rightly know what to call it," said the sergeant. "Talks like a Kraut° and dresses like a Kraut, but just look at it a minute."

Soon a dozen men stood in a circle around Joe, talking loudly, then softly, to   150
him, as though they thought getting through to him were a question of tone.

Every time Joe tried to explain his mission, they laughed in amazement.

"How he learn German? Tell me that."

"Where your daddy, boy?"

"Where your mammy, boy?"

"Sprecken zee Dutch,° boy? Looky there. See him nod. He talks it, all right."

"Oh, you're fluent, man, mighty fluent. Ask him some more."

"Go get the lieutenant," said the sergeant. "He can talk to this boy, and under-stand what he's tryin' to say. Look at him shake. Scared to death. Come here, boy; don't be afraid, now." He enclosed Joe in his great arms. "Just take it easy, now—   160
everything's gonna be all-l-l-l right. See what I got? By golly, I don't believe the boy's ever seen chocolate before. Go on—taste it. Won't hurt you."

°*ach!* a German exclamation, indicating someone is hurt or surprised

°*scoot* leave, go away, get out (usually used with children/animals)

°*doggone* an exclamation showing surprise

°*Kraut* (slang) a pejorative term for a German

°*sprecken zee Dutch* incorrect German; the soldier means to say in German, "Do you speak German?"

Joe, safe in a fort of bone and sinew, ringed by luminous eyes, bit into the chocolate bar. The pink lining of his mouth, and then his whole soul, was flooded with warm, rich pleasure, and he beamed.

"He smiled!"

"Look at him light up!"

"Doggone if he didn't stumble right into heaven! I mean!"

170   "Talk about displaced persons," said the sergeant, hugging Joe, "this here's the most displaced little old person I *ever* saw. Upside down and inside out and ever' which way."

"Here, boy—here's some more chocolate."

"Don't give him no more," said the sergeant reproachfully. "You want to make him sick?"

"Naw, sarge,° naw—don't wanna make him sick. No, sir."

"What's going on here?" The lieutenant, a small, elegant Negro, the beam of his flashlight dancing before him, approached the group.

"Got a little boy here, lieutenant," said the sergeant. "Just wandered into the battery. Must of crawled past the guards."

180   "Well, send him on home, sergeant."

"Yessir. I planned to." He cleared his throat. "But this ain't no ordinary little boy, lieutenant." He opened his arms so that the light fell on Joe's face.

The lieutenant laughed incredulously, and knelt before Joe. "How'd you get here?"

"All he talks is German, lieutenant," said the sergeant.

"Where's your home?" said the lieutenant in German.

"Over more water than you've ever seen," said Joe.

"Where do you come from?"

"God made me," said Joe.

190   "This boy is going to be a lawyer when he grows up," said the lieutenant in English. "Now, listen to me," he said to Joe, "what's your name, and where are your people?"

"Joe Louis," said Joe, "and you are my people. I ran away from the orphanage, because I belong with you."

The lieutenant stood, shaking his head, and translated what Joe had said.

The woods echoed with glee.

"Joe Louis! I *thought* he was awful big and powerful-lookin'!"

"Jus' keep away from that left—*tha's* all!"

"If he's Joe, he's sure found his people. He's got us there!"

200   "Shut up!" commanded the sergeant suddenly. "All of you just shut up. This ain't no joke! Ain't nothing funny in it! Boy's all alone in the world. Ain't no joke."

A small voice finally broke the solemn silence that followed. "Naw—ain't no joke at all."

"We better take the jeep and run him back into town, sergeant," said the lieutenant. "Corporal Jackson, you're in charge."

°*Sarge* short for Sergeant

"You tell 'em Joe was a *good* boy," said Jackson.

"Now, Joe," said the lieutenant in German, softly, "you come with the sergeant and me. We'll take you home."

Joe dug his fingers into the sergeant's forearms. "Papa! No—papa! I want to   210
stay with you."

"Look, sonny, I ain't your papa," said the sergeant helplessly. "I *ain't* your papa."

"Papa!"

"Man, he's glued to you, ain't he, sergeant?" said a soldier. "Looks like you ain't never goin' to pry him loose. You got yourself a boy there, sarge, and he's got hisself a papa."

The sergeant walked over to the jeep with Joe in his arms. "Come on, now," he said, "you leggo,° little Joe, so's I can drive. I can't drive with you hangin' on, Joe. You sit in the lieutenant's lap right next to me."   220

The group formed again around the jeep, gravely now, watching the sergeant try to coax Joe into letting go.

"I don't want to get tough, Joe. Come on—take it easy, Joe. Let go, now, Joe, so's I can drive. See, I can't steer or nothin' with you hanging on right there."

"Papa!"

"Come on, over to my lap, Joe," said the lieutenant in German.

"Papa!"

"Joe, Joe, looky," said a soldier. "Chocolate! Want some more chocolate, Joe? See? Whole bar, Joe, all yours. Jus' leggo the sergeant and move over into the lieutenant's lap."   230

Joe tightened his grip on the sergeant.

"Don't put the chocolate back in your pocket, man! Give it to Joe anyways," said a soldier angrily. "Somebody go get a case of D bars° off the truck, and throw 'em in the back for Joe. Give that boy chocolate enough for the nex' twenny years."

"Look, Joe," said another soldier, "ever see a wristwatch? Look at the wristwatch, Joe. See it glow, boy? Move over in the lieutenant's lap, and I'll let you listen to it tick. Tick, tick, tick, Joe. Come on, want to listen?"

Joe didn't move.

The soldier handed the watch to him. "Here, Joe, you take it anyway. It's yours."   240
He walked away quickly.

"Man," somebody called after him, "you crazy? You paid fifty dollars for that watch. What business a little boy got with any fifty-dollar watch?"

"No—I ain't crazy. Are you?"

"Naw, I ain't crazy. Neither one of us crazy, I guess. Joe—want a knife? You got to promise to be careful with it, now. Always cut *away* from yourself. Hear? Lieutenant, when you get back, you tell him always cut *away* from hisself."

"I don't want to go back. I want to stay with *papa*," said Joe tearfully.

°*leggo* let go
°*D bars* chocolate bars; military term during World War II

"Soldiers can't take little boys with them, Joe," said the lieutenant in German. "And we're leaving early in the morning."

"Will you come back for me?" said Joe.

"We'll come back if we can, Joe. Soldiers never know where they'll be from one day to the next. We'll come back for a visit, if we can."

"Can we give old Joe this case of D bars, lieutenant?" said a soldier carrying a cardboard carton of chocolate bars.

"Don't ask me," said the lieutenant. "I don't know anything about it. I never saw anything of any case of D bars, never heard anything about it."

"Yessir." The soldier laid his burden down on the jeep's back seat.

"He ain't gonna let go," said the sergeant miserably. "You drive, lieutenant, and me and Joe'll sit over there."

The lieutenant and the sergeant changed places, and the jeep began to move.

"'By, Joe!"

"You be a good boy, Joe!"

"Don't you eat all that chocolate at once, you hear?"

"Don't cry, Joe. Give us a smile."

"Wider, boy—that's the stuff!"

"Joe, Joe, wake up, Joe." The voice was that of Peter, the oldest boy in the orphanage, and it echoed damply from the stone walls.

Joe sat up, startled. All around his cot were the other orphans, jostling one another for a glimpse of Joe and the treasures by his pillow.

"Where did you get the hat, Joe—and the watch, and knife?" said Peter. "And what's in the box under your bed?"

Joe felt his head, and found a soldier's wool knit cap there. "Papa," he mumbled sleepily.

"Papa!" mocked Peter, laughing.

"Yes," said Joe. "Last night I went to see my papa, Peter."

"Could he speak German, Joe?" said a little girl wonderingly.

"No, but his friend could," said Joe.

"He didn't see his father," said Peter. "Your father is far, far away, and will never come back. He probably doesn't even know you're alive."

"What did he look like?" said the girl.

Joe glanced thoughtfully around the room. "Papa is as high as this ceiling," he said at last. "He is wider than that door." Triumphantly, he took a bar of chocolate from under his pillow. "And as brown as that!" He held out the bar to the others. "Go on, have some. There is plenty more."

"He doesn't look anything like that," said Peter. "You aren't telling the truth, Joe."

"My papa has a pistol as big as this bed, almost, Peter," said Joe happily, "and a cannon as big as this house. And there were hundreds and hundreds like him."

"Somebody played a joke on you, Joe," said Peter. "He wasn't your father. How do you know he wasn't fooling you?"

"Because he cried when he left me," said Joe simply. "And he promised to take me back home across the water as fast as he could." He smiled airily. "Not like the river, Peter—across more water than you've *ever* seen. He promised, and then I let him go."

ANALYZING THE STORY

ACTIVITY 2

Answer the following questions. Give evidence to support your answers and line numbers for each piece of evidence.

1. Where does the story take place and in what period of history?

2. Who are the important characters?

3. Where do the children live? Why are they there? Who cares for the children?

4. Describe Joe: his age, background, and language.

5. What does Peter tell Joe about his background? (lines 50–51) What does the nun tell Joe about his background? (lines 45–72)

6. What do the following comments about the American soldiers in Karlswald Village emphasize about them?

   "'And there were hundreds and hundreds like him.'" (line 289)
   ". . . Joe saw a massive brown man . . . ." (line 108)
   "'He's one of my people, sister!'" (line 116)
   "The lieutenant, a small, elegant Negro . . . ." (line 176)
   "'If he's Joe [Louis], he's sure found his people. He's got us there!'" (line 199)

7. The American soldiers speak a nonstandard dialect of English, as in the following examples:

   "'. . . boy, what you doin' here?'" (line 141)
   "'Where you come from?'" (line 143)
   "'Boy, how you get here—swim?'" (line 144)
   "'Where your daddy, boy?'" "'Where your mammy, boy?'" (lines 154–155)
   "'. . . he's got hisself a papa.'" (lines 216–217)
   "'. . . you leggo, little Joe . . . .'" (line 219)

   What are some grammatical characteristics of this dialect? In the story, do the American soldiers of all ranks use this dialect? What could this indicate?

8. What is the sergeant's first reaction when he sees Joe? What does he think? (lines 140–146)

9. What are the other soldiers' reactions? What gifts do they give him? In what way are these gifts special?

10. Why does Joe let go of the sergeant at the end of the story? (lines 292–295)

WRITING IN RESPONSE

Write briefly on these topics.

1. Describe your feelings about Joe and his situation. Then discuss the soldiers' reaction to Joe and why you think they feel the way they do.

2. What is your reaction to the dialect of English that the soldiers use in the story?

Elements of Literature

Point of View

ACTIVITY 3

In the chart, read each quotation from "D.P." and decide which **point of view** is represented—the narrator's **(third-person omniscient)** or a character's **(third-person limited)**. (See Appendix A for more information about terms in boldface type.) Name the character. Underline the key words in the passage that indicate whose point of view it is. The first one is done for you.

QUOTATION FROM THE STORY	LINE NUMBER(S)	POINT OF VIEW
1. "Eighty-one small sparks of human life <u>were kept</u> in an orphanage . . . ."	1	*Narrator*
2. "Every mild afternoon the nuns marched the children, two by two, through the woods . . . . "	8–9	
3. ". . . a lone, blue-eyed colored boy, six years old, turned and smiled with sweet uneasiness . . . . He nodded politely, murmuring a greeting in German, the only language he knew."	30–33	
4. "Peter . . . could remember . . . all sorts of food that Joe found impossible to imagine. Peter seemed superhuman to Joe . . . ."	55–56	
5. ". . . the carpenter came out to call something new to Joe, something that thrilled and terrified him."	93–94	
6. "Joe, safe in a fort of bone and sinew . . . bit into the chocolate bar. The pink lining of his mouth, and then his whole soul, was flooded with warm, rich pleasure . . . ."	163–165	

ACTIVITY 4

1. Choose two of the quotations in Activity 3. How does the point of view affect your understanding of the specific situation?

2. Is there a specific place in the story where the point of view changes and then remains in that point of view? Where is it? What is the author's purpose in doing this?

CREATIVE WRITING

Write a paragraph in the first person, as if you were Joe. Describe what you think and feel as you are held by the sergeant and surrounded by the first people of your race that you have ever seen. (lines 163–165)

Characterization

ACTIVITY 5

The characters in "D.P." reveal much about themselves and their motivations through their conversations and actions. In three groups, responding to one of the following questions for each group, discuss Joe and other significant characters. Report your answers and ideas to the class.

1. Joe asks the same question in different ways throughout the story. Examine the following quotations, find other examples in the text, and discuss what it is that Joe really wants to know about himself.

   • "'Sister, am I the son of an American soldier?'" (line 48)
   • "'Sister, . . . are Americans like me? Are they brown?'" (line 77)
   • "'My father—I just saw my father!'" (line 112)
   • "'He's one of my people, sister!'" (line 116)

2. Discuss the following questions as they relate to these five characters: the carpenter, the mechanic, the nun, Peter, and the sergeant. Support your ideas with evidence from the text.

   a. What kind of person is he or she?
   b. How does this character react to Joe?
   c. Does the character help Joe answer the questions about himself and his background? How?

3. Study the following two quotations. What do they reveal about Joe or about the characters who say them? Find other examples of quotations that reveal a specific personality trait of a character.

   • "'Full of arguments as you are, you won't argue with me about *him*. There we have an American!'" (lines 25–27)
   • "'Joe—when are you going to win the championship back?'" (lines 27–28)

WRITING IN RESPONSE

Respond briefly to these questions in writing. Compare your responses with those of two or three classmates.

1. What do you think about the way that Peter and the villagers react to Joe and make him feel? How do you explain their reactions?

2. If Joe remained in Germany, what do you think his life as a young adult in that era would be like?

Figurative Language

Symbolism

ACTIVITY 6

Vonnegut uses **symbolism** in "D.P." After your group completes the information about symbols (underlined) in the chart, be prepared to summarize the important points of your discussion for the class. Give evidence to support your answers and line numbers for each piece of evidence.

QUOTATION (Symbol Underlined)	ASSOCIATED QUALITIES	SYMBOL OF	SHARED QUALITIES	FURTHER ASSOCIATIONS
1. "Eighty-one small <u>sparks</u> of human life were kept in an orphanage . . . ." (line 1)	Sparks from a fire are explosive, lively, active, unpredictable.	The children from the orphanage	Energy, liveliness, unpredictability	This energetic, "free" image also contrasts with that of an orphanage, which we think of as a prisonlike, lonely, and sad place.
2. "Joe, safe in a <u>fort</u> of bone and sinew . . . ." (line 163)				
3. "Joe, safe in a fort of <u>bone and sinew</u> . . . ." (line 163)				
4. " 'Doggone if he didn't stumble right into <u>heaven</u>.' " (line 168)				

ACTIVITY 7

Answer the following questions about these symbols.

1. The sparrow:

    a. What has happened to the sparrow that the nun shows Joe?
    b. How does the sparrow react to its condition?
    c. Which character could the sparrow symbolize in the story? How are the
       two alike?

2. Chocolate:

    a. Had Joe ever tasted chocolate before?
    b. What is his reaction to the taste of chocolate?
    c. What could chocolate symbolize ? Explain.

3. Water:

    a. The nun tells Joe that America is across "'more water than you have ever
       seen.'" (line 68) Find two other similar mentions of water.
    b. What is the only body of water that Joe has seen?
    c. Literally, what body of water is the nun referring to?
    d. Symbolically, what could this large body of water represent to Joe?

4. Find one more symbol in the story and explain its meaning.

Metaphor

ACTIVITY 8

In the chart, look at the underlined **metaphor** in each quotation from the story.
Decide what its qualities are, what it is being compared to, and what qualities
those two things share. Complete the chart.

QUOTATION	QUALITIES	COMPARED TO	SHARED QUALITIES	FURTHER ASSOCIATIONS
1. "Peter was the oldest boy in the orphanage, an embittered old man of fourteen . . . ." (lines 53–54)				
2. "The sergeant stepped into a patch of moonlight . . . the image of an emperor." (lines 135–136)				

WRITING IN RESPONSE

Write briefly on these topics.

1. Do you think most authors want their readers to be conscious of symbolism as they read a story? Why or why not? Do you think readers should try to be conscious of symbolism as they read? Why or why not?

2. Choose one of the metaphors or symbols in the story and write about how it helps your understanding of the story.

Theme

ACTIVITY 9

A. Answer the following questions. Give evidence to support your answers and line numbers for each piece of evidence.

1. The German villagers, the nun, and Peter do not refer directly to the issue of race, yet they make assumptions about Joe based on stereotypes of people of his color. What are some of these assumptions? Are they correct, in Joe's case?

2. Discuss the sergeant's reactions to Joe and his situation. Does he seem to feel responsible for Joe in some way? What might the author be saying about social responsibility *in this situation?*

3. Joe is searching for his identity throughout the story. Where does Joe feel he belongs? In your opinion, where does he belong? How do you think people determine where they belong and feel comfortable—by racial, cultural, or national identities or by some other factor?

4. Honesty is an issue in the story. Discuss the nun, Peter, and the sergeant, considering the following:

   a. What do they say to Joe about his background?
   b. Why do you think they respond as they do to Joe's questions about himself?
   c. What is their effect on him?

5. The sergeant is honest with Joe in telling him that he is not his "papa," but at the end of the story Joe tells the boys in the orphanage that "he promised to take me back home. . . ." (lines 292–293) If, as Joe contends, the sergeant promised that, do you think he was being honest with Joe? Did he really intend to take him to America someday? Why do you think so?

B. Building on your group discussion of the questions in part A, formulate some **theme** statements for "D.P." and support these with evidence from the story. To find evidence in support of a theme, consider these elements of the story:

- The events and situations
- Figurative language, including metaphor and symbolism
- Details about the story's physical and historical setting
- Your analysis of the character's words, actions, and motivations

Study this example first.

> *Theme statement:* Searching for one's identity and knowing one's roots are essential for us as human beings.

> *Evidence:*
> "'Sister, am I the son of an American soldier?'" (line 48)
> "'What is an American?'" (line 62)
> "'Sister, . . . are Americans like me? Are they brown?'" (line 77)
> "'Are there many people like me?'" (line 79)
> "Joe stammered in German that he was looking for his father." (line 145)
> "'Will you come back for me?'" (line 251)

Exploring Further: *Comparing the Story and Film Versions of "D.P."*

Read through the questions below *before* viewing the film, so you can focus on specific things to consider. After you have seen Jonathan Demme's film version of the story "D.P.," discuss or write about the similarities and differences between the story and the film. Use the questions that follow to guide you.

Setting

1. How does the **setting** in the film and in the story differ? In what season does the film take place?
2. Why might the film director have made the change?

Characters

1. *Joe:*
   How old is Joe in the story?
   How old does he seem to be in the film?
   How is Joe described in the story?
   How does he look in the film?
   What is Joe searching for in the story? In the film? Are these similar or different?

2. *The sergeant:*

How is the sergeant described in the story? In the film?
What is the sergeant doing when we first see him in the story? In the film?
Why might the film director have made this change?

3. *Added scenes:*

Which scenes appear in the film that are not in the story?
Why might the film director have added these specific scenes?

4. *Theme:*

What themes are clearest in the story?
What themes does the film emphasize?
Discuss the similarities or differences in themes and the reasons for them.

WRITING IN RESPONSE

Write briefly on these topics.

1. Choose two of the changes the film director made and discuss why you think he made them. What effect do these changes have on your original perception of the story?

2. Discuss which you like better, the story or the film version of "D.P." Explain why.

ESSAY TOPICS

1. In "D.P." several characters, including the sergeant, the nun, and Peter, must face the issue of telling the truth, when the truth might be more painful than a lie. In an essay, discuss the issue of truth and its consequences for Joe in the story by considering two of the characters above. Consider how they present information about Joe's background to him, why they present it the way they do, and what effect the information has on Joe and his search for identity. In your conclusion, discuss your attitude toward telling the truth in the story's situation.

2. Develop a theme statement for "D.P." and support it with evidence from the story. Consider the following elements as you support your theme with quotations and other examples: the events and setting, metaphors and symbolism, and character details and analysis. In your conclusion, give your reaction to the theme you have discussed.

3. Focusing on the metaphors and symbolism in "D.P.," write an essay in which you show how these elements help further our understanding of Joe and his situation, his motivations, and his search for identity.

4. *If you have seen the film version of "D.P.":* Write a comparison of how the story and the film version of "D.P." differ in two of the following aspects: setting,

characters, scenes, and theme. How do these differences affect the story's original emphasis and message? Finally, discuss which you prefer, the story or the film, and explain why.

AUTHOR PROFILE

Kurt Vonnegut, Jr.

Kurt Vonnegut, Jr. (1922–   ) was born in Indianapolis, Indiana. He wrote *Welcome to the Monkey House: A Collection of Short Stories,* from which "D.P." is taken, in 1968. Now considered one of America's most respected novelists, Vonnegut was originally seen as too offbeat a writer to be seriously considered by most critics. His earliest works were categorized as science fiction, but they also transcend that single genre. Vonnegut's works show a distinctive humor and a lasting concern with questions about war, peace, technology, and human happiness. Vonnegut's experience in World War II, as one of the few survivors of the fire bombing of the city of Dresden, Germany, had an impact on the themes he pursues. Reviewer G. K. Wolfe, in the *Journal of Popular Science,* has said that "Vonnegut suggests that [the harsh realities of meaningless cruelty and death] will follow man wherever he goes, whatever he does, not because of a failure in man's vision of himself . . . but because, fortunately or unfortunately, they are part of what makes him human."

Some of Vonnegut's most famous novels include *The Sirens of Titan, Cat's Cradle, Breakfast of Champions, Slaughterhouse Five,* and his latest, written in 1997, *Timequake.*

CHAPTER 11

Mass of the Moon Eclipse

DENISE LEVERTOV

PREPARATION

ACTIVITY 1

Read this explanation of a lunar eclipse and answer the questions that follow.

An eclipse (obscuring) of the moon occurs when the earth blocks the light of the sun, thus casting the earth's shadow over the moon. For this to happen, the sun, the earth, and the moon must be lined up almost exactly, with the earth between the sun and the moon. Lunar eclipses are easily predicted by astronomers, since the paths and times of the orbits of the earth around the sun and the moon around the earth are known. It takes about eighteen years for the sun, the earth, and the moon to complete a cycle in relation to each other. Lunar eclipses generally occur once or twice each year; there are usually twenty-nine eclipses of the moon during each eighteen-year cycle.

1. Have you ever seen either a partial or a full eclipse of the moon? If so, what words would you use to describe it? How would you characterize the time that it takes for the earth's shadow to move across the moon?

2. Do you ever consciously slow down in order to pay close attention to some regularly occurring phenomenon in nature or society that you think other people fail to notice? Explain.

Mass of the Moon Eclipse

DENISE LEVERTOV

Not more slowly than frayed
human attention can bear, but slow
enough to be stately, deliberate, a ritual
we can't be sure will indeed move
from death into resurrection.   5
As the bright silver inch by inch
is diminished, options vanish,
life's allurements. The last sliver
lies face down, back hunched, a husk.

But then, obscured, the whole sphere can be seen   10
to glow from behind its barrier shadow: bronze,
unquenchable, blood-light. And slowly,
more slowly than desolation overcame, overtook
the light, the light
is restored, outspread in a cloudless pasture of   15
spring darkness where firefly planes
fuss to and fro, and humans
turn off their brief attention
in secret relief. No matter: the rite
contains its power, whether or not   20
our witness rises toward it;
grandeur plays out the implacable drama
without even flicking aside our trivial
absence, the impatience with which we
fail to respond.   25
                    And yet

we are spoken to, and sometimes
we do stop, do, do give ourselves leave
to listen, to watch. The moon,
the moon we do after all   30
love, is dying, are we to live
on in a world without moon? We swallow
a sour terror. Then
that coppery sphere, no-moon become once more
full-moon, visible in absence.   35
And still without haste, silver
increment by silver
increment, the familiar, desired,
disregarded brilliance
is given again, given and given.   40

ANALYZING THE POEM

ACTIVITY 2

Write for ten minutes in response to either or both of these questions. Share your ideas with your classmates.

1. How do you feel after reading "Mass of the Moon Eclipse"?

2. What does this poem make you think about or remember?

ACTIVITY 3

Answer the following questions, giving evidence where appropriate to support your answers and line numbers for each piece of evidence.

1. Describe or sketch the phases of the lunar eclipse, or eclipses, described in each of the following passages. The same phase may be described in more than one passage.

   a. "As the bright silver inch by inch
      is diminished . . .
      . . . The last sliver
      lies face down, back hunched, a husk." (lines 6–9)

   b. ". . . The moon,
      the moon we do after all
      love, is dying . . . " (lines 29–31)

   c. "But then, obscured, the whole sphere can be seen
      to glow from behind its barrier shadow . . ." (lines 10–11)

   d. ". . . And, slowly,
      more slowly than desolation overcame, overtook
      the light, the light
      is restored, outspread in a cloudless pasture of
      spring darkness . . ." (lines 12–16)

   e. ". . . Then
      that coppery sphere, no-moon become once more
      full-moon . . ." (lines 33–35)

   f. "And still without haste, silver
      increment by silver
      increment, the familiar, desired,
      disregarded brilliance
      is given again, given and given." (lines 36–40)

2. In the first stanza, Levertov describes the eclipse as a "ritual/we can't be sure will indeed move/from death to resurrection." (lines 3–5) She later refers to the "dying" moon. (line 31) In what ways is an eclipse like death and resurrection?

3. Based on your answer in question 2, label each of the passages in question 1 with one or more of the following words: *dying, death,* and *resurrection.* Compare your answers with classmates and discuss differences.

4. The words "And yet" (line 26) mark a shift in the action of the humans in the poem. In lines 1–25, how do humans respond to the eclipse? How do "we" respond in lines 26–40?

5. The poet uses the word *absence* twice. Find and highlight both references. What or who is absent in each passage?

6. What colors—or words that you may associate with color—does the poet use to describe the moon?

Elements of Literature

Figurative Language

Personification

ACTIVITY 4

Answer these questions about the moon in "Mass of the Moon Eclipse."

1. The following are definitions of "husk" (line 9):

   a. The outer covering of some vegetables, fruits, or seeds, especially the husk of corn

   b. A shell or covering that is worthless

   c. A framework that serves as support

   Why is the "last sliver" (line 8) of the moon described as a "husk"? Which of the preceding definitions might apply? Explain. How does this image of the moon compare with the image in lines 29–32? In lines 10–19? In lines 33–40?

2. Find examples where Levertov personifies the moon and/or the eclipse. For each example, be prepared to explain what human qualities the poet gives the moon and tell why she may be using the technique of **personification.** (See Appendix A for more information about terms in boldface type.)

   Example: "The last sliver lies face down, back hunched . . ." (lines 8–9)

   Levertov personifies the moon, giving it a "face" so that it can look down on us on the earth. In this case, however, the moon appears "face down," which may mean that it's not looking at us in this phase. Instead, its "back [is] hunched," possibly in pain or from picking up or carrying a heavy load. The "back hunched" could also be related to the crescent-like shape of the moon in this phase.

3. How can the night sky be like a "cloudless pasture/of spring darkness"? (lines 15–16)

4. There are two instances in the poem when the moon is "visible in absence." (line 35) What is the other one? Describe the moon or the moon's eclipse when it is "visible in absence."

Characterization

ACTIVITY 5

With a partner or in small groups, answer these questions about **characterization** in the poem.

1. There are no clearly defined characters in this poem. Levertov refers to "humans" and "we." Why does she do this?

2. Think of some things that can be frayed or worn out in places. In what ways can "human attention" be "frayed"? (lines 1–2) What or who could be fraying our attention?

3. Why might "humans/turn off their brief attention/in secret relief"? (lines 17–19) Write down or highlight specific words or phrases from the poem that describe what humans do or how they behave in lines 1–25 and 26–40.

4. Explain the meaning of "whether or not/our witness rises toward it." (lines 20–21)

5. In line 26, the action shifts, as humans "are spoken to." (line 27) Who or what is speaking?

6. How many times does the poet repeat the word *do* in lines 28–30, and what is the effect of this repetition?

7. In your view, does the poet describe two different eclipses, or does she describe one eclipse twice? Explain.

8. Why does the poet describe humans responding in two different ways?

ACTIVITY 6

Role-play the poem. Form small groups and follow these steps:

1. Divide the poem into Act I (lines 1–25) and Act II (lines 26–40). If you want, divide the role play further into scenes.

2. Cast the moon as a character and decide what other characters you will need. Discuss which character or characters will have lead role(s) in one or both of the acts.

3. Decide how to pace the action of various parts (scenes) in the poem. In other words, consider how quickly or slowly, or how deliberately or erratically, to move in each act or scene.

4. If you are going to use props or costumes, decide what they will be.

5. Perform the role play for the rest of the class.

6. After you watch all the role plays, write the answers to the questions in "Writing in Response," which follows.

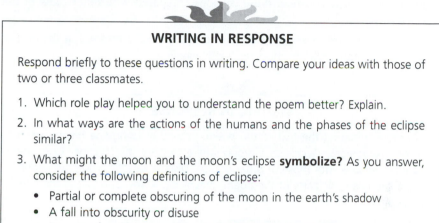

WRITING IN RESPONSE

Respond briefly to these questions in writing. Compare your ideas with those of two or three classmates.

1. Which role play helped you to understand the poem better? Explain.

2. In what ways are the actions of the humans and the phases of the eclipse similar?

3. What might the moon and the moon's eclipse **symbolize?** As you answer, consider the following definitions of eclipse:

   • Partial or complete obscuring of the moon in the earth's shadow
   • A fall into obscurity or disuse
   • Process of making something insignificant by comparison

Language and Style

Rhythm and Rhyme

A C T I V I T Y 7

Even though Levertov uses natural and conversational language, there is a regulated and formal strategy in the **rhythm** and sounds of the words. Levertov has also considered the placement of the words on the page. In addition to using periods and commas to punctuate her sentences, she uses line breaks to change or add meaning and create a rhythmic effect.

Examples:

a. The poet repeats "the light, the light" (line 14) on one line even though the word is used in different grammatical phrases. The first use of *light* refers to light diminishing, and the second use refers to light returning. By putting the words together in one line, she emphasizes the repetition of sound and the importance of light.

b. Levertov places together two similar sounding words, "overcame, overtook" (line 13), on the same line even though they are grammatically parts of different phrases. Here the repetition and placement on the same line seem to emphasize the two actions, *overcame* meaning "defeated" and *overtook* meaning "caught up and passed over." Reread lines 12–14.

Answer these questions alone or with a partner.

1. Find other places in the poem where the poet uses repetition of the same or similar words to create a rhythmic effect. How does this repetition influence the rate at which you read these sections compared with other parts of the poem?

2. Why do you think Levertov places "And yet" (line 26) by itself at the end of the second stanza? What effect does this have?

WRITING IN RESPONSE

In groups, reformat the text of the poem. Instead of using line breaks, write several paragraphs. Decide as a group where to place punctuation. Compare your paragraphs with those of other groups. Discuss whether you now understand the poem, or parts of the poem, differently. Is anything lost in the new version?

ACTIVITY 8

Although Levertov does not use **rhyme** at the end of lines, she creates internal rhymes of two kinds:

assonance   the repetition of vowel sounds

alliteration   the repetition of consonant sounds, especially at the beginning of words or in stressed syllables

1. Study the following example, which highlights assonance in boldface type and alliteration in italics. Notice the repetition of the vowel sound "i" as in "inch" and the sound "i" as in "life" (assonance) and the repetition of the consonant– vowel sound combinations in "hunch" and "husk" (alliteration).

> As the bright silver, **i**nch by **i**nch
> is dim**i**nished, options van**i**sh,
> l**i**fe's allurements. The last sl**i**ver
> l**i**es face down, back *h*unched, a *h*usk.

2. With a partner or in groups, find other places in the poem and mark the alliteration and assonance. What is the effect of these internal rhymes?

WRITING IN RESPONSE

Respond briefly to these questions in writing. Compare your responses to those of two or three classmates.

1. In what ways does the rhythm of the poem mirror the eclipse of the moon?

2. What does the rhythm of the poem reveal about humans and, in particular, about the way they respond to or fail to respond to the moon and its eclipse?

Exploring Further

Continue your analysis of "Mass of the Moon Eclipse" with these questions for discussion or writing.

1. As the earth's shadow passes in front of the moon, the poet says that "options vanish,/life's allurements." (lines 7–8) In your view, what are life's options and allurements? Why might it feel as if they are vanishing as the light of the moon is diminished?

2. In the second part of the poem, humans see the moon "dying" (line 31) and ask if they are "to live/on in a world without moon?" (lines 31–32) In what ways could the moon be dying? What feeling might "we" have, contemplating a "world without moon?"

3. Why, in the phrase "world without moon" (line 32), does the poet leave out the article "a" before "moon"? How does this change the meaning of the phrase?

4. The word *mass* in the poem's title has several meanings. Discuss how each of the following definitions could be related to the poem's theme.

   • The physical volume or bulk of a solid body
   • The measure of the quantity of matter that a body or an object contains
   • In some Christian churches, the celebration of the Eucharist or communion: the consuming of bread and wine to remember that Christ died so that people might live
   • A musical piece to accompany the celebration of the Eucharist

5. Choose a line, phrase, or image from the poem and explain what emotion it evokes in you. How and why do the poet's words create this emotion?

CREATIVE WRITING

Rewrite the "implacable drama" (line 22) of this poem as a play; that is, retell the action of the poem in the form of a drama. Add stage directions in italics, including set design, costuming, and directions for the actors.

ESSAY TOPICS

1. In an essay, discuss how Levertov uses language to mirror and give meaning to the moon's eclipse and to the actions and behavior of humans.

2. Explore the theme of paying attention in Levertov's poem. In your essay, include your interpretation of "absence" (line 24) and bearing "witness." (line 21)

3. What do you think is the "disregarded brilliance" (line 39) that is "given again, given and given"? (line 40) Why does the poem end with these two lines?

AUTHOR PROFILE

Denise Levertov

Denise Levertov (1923–1997) was born in England, came to the United States when she was twenty-five years old, and became a U.S. citizen in 1955. Levertov was educated entirely at home. Her poetry was strongly influenced by her mother's love of English and Welsh literature and folklore and her father's religious and mystical teachings. Levertov's father, a Russian Jew who converted to Christianity and became an Anglican minister, was a founding member of a Jewish mystical movement that celebrates the mystery of everyday events.

Levertov's poetry is filled with descriptions of everyday objects and events in which she finds joy as well as religious, personal, and political significance. This joy, as critic Sandra M. Gilbert notes, often comes from a "celebratory patience," a sense that if you wait confidently and for long enough, you will experience an epiphany, a moment in which you confirm life and renew joy.

A writer of over twenty volumes of verse and a teacher at universities throughout the United States, Levertov is considered one of the leading post–World War II American poets. Her poetry is characterized by natural speech rhythms and irregular line breaks to allow pauses for breathing. Many readers find her language clear, spontaneous, and accessible.

CHAPTER 12

Hills Like White Elephants

ERNEST HEMINGWAY

PREPARATION

ACTIVITY 1

With a partner or in small groups, discuss the following questions.

1. Have you ever seen a white elephant or a picture of one? What is your reaction to the image of a white elephant? Is it a positive or negative image for you?

2. Imagine the opening scene of a movie entitled *Hills Like White Elephants*. What would be in the landscape? How do you imagine the weather?

Hills Like White Elephants

ERNEST HEMINGWAY

The hills across the valley of the Ebro° were long and white. On this side there was no shade and no trees and the station was between two lines of rails in the sun. Close against the side of the station there was the warm shadow of the building and a curtain, made of strings of bamboo beads, hung across the open door into the bar, to keep out flies. The American and the girl with him sat at a table in the shade, outside the building. It was very hot and the express° from Barcelona would come in forty minutes. It stopped at this junction for two minutes and went on to Madrid.

"What should we drink?" the girl asked. She had taken off her hat and put it on the table.

"It's pretty hot," the man said.

"Let's drink beer."

"Dos cervezas,"° the man said into the curtain.

"Big ones?" a woman asked from the doorway.

"Yes. Two big ones."

The woman brought two glasses of beer and two felt° pads. She put the felt pads and the beer glasses on the table and looked at the man and the girl. The girl was looking off at the line of hills. They were white in the sun and the country was brown and dry.

"They look like white elephants," she said.

"I've never seen one," the man drank his beer.

"No, you wouldn't have."

"I might have," the man said. "Just because you say I wouldn't have doesn't prove anything."

The girl looked at the bead curtain. "They've painted something on it," she said. "What does it say?"

"Anis del Toro. It's a drink."

"Could we try it?"

The man called "Listen" through the curtain. The woman came out from the bar.

"Four reales."°

"We want two Anis del Toro."

"With water?"

"Do you want it with water?"

"I don't know," the girl said. "Is it good with water?"

"It's all right."

"You want them with water?" asked the woman.

°*Ebro* river in northern Spain
°*express* a train that makes very short stops between cities
°*dos cervezas* two beers
°*felt* material used as protective padding
°*reales* Spanish coins

"Yes, with water."

"It tastes like licorice,"° the girl said and put the glass down.

"That's the way with everything."   40

"Yes," said the girl. "Everything tastes of licorice. Especially all the things you've waited so long for, like absinthe."°

"Oh, cut it out."°

"You started it," the girl said. "I was being amused. I was having a fine time."

"Well, let's try and have a fine time."

"All right. I was trying. I said the mountains looked like white elephants. Wasn't that bright?"°

"That was bright."

"I wanted to try this new drink. That's all we do, isn't it—look at things and try new drinks?"   50

"I guess so."

The girl looked across at the hills.

"They're lovely hills," she said. "They don't really look like white elephants. I just meant the coloring of their skin through the trees."

"Should we have another drink?"

"All right."

The warm wind blew the bead curtain against the table.

"The beer's nice and cool," the man said.

"It's lovely," the girl said.

"It's really an awfully simple operation, Jig," the man said. "It's not really an op-   60
eration at all."

The girl looked at the ground the table legs rested on.

"I know you wouldn't mind it, Jig. It's really not anything. It's just to let the air in."

The girl did not say anything.

"I'll go with you and I'll stay with you all the time. They just let the air in and then it's all perfectly natural."

"Then what will we do afterward?"

"We'll be fine afterward. Just like we were before."

"What makes you think so?"   70

"That's the only thing that bothers us. It's the only thing that's made us unhappy."

The girl looked at the bead curtain, put her hand out and took hold of two of the strings of beads.

"And you think then we'll be all right and be happy."

"I know we will. You don't have to be afraid. I've known lots of people that have done it."

"So have I," said the girl. "And afterward they were all so happy."

°*licorice* a candy with a slightly sweet flavor

°*absinthe* a green bitter liquor

°*cut it out* stop it

°*bright* intelligent

"Well," the man said, "if you don't want to you don't have to. I wouldn't have
80   you do it if you didn't want to. But I know it's perfectly simple."

"And you really want to?"

"I think it's the best thing to do. But I don't want you to do it if you don't
really want to."

"And if I do it you'll be happy and things will be like they were and you'll
love me?"

"I love you now. You know I love you."

"I know. But if I do it, then it will be nice again if I say things are like white
elephants, and you'll like it?"

"I'll love it. I love it now but I just can't think about it. You know how I get
90   when I worry."

"If I do it you won't ever worry?"

"I won't worry about that because it's perfectly simple."

"Then I'll do it. Because I don't care about me."

"What do you mean?"

"I don't care about me."

"Well, I care about you."

"Oh, yes. But I don't care about me. And I'll do it and then everything will be
fine."

"I don't want you to do it if you feel that way."

100   The girl stood up and walked to the end of the station. Across on the other
side, were fields of grain and trees along the banks of the Ebro. Far away, beyond
the river, were mountains. The shadow of a cloud moved across the field of grain
and she saw the river through the trees.

"And we could have all this," she said. "And we could have everything and
every day we make it more impossible."

"What did you say?"

"I said we could have everything."

"We can have everything."

"No, we can't."

110   "We can have the whole world."

"No, we can't."

"We can go everywhere."

"No, we can't. It isn't ours any more."

"It's ours."

"No, it isn't. And once they take it away, you never get it back."

"But they haven't taken it away."

"We'll wait and see."

"Come on back in the shade," he said. "You mustn't feel that way."

"I don't feel any way," the girl said. "I just know things."

120   "I don't want you to do anything that you don't want to do—"

"Nor that isn't good for me," she said. "I know. Could we have another beer?"

"All right. But you've got to realize—"

"I realize," the girl said. "Can't we maybe stop talking?"

They sat down at the table and the girl looked across at the hills on the dry side of the valley and the man looked at her and at the table.

"You've got to realize," he said, "that I don't want you to do it if you don't want to. I'm perfectly willing to go through with it if it means anything to you."

"Doesn't it mean anything to you? We could get along."

"Of course it does. But I don't want anybody but you. I don't want any one else. And I know it's perfectly simple."   130

"Yes, you know it's perfectly simple."

"It's all right for you to say that, but I do know it."

"Would you do something for me now?"

"I'd do anything for you."

"Would you please please please please please please please stop talking?"

He did not say anything but looked at the bags against the wall of the station. There were labels on them from all the hotels where they had spent nights.

"But I don't want you to," he said, "I don't care anything about it."

"I'll scream," the girl said.

The woman came out through the curtains with two glasses of beer and put   140
them down on the damp felt pads. "The train comes in five minutes," she said.

"What did she say?" asked the girl.

"That the train is coming in five minutes."

The girl smiled brightly at the woman, to thank her.

"I'd better take the bags over to the other side of the station," the man said. She smiled at him.

"All right. Then come back and we'll finish the beer."

He picked up the two heavy bags and carried them around the station to the other tracks. He looked up the tracks but could not see the train. Coming back, he walked through the barroom, where people waiting for the train were drink-   150
ing. He drank an Anis at the bar and looked at the people. They were all waiting reasonably for the train. He went out through the bead curtain. She was sitting at the table and smiled at him.

"Do you feel better?" he asked.

"I feel fine," she said. "There's nothing wrong with me. I feel fine."

ANALYZING THE STORY

ACTIVITY 2

Answer the following questions. Give evidence from the story to support your answers where appropriate and include line numbers for each piece of evidence.

1. How would you describe the relationship between the man and the girl?

2. We know from line 13 that the man speaks Spanish. Who else in the story speaks Spanish?

3. Hemingway's **style** (see Appendix A for more information on terms in bold-face type) is often to leave off tags, or words identifying the speaker, from lines of dialogue. To be clear about who is speaking, go through the story and

write M (for man), G (for girl), or W (for woman) next to each line of dialogue that doesn't have a tag.

4. Look at a map of Spain. In what region do you think the train station could be located? How is the train station in the story similar to or different from train stations that you are familiar with or have seen in movies, on TV, or in photographs?

5. What are the man and the girl doing at the beginning of the story?

6. How old do you think the girl is? How old do you imagine the man to be?

7. Who is the woman, and why do you think the **narrator** refers to her as "the woman"?

8. Which character has a name? What might be Hemingway's reason for not giving all the characters names?

9. The story "Hills Like White Elephants" is set in Spain in the 1920s. How are our attitudes about the term *girl* different today than they were at that time?

10. Approximately how much time passes from the beginning of the story to the end?

11. Is the narrator one of the characters in the story? How much information does the narrator give us about the characters' thoughts or feelings?

12. What is the **point of view** of the story? How will this point of view make the story more challenging to read than if a character in the story were the narrator or if the story were told from the **third-person limited point of view?**

ACTIVITY 3

Use lines 60–99 to answer these questions. Give evidence from the story to support your answers and include line numbers for each piece of evidence.

1. Who first mentions the operation?

2. Does the girl seem to have a choice about having the operation?

3. What kind of operation are the man and the girl talking about?

4. What do we know about the procedures involved in the operation, and who tells us?

   a. Considering the time and place of the story, do you think the operation would be performed by a doctor in a hospital?

   b. What could the medical risks be for the girl?

   c. How do you think she feels about having the operation?

WRITING IN RESPONSE

In the preceding discussion, the class will have established that the operation is, in fact, an abortion. First, freewrite about your feelings on abortion. Then think about the story. Is "Hills Like White Elephants" primarily about abortion, or is it primarily about something else? Freewrite again about what you think the main topic of the story is.

Elements of Literature

Characterization

A C T I V I T Y   4

Because "Hills Like White Elephants" is written from the **third-person objective-observer point of view,** readers need to study the dialogue carefully in order to understand the thoughts, feelings, and personalities of the characters.

Using lines 1–99, analyze the dialogue between the man and the girl to answer the following questions.

1. In the following chart, list all arguments for the abortion and note the character who states them. How does the other character respond to each argument? The first one is done for you.

ARGUMENT	CHARACTER	RESPONSE	CHARACTER
"It's really an awfully simple operation . . . . '" (line 60)	*the man*	*". . . did not say anything." (line 65)*	*the girl*

2. List all the questions in the dialogue. Which character asks more questions? What are the questions about?

3. Which character says "I think" or "I know" more often?

4. In the beginning of the story the girl says the dry hills "'look like white elephants.'" (line 20) When the man says that he's "'never seen one,'" (line 21), the girl says "'No, you wouldn't have.'" (line 22) Why can we assume that the girl's reply is sarcastic; that is, she is responding to the man ironically or with a negative tone? Find other examples of sarcasm.

5. The girl looks again at the hills (lines 52–54) and remarks that "'They don't really look like white elephants. I just meant the coloring of their skins through the trees.'" To the reader, this statement seems unclear. It may have meaning

for the girl, but it is difficult to interpret since the narrator gives no direct clues about what she is thinking or feeling. Find other examples of statements that have no immediately clear meaning and discuss possible interpretations of those lines.

6. What does your analysis of the dialogue reveal about the man and the girl and their relationship?

CREATIVE WRITING

Choose something that is difficult to talk about, such as telling friends and family about a decision to take a year off school or informing a close friend that a mutual friend has a life-threatening illness. Write a dialogue in which two people discuss the difficult topic without mentioning it directly.

Setting

ACTIVITY 5

Underline every passage in the story where the landscape is described. Based on these descriptions, draw a complete sketch of the **setting** in which the story is set. Be prepared to support the accuracy of your sketch with evidence.

Include the following in your sketch and any other elements in the landscape that you think are important.

north (direction)	the fields of grain	the mountains
the Ebro River	the trees	the sun
the dry hills	the cloud	the beaded curtain
the train station	the table	the bar
the couple's bags	the valley	the two pairs of rails (train tracks)

ACTIVITY 6

In groups, use the individual sketches you prepared in Activity 5 to draw a group sketch of the landscape in the story. Draw it on the board or on large pieces of paper that can be displayed. Make the sketches in color. Then answer the questions below in your group. Use evidence from the text to support your answers.

1. Compare the sketches of the landscape from the different groups. Which ones do you think are most accurate? Why?

2. When the girl stands at the edge of the station, she can see the "fields of grain and trees along the banks of the Ebro" as well as the mountains and river. (line 101) Why does she say, "'And we could have all this . . . [a]nd every day we

make it more impossible'"? (lines 104–105) What are the possible meanings of the words *it, everything, everywhere,* and *they* in lines 104–116?

3. Romeo Giger, a critic and scholar of Hemingway's work, once wrote, "descriptions of landscapes [in Hemingway's writing] often reflect inner landscapes." What is an inner landscape? What do you think Giger means? How does his statement relate to "Hills Like White Elephants"?

WRITING IN RESPONSE

1. Freewrite about the connection between Hemingway's descriptions of the landscape and the characters. What conclusions can you draw about the inner landscapes of the characters?

2. Sketch and/or freewrite about your own inner landscapes.

Characterization

ACTIVITY 7

In their speech, the characters in Hemingway's story reveal important information about themselves. Answer the following questions. Include evidence from the story and line numbers for each piece of evidence.

1. What things does each character observe and respond to both in and around the train station? Examples have been done for you.

WHAT THE MAN OBSERVES/RESPONDS TO	WHAT THE GIRL OBSERVES/RESPONDS TO
"... the man looked at [the girl] and at the table." (line 125)	"[The hills] look like white elephants...." (line 20)

2. What is different about how each character observes and responds to his or her surroundings? What do their observations and responses suggest about each of them?

3. Hemingway does not use adjectives to describe his characters. He merely reports their speech and actions. Create a list of adjectives to describe the personalities of the two main characters in "Hills Like White Elephants." Be prepared to support your choices with evidence from the story. Examples have been done for you.

ADJECTIVES THAT DESCRIBE THE GIRL	ADJECTIVES THAT DESCRIBE THE MAN
imaginative (She sees the hills as "white elephants.")	*persistent (He won't stop referring to the "operation.")*

4. What does your analysis of the girl and the man reveal about their relationship?

Figurative Language

Simile

In the story, Hemingway uses **figurative language** in the form of a **simile** "hills like white elephants," which gives the reader clues about the characters and the conflict.

ACTIVITY 8

Answer the following questions.

1. Below are four definitions of *white elephant* from *The American Heritage Dictionary*. Which of these definitions are you familiar with? Are any surprising to you? Which apply to the story "Hills Like White Elephants"?

   • A rare whitish or light-gray form of the Asian elephant, often regarded with special respect in regions of Southeastern Asia
   • A rare and expensive possession that is financially a burden to maintain; a thing or gift regarded with reservations; something doubtful or limited in value
   • An article, ornament, or household utensil no longer wanted by its owner
   • An endeavor or venture that proves to be an obvious failure

2. Bernard Oldsey, a critic and scholar of Hemingway's work, says, "Hemingway was as careful and precise in the selection of titles as he was in the actual writing and revision of his works." Considering your discussion of the definitions in item 1 and ideas you may have about the story, explain how Oldsey's statement relates to "Hills Like White Elephants."

3. Think about the river, the trees, the tracks, and other **images** in the story and what they might represent. Go back to the list that you used when you drew your sketch of the landscape in Activity 5.

   a. What possible meanings are connected to these images?
   b. What images help us understand the characters, their relationship, or the choices they are facing?

WRITING IN RESPONSE

Freewrite about what you think the outcome of the story will be and what decisions you think the girl will make.

Exploring Further

Write or discuss the answers to these questions. Give evidence from the story to support your answers and include line numbers for each piece of evidence.

1. Compare the dialogue in lines 60–99 with the dialogue in lines 117–139. How has the discussion changed? How have the characters changed?

2. At the end of the story, the girl smiles three times. (lines 144–153)

   a. In what three situations does she smile?
   b. Is it surprising that she smiles? Why or why not?
   c. How are these smiles similar to or different from other ways she has responded?
   d. Why do you think she smiles?

3. Based on your responses to question 2, what do you think the girl will do about the abortion and about her relationship with the man? Explain your answer.

4. The characters in Hemingway's stories and novels often face difficult and even life-threatening situations, such as war, bullfights, or dangerous missions. Hemingway's ideas about human behavior are revealed by the way his characters respond to physical danger and emotional stress. In Hemingway's words, courage is "grace under pressure."

   a. What kind of behavior is *graceful*? Is this a positive or negative word? In what situations do we use the word *grace* or the other forms of this word, such as gracious or gracefully, to describe a person's behavior?
   b. What other words are associated with the word *pressure*? Is this a positive or negative word? Give examples of situations or conditions that show pressure.
   c. What does "grace under pressure" mean?

   How does the story "Hills Like White Elephants" illustrate Hemingway's ideas about courage? Does the behavior of either the man or the girl fit Hemingway's definition of "grace under pressure"? Explain.

WRITING IN RESPONSE

Respond briefly to these questions in writing.

1. Based on your analysis of the dialogue and the characters' behavior, would you have encouraged the girl to respond to the man in the way that she did, or would you encourage her to act differently? Explain.

2. As a reader, do you feel sympathy toward either or both of the main characters? Explain.

3. How do Hemingway's ideas about courage relate to "Hills Like White Elephants"?

ESSAY TOPICS

1. Write an essay that shows what you think the girl will do about the abortion and her relationship with the man. Will she have the abortion? Will she stay with the man?

2. Consider Hemingway's definition of courage as "grace under pressure" and how it relates to the story "Hills Like White Elephants." Write an essay that shows whether or not the girl's behavior fits Hemingway's definition of courage.

3. The narrator of "Hills Like White Elephants" tells the story as an objective observer who describes the setting minimally and gives us incomplete portraits of the characters through their limited dialogue and actions. Furthermore, the narrator offers no background to help us understand the situation, the relationship between the man and the girl, or the thoughts or feelings of the characters.

   Write an essay in which you explore the effect this style of narration has on the story. How can the story—its characters and outcome—be understood in different ways based on different interpretations of the limited information? Support your analyses with evidence from the story.

4. Hemingway said this about his writing: "I always try to write on the principle of the iceberg. There is 7/8 of it below the water for every eighth that shows." How does Hemingway's writing reflect this principle? Interpret the meaning of Hemingway's statement as it relates to the story: the characters, their relationship, the setting, and the outcome.

Ernest Hemingway

Ernest Hemingway (1899–1961), journalist, novelist, and short story writer, was born in Oak Park, Illinois. As a reporter for the *Kansas City Star,* a newspaper known for its distinct style of writing, he learned to write "short sentences, short paragraphs, and positive vigorous English" with "authenticity, selectivity, precision, clarity, and immediacy." Hemingway referred to the training he received at the *Star* as "the best rules I ever learned for the business of writing. I've never forgotten them." Ernest Hemingway was awarded the Nobel Prize for Literature in 1954.

Hemingway's experiences in Europe and Africa provided him with material and settings for many of his most famous works: Italy, the setting for *A Farewell to Arms,* where, at the age of nineteen, he was wounded while working as an ambulance driver during World War I; Spain, the setting for *The Sun Also Rises* and *For Whom The Bell Tolls,* where he developed his passion for bullfights and fought in the Spanish Civil War; and Africa, the setting for *The Snows of Kilimanjaro,* where he hunted wild animals and was severely injured in two airplane crashes. Fascination with Hemingway's life, his unique style of writing, and his numerous and often controversial relationships with women has contributed to transforming him into a legendary figure of American literature and culture.

CHAPTER 13

On the Road

PREPARATION

ACTIVITY 1

With a partner or in small groups, discuss the following questions.

1. "On the Road" was published in 1935, during the Great Depression in the United States. What do you know about that period in American history? What was the economic situation? How would the Depression have affected people who were already poor, uneducated, and had few opportunities?

2. Langston Hughes, an African-American writer, belonged to a group of artists, writers, and playwrights who contributed to the Harlem Renaissance (1919–1940), a time of bold creativity and expression for African-American artists. What do you know about Harlem? What do you think the Harlem Renaissance writers might have written about?

3. "On the Road" is about a poor, homeless African-American man who refers to people drawing "the color line" (line 18) when he looks for shelter. What do you imagine the "color line" to be? Explain.

ACTIVITY 2

Study and discuss the definitions for each group of terms. Then answer the questions.

1. *Terms that refer to the church* Based on the following definitions, how would you describe what a minister, reverend, or holy man would do as part of his service? Give specific examples.

to minister: to attend to the wants and needs of other people
to revere: to have great respect for a person's kindness, good qualities, and
   good actions
to be holy: to live according to a strict, highly moral or deeply religious belief system

2. *Terms that refer to the Great Depression*   How would the Depression have affected the number of hobos in America?

hobo: an unemployed homeless person who traveled from place to place,
   often by jumping onto freight trains and riding in empty cars
relief shelter: a public shelter for people who had no other place to go to
   sleep or eat

3. During the Depression, how do you think the race of a poor person affected
the kind of assistance he or she could receive, especially considering that an
unspoken "color line" existed?

WRITING IN RESPONSE

Write briefly on this topic.

Considering what you discussed in Activities 1 and 2, what do you think "On
the Road" is about? Make predictions about who the characters might be, what
they might do, and their possible interactions with each other.

On the Road

LANGSTON HUGHES

He was not interested in the snow. When he got off the freight, one early evening during the depression, Sargeant never even noticed the snow. But he must have felt it seeping down his neck, cold, wet, sopping in his shoes. But if you had asked him, he wouldn't have known it was snowing. Sargeant didn't see the snow, not even under the bright lights of the main street, falling white and flaky against the night. He was too hungry, too sleepy, too tired.

The Reverend Mr. Dorset, however, saw the snow when he switched on his porch light, opened the front door to his parsonage,° and found standing there before him a big black man with snow on his face, a human piece of night with
10   snow on his face—obviously unemployed.

Said the Reverend Mr. Dorset before Sargeant even realized he'd opened his mouth: "I'm sorry. No! Go right on down this street four blocks and turn to your left, walk up seven and you'll see the Relief Shelter. I'm sorry. No!" He shut the door.

Sargeant wanted to tell the holy man that he had already been to the Relief Shelter, been to hundreds of relief shelters during the depression years, the beds were always gone and supper was over, the place was full, and they drew the color line anyhow. But the minister said "No," and shut the door. Evidently he didn't want to hear about it. And he *had* a door to shut.
20   The big black man turned away. And even yet he didn't see the snow, walking right into it. Maybe he sensed it, cold, wet, sticking to his jaws, wet on his black hands, sopping in his shoes. He stopped and stood on the sidewalk hunched over—hungry, sleepy, cold—looking up and down. Then he looked right where he was—in front of a church. Of course! A church! Sure, right next to a parson-age, certainly a church.

It had *two* doors.

Broad white steps in the night all snowy white. Two high arched doors with slender stone pillars on either side. And way up, a round lacy window with a stone crucifix in the middle and Christ on the crucifix in stone. All this was pale
30   in the street lights, solid and stony pale in the snow.

Sargeant blinked. When he looked up, the snow fell into his eyes. For the first time that night he *saw* the snow. He shook his head. He shook the snow from his coat sleeves, felt hungry, felt lost, felt not lost, felt cold. He walked up the steps of the church. He knocked at the door. No answer. He tried the handle. Locked. He put his shoulder against the door and his long black body slanted like a ramrod. He pushed. With loud rhythmic grunts, like the grunts in a chain-gang° song, he pushed against the door.

"I'm tired ... Huh! ... Hongry ... Uh! ... I'm sleepy ... Huh! I'm cold ... I got to sleep somewheres," Sargeant said. "This here is a church, ain't it? Well, uh!"
40   He pushed against the door.

°*parsonage* home for a minister of a church
°*chain-gang* prisoners who are chained together at the ankles as they move or work

Suddenly, with an undue cracking and screaking, the door began to give way to the tall black Negro who pushed ferociously against it.

By now two or three white people had stopped in the street, and Sargeant was vaguely aware of some of them yelling at him concerning the door. Three or four more came running, yelling at him.

"Hey!" they said. "Hey!"

"Uh-huh," answered the big tall Negro, "I know it's a white folks' church, but I got to sleep somewhere." He gave another lunge at the door. "Huh!"

And the door broke open.

But just when the door gave way, two white cops arrived in a car, ran up the   50
steps with their clubs, and grabbed Sargeant. But Sargeant for once had no intention of being pulled or pushed away from the door.

Sargeant grabbed, but not for anything so weak as a broken door. He grabbed for one of the tall stone pillars beside the door, grabbed at it and caught it. And held it. The cops pulled and Sargeant pulled. Most of the people in the street got behind the cops and helped them pull.

"A big black unemployed Negro holding onto our church!" thought the people. "The idea!"°

The cops began to beat Sargeant over the head, and nobody protested. But he held on.   60

And then the church fell down.

Gradually, the big stone front of the church fell down, the walls and the rafters, the crucifix and the Christ. Then the whole thing fell down, covering the cops and the people with bricks and stones and debris. The whole church fell down in the snow.

Sargeant got out from under the church and went walking on up the street with the stone pillar on his shoulder. He was under the impression that he had buried the parsonage and the Reverend Mr. Dorset who said, "No!" So he laughed, and threw the pillar six blocks up the street and went on.

Sargeant thought he was alone, but listening to the *crunch, crunch, crunch*   70
on the snow of his own footsteps, he heard other footsteps, too, doubling his own. He looked around, and there was Christ walking along beside him, the same Christ that had been on the cross on the church—still stone with a rough stone surface, walking along beside him just like he was broken off the cross when the church fell down.

"Well, I'll be dogged,"° said Sargeant. "This here's the first time I ever seed° you off the cross."

"Yes," said Christ, crunching his feet in the snow. "You had to pull the church down to get me off the cross."

"You glad?" said Sargeant.   80

"I sure am," said Christ.

They both laughed.

° *"The idea!"* "how dare he!"; "he has no right to do that!"

° *"Well, I'll be dogged."* "I can hardly believe it."

° *"I ever seed."* "I have ever seen."

"I'm a hell of a fellow, ain't I?" said Sargeant. "Done pulled the church down!"

"You did a good job," said Christ. "They have kept me nailed on a cross for nearly two thousand years."

"Whee-ee-e!" said Sargeant. "I know you are glad to get off."

"I sure am," said Christ.

They walked on in the snow. Sargeant looked at the man of stone.

"And you have been up there two thousand years?"

90   "I sure have," Christ said.

"Well, if I had a little cash," said Sargeant, "I'd show you around a bit."

"I been around," said Christ.

"Yeah, but that was a long time ago."

"All the same," said Christ, "I've been around."

They walked on in the snow until they came to the railroad yards. Sargeant was tired, sweating and tired.

"Where you goin'?" Sargeant said, stopping by the tracks. He looked at Christ. Sargeant said, "I'm just a bum on the road. How about you? Where you goin'?"

"God knows," Christ said, "but I'm leavin' here."

100   They saw the red and green lights of the railroad yard half veiled by the snow that fell out of the night. Away down the track they saw a fire in a hobo jungle.

"I can go there and sleep," Sargeant said.

"You can?"

"Sure," said Sargeant. "That place ain't got no doors."

Outside the town, along the tracks, there were barren trees and bushes below the embankment, snow-gray in the dark. And down among the trees and bushes there were makeshift houses made out of boxes and tin and old pieces of wood and canvas. You couldn't see them in the dark, but you knew they were there if you'd ever been on the road, if you had ever lived with the homeless and hungry

110   in a depression.

"I'm side-tracking," Sargeant said. "I'm tired."

"I'm gonna make it on to Kansas City," said Christ.

"O.K.," Sargeant said. "So long!"

He went down into the hobo jungle and found himself a place to sleep. He never did see Christ no more. About 6:00 A.M. a freight came by. Sargeant scrambled out of the jungle with a dozen or so more hobos and ran along the track, grabbing at the freight. It was dawn, early dawn, cold and gray.

"Wonder where Christ is by now?" Sargeant thought. "He musta gone on way on down the road. He didn't sleep in this jungle."

120   Sargeant grabbed the train and started to pull himself up into a moving coal car, over the edge of a wheeling coal car. But strangely enough, the car was full of cops. The nearest cop rapped Sargeant soundly across the knuckles with his night stick. Wham! Rapped his big black hands for clinging to the top of the car. Wham! But Sargeant did not turn loose. He clung on and tried to pull himself into the car. He hollered at the top of his voice, "Damn it, lemme° in this car!"

°*lemme* let me

"Shut up," barked the cop. "You crazy coon!"° He rapped Sargeant across the knuckles and punched him in the stomach. "You ain't out in no jungle now. This ain't no train. You in jail."

Wham! across his bare black fingers clinging to the bars of his cell. Wham! be- 130
tween the steel bars low down against his shins.

Suddenly Sargeant realized that he really was in jail. He wasn't on no train. The blood of the night before had dried on his face, his head hurt terribly, and a cop outside in the corridor was hitting him across the knuckles for holding onto the door, yelling and shaking the cell door.

"They musta took me to jail for breaking down the door last night," Sargeant thought, "that church door."

Sargeant went over and sat on a wooden bench against the cold stone wall. He was emptier than ever. His clothes were wet, clammy cold wet, and shoes sloppy with snow water. It was just about dawn. There he was, locked up behind 140
a cell door, nursing his bruised fingers.

The bruised fingers were his, but not the *door.*

Not the *club,* but the fingers.

"You wait," mumbled Sargeant, black against the jail wall. "I'm gonna break down this door, too."

"Shut up—or I'll paste you one,"° said the cop.

"I'm gonna break down this door," yelled Sargeant as he stood up in his cell.

Then he must have been talking to himself because he said, "I wonder where Christ's gone? I wonder if he's gone to Kansas City?"

ANALYZING THE STORY

ACTIVITY 3

Divide these questions among two or more small groups. Each group reports its answers to the class.

1. Who are the two main characters at the beginning of the story? Is the **narrator** a character in the story? What is the **point of view** of the story? (See Appendix A for more information about terms in boldface type.)

2. Describe the **setting** of the story with specific details.

3. What is the reaction of the Reverend Mr. Dorset when he finds Sargeant on his front porch? What is your reaction to Dorset's perception of Sargeant as "a human piece of night with snow on his face—obviously unemployed"? (lines 9–10)

4. How does Sargeant want to respond to the Reverend? Why can't he? (lines 15–19)

5. What does Sargeant do when he sees the church? (lines 31–42)

°*coon* a derogatory term for an African-American person
°*paste you one* hit you hard

6. What happens when the white people and then the police arrive on the scene? How does Sargeant act? (lines 43–60)

7. What finally happens to the church? (lines 61–65) Is this possible? What do you think may have really happened? Why?

8. Describe the Christ that appears beside Sargeant. What is unusual about him? (lines 72–75)

9. What are Sargeant's plans for what he will do next? What are Christ's plans? How are their plans different? (lines 97–115)

10. Describe what happens to Sargeant in the "moving coal car." What really happens to him? (lines 120–129)

11. How does the cop respond to Sargeant? What specific language does he use? What do the cop's comments tell about him? (lines 127–135)

12. Mark in your text where Sargeant's "dream" begins and where it ends. What causes the beginning of his dream? What causes the end of his dream?

Elements of Literature

Characterization

ACTIVITY 4

Do this activity with a partner or in small groups.

1. "On the Road" contains many examples of what Sargeant is and is not aware of about his situation. Complete the following chart to compare these two states of mind in Sargeant.

    Note: In some cases, the narrator speculates or guesses about what Sargeant might be aware of. These guesses belong in the "not aware of" category. Look for lines that contain words of possibility, such as *must have* and *maybe*.

WHAT SARGEANT IS AWARE OF		WHAT SARGEANT IS NOT AWARE OF	
line 6	"He was too hungry, too sleepy, too tired."	line 2	"Sargeant never even noticed the snow."
lines 15–18	Sargeant knows what Relief Shelters are like.	lines 2–3	"But he must have felt it seeping down his neck, cold, wet, sopping in his shoes."

2. After you complete the chart, discuss the contrasts between what Sargeant is aware of and what he is not aware of about his situation. What are the causes of his misery?

CREATIVE WRITING

In one or two paragraphs, use **imagery** to fully describe a person or a place. Describe a character who experiences a strong physical response to something, either positive or negative, or choose a place that appeals to the five senses. In your description, appeal to your reader's mental senses of smell, touch, taste, sight, and hearing.

ACTIVITY 5

Role play Form small groups and follow these steps.

1. The role play includes the story events in lines 1–61. Decide who will play the roles of Sargeant, the Reverend Mr. Dorset, the individuals in the street, and the cops.

2. Using the story and what you have learned from class discussion, develop a role play up to the collapse of the church. Your role play should illustrate the events, the dialogue, and how the characters respond and behave. Do not read lines directly from the story.

3. Each group performs its role play for the class.

4. Discuss how different groups interpreted the characters and their words and actions. Which performances seem to represent the text most accurately? Why?

WRITING IN RESPONSE

Write briefly on this topic. Compare your ideas with those of two or three classmates.

In the story the white people react violently to Sargeant as he expresses his frustration when he can't find shelter in the church. Do you think such an incident could happen in the United States today? Explain why or why not.

Irony

ACTIVITY 6

In "On the Road," Hughes makes use of **irony** to show contradictions in the events of the story and the attitudes and behavior of the characters.

In one example of **situational irony,** the words and actions of the Reverend Mr. Dorset make a point about the church:

> "Said the Reverend Mr. Dorset before Sargeant even realized he'd opened his mouth: 'I'm sorry. No! Go right on down this street four blocks and turn to your left, walk up seven and you'll see the Relief Shelter. I'm sorry. No!' He shut the door." (lines 11–14)

Since the reverend is a minister of a church, a "holy man," (line 15) we expect him to help Sargeant, yet he refuses to assist him in his search for shelter. What message might Hughes want to convey through this irony?

In groups, read the following examples of irony and answer the questions. Be prepared to explain the irony and the point Hughes might want to make.

1. "'Uh-huh,' answered the big tall Negro, 'I know it's a white folks' church, but I got to sleep somewhere.'" (lines 47–48)

   What words and phrases show irony in these lines? Why?

2. "'A big black unemployed Negro holding onto our church!' thought the people. 'The idea!'" (lines 57–58)

   What is implied by "big black unemployed Negro"? What is ironic about the words *our* and *the idea?*

3. "'Well, I'll be dogged,' said Sargeant. 'This here's the first time I ever seed you off the cross.'" (lines 76–77)

   Sargeant is surprised to see Christ off the cross and walking with him, a poor, black man. Yet when Christ was alive, he walked and talked with people regardless of their class and race. How do Sargeant's words reveal irony in relationship to the church?

4. "'They have kept me nailed on a cross for nearly two thousand years.'" (lines 84–85)

   Who does "they" refer to? As followers of the teachings of Christ, what would we expect the church people to do to carry out Christ's work? What is ironic about the word *nailed?*

5. "'You had to pull the church down to get me off the cross.'" (lines 78–79)

   Why is it ironic that the entire church building had to come down before Christ could walk freely? How might the church falling down represent something more than the falling down of one building?

6. "'Well, if I had a little cash,' said Sargeant, 'I'd show you around a bit.'"
   "'I been around,' said Christ."
   "'Yeah, but that was a long time ago.'"
   "'All the same,' said Christ, 'I've been around.'" (lines 91–94)

   What does Sargeant offer to do? What does Christ mean by "I've been around"? How much has actually changed since Christ was alive? Why is this ironic?

WRITING IN RESPONSE

Write briefly on these topics. Focus on the characters in "On the Road" as you respond to the topics.

1. Is the character of Christ in the story someone you would like to know? Why or why not?

2. Why do you think Hughes portrays Christ as a "man of stone" (line 88) who doesn't seem interested in Sargeant's situation and only wants to leave for the city? (line 112) Explain.

3. In what ways does Sargeant appear naive or oblivious—that is, as someone who neither understands nor is aware of his situation or the intentions of the people around him? Discuss examples from the story. Why do you think Hughes portrays Sargeant in this way? Explain.

Figurative Language

Symbolism

In "On the Road" Hughes gives the reader clues to understanding the **themes** of the story through his use of **symbolism.**

ACTIVITY 7

Answer the following questions in groups. Each group will answer all the questions on either "snow" or "doors." Give evidence from the story to support your answers, if necessary, and include line numbers for each piece of evidence. Be prepared to explain the context in which the examples appear and to report your conclusions to the class.

Snow

Brainstorm all the words you associate with *snow*. Discuss which of those words relate to the story "On the Road" and why. Then underline all the references to *snow* in the story.

1. How does the snow affect Sargeant? Explain with examples.

2. Before and after Sargeant's "dream," the snow is "cold, wet . . . sopping in his shoes" (lines 21–22) and makes his clothes "wet, clammy cold wet, and shoes sloppy with snow water." (lines 139–140) Yet during Sargeant's dream, he can hear the "*crunch, crunch, crunch* on the snow of his own footsteps" (lines 70–71) and Christ "crunching his feet in the snow." (line 78) What causes snow to crunch? What is the difference between the snow in Sargeant's dream and the snow outside his dream?

3. What is the difference between how the snow affects Sargeant in his dream and outside his dream? Why? What might Hughes be trying to show?

4. How might the snow function as a symbol in the story? What might it represent? Explain.

Doors

Brainstorm all the words you associate with *doors*. Discuss which of those words relate to the story and why. Then circle all the references to doors in the story.

5. Explain the significance of the following examples:

   a. "And he *had* a door to shut." (line 19)
   b. "It had *two* doors." (line 26)
   c. Sargeant chooses "one of the tall stone pillars beside the door" rather than "anything so weak as a broken door." (lines 53–54)

6. What do you discover when you circle all the references to *doors* in the story? Why might this be important?

7. What is the difference between how the doors affect Sargeant in his dream and outside his dream? Why? What might Hughes be trying to show?

8. How might the doors function as a symbol in the story? What might they represent? Explain.

Exploring Further

Write or discuss the answers to these questions. Give evidence from the story to support your answers and include line numbers for each piece of evidence.

1. How does "On the Road" reveal hypocrisy in people and institutions?

2. Why is Christ so glad to get off the cross? (lines 84–90) When Sargeant asks, "'Where you goin'?'" why does Christ say, "'God knows . . . but I'm leavin' here'"? (lines 98–99)

3. Do you think there are any ways in which Sargeant is responsible for the situations he finds himself in? Explain.

4. What is significant about the "moving coal car" (lines 120–121) at the end of his dream?

5. Explain the significance of the following lines: "The bruised fingers were his, but not the *door*" (line 142) and "Not the *club,* but the fingers." (line 143)

6. In what ways has Sargeant's situation changed at the end of the story? Is it better or worse? Do you think Sargeant himself has changed as a result of his experience? Explain.

7. When Sargeant and Christ go their separate ways, the narrator begins to tell the story using *double negatives* when he says, "He <u>never</u> did see Christ <u>no</u> more." (lines 114–115) Find other examples of double negatives in the story. Why are these examples important?

8. In the story, Sargeant dreams about a walk with Christ and about being in a moving coal car. What causes Sargeant to have these dreams? Why might it be important to recognize that Sargeant is not just dreaming as we do when we're asleep, but that he has been knocked unconscious? What might Hughes want to show about Sargeant?

9. Discuss the possible significance of the names of the characters Sargeant and the Reverend Mr. Dorset. What is a sergeant and what does a sergeant do? Divide "Dorset" into two parts. What do you discover? How might these names help illustrate Hughes' point in the story?

10. In the Bible, Samson, a man of great physical strength, is captured by enemies who discover the secret of his strength is in his hair and cut his hair while he is sleeping. Rejoicing that they now have power over him, they blind him and lead him in chains to a great temple filled with people. As the people make fun of him, Samson prays to have his strength restored for a moment. Standing between two main pillars of the temple, Samson pushes with all the strength he can find. The temple falls down, and everyone is killed.

   In what ways is the story of Sargeant similar to the story of Samson? How is it different? Why do you think Hughes has chosen to make this parallel?

ESSAY TOPICS

1. Using the character of Christ, the symbol of snow, or the symbol of doors as a focus for your essay, illustrate what for you is the most significant message in "On the Road." Discuss how the character of Christ or the symbol you choose functions within the story to make your point clear.

2. Write an essay that illustrates how the irony in "On the Road" reveals a strong message about people and institutions. Include a discussion of the following *elements* from the story: the dialogue, the events, the characters and their actions, and the outcome.

3. Write an essay that focuses on the character of Sargeant and how he reveals Hughes's message in "On the Road." Include the following in your discussion: Sargeant's motivations, his understanding of the causes of his situation, and who or what he might represent. As you develop your ideas, think about how different readers might interpret Hughes's message differently, depending on their backgrounds.

AUTHOR PROFILE

Langston Hughes

Langston Hughes (1902–1967), poet, playwright, essayist, and short story writer, was born in Joplin, Missouri, and graduated from Lincoln University, an historically black college. At the age of eighteen, Hughes published one of his most well-known poems,

"The Negro Speaks of Rivers." Creative and experimental, Hughes incorporated authentic dialect in his work, adapted traditional poetic forms to embrace the cadences and moods of blues and jazz, and developed characters and themes that reflected elements of lower-class black culture. For these innovations, Hughes was criticized, yet he fearlessly persisted and responded by saying, "We younger Negro artists who create now intend to express our individual dark-skinned selves without fear or shame."

With his ability to fuse serious content with humorous style, Hughes attacked racial prejudice in a way that was "natural, humorous, restrained, yet powerful." Hughes is credited for ten volumes of poetry, sixty-six published short stories, over one hundred published essays, and more than twenty dramas, operas, and musicals. Known for his modesty and generosity as well as his accomplishments, Langston Hughes affectionately earned the title "Poet Laureate of the Negro Race" and is said to be "the most representative writer in the history of African-American literature."

CHAPTER 14

The Local Production of Cinderella

ALLEGRA GOODMAN

PREPARATION

ACTIVITY 1

Locate Hawaii on a map as you answer the following questions.

1. What do you know about Hawaii? Who are the native people? What is the climate like? What effect might Hawaii's location have had on its history?

2. In the nineteenth century, many European Americans from the continental United States went to Hawaii to create huge sugar and pineapple plantations. These plantations required more workers than the owners could find on the islands. Where do you think the rest of their large labor force came from? What effect would these circumstances have on the people and history of Hawaii?

ACTIVITY 2

Read the following excerpts from "The Local Production of Cinderella" and answer the questions.

1. "The missionaries came to Hawaii in their Victorian dresses, whalebones* and jet buttons. Imagine the black dresses soaking up the heat.

    Missionaries planted roses—a buffet for gnats and slugs, caterpillars and aphids,† not to mention black mold." (lines 67–70)

    What does this passage imply about the wisdom of the missionaries?

---

*corsets: long, stiff, tight undergarments for women
†insects that destroy crops

2. "The tide will come in up to the mountaintops. Hotels will dissolve like sand castles. . . . Honolulu will become a lost city, whales swishing through lobbies. Green sea turtles nosing empty rooms." (lines 88–91)

   What does this passage suggest about the power of civilization? Could something like this really happen?

The Local Production of Cinderella

Allegra Goodman

You couldn't tell anymore that they had separate desks. For fifteen years, Roselva and Helen had worked together at H.D.H.S., the Hawaii Department of Human Services, and their two gray steel desks, pushed together in the Great Hall of the State Administration Building, were covered with layers of notes and client files and forms to be filled out. This was in 1978, and they worked on twin sea-foam-green I.B.M. Selectric typewriters.

Roselva was Chinese-Hawaiian-Portuguese. She was a religious woman and attended Calvary-by-the-Sea Church. Her skin was deeply tanned, her short hair smooth and black. Her features were soft, as were her brown eyes. She had a gentle face, and was always patient with her clients, whether they were run- 10 aways or battered wives, drug-addicted mothers or schizophrenic homeless people. She believed in her job; she believed in human services. Helen, on the other hand, had grown up on the mainland, in Maine, and was of German-Lutheran ancestry. Her skin was fair, her eyes dark. Her voice was weary. She talked all the time about how she wanted to leave social work and do something for herself— music or fine cooking or writing. The clients depressed her. She thought some people were just bad.

Of all the teams in the Great Hall, Roselva and Helen had been together the longest. They were true partners as they sifted the stacks of paperwork before them; effortlessly, they plucked forms from their shared mess. Often they took 20 brown bags from their desk drawers and ate lunch together while they worked. On easy days, or after home visits, they ate outside, sitting on a dark-green bench in Tamarind Park. In the enormous shade of a monkeypod tree, they would talk about Helen's daughters and Roselva's son, Thad, about their husbands, and about cleaning house.

On this day at the end of May, walking back to the office after lunch, they crossed South Beretania Street while they talked about Roselva's big night coming up. Thad's girlfriend, Clarysse, was a ballet major at Chaminade University of Honolulu, and that night she was going to dance the title role in "Cinderella." Everyone was going—Roselva's family, and Clarysse's. Helen and her husband, 30 Sid, had tickets, too.

"I'm so nervous," Roselva confessed.

"Why?" asked Helen. "You don't have to get up and dance onstage."

"I'm nervous for Clarysse," Roselva said. "When she gets up there, I'm going to get butterflies for sure. She's my daughter, practically."

Helen sighed. For six years, Thad and Clarysse had been planning to get married. "Have they set a new date?" Helen asked.

"No," Roselva said. "I think her parents—"

"Yeah, they're pigs," Helen said. She often finished Roselva's sentences, although not with the words Roselva would have chosen. "She's still holding out 40 for the big wedding, huh? Or maybe she doesn't really want to marry Thad."

"Of course she does!"

All around them, lawyers in suits were streaming back to work. Men in aloha shirts and dress pants were walking up the steps to the state capitol building, with its open crater roof.

"Maybe they'll elope," Helen said.

Roselva was distracted. She was feeling guilty. That morning, she had read some of Helen's private writing. She had not done anything so clearly wrong since she was a child. She had come in to work a few minutes early, and put her purse in the file drawer, the way she always did. She began sorting through the papers in the "in" box, and there among them was a letter from Helen. It was written in black ink on the good heavyweight bond paper. But it wasn't a letter to Roselva, or to anyone in particular. It was addressed, "Dear People of Hawaii." Roselva looked away. Then she glanced back. She hesitated just a moment. And then, in the empty Department of Human Services, she read the whole thing. Then she read it again. It made her queasy, but she couldn't stop. It was a cuckoo letter. Some kind of scary joke. This could not be Helen's writing, she thought. And yet it was her handwriting. This was not the Helen she knew. She wanted to hide the letter somewhere, stuff it away where she couldn't see it. But she put it back where she'd found it, among the pink, yellow, and white forms on the desk.

The letter still sat there when they returned from lunch. Maybe it was a warning sign. Maybe it was a plea for help. In which case Roselva should speak up. That was what she always told her clients' families: first ask if anything is wrong.

As soon as Helen got up to go to the ladies' room, Roselva scooted forward in her swivel chair and slid the letter out once more.

Dear People of Hawaii:

The missionaries came to Hawaii in their Victorian dresses, whalebones and jet buttons. Imagine the black dresses soaking up the heat.

Missionaries planted roses—a buffet for gnats and slugs, caterpillars and aphids, not to mention black mold.

Now the universities plant their sick ideas. People of Hawaii, professors spread their ideology over you each day. They twist your history. Why do you sit silently in the valleys? Why do you sit patiently in the classrooms? Cut the white men down whether from New York or Michigan. Cut them down and plant them. Let them become succulent plants, night-blooming cereus° blossoming under the moon. Heads of coral for the reef fish.

O People of Hawaii, I see your shopping malls and hotel luaus but then I see your revolution. A red tide, a taste of salt.

A new Queen rises in the fountain at the foot of Diamond Head. She wears a twelve-strand necklace of braided human hair, and a pendant of polished ivory. She outlaws ukuleles and slack-key guitars. But will the people rise up from their lei stands by the airport and romp across the asphalt back to the green valleys to reclaim their taro patches? Will you leave the front desks at the hotels and go back to plait pili grass and hold your ancient games? Stick throwing, javelin, smooth black rock bowling, and wrestling.

°*cereus* a tropical night-blooming cactus

Without knowing it, Roselva had begun to read this letter aloud to herself. "The Queen will die," she whispered. "The dolphins will rise up and circle each island. The tide will come in up to the mountaintops. Hotels will dissolve like sand castles. In catamarans the children will sail from Pearl Harbor, gliding over sunken battleships. Honolulu will become a lost city, whales swishing through lobbies. Green sea turtles nosing empty rooms. The great white shark with pin-point eyes will swim through sunken streets. There will be no humans left but bones and graves under the water."

What was this? What was this writing? It was like a love letter never sent. Or a speech Helen never gave. It was a crazy letter, some kind of crazy story. But Helen never acted crazy in real life. She was sarcastic in real life, always talking about her husband, Sid, who taught at the university, and their three teen-age daughters. The professor and the princesses, she called them. Helen was cynical, maybe, but she'd never said a word about the old Hawaii. She talked about the old movies at the Honolulu Academy of the Arts—Fred Astaire and Ginger Rogers.° This letter wasn't Helen. And the place Helen described—the turtles and water? What was that place? Not Honolulu.

"Let me give you a piece of advice," Helen said.

Roselva practically jumped out of her chair. Helen was back from the ladies' room. "Advice?" she asked.

"If you really want the kids to get married, offer to pay for the wedding."

Helen was talking about Thad and Clarysse, but Roselva's mind was still with the dolphins and the rising tide. That afternoon, she hung back a little until Helen left. She gathered up the letter along with the other papers on the desk and put the whole pile in her silk-screened orchid-pattern canvas tote bag.

Roselva's house was hot. She and her husband, Jimmy, lived in Niu Valley, and they had glassed in the lanai° in the back. They had wanted a den, but they got a greenhouse effect. A ranch with three bedrooms and two plumeria° trees in front, it was a tract house° like every other one in the flat bottom of the valley. Roselva pulled up after work and parked her Dodge Omni in the carport. The car had a pyramidal sign on the roof, with "Student Driver" on one side and "Jimmy's Auto School" on the other. This was her husband's business, and his car, a green 1975 Pontiac, had a similar sign on its roof.

Indoors, Roselva opened the jalousies° to cool down the living room and kitchen. Thad was already home. Jimmy would be next. The dance performance was that night, and her best friend was turning crazy on her. As if she didn't have enough to worry about. Of course, who told her to go around reading other people's private mail?

°*Fred Astaire and Ginger Rogers* the famous dancing couple of the 1930s and 1940s
°*lanai* Hawaiian porch or covered patio
°*plumeria* a tropical shrub with large, showy, fragrant flowers
°*tract house* an inexpensive house built in a development of similar houses
°*jalousies* shutters with adjustable slats

She stood at the counter, her brain zinging. She tried to cool down and watch Thad eat. He was wearing gym shorts and an ancient T-shirt printed "13th Annual Haleiwa Surfing Classic." Long ago, Clarysse's parents, Edwin and Mitsuko, had announced that they were never going to pay for any wedding between Clarysse and Thad. Clarysse's parents tolerated Thad, but they did not approve of him. They thought their daughter should marry someone with a career like law or
130   medicine, who could support a ballerina daughter. Clarysse's father owned a pool-cleaning-supplies store, and her mother taught the art of ikebana.°

Thad bolted down his chicken and rice. He got up to look for a glass, then leaned over and drank from the kitchen tap as if it were a water fountain.

"Thad," Roselva said.

"Gotta go, Mom," he told her.

"It's still early yet," she said.

"Call is six o'clock!" he told her. He ran out to the driveway and started up Roselva's car. He was taking Clarysse down to the Chaminade University theatre.

Any minute, Jimmy would come home. Roselva changed into a deep-green
140   muumuu. She tried to read the newspaper. She opened the refrigerator and checked on the leis for Clarysse: a three-strand lei of pink Maui rosebuds and a matching haku lei of pink rosebuds, tiny orchids, and ferns, woven into a garland. The leis rested on damp paper towels in their clear plastic boxes.

The door slammed. It was Jimmy, in the living room. She heard him take his keys and wallet and smash them down onto the coffee table. She knew exactly what had happened. Jeannine Chung had failed her driving test. Patiently, painstakingly, Jimmy had been teaching this student, and had brought her along to a point where she was ready to take the exam. More than ready: prepared to ace that driving test. Jimmy had brought her to the D.M.V.,° let her take his driv-
150   ing-school car out on the test drive with the state examiner, gently pushed his student out of the nest—and the kid had flopped. Randall or Mike or one of the other examiners—Jimmy knew them all—had shuddered in the car and screamed at Jeannine, "*Never* do that. Never, *never* do that. Return to the testing station. Get out of the vehicle. Zero. You flunk!" Jimmy was Jeannine's instructor, and he was disgraced. Roselva knew how hard this hit him. He was the most careful teacher in the world. He never took a student to the D.M.V. until he or she was a perfect driver. But once in a while it all went wrong. Jimmy's flawless student driver would get to the test and fall apart. Panic while turning left into traffic. Fail to line up properly while parking. Block an intersection and turn into
160   a snivelling mess.

Jimmy didn't say a word while they ate dinner. He didn't speak as they got into his car and drove to Chaminade. Roselva wanted to tell him what she'd done, and ask his advice. But she knew better than to open her mouth.

The car jerked ahead in the rush-hour traffic. Tight-lipped, Jimmy accelerated to catch the tail end of a green light. They lurched forward. "Stop that!" Jimmy said to Roselva.

°*ikebana* the Japanese art of flower arranging
°*D.M.V.* Department of Motor Vehicles, where driving licenses are issued

"Stop what?" she asked. Then she looked down at her feet. Without realizing it she had been correcting Jimmy's driving with the car's specially added instructional passenger-side brake. Jimmy used the brake all the time to curb his wayward driving students, but he couldn't stand it when Roselva used the brake on him.

When they got to Chaminade, Jimmy let her out in front of the white, Spanish-style auditorium and drove off to park. Thad was waiting outside the auditorium door, and Roselva gave him the leis for Clarysse. Then she gave the usher her ticket and opened the door to the auditorium. The place was chilly, full of expectant talk. She went down the center aisle, past rows full of people. She was looking for Clarysse's parents, or for empty seats, but all she found were rows filled with strangers, and seats that were saved with programs folded over their backs. Then she heard someone calling her from down front.

"Roselva!" Helen was standing there, in the center of the third row. She had saved seats for her and Jimmy. Thad was there already, sitting next to her. Sid hadn't been able to come, Helen said.

"Thanks." Roselva squeezed in next to Helen. "Jimmy's parking. Oh, there he is." Her voice was breathy; she was so nervous. She should say something to Helen. She should speak up right now. The red velvet curtain loomed in front of her. The lights went down. She felt a sympathetic stagefright. When Jimmy took his seat she said a silent prayer. Lord Jesus, help us. Help Clarysse dance. And forgive me for what I did today. Show me the way.

Music started up from speakers in the wings. The curtains parted and the Chaminade dance majors appeared. Roselva had to put her glasses on in a hurry. The dancers jumped and pranced to the strains of Prokofiev, some more graceful and some less so, the women sometimes tall and willowy, in their tights and tutus, but sometimes short, with big thighs. Roselva's seat was excellent, almost too good. She could see the sweat trickling on the ballerinas' faces, glistening in their hair. When the dancers spun and turned, sweat flew off them as if they had been swimming and had just sprung out of the water.

Helen nudged Roselva. There was Clarysse. Her body was slender and her skin fair. Her makeup made her look almost European. She had blushing pink cheeks and wide, blue-shadowed eyes. In her costume of gold lace, she descended the grand staircase at the ball. Her black hair was beautifully pinned up, her head suddenly small.

When Clarysse danced with her prince, she became more ordinary. The prince was a paid ringer° from the Honolulu Opera Theatre, and he had a distant, professional manner. He looked less like an ardent lover than like a seasoned horse trainer as he led Clarysse this way and that. Her toe shoes clopped delicately on the wood floor of the stage as he took her through her paces. Oh, poor Thad, Roselva thought. What was he going to do with a dance major? How was he ever going to support her? But then, when Clarysse went into a solo, Roselva almost forgot her worries. When she sprang up in the air and beat her pointed feet, Roselva cheered silently against gravity. Even when Clarysse landed

°*ringer* a professional brought in for a performance from outside the nonprofessional group

on the ground, she fell back lightly. She was on the verge of flying. Any second it was going to happen—Clarysse would become a princess and a bride, the fairy-tale star of her dream wedding.

All the way home, Roselva wished she had spoken to Helen. There Helen had been all evening, sitting and applauding with her. She had come to Clarysse's performance and sat at Roselva's side. And what had Roselva done? Only be-trayed her colleague, her friend of fifteen years. In the car, Roselva couldn't stop thinking about Helen's words. The missionaries in their Victorian dresses. White men becoming succulent plants. What was that all about?

220   "Jimmy," she said. "You notice anything about Helen?"

"No," he said.

A red tide and a taste of salt, she thought. The white shark with pinpoint eyes.

At home in their bedroom, Roselva changed into her nightgown. Jimmy was lying in his underwear watching the news. His eyes were half closed.

"Helen wrote a letter," Roselva said. "I never should have read it, but—I'm wor-ried she's sick. You think she's sick?" She tapped her head.

Jimmy didn't answer.

Roselva turned off the television. In a flash Jimmy opened his eyes. "I was watching that," he said.

230   "Can I show you this?" Roselva took Helen's letter from her bag. She handed Jimmy his reading glasses and he read. He read the whole thing in silence, then handed it back.

"You sure that's Helen's?" he said.

"It's her handwriting," Roselva said.

"Maybe she copied it."

"Where would she copy something like that from?"

Jimmy shrugged.

"I just found it on the desk," Roselva said, "and now I can't figure out what to do."

240   "Put it back," Jimmy suggested.

"And what if it's some kind of call for help?"

"We just saw her," Jimmy said. He had turned on the news again. His eyes were starting to close.

Roselva bent her head down close to the words in the letter. Then she had an inspiration. "Jimmy," she said. "This letter is a prophecy."

"Prophecy for what?"

"For the future," Roselva said. Her voice was hushed. "Look," she said. "The dol-phins will rise up. The water will cover the city. There will be no humans left."

Jimmy opened his eyes. "What type prophecy is that?" he said.

250   "Armageddon° type," Roselva replied. She lay down on the bed. For the first time that day, she felt some relief.

°*Armageddon* the end of the world, when good and evil have their final battle (biblical reference)

As soon as she came in on Monday morning, Roselva saw the newspaper clip-pings on the desk. Helen had clipped the review from her copy of the Sunday paper:

LOCAL PRODUCTION OF CINDERELLA TAKES WING

Chaminade University's spring offering, "Cinderella," sparkled with innovative choreography, energetic dancing, and dazzling costumes.

In the demanding title role, Clarysse Leong danced with verve and elegant ex-tension. She was a lovely presence on the stage, and we hope to see much more of her in years to come.

260

"'Verve,'" Helen said to Roselva. "Not bad."

"Not too shabby," Roselva agreed.

"But you have to wonder what she's going to do with herself after graduation."

Roselva stared at Helen. "That's exactly what I was thinking at the performance."

"Poor Thad," Helen said.

"Poor Thad! That's just what I was thinking." Roselva shook her head.

But Helen was already at the steel file cabinet, gathering folders. They had a visit out on the North Shore. A homeless Tongan family camped out on the beach. Roselva felt sad whenever they drove out there. The family tent leaked. Mr. Tafesau was always trying to use the pay phone up the road to look for work trimming trees.

270

"Don't you start getting down already," Helen said, looking over at her.

"I can't believe it," Roselva whispered. "You've been reading my mind."

"Oh, Roselva, quit it." Helen took out her car keys.

"I mean, I read your letter." Roselva took it out of her bag and placed it on Helen's desk. "I'm sorry," she said.

For just a second Helen was taken aback. Then she shrugged. "My shrink says I should write. He says I have a lot of anger. I'm working on that."

280

"You're blessed," Roselva said.

"Yeah, I guess," Helen said. "I'm blessed with a lousy marriage, scum for clients, a daughter sleeping with her entire senior class."

"You're blessed with prophecy," Roselva said. "You see how it's all going to be."

"Oh, Roselva," Helen said. "I can't see two steps in front of me."

Roselva shook her head. "Look at this." She picked up Helen's letter. "No more selling leis. Whales in the lobby."

Helen took the letter, crumpled it up, and tossed it in the trash bin next to her desk.

290

Roselva blinked. She nearly went to fish the letter out again.

"That's just made up," Helen said. "None of that's going to happen."

"No, no," Roselva insisted. "You have the gift, you know the future."

"Fine. If you believe in that kind of thing. It's like you believe in angels and Heaven and Hell."

"I do," Roselva said.

Helen shrugged. "O.K. I'm not going to argue with you."

"And what do you believe?"

"When you're dead, you're dead," Helen said. "That's the beauty of it. You just
300 stop."

"And then what?"

"Then nothing."

"I can't believe that's true."

"That's why they invented Heaven," Helen said.

"It's not," Roselva said.

"O.K., whatever you say," said Helen. "Listen, if you get up there, I'll go with
you."

"But not too soon," Roselva said.

"It'll be like this," Helen said, and she leaned close. Roselva looked at her
310 earnestly—just a little bit on guard, since Helen loved to make fun. And Helen
said in her weary, half-serious voice, "We'll grow very old. And then we'll go to
Heaven in clouds of smoke. Or to the shark palace. Wherever we go we'll kick
off our shoes, and it'll all be the same. I'm still going to be working with you."

ANALYZING THE STORY

ACTIVITY 3

Answer the following questions. Give evidence from the story to support
your answers, where appropriate, and include line numbers for each piece of
evidence.

1. What do we know about the backgrounds of Roselva and Helen? Why do
   you think the writer chose to give this specific information about them?

2. How do Roselva and Helen differ in their attitudes toward their clients? Do
   they have the same clients?

3. What do we know about Helen's family?

4. Who are Thad and Clarysse? How old do you think they are? Why do
   Clarysse's parents not approve of Thad? Can you think of any other reasons
   besides the ones they give?

5. Where does Roselva find Helen's letter? Why is this significant?

6. When Roselva reads the letter, she thinks it is crazy. Why? Do you agree?

7. Why is Roselva relieved when she decides that the letter is a prophecy? What
   does this tell us about Roselva?

8. Were you surprised at Helen's reaction when she learns that Roselva has read
   her letter? Why or why not? Why do you think Helen throws the letter away?

9. Why do you think Helen is going to a psychiatrist?

10. Do you think Helen is being serious or making fun about going to heaven
    with Roselva at the end of the story? Explain.

Elements of Literature

Characterization

ACTIVITY 4

Work with a partner or small group and read "The Local Production of Cinderella" again. Then, without referring to the story, try to answer these three questions about each quotation. If necessary, refer to the indicated lines to verify your answers.

- Who says it and why?
- What does it reveal about the character?
- How does it make the other character feel?

1. "'I'm so nervous.'" (line 32)

2. "'Yeah, they're pigs.'" (line 39)

3. "'Or maybe she doesn't really want to marry Thad.'"
   "'Of course she does!'" (lines 41–42)

4. "'Maybe they'll elope.'" (line 46)

5. "Cut the white men down whether from New York or Michigan." (lines 73–74)

6. "'Oh, Roselva, quit it.'" (line 276)

7. "'When you're dead, you're dead. . . . That's the beauty of it. You just stop.'" (lines 299–300)

8. "'We'll grow very old. And then we'll go to heaven in clouds of smoke. Or to the shark palace.'" (lines 311–312)

WRITING IN RESPONSE

Write a brief response to the following question.

Based on your conclusions in Activity 4, what important differences do you find between Roselva and Helen? Why do you think these two women are such good friends?

Point of View

ACTIVITY 5

Answer the following questions with a partner.

1. At what point does the story become limited to one character's **point of view?** (See Appendix A for more information about terms in boldface type.) Whose is it? How do you know?

2. "The Local Production of Cinderella" is written from a **third-person limited point of view;** that is, the descriptions of events are the perceptions of one character. Read the statements in the following chart and decide if they are factual descriptions of events or interpretations of events. Then explain what the statements reveal about the point of view of the story. The first one has been done for you.

STATEMENT	FACT OR INTERPRETATION	EXPLANATION
a. Helen is going crazy.	*Interpretation*	*Roselva is shocked at what is a new side of Helen for her. The only explanation: she's crazy.*
b. The place described in the letter is not Honolulu.		
c. Roselva should say something to Helen.		
d. "The red velvet curtain loom[s]" before Roselva. (line 185)		
e. Roselva's seat is bad.		
f. Roselva has betrayed her friend by reading the letter.		

Figurative Language

ACTIVITY 6

Helen's letter is full of **figurative language** and other comparisons. Find four or five examples in the letter and answer these questions.

1. What does the *comparison* or *figure of speech* mean?
2. What does it tell us about what Helen thinks may happen to Hawaii?

Example: ". . . I see your revolution. A red tide,* a taste of salt." (lines 77–78)
Answer: Helen sees a bloody revolution, salty with tears and bent on destruction, which she compares with a toxic red tide of salty ocean water.

---

*Red tide is an unhealthy tide but occurs naturally when a proliferation of a certain kind of protozoan causes the water to be toxic. Gathering shellfish is not allowed during a red tide.

Tone

ACTIVITY 7

Helen's letter has a distinctive **tone** revealing the attitude of the author. Read the following excerpts from her letter and answer these two questions about each one.

- How do these phrases and repetitions create a tone for the letter that is different from the tone of the rest of the story?
- What does the tone tell us about Helen?

1. "Dear people of Hawaii: . . ." (line 66)
2. "O people of Hawaii . . ." (line 77)
3. "Why do you . . . ? Why do you . . . ?" (lines 72–73)
4. "Cut . . . Cut . . ." (lines 73, 74)
5. "Let them . . ." (line 75)
6. "But will the people . . . ? Will you . . . ?" (lines 81–83)
7. "The Queen will . . . The dolphins will . . . The tide will . . . Hotels will . . ." (lines 87–88)

WRITING IN RESPONSE

Write briefly on this topic.

Helen's letter is described as ". . . like a love letter never sent. Or a speech Helen never gave." (lines 94–95) In what ways is the letter like a love letter? A letter never sent? A speech? A speech never given?

CREATIVE WRITING

Cut Helen's letter down to a brief poem. Use exact words, phrases, and figurative language from the letter. Retain the tone and the main point of the letter in your poem. When you are finished, compare your poem with others in the class and discuss with your classmates whether this was an easy or difficult task and why.

Theme

ACTIVITY 8

A. Read "between the lines" of the letter to answer the following questions about Hawaii *from Helen's perspective*. Explain your answers.

1. How might professors "twist . . . history"? (line 72)
2. What is so wrong with a hotel luau that it would help provoke a revolution?
3. Who is the new Queen? (What is the significance of queens in Hawaii?)
4. Who works at the airport lei stands and at the front desks of the hotels?
5. Whose revolution is the letter talking about?
6. When Honolulu is gone, who will be left? What is her point?

B. Answer the following questions to determine what the author may be trying to say about Hawaii and other colonized areas of the world.

1. What is the connection between the letter and Helen's referring to her family as "the professor and the princesses"? (line 98) Where does she place herself and/or her family in her greater vision of Hawaii?
2. Would you expect a letter like Helen's to be written by someone who had some native Hawaiian background or by someone whose ancestors were European American? Depending on your answer, do you find a **paradox** related to who wrote the letter and who thought it was crazy? Explain.

ACTIVITY 9

Do the following pairs of sentences refer to similar ideas and feelings or to different ones? What does each answer imply about the friendship between Helen and Roselva?

1. The way Roselva would have finished sentences if she had had the chance
   The way Helen finished them for her
2. Roselva's attitude toward her job and her clients
   Helen's attitude toward them
3. Roselva's marriage and home life
   Helen's marriage and home life
4. Roselva's feelings toward Clarysse
   Helen's feelings toward her daughters
5. The intended message of the letter
   Roselva's interpretation of the letter

ACTIVITY 10

In pairs, role-play a discussion between Helen and Roselva about the contents of the letter.

Note for the Roselva character: Try as hard as possible to find out what is really going on with Helen.

Note for the Helen character: Reveal why Helen wrote the letter and what she meant by what she said.

As a class, discuss what you found out about Roselva and Helen through the role plays.

Exploring Further

Skim the story and underline (or highlight) all proper nouns, excluding the names of the characters. Then answer the following questions in groups. Compare your answers with those of the rest of the class.

1. The writer mentions many specific places, such as the Great Hall of the State Administration Building (lines 3–4) or the Calvary-by-the-Sea Church. (line 8) Find other examples of specific places named in the story. Would Goodman expect all her readers to know Honolulu well enough to be familiar with them? What might be Goodman's purpose in mentioning these places?

2. Goodman is also specific about certain other details by using proper nouns for them, such as what is written on Thad's T-shirt, brands of cars, and so on. What might be the author's purpose for doing this?

3. The ballet in the story is Sergei Prokofiev's *Cinderella*. (line 29) What reasons can you think of for the author's choice? Who or what in Goodman's story is similar to Cinderella?

ESSAY TOPICS

1. Choose one of the following titles for an essay in which you focus on either Helen or Roselva.

   Hotels of Sand   Blessed   Sorry   Collective Guilt

2. "The Local Production of Cinderella" reveals some contradictions in the friendship between Helen and Roselva. One such contradiction is Roselva's guilt and concern over reading Helen's letter and Helen's reaction of apparent disinterest. Write an essay that focuses on the contradictions in the relationship between Helen and Roselva. What do those contradictions reveal about the friendship?

3. What do we learn about Roselva from her interaction with her husband? Write an essay that shows how Roselva's relationship with her husband gives further insight into Roselva's character.

AUTHOR PROFILE

Allegra Goodman

Allegra Goodman was raised in a small, conservative Jewish community in Honolulu. While she was still a child, her parents—both professors at the University of Hawaii— encouraged her to write. They read her work with enthusiasm and formed their own family writer's workshop. By the time Goodman was a freshman at Harvard, she had her first short story published. Her first collection of stories, *Total Immersion,* appeared in 1989, the year of her graduation. After leaving Harvard she went on to receive her Ph.D. in English Literature from Stanford. Goodman's second collection of stories, *The Family Markowitz,* became a bestseller when she was only twenty-nine. Along with her award-winning first novel, *Kaaterskill Falls,* these entertaining and complex works have made her both a popular and a respected young American writer. Other stories have appeared in *The New Yorker* and *Prize Stories of 1995,* and she has received an O. Henry Award.

Goodman is known for her clearly detailed characterizations and the confidence and wit of her style. She writes primarily about Jewish life in the United States, poking warm fun as it wavers between assimilation and redevelopment of its cultural identity. However, she does not inject her own life story into her work. Rather, as she once said, she writes the stories of other people as if they were autobiographies. Goodman also believes fiction can be popular and literary at the same time, just as people can love mass-produced candy bars and appreciate gourmet chocolate.

CHAPTER 15

One Human Hand

LI-YOUNG LEE

PREPARATION

ACTIVITY 1

With a partner or in small groups, answer the following questions.

1. Think about an older person in your life—a parent, grandparent, aunt, uncle, older sibling, or close friend. When you call up an image of this person in your mind, what possession do you most often associate with that person? Explain why you think this possession is or was important for that person. How does the possession help you understand the person?

2. Look at the brush paintings of the two birds. The title of the piece you are about to read is "One Human Hand." What possible connections can you think of between the paintings and the title?

3. This **prose poem** (see Appendix A for more information on terms in bold-face type) is an excerpt from Li-Young Lee's book, *The Winged Seed, A Remembrance.* In this excerpt, he writes about his father, who immigrated with his family to the United States from Indonesia. What qualities do you associate with a remembrance, or memoir?

One Human Hand

Li-Young Lee

I remember how on certain Sunday evenings my father would show us his best-
loved possessions, unrolling across our dining-room table the hundred-year-old
scrolls he'd carried over the sea from China. He showed them to us in the order
he remembered having collected them, and the first one, unscrolled, revealed
first the black claws, and then the long legs, and at last the whole height of a   5
standing cranc, long-beaked, with coarse head and neck feathers, and one fierce
eye. The second scroll was mostly white except for the blight-struck pine, and
one bird perched at the tip: a shrike, surviving, last carrier of seed and stones in
his little gizzard. The scrolls in my father's house, stored in room after room, or
hung in the halls, were so many any breeze could send their silk dancing and   10
their bones all knocking against the walls. He spent every day in August, his vacation time, painting from morning to evening, filling sheet after sheet of rice
paper with washes of ink. I watched him lean over the table and his hand flee,
or seem to flee, the ink running past the brush and into the very bird. It was
birds he painted, one after another. *To make you see flying in a standing body,*   15
he said, his arm moving up and down to be flying, pushing backward to be drawing nigh, backing up into the future in order to be coming into what's passed.
One human hand, a bird, resigned to let time resolve it in paper and ink. It takes
one bird to write the central action of the air, lending its wings to gravity, in
order to be aloft.   20

ANALYZING THE POEM

ACTIVITY 2

Work on these questions with a partner or group.

1. Look through the poem and find words to put in each of the four categories
   in the chart. Some words may fit in more than one category. Then discuss
   what you know and can guess about the meanings of the words, in the context of the poem. Use the glossary and a dictionary to help you.

HANDS	BIRDS	ART/PAINTING	CHINESE CULTURE
unrolling	claws	scrolls	scrolls

2. After reading the poem, which one or two images linger in your mind? What
   questions do you have? Discuss.

A C T I V I T Y   3

Answer the following questions. Give evidence from the poem to support your answers and line numbers for each piece of evidence.

1. Who are the main characters? How are they related to each other?

2. Who could the "us" be in lines 1 and 3?

3. In what order did the father choose to show the pictures? Why?

4. What color does the **narrator** see in the first scroll? What part of the bird does he first see? What color does the narrator see in the second scroll? Why do you think the narrator chose to describe only images that are black or white? What associations do you have with these colors?

5. How old do you think the narrator was when he saw his father unroll the scrolls? What makes you think so?

6. How old do you think the narrator was when he wrote this memoir? Why do you think so?

7. What does the narrator really see when he sees "his [father's] hand flee, or seem to flee"? (lines 13–14) With your classmates, demonstrate the motion that you think the narrator sees.

Elements of Literature

Figurative Language

Symbolism

A C T I V I T Y   4

"One Human Hand" contains **symbolism** that can help readers interpret the meanings of the poem. Follow these steps to help you interpret the symbols.

1. In groups, choose one of the following three images and study the list of their associated details.

   The first scroll

   | black claws | long legs | | the whole crane, standing |
   | the long beak | coarse head and neck feathers | | one fierce eye |

   The second scroll

   | mostly white | a blight-struck pine | | bird perched on the |
   | a survivor | seeds and stones in his little gizzard | | tip—a shrike |

   Many scrolls

   | stored in room after room | hung in the halls | | any breeze |
   | [the scrolls'] silk dancing | [the scrolls'] bones knocking | | |

2. Next, work together to determine a literal understanding of the image. In other words, what do you actually see in your mind? Sketch the image in full detail.

3. Discuss the connotations of each detail and the whole image. What do you associate with the details, with the specific words, and with the whole image? Keep in mind that each detail relates to the image as a whole.

4. Finally, be prepared to explain to the class both your literal understanding of the image you chose and your understanding of the connotations of that image.

ACTIVITY 5

1. Trace the actions of the father's hand, from the beginning to the end of the prose poem. In the order it occurs, list each motion that the father's hand performs.

   Example   1. hand "would show" (line 1)
   　　　　　　 2. hand "unrolling" (line 2)

   What do you notice about the progression of the verbs and the changes in tense? In which line does a shift in action occur? What does this suggest about the difference between the father's possessions and the father's painting?

2. The author tells us that his father painted birds in order to make us "see flying in a standing body." (line 15) *Flying* and *standing* are contrasting images.

   a. Use your imagination to combine the following people, images, or ideas into contrasting pairs.

father	crane	black	bird	hands
what's passed	gravity	write	ink	aloft
paint	white	paper	black	future
Li-Young Lee	shrike	silk dancing		

   b. Explain why you chose the combinations you did.
   c. A bird cannot literally be flying and standing at the same time, but you can probably imagine the two actions merging into a single image. Explain to a partner how one of the contrasting image pairs you have chosen is both different and similar.

3. At the end of the prose poem, does the hand become more like a bird? Why might the author use the following verbs (italics added)? What is significant about the action described here?

   "*resigned* to let time resolve it in paper" (line 18)
   "*write* the central action of the air" (line 19)
   "*lending* its wings to gravity" (line 19)

WRITING IN RESPONSE

Write a paragraph in which you describe one image from "One Human Hand." Explain what you think it means and how it helps you to understand the poem.

Language and Style

ACTIVITY 6

In writing fiction, authors invent **plots,** characters, **settings**—whole stories. As readers, you don't expect to find any personal information about the author in a fictional story. In a memoir or autobiography, on the other hand, the author invites readers to believe that the story actually happened and the characters are real people.

Answer the following questions in pairs or small groups.

1. How might the purpose of a memoir be different from the purpose of a work of fiction or poetry?

2. How might this purpose affect the language and style of "One Human Hand," which is a memoir?

3. "One Human Hand" is also a prose poem. How does Lee use elements of poetry with his autobiographical information?

4. What might Lee have written differently in "One Human Hand" if it were a piece of fiction? What might stay the same?

WRITING IN RESPONSE

Respond briefly to these questions in writing. Compare your responses with those of two or three classmates.

1. If you were going to write a memoir, what time of your life would you focus on? Why?

2. What part of your life would you choose to write fiction about? Why?

Exploring Further

Continue analyzing "One Human Hand" with these questions.

1. Why do you think the father shows the scrolls to his son? What do you think the son learns about the father?

2. The prose poem begins with "possessions" (line 2) and ends with "one bird . . . aloft." (lines 18–20) How are these two images different? How would you describe how the piece moves, considering where it begins and where it ends?

3. List all the phrases describing motion in lines 13–17. Do these motions mostly describe the father's painting or a bird's flying? What could the narrator be suggesting about the relationship between the father, his hand painting, and the bird?

4. The narrator describes his father's arm as "pushing backward to be drawing nigh" (lines 16–17) and as "backing up into the future in order to be coming

into what's passed." (line 17) What could these lines of apparent contradiction mean?

5. How are a human hand and a bird alike?

6. In the prose poem the father is an artist. We also know that the narrator, his son, is a writer. What words near the end of the poem show a connection between the father as artist and the son as writer?

7. What do you think the poem says about the purpose of art in the father's life? In the son's life?

CREATIVE WRITING

"One Human Hand" is told from the point of view of the son. How would it be different if it were told from the father's point of view? Imagine you are the father and tell the story from his point of view. Use first-person "I."

ESSAY TOPICS

1. In his memoir, *The Winged Seed, a Remembrance,* the paragraphs that make up "One Human Hand" are not set off from the rest of the text and have no title. In an essay, explain why you think Lee, when he extracted this part as a prose poem for publication, titled it "One Human Hand."

2. What do the father's possessions tell you about who he is? Explain in an essay.

3. What does the poem tell you about the relationship between the son and his father? Write an essay in which you consider what the son understands about the father, what he has learned, and how the two are similar.

4. In an essay, focus on **symbolism.** How do the symbols in "One Human Hand" help you understand the father, the son, or a theme?

AUTHOR PROFILE

Li-Young Lee

Li-Young Lee was born in 1957 in Jakarta, Indonesia, of Chinese parents. After Lee's father was jailed for a year for political reasons, Lee's family fled Indonesia and traveled to Hong Kong, where Lee's father worked as a preacher, then to Macau and Japan. Finally, when Lee was six years old, his family settled in the United States. They lived in a small town in Pennsylvania where Lee's father became the minister of an all-white Presbyterian church. Lee studied at the University of Pittsburgh, the University of Arizona, and the State University of New York at Brockport. He has taught at many universities, including Northwestern University and the University of Iowa. Lee is the author of two award-winning books of poetry, *Rose* and *The City in Which I Love You.*

Family is an important theme in Lee's poetry and in his memoir. Many of his poems include explicit references to his mother, father, siblings, wife, and children. He writes of specific places as well, such as Shanghai, Malaysia, and his bathroom in Chicago, where his wife bathes their child. He concludes the poem "With Ruins" with "It's a place/for those who own no place . . . ."

In all his writings, Lee remembers his family's past and writes of his experience as an immigrant to the United States. In the last three lines of his second book of poems he writes, "I daily face,/this immigrant,/this man with my own face" (Lee, 1990). Lee lives and writes in Chicago.

CHAPTER 16

The Magic Barrel

BERNARD MALAMUD

PREPARATION

ACTIVITY 1

With a partner or in small groups, discuss the following questions and do the activities.

1. "If [a short story writer] is lucky, serious things may seem funny." This was Bernard Malamud's reply when he was asked why he loved writing short stories. Based on these words, what kind of story do you think "The Magic Barrel" is?

2. What are barrels commonly used for? Brainstorm a list of common or possible uses for a barrel. Then brainstorm a list of improbable uses for a barrel. Use your imagination.

3. What could be "magical" about a barrel? Based on your ideas, formulate possible definitions of *magic*. What other things, places, or events do we often describe as magical?

4. Have you ever been attracted to someone whose behavior you consider wild? What did the wild behavior consist of? What might be the basis of your attraction to it?

ACTIVITY 2

To prepare to read "The Magic Barrel," read the following descriptions of places in New York City and aspects of Jewish culture. On a map of New York, locate all the places mentioned.

- *Manhattan* is the most famous of the five boroughs, or districts, of New York City. Wall Street, the Empire State Building, and Central Park are all located there. Downtown and midtown Manhattan are both commercial and residential, but uptown Manhattan is primarily residential. Although there have always been different economic levels of uptown neighborhoods, at the time this story takes place, with some exceptions, the farther uptown you went, the less expensive the neighborhoods became. The *Bronx* is the borough even farther uptown (north) than uptown Manhattan. In the time this story is set, some areas of the Bronx were still middle class, but many neighborhoods were becoming poor.

- *Yeshiva University* is a famous Jewish theological seminary where young men and women are trained to become rabbis, the leaders in Jewish places of worship. At the time of the story, however, all students were male, and the main campus was located in uptown Manhattan, near Riverside Park and the Hudson River in one of the more expensive uptown neighborhoods. *Riverside Drive* runs north-south along Riverside Park and is lined on one side with expensive apartment buildings overlooking the Hudson River.

- New York City is undeniably the center of American Jewish culture. There are more Jews in the New York metropolitan area than in all of Israel. The heart of this Jewish culture is on the lower East Side of Manhattan, in a small, relatively poor neighborhood founded more than a century ago by Jewish immigrants from Europe. This neighborhood has retained many aspects of Jewish culture that have been lost elsewhere in the United States. The ancient custom of hiring a matchmaker to find a husband or wife, for example, is still practiced here by some people. There are also daily newspapers printed in Yiddish as well as English for Jewish readers all around the city. One of these newspapers is called the *Jewish Daily Forward*, sometimes referred to simply as the *Forward*.

- A little farther uptown, but still considered downtown, was the Yiddish theater district along *Second Avenue* in Manhattan. Yiddish theater was, essentially, the Jewish-American form of theater that became a rich source of American plays, playwrights, and performers during the first half of the twentieth century.

- The Rothschild* name is commonly used as a synonym for wealth.

---

*The Rothschild family, whose fortunes span the late eighteenth through the early twentieth centuries, made their money as bankers and industrialists in England, France, and later in the United States. The particular Rothschild mentioned in the story may be Meyer Rothschild (1840–1915).

The Magic Barrel

BERNARD MALAMUD

Not long ago there lived in uptown New York, in a small, almost meager room, though crowded with books, Leo Finkle, a rabbinical student in the Yeshiva University. Finkle, after six years of study, was to be ordained in June and had been advised by an acquaintance that he might find it easier to win himself a congregation if he were married. Since he had no present prospects of marriage, after two tormented days of turning it over in his mind, he called in Pinye Salzman, a marriage broker whose two-line advertisement he had read in the *Forward*.

The matchmaker appeared one night out of the dark fourth-floor hallway of the graystone rooming house where Finkle lived, grasping a black, strapped portfolio that had been worn thin with use. Salzman, who had been long in the business, was of slight but dignified build, wearing an old hat, and an overcoat too short and tight for him. He smelled frankly of fish, which he loved to eat, and although he was missing a few teeth, his presence was not displeasing, because of an amiable manner curiously contrasted with mournful eyes. His voice, his lips, his wisp of beard, his bony fingers were animated, but give him a moment of repose and his mild blue eyes revealed a depth of sadness, a characteristic that put Leo a little at ease although the situation, for him, was inherently tense.

He at once informed Salzman why he had asked him to come, explaining that his home was in Cleveland, and that but for his parents, who had married comparatively late in life, he was alone in the world. He had for six years devoted himself almost entirely to his studies, as a result of which, understandably, he had found himself without time for a social life and the company of young women. Therefore he thought it the better part of trial and error—of embarrassing fumbling—to call in an experienced person to advise him on these matters. He remarked in passing that the function of the marriage broker was ancient and honorable, highly approved in the Jewish community, because it made practical the necessary without hindering joy. Moreover, his own parents had been brought together by a matchmaker. They had made, if not a financially profitable marriage—since neither had possessed any worldly goods to speak of—at least a successful one in the sense of their everlasting devotion to each other. Salzman listened in embarrassed surprise, sensing a sort of apology. Later, however, he experienced a glow of pride in his work, an emotion that had left him years ago, and he heartily approved of Finkle.

The two went to their business. Leo had led Salzman to the only clear place in the room, a table near a window that overlooked the lamp-lit city. He seated himself at the matchmaker's side but facing him, attempting by an act of will to suppress the unpleasant tickle in his throat. Salzman eagerly unstrapped his portfolio and removed a loose rubber band from a thin packet of much-handled cards. As he flipped through them, a gesture and sound that physically hurt Leo, the student pretended not to see and gazed steadfastly out the window. Although it was still February, winter was on its last legs, signs of which he had for the first time in years begun to notice. He now observed the round white

moon, moving high in the sky through a cloud menagerie, and watched with half-open mouth as it penetrated a huge hen, and dropped out of her like an egg laying itself. Salzman, though pretending through eyeglasses he had just slipped on, to be engaged in scanning the writing on the cards, stole occasional glances at the young man's distinguished face, noting with pleasure the long, severe scholar's nose, brown eyes heavy with learning, sensitive yet ascetic lips, and a
50   certain, almost hollow quality of the dark cheeks. He gazed around at shelves upon shelves of books and let out a soft, contented sigh.

When Leo's eyes fell upon the cards, he counted six spread out in Salzman's hand.

"So few?" he asked in disappointment.

"You wouldn't believe me how much cards I got in my office," Salzman replied. "The drawers are already filled to the top, so I keep them now in a barrel, but is every girl good for a new rabbi?"

Leo blushed at this, regretting all he had revealed of himself in a curriculum vitae he had sent to Salzman. He had thought it best to acquaint him with his
60   strict standards and specifications, but in having done so, he felt he had told the marriage broker more than was absolutely necessary.

He hesitantly inquired, "Do you keep photographs of your clients on file?"

"First comes family, amount of dowry, also what kind promises," Salzman replied, unbuttoning his tight coat and settling himself in the chair. "After comes pictures, rabbi."

"Call me Mr. Finkle. I'm not yet a rabbi."

Salzman said he would, but instead called him doctor, which he changed to rabbi when Leo was not listening too attentively.

Salzman adjusted his horn-rimmed spectacles, gently cleared his throat and
70   read in an eager voice the contents of the top card:

"Sophie P. Twenty four years. Widow one year. No children. Educated high school and two years college. Father promises eight thousand dollars. Has wonderful wholesale business. Also real estate. On the mother's side comes teachers, also one actor. Well known on Second Avenue."

Leo gazed up in surprise. "Did you say a widow?"

"A widow don't mean spoiled, rabbi. She lived with her husband maybe four months. He was a sick boy she made a mistake to marry him."

"Marrying a widow has never entered my mind."

"This is because you have no experience. A widow, especially if she is young
80   and healthy like this girl, is a wonderful person to marry. She will be thankful to you the rest of her life. Believe me, if I was looking now for a bride, I would marry a widow."

Leo reflected, then shook his head.

Salzman hunched his shoulders in an almost imperceptible gesture of disappointment. He placed the card down on the wooden table and began to read another.

"Lily H. High school teacher. Regular. Not a substitute. Has savings and new Dodge car. Lived in Paris one year. Father is successful dentist thirty-five years. Interested in professional man. Well Americanized family. Wonderful opportunity."

"I knew her personally," said Salzman. "I wish you could see this girl. She is a   90
doll. Also very intelligent. All day you could talk to her about books and theater
and what not. She also knows current events."

"I don't believe you mentioned her age?"

"Her age?" Salzman said, raising his brows. "Her age is thirty-two years."

Leo said after a while. "I'm afraid that seems a little too old."

Salzman let out a laugh. "So how old are you, rabbi?"

"Twenty-seven."

"So what is the difference, tell me, between twenty-seven and thirty-two? My
own wife is seven years older than me. So what did I suffer?—Nothing. If Rothschild's daughter wants to marry you, would you say on account of her age, no?"   100

"Yes," Leo said dryly.

Salzman shook off the no in the yes. "Five years don't mean a thing. I give you
my word that when you will live with her for one week you will forget her age.
What does it mean five years—that she lived more and knows more than somebody who is younger? On this girl, God bless her, years are not wasted. Each one
that it comes makes better the bargain."

"What subject does she teach in high school?"

"Languages. If you heard the way she speaks French, you will think it is music.
I am in the business twenty-five years, and I recommend her with my whole
heart. Believe me, I know what I'm talking, rabbi."   110

"What's on the next card?" Leo said abruptly.

Salzman reluctantly turned up the third card:

"Ruth K. Nineteen years. Honor student. Father offers thirteen thousand cash
to the right bridegroom. He is a medical doctor. Stomach specialist with marvelous practice. Brother in law owns own garment business. Particular people."

Salzman looked as if he had read his trump card.°

"Did you say nineteen?" Leo asked with interest.

"On the dot."

"Is she attractive?" He blushed. "Pretty?"

Salzman kissed his finger tips. "A little doll. On this I give you my word. Let me   120
call the father tonight and you will see what means pretty."

But Leo was troubled. "You're sure she's that young?"

"This I am positive. The father will show you the birth certificate."

"Are you positive there isn't something wrong with her?" Leo insisted.

"Who says there is wrong?"

"I don't understand why an American girl her age should go to a marriage
broker."

A smile spread over Salzman's face.

"So for the same reason you went, she comes."

Leo flushed. "I am pressed for time."   130

Salzman, realizing he had been tactless, quickly explained. "The father came,
not her. He wants she should have the best, so he looks around himself. When
we will locate the right boy he will introduce him and encourage. This makes a

°*trump card* in a card game, a card that will beat all others

better marriage than if a young girl without experience takes for herself. I don't have to tell you this."

"But don't you think this young girl believes in love?" Leo spoke uneasily.

Salzman was about to guffaw but caught himself and said soberly, "Love comes with the right person, not before."

Leo parted dry lips but did not speak. Noticing that Salzman had snatched a glance at the next card, he cleverly asked, "How is her health?"

140

"Perfect," Salzman said, breathing with difficulty. "Of course, she is a little lame on her right foot from an auto accident that it happened to her when she was twelve years, but nobody notices on account she is so brilliant and also beautiful."

Leo got up heavily and went to the window. He felt curiously bitter and up-braided himself for having called in the marriage broker. Finally, he shook his head.

"Why not?" Salzman persisted, the pitch of his voice rising.

"Because I detest stomach specialists."

"So what do you care what is his business? After you marry her do you need him? Who says he must come every Friday night in your house?"

150

Ashamed of the way the talk was going, Leo dismissed Salzman, who went home with heavy, melancholy eyes.

Though he had felt only relief at the marriage broker's departure, Leo was in low spirits the next day. He explained it as arising from Salzman's failure to pro-duce a suitable bride for him. He did not care for his type of clientele. But when Leo found himself hesitating whether to seek out another matchmaker, one more polished than Pinye, he wondered if it could be—his protestations to the con-trary,° and although he honored his father and mother—that he did not, in essence, care for the match-making institution? This thought he quickly put out of mind yet found himself still upset. All day he ran around in the woods—

160

missed an important appointment, forgot to give out his laundry, walked out of a Broadway cafeteria without paying and had to run back with the ticket in his hand; had not even recognized his landlady in the street when she passed with a friend and courteously called out, "A good evening to you, Doctor Finkle." By nightfall, however, he had regained sufficient calm to sink his nose into a book and there found peace from his thoughts.

Almost at once there came a knock on the door. Before Leo could say enter, Salzman, commercial cupid, was standing in the room. His face was gray and meager, his expression hungry, and he looked as if he would expire on his feet. Yet the marriage broker managed, by some trick of the muscles, to display a broad smile.

170

"So good evening. I am invited?"

Leo nodded, disturbed to see him again, yet unwilling to ask the man to leave.

Beaming still, Salzman laid his portfolio on the table. "Rabbi, I got for you tonight good news."

"I've asked you not to call me rabbi. I'm still a student."

"Your worries are finished. I have for you a first-class bride."

"Leave me in peace concerning this subject." Leo pretended lack of interest.

°*protestations to the contrary* claims that the opposite was true

"The world will dance at your wedding."

"Please, Mr. Salzman, no more."

"But first must come back my strength," Salzman said weakly. He fumbled with   180
the portfolio straps and took out of the leather case an oily paper bag, from
which he extracted a hard, seeded roll and a small, smoked white fish. With a
quick motion of his hand he stripped the fish out of its skin and began raven-
ously to chew. "All day in a rush," he muttered.

Leo watched him eat.

"A sliced tomato you have maybe?" Salzman hesitantly inquired.

"No."

The marriage broker shut his eyes and ate. When he had finished he carefully
cleaned up the crumbs and rolled up the remains of the fish, in the paper bag. His
spectacled eyes roamed the room until he discovered, amid some piles of books, a   190
one-burner gas stove. Lifting his hat he humbly asked, "A glass tea you got, rabbi?"

Conscience-stricken, Leo rose and brewed the tea. He served it with a chunk
of lemon and two cubes of lump sugar, delighting Salzman.

After he had drunk his tea, Salzman's strength and good spirits were restored.

"So tell me, rabbi," he said amiably, "you considered some more the three
clients I mentioned yesterday?"

"There was no need to consider."

"Why not?"

"None of them suits me."

"What then suits you?"   200

Leo let it pass because he could give only a confused answer.

Without waiting for a reply, Salzman asked, "You remember this girl I talked to
you—the high school teacher?"

"Age thirty-two?"

But, surprisingly, Salzman's face lit in a smile. "Age twenty-nine."

Leo shot him a look. "Reduced from thirty-two?"

"A mistake," Salzman avowed. "I talked today with the dentist. He took me to
his safety deposit box and showed me the birth certificate. She was twenty-nine
last August. They made her a party in the mountains where she went for her vacation. When her father spoke to me the first time I forgot to write the age and I   210
told you thirty-two, but now I remember this was a different client, a widow."

"The same one you told me about? I thought she was twenty-four?"

"A different. Am I responsible that the world is filled with widows?"

"No, but I'm not interested in them, nor for that matter, in school teachers."

Salzman pulled his clasped hands to his breast. Looking at the ceiling he de-
voutly exclaimed, "Yiddishe kinder,° what can I say to somebody that he is not
interested in high school teachers? So what then you are interested?"

Leo flushed but controlled himself.

"In what else will you be interested," Salzman went on, "if you not interested
in this fine girl that she speaks four languages and has personally in the bank ten   220
thousand dollars? Also her father guarantees further twelve thousand. Also she

°*Yiddishe kinder* Jewish children

has a new car, wonderful clothes, talks on all subjects, and she will give you a first-class home and children. How near do we come in our life to paradise?"

"If she's so wonderful, why wasn't she married ten years ago?"

"Why?" said Salzman with a heavy laugh. "—Why? Because she is *partikiler*.° This is why. She wants the *best*."

Leo was silent, amused at how he had entangled himself. But Salzman had aroused his interest in Lily H., and he began seriously to consider calling on her. When the marriage broker observed how intently Leo's mind was at work on the facts he had supplied, he felt certain they would soon come to an agreement.

230

Late Saturday afternoon, conscious of Salzman, Leo Finkle walked with Lily Hirschorn along Riverside Drive. He walked briskly and erectly, wearing with distinction the black fedora he had that morning taken with trepidation out of the dusty hat box on his closet shelf, and the heavy black Saturday coat he had thoroughly whisked clean. Leo also owned a walking stick, a present from a distant relative, but quickly put temptation aside and did not use it. Lily, petite and not unpretty, had on something signifying the approach of spring. She was au courant,° animatedly, with all sorts of subjects, and he weighed her words and found her surprisingly sound—score another for Salzman, whom he uneasily

240   sensed to be somewhere around, hiding perhaps high in a tree along the street, flashing the lady signals with a pocket mirror; or perhaps a cloven-hoofed Pan,° piping nuptial ditties° as he danced his invisible way before them, strewing wild buds on the walk and purple grapes in their path, symbolizing fruit of a union,° though there was of course still none.

Lily startled Leo by remarking, "I was thinking of Mr. Salzman, a curious figure, wouldn't you say?"

Not certain what to answer, he nodded.

She bravely went on, blushing, "I for one am grateful for his introducing us. Aren't you?"

250   He courteously replied, "I am."

"I mean," she said with a little laugh—and it was all in good taste, or at least gave the effect of being not in bad—"do you mind that we came together so?"

He was not displeased with her honesty, recognizing that she meant to set the relationship aright,° and understanding that it took a certain amount of experience in life, and courage, to want to do it quite that way. One had to have some sort of past to make that kind of beginning.

He said that he did not mind. Salzman's function was traditional and honorable—valuable for what it might achieve, which, he pointed out, was frequently nothing.

°*partikiler* Salzman's pronunciation of "particular"

°*au courant* knowledgeable about current events and styles

°*Pan* a mythical creature, half man and half goat

°*piping nuptial ditties* playing wedding songs on a flute

°*fruit of the union* children from a marriage

°*set the relationship aright* be straightforward or correct a misunderstanding

Lily agreed with a sigh. They talked on for a while and she said after a long si- 260
lence, again with a nervous laugh, "Would you mind if I asked you something a
little bit personal? Frankly, I find the subject fascinating." Although Leo shrugged,
she went on half embarrassedly, "How was it that you came to your calling? I
mean was it a sudden passionate inspiration?"

Leo, after a time, slowly replied, "I was always interested in the Law."

"You saw revealed in it the presence of the Highest?"

He nodded and changed the subject. "I understand that you spent a little time
in Paris, Miss Hirschorn?"

"Oh, did Mr. Salzman tell you, Rabbi Finkle?" Leo winced but she went on, "It
was ages ago and almost forgotten. I remember I had to return for my sister's 270
wedding."

And Lily would not be put off. "When," she asked in a trembly voice, "did you
become enamored of God?"

He stared at her. Then it came to him that she was talking not about Leo
Finkle, but of a total stranger, some mystical figure, perhaps even passionate
prophet that Salzman had dreamed up for her—no relation to the living or dead.
Leo trembled with rage and weakness. The trickster had obviously sold her a bill
of goods,° just as he had him, who'd expected to become acquainted with a
young lady of twenty-nine, only to behold, the moment he laid eyes upon her
strained and anxious face, a woman past thirty-five and aging rapidly. Only his 280
self control had kept him this long in her presence.

"I am not," he said gravely, "a talented religious person," and in seeking words to
go on, found himself possessed by shame and fear. "I think," he said in a strained
manner, "that I came to God not because I loved him, but because I did not."

This confession he spoke harshly because its unexpectedness shook him.

Lily wilted. Leo saw a profusion of loaves of bread go flying like ducks high
over his head, not unlike the winged loaves by which he had counted himself to
sleep last night. Mercifully, then, it snowed, which he would not put past Salzman's machinations.

He was infuriated with the marriage broker and swore he would throw him 290
out of the room the minute he reappeared. But Salzman did not come that night,
and when Leo's anger had subsided, an unaccountable despair grew in its place.
At first he thought this was caused by his disappointment in Lily, but before long
it became evident that he had involved himself with Salzman without a true
knowledge of his own intent. He gradually realized—with an emptiness that
seized him with six hands—that he had called in the broker to find him a bride
because he was incapable of doing it himself. This terrifying insight he had de-
rived as a result of his meeting and conversation with Lily Hirschorn. Her prob-
ing questions had somehow irritated him into revealing—to himself more than
her—the true nature of his relationship to God, and from that it had come upon 300
him, with shocking force, that apart from his parents, he had never loved anyone.
Or perhaps it went the other way, that he did not love God so well as he might,
because he had not loved man. It seemed to Leo that his whole life stood starkly

°*sold her a bill of goods* lied to her to catch her interest

revealed and he saw himself for the first time as he truly was—unloved and love-less. This bitter but somehow not fully unexpected revelation brought him to a point of panic controlled only by extraordinary effort. He covered his face with his hands and cried.

The week that followed was the worst of his life. He did not eat and lost weight. His beard darkened and grew ragged. He stopped attending seminars and
310   almost never opened a book. He seriously considered leaving the Yeshiva, al-though he was deeply troubled at the thought of the loss of all his years of study—saw them like pages torn from a book, strewn over the city—and at the devastating effect of this decision upon his parents. But he had lived with knowl-edge of himself, and never in the Five Books and all the Commentaries—mea culpa°—had the truth been revealed to him. He did not know where to turn, and in all this desolating loneliness there was no *to whom,* although he often thought of Lily but not once could bring himself to go downstairs and make the call. He be-came touchy and irritable, especially with his landlady, who asked him all manner of personal questions; on the other hand, sensing his own disagreeableness, he
320   waylaid her on the stairs and apologized abjectly, until mortified, she ran from him. Out of this, however, he drew the consolation° that he was a Jew and that a Jew suffered. But gradually, as the long and terrible week drew to a close, he re-gained his composure and some idea of purpose in life: to go on as planned. Al-though he was imperfect, the ideal was not. As for his quest of a bride, the thought of continuing afflicted him with anxiety and heartburn, yet perhaps with this new knowledge of himself he would be more successful than in the past. Perhaps love would now come to him and a bride to that love. And for this sanctified seeking who needed a Salzman?

The marriage broker, a skeleton with haunted eyes, returned that very night. He
330   looked, withal, the picture of frustrated expectancy—as if he had steadfastly waited the week at Miss Lily Hirschorn's side for a telephone call that never came.

Casually coughing, Salzman came immediately to the point: "So how did you like her?"

Leo's anger rose and he could not refrain from chiding the matchmaker: "Why did you lie to me, Salzman?"

Salzman's pale face went dead white, the world had snowed on him.

"Did you not state that she was twenty-nine?" Leo insisted.

"I gave you my word—"

"She was thirty-five, if a day. *At least* thirty-five."
340   "Of this don't be too sure. Her father told me—"

"Never mind. The worst of it was that you lied to her."

"How did I lie to her, tell me?"

"You told her things about me that weren't true. You made me out to be more, consequently less than I am. She had in mind a totally different person, a sort of semimystical Wonder Rabbi."

"All I said, you was a religious man."

°*mea culpa* Latin for "my fault"
°*drew the consolation* found something positive in a bad situation

"I can imagine."

Salzman sighed. "This is my weakness that I have," he confessed. "My wife says to me I shouldn't be a salesman, but when I have two fine people that they would be wonderful to be married, I am so happy that I talk too much." He smiled wanly.   350
"This is why Salzman is a poor man."

Leo's anger left him. "Well, Salzman, I'm afraid that's all."

The marriage broker fastened hungry eyes on him.

"You don't want any more a bride?"

"I do," said Leo, "but I have decided to seek her in a different way. I am no longer interested in an arranged marriage. To be frank, I now admit the necessity of premarital love. That is, I want to be in love with the one I marry."

"Love?" said Salzman, astounded. After a moment he remarked "For us, our love is our life, not for the ladies. In the ghetto they—"

"I know, I know," said Leo. "I've thought of it often. Love, I have said to myself,   360
should be a by-product of living and worship rather than its own end. Yet for myself I find it necessary to establish the level of my need and fulfill it."

Salzman shrugged but answered, "Listen, rabbi, if you want love, this I can find for you also. I have such beautiful clients that you will love them the minute your eyes will see them."

Leo smiled unhappily. "I'm afraid you don't understand."

But Salzman hastily unstrapped his portfolio and withdrew a manila packet from it.

"Pictures," he said, quickly laying the envelope on the table.

Leo called after him to take the pictures away, but as if on the wings of the   370
wind, Salzman had disappeared.

March came. Leo had returned to his regular routine. Although he felt not quite himself yet—lacked energy—he was making plans for a more active social life. Of course it would cost something, but he was an expert at cutting corners; and when there were no corners left he would make circles rounder. All the while Salzman's pictures had laid on the table, gathering dust. Occasionally as Leo sat studying, or enjoying a cup of tea, his eyes fell on the manila envelope, but he never opened it.

The days went by and no social life to speak of developed with a member of the opposite sex—it was difficult, given the circumstances of his situation. One   380
morning Leo toiled up the stairs to his room and stared out the window at the city. Although the day was bright his view of it was dark. For some time he watched people in the street below hurrying along and then turned with a heavy heart to his little room. On the table was the packet. With a sudden relentless gesture he tore it open. For a half-hour he stood by the table in a state of excitement, examining the photographs of the ladies Salzman had included. Finally, with a deep sigh he put them down. There were six, of varying degrees of attractiveness, but look at them long enough and they all became Lily Hirschorn; all past their prime, all starved behind bright smiles, not a true personality in the lot. Life, despite their frantic yoohooings,° had passed them by; they were pictures in a brief   390

°*yoohooings* calling out to get attention

case that stunk of fish. After a while, however, as Leo attempted to return the photographs into the envelope, he found in it another, a snapshot of the type taken by
a machine for a quarter. He gazed at it a moment and let out a cry.

Her face deeply moved him. Why, he could at first not say. It gave him the impression of youth—spring flowers, yet age—a sense of having been used to the
bone, wasted; this came from the eyes, which were hauntingly familiar, yet absolutely strange. He had a vivid impression that he had met her before, but try as
he might he could not place her although he could almost recall her name, as
if he had read it in her own handwriting. No, this couldn't be; he would have re-
400   membered her. It was not, he affirmed, that she had an extraordinary beauty—
no, though her face was attractive enough; it was that *something* about her
moved him. Feature for feature, even some of the ladies of the photographs
could do better; but she leaped forth to his heart—had *lived*, or wanted to—
more than just wanted, perhaps regretted how she had lived—had somehow
deeply suffered: it could be seen in the depths of those reluctant eyes, and from
the way the light enclosed and shone from her, and within her, opening realms
of possibility: this was her own. Her he desired. His head ached and eyes narrowed with the intensity of his gazing, then as if an obscure fog had blown up in
the mind, he experienced fear of her and was aware that he had received an im-
410   pression, somehow, of evil. He shuddered, saying softly, it is thus with us all. Leo
brewed some tea in a small pot and sat sipping it without sugar, to calm himself.
But before he had finished drinking, again with excitement he examined the
face and found it good: good for Leo Finkle. Only such a one could understand
him and help him seek whatever he was seeking. She might, perhaps, love him.
How she had happened to be among the discards in Salzman's barrel he could
never guess, but he knew he must urgently go find her.

Leo rushed downstairs, grabbed up the Bronx telephone book, and searched
for Salzman's home address. He was not listed, nor was his office. Neither was he
in the Manhattan book. But Leo remembered having written down the address
420   on a slip of paper after he had read Salzman's advertisement in the "personals"
column of the *Forward*. He ran up to his room and tore through his papers,
without luck. It was exasperating. Just when he needed the matchmaker he was
nowhere to be found. Fortunately Leo remembered to look in his wallet. There
on a card he found his name written and a Bronx address. No phone number
was listed, the reason—Leo now recalled—he had originally communicated with
Salzman by letter. He got on his coat, put a hat on over his skull cap° and hurried
to the subway station. All the way to the far end of the Bronx he sat on the edge
of his seat. He was more than once tempted to take out the picture and see if
the girl's face was as he remembered it, but he refrained, allowing the snapshot
430   to remain in his coat pocket, content to have her so close. When the train pulled
into the station he was waiting at the door and bolted out. He quickly located
the street Salzman had advertised.

The building he sought was less than a block from the subway, but it was not
an office building, nor even a loft, nor a store in which one could rent office

---

°*skull cap* a small cap sometimes worn by Jewish men

space. It was a very old tenement house. Leo found Salzman's name in pencil on a soiled tag under the bell and climbed three dark flights to his apartment. When he knocked, the door was opened by a thin, asthmatic, gray-haired woman, in felt slippers.

"Yes?" she said, expecting nothing. She listened without listening. He could have sworn he had seen her, too, before you knew it was an illusion.   440

"Salzman—does he live here? Pinye Salzman," he said, "the matchmaker?"

She stared at him a long minute. "Of course."

He felt embarrassed. "Is he in?"

"No." Her mouth, though left open, offered nothing more.

"The matter is urgent. Can you tell me where his office is?"

"In the air." She pointed upward.

"You mean he has no office?" Leo asked.

"In his socks."

He peered into the apartment. It was sunless and dingy, one large room divided by a half-open curtain, beyond which he could see a sagging metal bed.   450
The near side of a room was crowded with rickety chairs, old bureaus, a three-legged table, racks of cooking utensils, and all the apparatus of a kitchen. But there was no sign of Salzman or his magic barrel, probably also a figment of the imagination.° An odor of frying fish made Leo weak to the knees.

"Where is he?" he insisted. "I've got to see your husband."

At length she answered, "So who knows where he is? Every time he thinks a new thought he runs to a different place. Go home, he will find you."

"Tell him Leo Finkle."

She gave no sign she had heard.

He walked downstairs, depressed.   460

But Salzman, breathless, stood waiting at his door.

Leo was astounded and overjoyed. "How did you get here before me?"

"I rushed."

"Come inside."

They entered. Leo fixed tea, and a sardine sandwich for Salzman. As they were drinking he reached behind him for the packet of pictures and handed them to the marriage broker.

Salzman put down his glass and said expectantly, "You found somebody you like?"

"Not among these."   470

The marriage broker turned away.

"Here is the one I want." Leo held forth the snapshot.

Salzman slipped on his glasses and took the picture into his trembling hand. He turned ghastly and let out a groan.

"What's the matter?" cried Leo.

"Excuse me. Was an accident this picture. She isn't for you."

Salzman frantically shoved the manila packet into his portfolio. He thrust the snapshot into his pocket and fled down the stairs.

°*figment of the imagination* something imagined

Leo, after momentary paralysis, gave chase and cornered the marriage broker
480   in the vestibule. The landlady made hysterical outcries but neither of them
listened.

"Give me back the picture, Salzman."

"No." The pain in his eyes was terrible.

"Tell me who she is then."

"This I can't tell you. Excuse me."

He made to depart, but Leo, forgetting himself, seized the matchmaker by his
tight coat and shook him frenziedly.

"Please," sighed Salzman. *"Please."*

Leo ashamedly let him go. "Tell me who she is," he begged. "It's very important
490   for me to know."

"She is not for you. She is a wild one—wild, without shame. This is not a bride
for a rabbi."

"What do you mean wild?"

"Like an animal. Like a dog. For her to be poor was a sin. This is why to me
she is dead now."

"In God's name, what do you mean?"

"Her I can't introduce to you," Salzman said.

"Why are you so excited?"

"Why, he asks," Salzman said, bursting into tears. "This is my baby, my Stella,
500   she should burn in hell."

Leo hurried up to bed and hid under the covers. Under the covers he
thought his life through. Although he soon fell asleep he could not sleep her
out of his mind. He woke, beating his breast. Though he prayed to be rid of her,
his prayers went unanswered. Through days of torment he endlessly struggled
not to love her; fearing success, he escaped it. He then concluded to convert
her to goodness, himself to God. The idea alternately nauseated and exalted
him.°

He perhaps did not know that he had come to a final decision until he en-
countered Salzman in a Broadway cafeteria. He was sitting alone at a rear table,
510   sucking the bony remains of a fish. The marriage broker appeared haggard, and
transparent to the point of vanishing.

Salzman looked up at first without recognizing him. Leo had grown a pointed
beard and his eyes were weighted with wisdom.

"Salzman," he said, "love has at last come to my heart."

"Who can love from a picture?" mocked the marriage broker.

"It is not impossible."

"If you can love her, then you can love anybody. Let me show you some new
clients that they just sent me their photographs. One is a little doll."

"Just her I want," Leo murmured.
520   "Don't be a fool, doctor. Don't bother with her."

°*exalted him* filled him with joy

"Put me in touch with her, Salzman," Leo said humbly. "Perhaps I can be of service."

Salzman had stopped eating and Leo understood with emotion that it was now arranged.

Leaving the cafeteria, he was, however, afflicted by a tormenting suspicion that Salzman had planned it all to happen this way.

Leo was informed by letter that she would meet him on a certain corner, and she was there one spring night, waiting under a street lamp. He appeared, carrying a small bouquet of violets and rosebuds. Stella stood by the lamp post, smoking. She wore white with red shoes, which fitted his expectations, although in a troubled moment he had imagined the dress red, and only the shoes white. She waited uneasily and shyly. From afar he saw that her eyes—clearly her father's—were filled with desperate innocence. He pictured, in her, his own redemption. Violins and lit candles° revolved in the sky. Leo ran forward with flowers outthrust. 530

Around the corner, Salzman, leaning against a wall, chanted prayers for the dead.

ANALYZING THE STORY

ACTIVITY 3

Answer the following questions. Give evidence from the story to support your answers, where appropriate, and include line numbers for each piece of evidence.

1. In what season does the story begin and in what season does it end? What associations do you have with each of these times of year?

2. What reasons does Leo Finkle give to Pinye Salzman about why he wants to hire a matchmaker?

3. What is the barrel that is referred to in the title of the story?

4. How many cards does Salzman bring to show Leo, and what is the condition of those cards? What does this suggest about Salzman's work?

5. At the beginning of the story, how has Salzman been feeling about his work lately? What might be one reason he feels this way?

6. The following excerpts are Salzman's descriptions of the prospective brides. What kind of information about the women is missing from all of the descriptions?

   - "'Twenty four years. Widow one year. No children. Educated high school and two years college. Father promises eight thousand dollars. Has wonderful wholesale business. Also real estate. On the mother's side comes teachers, also one actor. Well known on Second Avenue.'" (lines 71–74)

°*violins and lit candles* items used in a Jewish wedding ceremony; in a nonreligious setting, these items are associated with romance

- "'High school teacher. Regular. Not a substitute. Has savings and new Dodge car. Lived in Paris one year. Father is successful dentist thirty-five years. Interested in professional man. Well Americanized family. Wonderful opportunity.'" (lines 87–89)
- "'Nineteen years. Honor student. Father offers thirteen thousand cash to the right bridegroom. He is a medical doctor. Stomach specialist with marvelous practice. Brother in law owns own garment business. Particular people.'" (lines 113–115)

7. What do the descriptions in the preceding items remind you of in modern publications? Read the excerpts aloud. Who might use descriptions such as these? Where might you read such descriptions?

8. Does Leo seem interested in the qualities that Salzman points out in his descriptions? What kinds of questions does Leo ask Salzman after the matchmaker describes each client? What does Leo specifically ask after Salzman describes Sophie P.? After Lily H.? After Ruth K.?

9. What happens while Lily and Leo are on their date? What does Lily say, and why does this make Leo angry?

10. What are your impressions of Stella based on what Leo sees in the picture, what her father says about her, and her brief appearance at the end of the story?

11. What elements of magic have you noticed in the story? Find at least four places in the story when something magical happens. How and when does Salzman come and go at these times? What is magical about Salzman's barrel?

Elements of Literature

Characterization

ACTIVITY 4

The following chart is designed to help you record important information about the characters and is divided into three sections based on the story's **plot.** (See Appendix A for more information about terms in boldface type.) In the first section, readers are introduced to the characters, and a conflict is established. The conflict becomes increasingly complicated until, in the second part, it reaches a climax. In the third part, the action begins to fall as the conflict is resolved, although in an ambigious way.

1. For each quotation from the story cited by line number in the chart, do the following:
   a. Write a few notes about what each character says, thinks, or does.
   b. Write the physical description of each character (if any), noting, in particular, references to the eyes.

   The first one is done for you.

LEO FINKLE		PINYE SALZMAN	
LINES	NOTES	LINES	NOTES
Part 1		Part 1	
19–34	*alone in the world; devoted to studies*	8–18	*slight but dignified build; old hat, overcoat too short and tight; smells of fish*
35–51		67–68	
139–140		150–151	
		180–194	
Part 2		Part 2	
290–328		329–331	
Part 3		Part 3	
372–378		508–511	
501–507		523–524	
512–513			

2. Use the information in the chart to answer these questions. Be prepared to explain your answers to the class.

Leo Finkle and Pinye Salzman

a. List all the similarities and differences between the two men, noting age, appearance, habits, behavior, and beliefs.
b. As the story progresses, what changes do you notice in Salzman's physical appearance? What might be happening to him?
c. What changes do you notice in Leo's physical appearance? The **narrator** refers to Leo's eyes near the end of the story. (line 513) What has happened to him?

d. Leo asks Salzman not to call him rabbi since he isn't a rabbi yet. Salzman agrees, but then resumes calling him rabbi "when Leo is not listening too attentively." (line 68) Why do you think Salzman does this, and what does the behavior suggest about his character?

e. Does Salzman like Leo when they first meet? Explain. Find specific evidence.

f. In the beginning of the story, Salzman's "mild blue eyes" and their "depth of sadness" make Leo feel "at ease." (lines 16–17) As the story progresses, how do Leo's feelings about Salzman change? Find at least three examples. Explain the possible reasons for the change.

Stella

a. From lines 394–410 and lines 529–533, divide the words and phrases that describe Stella into two lists that suggest contrasting characteristics.

REFERENCES WITH POSITIVE CONNOTATIONS	REFERENCES WITH NEGATIVE CONNOTATIONS
"youth" (line 395) "spring flowers" (line 395)	"used to the bone" (lines 395–396)

b. What do the descriptions in the chart suggest about what Stella has done in her life?

WRITING IN RESPONSE

Respond briefly to these questions in writing. Compare your responses with those of two or three classmates.

1. How would you describe the relationship between Leo Finkle and Pinye Salzman? In what ways, either directly or indirectly, does Salzman help Leo to understand who he is and what he wants?

2. Why do you think Leo is attracted to Stella?

Point of View

ACTIVITY 5

Discuss the following questions with a partner.

1. Malamud mostly uses **third-person omniscient point of view.** In "The Magic Barrel," however, he occasionally shifts to **third-person limited point of view,** giving us insight into the thoughts and feelings of a particular character. In each of the following quotations, whose point of view is represented? Underline key words that reveal the point of view.

   a. "Salzman, though pretending through eyeglasses he had just slipped on, to be engaged in scanning the writing on the cards, stole occasional glances at the young man's distinguished face, noting with pleasure the long, severe scholar's nose . . . ." (lines 46–49)

      Point of view: _____

   b. "Salzman, realizing he had been tactless, quickly explained." (line 131)

      Point of view: _____

   c. "Leo was silent, amused at how he had entangled himself." (line 227)

      Point of view: _____

   d. "She was au courant, animatedly, with all sorts of subjects, and he weighed her words and found her surprisingly sound—score another for Salzman, whom he uneasily sensed to be somewhere around . . . ." (lines 237–240)

      Point of view: _____

   e. "[Leo] gradually realized—with an emptiness that seized him with six hands—that he had called in the broker to find him a bride because he was incapable of doing it himself." (lines 295–297)

      Point of view: _____

   f. "How she had happened to be among the discards in Salzman's barrel he could never guess, but he knew he must urgently go find her." (lines 415–416)

      Point of view: _____

   g. "Leaving the cafeteria, he was, however, afflicted by a tormenting suspicion that Salzman had planned it all to happen this way." (lines 525–526)

      Point of view: _____

2. When Malamud uses a third-person limited point of view, whose point of view—Leo's or Salzman's—does he most often use?

WRITING IN RESPONSE

Write briefly on this topic.

In "The Magic Barrel," we learn a great deal about Leo's thoughts and feelings and how they change during the course of the story. However, the narrator gives us only occasional insights into Salzman's mind. Discuss how this manipulation of point of view adds to the "magic" of the story. Consider whether we should trust Leo's "suspicion that Salzman had planned it all to happen this way." (lines 525–526)

Foreshadowing

A C T I V I T Y   6

Foreshadowing is part of the magic and the humor in "The Magic Barrel." Malamud drops hints throughout the story about events or situations that will develop later.

Answering the following questions should help you explain how the related passages from the story illustrate foreshadowing.

1. Can you find hints toward the beginning of the story that might suggest Salzman planned to arrange a meeting between Leo and Stella from the beginning?

2. Salzman is described as "a skeleton with haunted eyes. . . . He looked . . . the picture of frustrated expectancy . . . ." (lines 329–330) What could he be expecting? Think of all the possibilities.

3. After Leo tells Salzman that what he wants is love, not just a bride, Salzman says ". . . if you want love, this I can find for you also. I have such beautiful clients that you will love them the minute your eyes will see them." (lines 363–365) Does the matchmaker fulfill his promise? Explain.

4. When Leo goes to Salzman's house, a "thin, asthmatic, gray-haired woman, in felt slippers" (lines 437–438) answers the door and "listen[s] without listening." (line 439) Who do you think the woman is, and why does Leo think "he had seen her, too"? (line 440)

WRITING IN RESPONSE

Respond briefly to these questions in writing. Compare your ideas with those of two or three classmates.

This story begins with "Not long ago there lived . . . ." These words often begin fairytales. Consider some typical fairytale plots that you know and their endings. Then explain how events toward the end of "The Magic Barrel" are foreshadowed by the first words of the story.

Exploring Further

Write or discuss the answers to these questions. Give evidence from the story to support your answers, and include line numbers for each piece of evidence.

Understanding Magical Elements

1. Toward the beginning of the story, Salzman appears "one night out of the dark." When and how does Salzman appear and disappear throughout the rest of the story?

2. Leo feels Salzman's presence in many instances when Salzman isn't actually there. How can you explain this?

3. According to Salzman's wife, where is the matchmaker's office? What are possible meanings of "in his socks"? (line 448)

4. What is magical about Salzman's barrel?

5. Do you think Salzman is someone or something other than who or what he appears to be? Explain.

Understanding Major Themes

1. What two important things does Leo learn about himself during his date with Lily and as a result of her question? (lines 290–307)

2. At the end of the story, Leo begs Salzman to "put [him] in touch with [Stella]." (line 521) He then says, "'Perhaps I can be of service.'" (lines 521–522) What could he mean by "be of service"?

3. Near the end of the story, Leo falls madly in love with the photo of Stella and concludes that he will "convert her to goodness, himself to God." (lines 505–506) Here, Leo is speaking of redemption. In the secular (nonreligious) sense, *redemption* means saving or rescuing oneself or someone else. Who is redeemed—and by whom—in the secular sense? In what ways is this character (or are these characters) saved and from what?

4. Why and for whom do you think Salzman recites the prayer for the dead at the end of the story? Consider all possibilities. First read this explanation: The "prayers for the dead" (lines 536–537) are part of the Kaddish, which is a prayer that concludes most public Jewish services. Typically, the entire congregation, or sometimes only those who are mourning the loss of a loved one, may be asked to stand and recite the Kaddish. This prayer is recited to remember the dead, but there is no mention of death in the prayer itself. The prayer praises and honors God.

WRITING IN RESPONSE

Write briefly on these topics.

1. Do you think that Salzman had "planned it [Leo's meeting Stella] all to happen this way" as Leo suggests? (line 526) Or do you think their meeting is simply part of the magic of this story? Is the answer important? Why or why not?

2. Discuss the story's ending as one of the magical elements.

ESSAY TOPICS

1. Malamud, in concluding an explanation of why he loved to write short stories, observed that "if [a writer] is lucky, serious things may seem funny." The idea that something can be both serious and funny is a **paradox.** In an essay, discuss the use of paradoxes in "The Magic Barrel," showing how they are related to your understanding of the story.

2. What is magic about "The Magic Barrel"? In an essay, discuss the magical elements in the theme, in the foreshadowing of events, in the setting, in the characters, and in the figurative language.

3. Near the end of "The Magic Barrel," Leo falls madly in love with Stella in the photo and concludes that he will "convert her to goodness, himself to God." (lines 505–506) Examine the story "The Magic Barrel" as a story of redemption. How is Leo redeemed? How is Stella redeemed? How is Salzman redeemed?

AUTHOR PROFILE

Bernard Malamud

Bernard Malamud (1914–1986) was born and raised in Brooklyn, New York. His parents, Russian-Jewish immigrants, and their lives became sources for much of Malamud's early writing. He said, "Without understanding why, I was thinking about my father's immigrant life—how he earned his living and what he paid for it, and about my mother's, diminished by fear and suffering . . . as I invented the characters who be-came their fictional counterparts." Suffering that leads to personal insight is at the cen-ter of much of Malamud's work. His male characters, often alone or alienated, must cast off egocentric notions of themselves in order to grow and to find commitment in relationships with others. Malamud's female characters are often minor and one di-mensional, helping only in the development of the central conflict of a male character.

Malamud often develops his concern for inner change and fulfillment in a parable, or fablelike style. He writes about human values and, in particular, love in a highly sym-bolic, sometimes fantastic or bizarre, fashion. His tone is often ironic, revealing his own attitude about the nature of human existence.

Malamud sold his first short story in 1949 and won the National Book Award in 1959 for the stories collected in the anthology *The Magic Barrel*. His novels include *The Natural* (1952), a baseball fantasy subsequently made into a movie; *The Assistant* (1957); and *The Fixer* (1966), also made into a movie.

CHAPTER 17

Romero's Shirt

DAGOBERTO GILB

PREPARATION

ACTIVITY 1

With a partner or in small groups, discuss the following questions.

1. On a map of the state of Texas, find the city of El Paso. What do you notice about where it is located? What important landmarks are nearby? What effect would the location of El Paso have on its people and economy?

2. What do you imagine the climate, land, and vegetation to be like in and around El Paso?

3. How would Mexico's closeness to El Paso affect the labor market in that city? What types of jobs would Mexican immigrants and day laborers do in and around El Paso?

4. Read the following description of the main character of "Romero's Shirt." From this description, what inferences can you make about this man and his background?

   ". . . a man not unlike many in this country, [who] has had jobs in factories, shops, and stores. He has painted houses, dug ditches, planted trees, hammered, sawed, bolted, snaked pipes, picked cotton and chile and pecans, each and all for wages." (lines 1–4)

Romero's Shirt

Dagoberto Gilb

Juan Romero, a man not unlike many in this country, has had jobs in factories, shops, and stores. He has painted houses, dug ditches, planted trees, hammered, sawed, bolted, snaked pipes,° picked cotton and chile° and pecans, each and all for wages. Along the way he has married and raised his children and several years ago he finally arranged it so that his money might pay for the house he and his family live in. He is still more than twenty years away from being the owner. It is a modest house even by El Paso standards. The building, in an adobe° style, is made of stone which is painted white, though the paint is gradually chipping off or being absorbed by the rock. It has two bedrooms, a den which is used as an-   10
other, a small dining area, a living room, a kitchen, one bathroom, and a garage which, someday, he plans to turn into another place to live. Although in a development facing a paved street and in a neighborhood, it has the appearance of being on almost half an acre. At the front is a garden of cactus—nopal, ocotillo, and agave—and there are weeds that grow tall with yellow flowers which seed into thorn-hard burrs. The rest is dirt and rocks of various sizes, some of which have been lined up to form a narrow path out of the graded dirt, a walkway to the front porch—where, under a tile and one-by tongue and groove overhang, are a wooden chair and a love seat, covered by an old bedspread, its legless frame on the red cement slab. Once the porch looked onto oak trees. Two of them are dried-out stumps; the remaining one has a limb or two which still can   20
produce leaves, but with so many amputations, its future is irreversible. Romero seldom runs water through a garden hose, though in the back yard some patchy grass can almost seem suburban, at least to him, when he does. Near the corner of his land, in the front, next to the sidewalk, is a juniper shrub, his only bright green plant, and Romero does not want it to yellow and die, so he makes special efforts on its behalf, washing off dust, keeping its leaves neatly pruned and shaped.

These days Romero calls himself a handyman. He does odd jobs, which is exactly how he advertises—"no job too small"—in the throwaway paper.° He hangs wallpaper and doors, he paints, lays carpet, does just about anything some-   30
one will call and ask him to do. It doesn't earn him much, and sometimes it's barely enough, but he's his own boss, and he's had so many bad jobs over those other years, ones no more dependable, he's learned that this suits him. At one time Romero did want more, and he'd believed that he could have it simply through work, but no matter what he did his children still had to be born at the county hospital. Even years later it was there that his oldest son went for serious medical treatment because Romero couldn't afford the private hospitals. He tried not to worry about how he earned his money. In Mexico, where his parents

°*snaked pipes* cleaned pipes with long, flexible metal cord
°*chile* pepper, ranging from mild to hot in flavor
°*adobe* sun-dried brick
°*throwaway paper* free newspaper for advertising jobs and items for sale

40   were born and he spent much of his youth, so many things weren't available, and any work which allowed for food, clothes, and housing was to be honored—by the standards there, Romero lived well. Except this wasn't Mexico, and even though there were those who did worse even here, there were many who did better and had more, and a young Romero too often felt ashamed by what he saw as his failure. But time passed, and he got older. As he saw it, he didn't live in poverty, and *here,* he finally came to realize, was where he was, where he and his family were going to stay. Life in El Paso was much like the land—hard, but one could make do with what was offered. Just as his parents had, Romero always thought it was a beautiful place for a home.

50   Yet people he knew left—to Houston, Dallas, Los Angeles, San Diego, Denver, Chicago—and came back for holidays with stories of high wages and acquisition. And more and more people crossed the river, in rags, taking work, his work, at any price. Romero constantly had to discipline himself by remembering the past, how his parents lived; he had to teach himself to appreciate what he did have. His car, for example, he'd kept up since his early twenties. He'd had it painted three times in that period and he worked on it so devotedly that even now it was in as good a condition as almost any car could be. For his children he tried to offer more—an assortment of clothes for his daughter, lots of toys for his sons. He denied his wife nothing, but she was a woman who asked for little. For him-self, it was much less. He owned some work clothes and T-shirts necessary for his

60   jobs as well as a set of good enough, he thought, shirts he'd had since before the car. He kept up a nice pair of custom boots, and in a closet hung a pair of slacks for a wedding or baptism or important mass. He owned two jackets, a leather one from Mexico and a warm nylon one for cold work days. And he owned a wool plaid Pendleton shirt, his favorite piece of clothing, which he'd bought right after the car and before his marriage because it really was good-looking be-sides being functional. He wore it anywhere and everywhere with confidence that its quality would always be both in style and appropriate.

The border was less than two miles below Romero's home, and he could see, down the dirt street which ran alongside his property, the desert and mountains

70   of Mexico. The street was one of the few in the city which hadn't yet been paved. Romero liked it that way, despite the run-off problems when heavy rains passed by, as they had the day before this day. A night wind had blown hard be-hind the rains, and the air was so clean he could easily see buildings in Juárez.° It was sunny, but a breeze told him to put on his favorite shirt before he pulled the car up alongside the house and dragged over the garden hose to wash it, which was something he still enjoyed doing as much as anything else. He was orga-nized, had a special bucket, a special sponge, and he used warm water from the kitchen sink. When he started soaping the car he worried about getting his shirt sleeves wet, and once he was moving around he decided a T-shirt would keep

80   him warm enough. So he took off the wool shirt and draped it, conspicuously, over the juniper near him, at the corner of his property. He thought that if he

°*Juárez* city in the Mexican state of Chihuahua

couldn't help but see it, he couldn't forget it, and forgetting something outside
was losing it. He lived near a school, and teenagers passed by all the time, and
also there was regular foot-traffic—many people walked the sidewalk in front of
his house, many who had no work.

After the car was washed, Romero went inside and brought out the car wax.
Waxing his car was another thing he still liked to do, especially on a weekday
like this one when he was by himself, when no one in his family was home. He
could work faster, but he took his time, spreading with a damp cloth, waiting,
then wiping off the crust with a dry cloth. The exterior done, he went inside the   90
car and waxed the dash, picked up some trash on the floorboard, cleaned out
the glove compartment. Then he went for some pliers he kept in a toolbox
in the garage, returned and began to wire up the rear license plate which had
lost a nut and bolt and was hanging awkwardly. As he did this, he thought of
other things he might do when he finished, like prune the juniper. Except his
old shears had broken, and he hadn't found another used pair, because he
wouldn't buy them new.

An old man walked up to him carrying a garden rake, a hoe, and some shears.
He asked Romero if there was some yard work needing to be done. After spring,
tall weeds grew in many yards, but it seemed a dumb question this time of year,   100
particularly since there was obviously so little ever to be done in Romero's yard.
But Romero listened to the old man. There were still a few weeds over there, and
he could rake the dirt so it'd be even and level, he could clip that shrub, and
probably there was something in the back if he were to look. Romero was
usually brusque with requests such as these, but he found the old man unique
and likeable and he listened and finally asked how much he would want for all
those tasks. The old man thought as quickly as he spoke and threw out a number. Ten. Romero repeated the number, questioningly, and the old man backed
up, saying well, eight, seven. Romero asked if that was for everything. Yes sir, the
old man said, excited that he'd seemed to catch a customer. Romero asked if he   110
would cut the juniper for three dollars. The old man kept his eyes on the ever-
green, disappointed for a second, then thought better of it. Okay, okay, he said,
but, I've been walking all day, you'll give me lunch? The old man rubbed his
striped cotton shirt at his stomach.

Romero liked the old man and agreed to it. He told him how he should follow
the shape which was already there, to cut it evenly, to take a few inches off all of
it just like a haircut. Then Romero went inside, scrambled enough eggs and chile
and cheese for both of them and rolled it all in some tortillas. He brought out a
beer.

The old man was clearly grateful, but since his gratitude was keeping the   120
work from getting done—he might talk an hour about his little ranch in Mexico,
about his little turkeys and his pig—Romero excused himself and went inside.
The old man thanked Romero for the food, and, as soon as he was finished with
the beer, went after the work sincerely. With dull shears—he sharpened them, so
to speak, against a rock wall—the old man snipped garishly, hopping and jumping around the bush, around and around. It gave Romero such great pleasure to
watch that this was all he did from his front window.

The work didn't take long, so, as the old man was raking up the clippings, Romero brought out a five-dollar bill. He felt that the old man's dancing around

130   that bush, in those baggy old checkered pants, was more inspiring than religion, and a couple of extra dollars was a cheap price to see old eyes whiten like a boy's.

The old man was so pleased that he invited Romero to that little ranch of his in Mexico where he was sure they could share some aguardiente,° or maybe Romero could buy a turkey from him—they were skinny but they could be fattened—but in any case they could enjoy a bottle of tequila° together, with some sweet lemons. The happy old man swore he would come back no matter what, for he could do many things for Romero at his beautiful home. He swore he would return, maybe in a week or two, for surely there was work that needed to be done in the back yard.

140   Romero wasn't used to feeling so virtuous. He so often was disappointed, so often dwelled on the difficulties of life, that he had become hard, guarding against compassion and generosity. So much so that he'd even become spare with his words, even with his family. His wife whispered to the children that this was because he was tired, and, since it wasn't untrue, he accepted it as the explanation too. It spared him that worry, and from having to discuss why he liked working weekends and taking a day off during the week, like this one. But now an old man had made Romero wish his family were there with him so he could give as much, *more*, to them too, so he could watch their spin-around dances— he'd missed so many—and Romero swore he would take them all into Juárez

150   that night for dinner. He might even convince them to take a day, maybe two, for a drive to his uncle's house in Chihuahua instead, because he'd promised that so many years ago—so long ago they probably thought about somewhere else by now, like San Diego, or Los Angeles. Then he'd take them there! They'd go for a week, spend whatever it took. No expense could be so great, and if happiness was as easy as some tacos and a five-dollar bill, then how stupid it had been of him not to have offered it all this time.

Romero felt so good, felt such relief, he napped on the couch. When he woke up he immediately remembered his shirt, that it was already gone before the old man had even arrived—he remembered they'd walked around the juniper before

160   it was cut. Nevertheless, the possibility that the old man took it wouldn't leave Romero's mind. Since he'd never believed in letting down, giving into someone like that old man, the whole experience became suspect. Maybe it was part of some ruse which ended with the old man taking his shirt, some food, money. This was how Romero thought. Though he held a hope that he'd left it somewhere else, that it was a lapse of memory on his part—he went outside, inside, looked everywhere twice, then one more time after that—his cynicism had flowered, colorful and bitter.

Understand that it was his favorite shirt, that he'd never thought of replacing it and that its loss was all Romero could keep his mind on, though he knew very

°*aguardiente* Latin American liquor made from sugar cane
°*tequila* Mexican liquor made from maguey, a type of cactus

well it wasn't a son, or a daughter, or a wife, or a mother or father, not a disaster   170
of any kind. It was a simple shirt, in the true value of things not very much to
lose. But understand also that Romero was a good man who tried to do what
was right and who would harm no one willfully. Understand that Romero was a
man who had taught himself to not care, to not want, to not desire for so long
that he'd lost many words, avoided many people, kept to himself, alone, almost always, even when his wife gave him his meals. Understand that it was his favorite
shirt and though no more than that, for him it was no less. Then understand how
he felt like a fool paying that old man who, he considered, might even have
taken it, like a fool for feeling so friendly and generous, happy, when the shirt
was already gone, like a fool for having all those and these thoughts for the love   180
of a wool shirt, like a fool for not being able to stop thinking them all, but especially the one reminding him that this was what he had always believed in, that
loss was what he was most prepared for. And so then you might understand why
he began to stare out the window of his home, waiting for someone to walk by
absently with it on, for the thief to pass by, careless. He kept a watch out the
window as each of his children came in, then his wife. He told them only what
had happened and, as always, they left him alone. He stared out that window
onto the dirt street, past the ocotillos and nopales and agaves, the junipers and
oaks and mulberries in front of other homes of brick or stone, painted or not,
past them to the buildings in Juárez, and he watched the horizon darken and the   190
sky light up with the moon and stars, and the land spread with shimmering
lights, so bright in the dark blot of night. He heard dogs barking until another
might bark farther away, and then another, back and forth like that, the small rec-
tangles and squares of their fences plotted out distinctly in his mind's eye as his
lids closed. Then he heard a gust of wind bend around his house, and then came
the train, the metal rhythm getting closer until it was as close as it could be, the
steel pounding the earth like a beating heart, until it diminished and then faded
away and then left the air to silence, to its quiet and dark, so still it was like
death, or rest, sleep, until he could hear a grackle,° and then another gust of
wind, and then finally a car.   200

He looked in on his daughter still so young, so beautiful, becoming a woman
who would leave that bed for another, his sons still boys when they were
asleep, who dreamed like men when they were awake, and his wife, still young
in his eyes in the morning shadows of their bed.

Romero went outside. The juniper had been cut just as he'd wanted it. He got
cold and came back in and went to the bed and blankets his wife kept so clean,
so neatly arranged as she slept under them without him, and he lay down beside her.

°*grackle* a bird that makes a whistling or "clacking" sound

ANALYZING THE STORY

ACTIVITY 2

Answer the following questions with a partner or in small groups. Give evidence from the story to support your answers and include line numbers for each piece of evidence.

1. Describe Juan Romero. Include his approximate age, his occupation, his lifestyle, his home, his family, where he was born, and how he grew up.

2. Why is Romero so fond of his favorite shirt? How does he describe it? Do you think the shirt is expensive? Why or why not? What does Romero's description of his shirt tell you about him?

3. What does Romero's process of washing and waxing his car reveal about him? Where is the shirt during this time? Why does Romero decide to put it there?

4. Describe the interaction between the old man and Romero. How is the old man successful in getting Romero to agree to hire him to do work in the yard? What else does he convince Romero to do? Is Romero's behavior unusual for him? Explain.

5. Why does it give "Romero such great pleasure to watch [the old man] that this was all he did from his front window"? (lines 126–127)

6. How does the old man express his gratitude toward Romero? How does Romero respond?

7. What does Romero decide to do for his family as a result of his interaction with the old man? Why do you think Romero wants to do this?

8. After his nap, when Romero remembers his shirt, how do his feelings about the old man and his earlier interactions with him change?

9. Why do you think Romero "kept a watch out the window" until his family came home? (lines 185–186)

10. What do we learn about Romero and his relationship with his family when he "told them only what had happened and, as always, they left him alone." (lines 186–187) Why is the word *only* important? What didn't he tell them?

WRITING IN RESPONSE

In a few paragraphs, describe a favorite possession of yours or describe someone else's. Why is this possession important? How does the owner feel about it? What does it reveal about you or the person who owns it?

Elements of Literature

Characterization

ACTIVITY 3

Answer the following questions about **characterization** in "Romero's Shirt." (See Appendix A for more information about terms in boldface type.)

1. Reread lines 140–167. Then fill out the following chart with what you learn about Romero from his interaction with the old man: his past, his relationships, and his attitudes and values. Refer to the examples and provide line numbers as support.

ROMERO'S PAST	ROMERO'S RELATIONSHIPS	ROMERO'S ATTITUDES AND VALUES
disappointing and difficult (lines 140–141)	*didn't communicate openly with his family (lines 142–143)*	*wasn't used to feeling virtuous (line 140)*
		guarded against compassion and generosity (lines 141–142)

2. Explain what Romero's interaction with the old man reveals about Romero in the following two passages:
   - Romero "felt that the old man's dancing around the bush . . . was more inspiring than religion, and a couple of extra dollars was a cheap price to see old eyes whiten like a boy's." (lines 129–131)
   - "Romero felt so good, felt such relief, he napped on the couch." (line 157)

3. When Romero woke after his nap, "he immediately remembered his shirt, that it was already gone before the old man had even arrived. . . . Nevertheless, the possibility that the old man took it wouldn't leave [his] mind." (lines 158–161) Why is this the case?

4. Discuss the significance of the following lines: "Though he held a hope that he'd left [the shirt] somewhere else, that it was a lapse of memory on his part— he went outside, inside, looked everywhere twice, then one more time after that—his cynicism had flowered, colorful and bitter." (lines 164–167) Why is Romero cynical?

WRITING IN RESPONSE

Write briefly on this topic.

When Romero agrees to hire the old man to work in the yard, he does something he had never believed in doing: "letting down, giving into someone like that old man . . . ." (lines 161–162) What does Romero gain and/or lose in making this decision?

Point of View

ACTIVITY 4

With a partner or in small groups, answer these questions about **point of view.**

1. What is the point of view of the story in lines 28–167? What verbs give clues to Romero's thoughts, feelings, or values in this section? Discuss some of the examples and explain how they illustrate the point of view.

2. How does the point of view in the story shift in line 168? What is the subject of the verb *understand* in lines 168–177? Why do you think Gilb makes this change to **second-person point of view?** What is the effect of this shift?

3. Notice the repetition in lines 168–185. Circle *understand* and underline *like a fool* every time they appear. Why does Gilb repeat these words? How is the clause "you might understand" in line 183 different from previous uses of the verb *understand*? Why is this significant?

Setting

ACTIVITY 5

In pairs or in small groups, sketch the **setting:** Romero's home, yard, and the surrounding landscape.

• Include the details that are described in the excerpted lines that follow.

• Draw the sketches on the board or on large paper that can be displayed. Make the sketches in color.

• Discuss how the author's choice of language to describe these setting elements gives us insights into Romero's character. For example in excerpt 2, how is Romero like a flower that seeds "into thorn-hard burrs"?

• Use evidence from the story to support your answers.

1. Romero's "modest house . . . made of stone which is painted white, though the paint is gradually chipping off or being absorbed by the rock" (lines 7–9)

2. "a garden of cactus" and the "weeds that grow tall with yellow flowers which seed into thorn-hard burrs" (lines 13–15)

3. the "dirt and rocks of various sizes . . . which have been lined up to form a narrow path" (lines 15–16)

4. the "love seat, covered by an old bedspread, its legless frame on the red cement slab" (lines 18–19)

5. The oak trees, two of which "are dried-out stumps; the remaining one [with] a limb or two which still can produce leaves, but with so many amputations, its future is irreversible" (lines 20–21)

6. The juniper shrub "[n]ear the corner of his land, in the front, next to the sidewalk . . . his only bright green plant" (lines 23–25)

7. "patchy grass" in the back yard which "can seem almost suburban, at least to him" (lines 22–23)

8. "the dirt street which ran alongside [Romero's] property" which he "liked . . . that way, despite the run-off problems when heavy rains passed by" with "the border . . . less than two miles below Romero's home," and "the desert and mountains of Mexico" (lines 69–72)

CREATIVE WRITING

In a few paragraphs, write a description of a setting.

- Describe your own home, apartment, garden, shop, or other personal space, or that of someone you know.

- Give details about the setting in such a way that they reveal information about the person's personality, hopes, dreams, fears, or values without telling about the person directly.

- Ask a partner to read your description and explain what he or she understands about the person from your description of the setting.

WRITING IN RESPONSE

Respond briefly to this question in writing. Compare your responses with those of two or three classmates.

What do we learn about Romero from the description of the setting?

Exploring Further

Continue your analysis of "Romero's Shirt" with these questions for discussion or writing.

1. Reread lines 185–195. How would you describe the **mood,** or the feeling, in this scene of the story? What words or phrases create the mood? Find other examples of passages that create distinct moods and describe them.

2. The **narrator** describes the wind, a train as it approaches and moves away, and the silent air "quiet and dark, so still it was like death, or rest, sleep, until he could hear a grackle, and then another gust of wind, and then finally a car." (lines 195–200) How do these **images** help in understanding the story?

3. How might the image of the train function as **symbolism** in the story?

4. What do we learn about Romero and his feelings for his family in lines 201–208? What does the author want us to understand about the differences between the way that Romero thinks and feels on the inside and the way he responds on the outside? Why is the last sentence of the story especially significant?

5. What happens to Romero's shirt? Is it important? Why or why not? What does the shirt represent?

ACTIVITY 6

Role Play   In a role play, you can explore how the story might be different if the characters behaved differently and tried to communicate with each other.

Scene from the Story

Romero "kept a watch out the window as each of his children came in, then his wife. He told them only what had happened and, as always, they left him alone." (lines 185–187)

Change in the Scene

Instead of Romero's telling his family "only what happened" and his family's leaving him alone, for your role play, Romero tells his family his thoughts and feelings about his interaction with the old man. Romero's family then responds with their feelings about what Romero tells them. What kinds of things would they say to each other?

Form small groups and follow these steps.

1. Decide who will play the roles of Romero, his wife, his daughter, his sons.

2. Using the story and what you have learned from class discussion about Romero and his relationship with his family, develop a role play that demonstrates what would happen if the characters tried to communicate with one another.

- Your role play should illustrate the different characters' thoughts and feelings, as well as how they respond to and behave toward each other.
- For the characters other than Romero, you will need to infer what they think and feel based on what you have learned about them through Romero.

3. Each group performs its role play.

4. Discuss how different groups interpreted the characters and their words and actions. Based on what you know from the text about the characters, which performances are the most convincing? Why?

ESSAY TOPICS

1. What role does the old man play in helping us understand Romero's thoughts, feelings, and struggles?

2. How does the setting, the physical world of the story, help us understand Romero and his emotional world?

3. Imagine that you are Romero's wife, son, or daughter. What would you like to tell him or have him know or understand?

4. How is the image of the train a symbol of Romero's experience in the story?

5. Why do you think Gilb chose the title "Romero's Shirt" for the story?

AUTHOR PROFILE

Dagoberto Gilb

Dagoberto Gilb (1950–   ) grew up in Los Angeles and graduated from the University of California at Santa Barbara. Gilb's mother emigrated from Mexico City as a child, and his father, a World War II sergeant of German ancestry, supervised a laundry in Central Los Angeles. When he was young, Gilb's parents separated, and he grew up in the care of his mother. To help finance his writing and support his family, Gilb worked in construction as a laborer and carpenter. In 1976 Gilb and his family moved to El Paso, a place he refers to as "the Ellis Island of Chicanos" and appreciates for its dry, spare, and isolated beauty.

Gilb's central characters are often working class men struggling with life's daily dilemmas: bounced paychecks, greedy landladies, envious co-workers. His stories feature Chicano/Latino protagonists who find themselves in precarious situations, in part because of their own doing. In Gilb's words, a writer should "[w]rite from the gut and soul. Spill it. Write from *las alturas* [the heights] and from *los hoyos* [the depths]."

At first not recognized by New York publishers, Gilb won several awards for *The Magic of Blood*: the Texas Institute of Letters' award for best fiction, PEN'S Ernest Hemingway Foundation Award, and finalist for the PEN/Faulkner Award. Gilb's novels include *The Last Known Residence of Mickey Acuña* and *20 lbs.*

CHAPTER 18

Sunday in the Park

BEL KAUFMAN

PREPARATION

ACTIVITY 1

Freewrite briefly on these topics and then discuss them with a partner or in small groups.

1. What feelings or **images** (see Appendix A for more information about terms in boldface type) do you associate with the phrase "Sunday in the park"? What kind of scene does it bring to mind? Describe it in detail.

2. When you are confronted with an unpleasant situation in public (for example, someone taking a parking space you've been waiting for or being rude or challenging in some other way), how do you handle the situation? Do you confront the offender or keep quiet? Why?

Sunday in the Park

BEL KAUFMAN

It was still warm in the late-afternoon sun, and the city noises came muffled through the trees in the park. She put her book down on the bench, removed her sunglasses, and sighed contentedly. Morton was reading the *Times Magazine*° section, one arm flung around her shoulder; their three-year-old son, Larry, was playing in the sandbox; a faint breeze fanned her hair softly against her cheek. It was five-thirty of a Sunday afternoon, and the small playground, tucked away in a corner of the park, was all but deserted. The swings and seesaws stood motionless and abandoned, the slides were empty, and only in the sandbox two little boys squatted diligently side by side. *How good this is,* she thought, and almost smiled at her sense of well-being. They must go out in the sun more often; Morton was so   10
city-pale, cooped up all week inside the gray factorylike university. She squeezed his arm affectionately and glanced at Larry, delighting in the pointed little face frowning in concentration over the tunnel he was digging. The other boy suddenly stood up and with a quick, deliberate swing of his chubby arm threw a spadeful of sand at Larry. It just missed his head. Larry continued digging; the boy remained standing, shovel raised, stolid and impassive.

"No, no, little boy." She shook her finger at him, her eyes searching for the child's mother or nurse.° "We mustn't throw sand. It may get in someone's eyes and hurt. We must play nicely in the nice sandbox." The boy looked at her in unblinking expectancy. He was about Larry's age but perhaps ten pounds heavier, a   20
husky little boy with none of Larry's quickness and sensitivity in his face. Where was his mother? The only other people left in the playground were two women and a little girl on roller skates leaving now through the gate, and a man on a bench a few feet away. He was a big man, and he seemed to be taking up the whole bench as he held the Sunday comics close to his face. She supposed he was the child's father. He did not look up from his comics, but spat once deftly out of the corner of his mouth. She turned her eyes away.

At that moment, as swiftly as before, the fat little boy threw another spadeful of sand at Larry. This time some of it landed on his hair and forehead. Larry looked up at his mother, his mouth tentative; her expression would tell him   30
whether to cry or not.

Her first instinct was to rush to her son, brush the sand out of his hair, and punish the other child, but she controlled it. She always said that she wanted Larry to learn to fight his own battles.

"Don't *do* that, little boy," she said sharply, leaning forward on the bench. "You mustn't throw sand!"

The man on the bench moved his mouth as if to spit again, but instead he spoke. He did not look at her, but at the boy only.

"You go right ahead, Joe," he said loudly. "Throw all you want. This here is a   40
public sandbox."

°*Times Magazine* feature section of the *New York Times* newspaper
°*nurse* a full-time baby-sitter, generally hired by wealthy families

She felt a sudden weakness in her knees as she glanced at Morton. He had become aware of what was happening. He put his *Times* down carefully on his lap and turned his fine, lean face toward the man, smiling the shy, apologetic smile he might have offered a student in pointing out an error in his thinking. When he spoke to the man, it was with his usual reasonableness.

"You're quite right," he said pleasantly, "but just because this is a public place . . ."

The man lowered his funnies° and looked at Morton. He looked at him from head to foot, slowly and deliberately. "Yeah?" His insolent voice was edged with menace. "My kid's got just as good right here as yours, and if he feels like throwing sand, he'll throw it, and if you don't like it, you can take your kid the hell out of here."

The children were listening, their eyes and mouths wide open, their spades forgotten in small fists. She noticed the muscle in Morton's jaw tighten. He was rarely angry; he seldom lost his temper. She was suffused with a tenderness for her husband and an impotent rage against the man for involving him in a situation so alien and so distasteful to him.

"Now, just a minute," Morton said courteously, "you must realize . . ."

"Aw, shut up," said the man.

Her heart began to pound. Morton half rose; the *Times* slid to the ground. Slowly the other man stood up. He took a couple of steps toward Morton, then stopped. He flexed his great arms, waiting. She pressed her trembling knees together. Would there be violence, fighting? How dreadful, how incredible . . . She must do something, stop them, call for help. She wanted to put her hand on her husband's sleeve, to pull him down, but for some reason she didn't.

Morton adjusted his glasses. He was very pale. "This is ridiculous," he said unevenly. "I must ask you . . ."

"Oh, yeah?" said the man. He stood with his legs spread apart, rocking a little, looking at Morton with utter scorn. "You and who else?"°

For a moment the two men looked at each other nakedly. Then Morton turned his back on the man and said quietly, "Come on, let's get out of here." He walked awkwardly, almost limping with self-consciousness, to the sandbox. He stooped and lifted Larry and his shovel out.

At once Larry came to life; his face lost its rapt expression and he began to kick and cry. "I don't *want* to go home, I want to play better, I don't *want* any supper, I don't *like* supper. . . ." It became a chant as they walked, pulling their child between them, his feet dragging on the ground. In order to get to the exit gate they had to pass the bench where the man sat sprawling again. She was careful not to look at him. With all the dignity she could summon, she pulled Larry's sandy, perspiring little hand, while Morton pulled the other. Slowly and with head high she walked with her husband and child out of the playground.

°*funnies* comics section of a newspaper
° *"You and who else?"* "How will you make me do anything?"

Her first feeling was one of relief that a fight had been avoided, that no one was hurt. Yet beneath it there was a layer of something else, something heavy and inescapable. She sensed that it was more than just an unpleasant incident, more than defeat of reason by force. She felt dimly it had something to do with her and Morton, something acutely personal, familiar and important.

Suddenly Morton spoke. "It wouldn't have proved anything."

"What?" she asked.

"A fight. It wouldn't have proved anything beyond the fact that he's bigger than I am."   90

"Of course," she said.

"The only possible outcome," he continued reasonably, "would have been—what? My glasses broken, perhaps a tooth or two replaced, a couple of days' work missed—and for what? For justice? For truth?"

"Of course," she repeated. She quickened her step. She wanted only to get home and to busy herself with her familiar tasks; perhaps then the feeling, glued like heavy plaster on her heart, would be gone. *Of all the stupid, despicable bullies,* she thought, pulling harder on Larry's hand. The child was still crying. Always before she had felt a tender pity for his defenseless little body, the frail   100
arms, the narrow shoulders with sharp, winglike shoulder blades, the thin and unsure legs, but now her mouth tightened in resentment.

"Stop crying," she said sharply. "I'm ashamed of you!" She felt as if all three of them were tracking mud along the street. The child cried louder.

If there had been an issue involved, she thought, *if there had been something to fight for . . . But what else could he possibly have done? Allow himself to be beaten? Attempt to educate the man? Call a policeman? "Officer, there's a man in the park who won't stop his child from throwing sand on mine. . . ."* The whole thing was as silly as that, and not worth thinking about.

"Can't you keep him quiet, for Pete's sake?" Morton said irritably.   110

"What do you suppose I've been trying to do?" she said.

Larry pulled back, dragging his feet.

"If you can't discipline this child, I will," Morton snapped, making a move toward the boy.

But her voice stopped him. She was shocked to hear it, thin and cold and penetrating with contempt. "Indeed?" she heard herself say. "You and who else?"

ANALYZING THE STORY

ACTIVITY 2

Answer the following questions. Give evidence from the story to support your answers, where appropriate, and include line numbers for each piece of evidence.

1. Describe each character in the story. Fill in the chart.

	AGE	APPEARANCE	PERSONALITY TRAITS
Morton			
The wife			
Larry			
The big man			
Joe			

2. What are the similarities between Morton and his son, Larry? Between the big
   man and his son, Joe?

3. What do you think Morton does for a living? How do you know this?

4. What socioeconomic class do Morton and his wife belong to? What socioeconomic class do the big man and his son belong to? What evidence supports your answers? Consider what you know about the characters' actions,
   appearance, occupations, and language.

5. Why do you think the following lines in the story are italicized?

   "How good this is" (line 9)
   "Of all the stupid, despicable bullies" (lines 98–99)
   "If there had been an issue . . ." through *"throwing sand on mine . . . ."*
      (lines 105–108)

6. What is the **point of view** of "Sunday in the Park"? (See Appendix A for more
   information about terms in boldface type.) Answer the following questions to
   help you determine what it is:

   a. Is the narrator using first or third person?
   b. Does the story tell us what all of the characters are thinking and feeling
      (**omniscient**), or does it show us the thoughts and feelings of mainly one
      character (**limited**)?

WRITING IN RESPONSE

Write briefly on this topic.

In your opinion, what makes a person's social class obvious? Explain, using specific examples. Is class important in being able to get along with someone? Share what you have written with classmates.

Elements of Literature

Characterization

ACTIVITY 3

Work in groups.

1. Focus on two characters: the wife and her husband, Morton.

   a. Identify words and passages in the story that describe these characters' personality traits or attitudes or that suggest their values.
   b. In column 2 of the chart, write adjectives or descriptive phrases to explain these traits or values.
   c. In column 3, record specific pieces of evidence from the story that demonstrate these traits or values.

   An example is done for you.

CHARACTER	ADJECTIVE/ DESCRIPTIVE PHRASE	EVIDENCE FROM STORY
Wife	content (beginning of story)	• "sighed contentedly" (line 3) • "How good this is" (line 9) • "almost smiled at her sense of well-being" (lines 9–10)
Morton		

2. In your group, choose three adjectives or descriptive phrases from your list that describe either the wife or Morton. Write only the name of the character and the evidence on the board. (Do not write the adjective or phrase.) Ask the class to determine the trait or value being described.

ACTIVITY 4

Write and dramatize a scene based on lines 1–52 from "Sunday in the Park." You may do this in groups or as a class. Follow these steps.

A. To help you understand the scene in the story, discuss these questions about the characters and their actions, feelings, and intentions.

1. The wife describes the place where her husband works as "the gray factory-like university." (line 11) What could her description imply that she feels about her husband's work?

2. When the wife scolds Joe for throwing sand, he "[looks up] at her in un-blinking expectancy." (lines 19–20) What do you think Joe expects? How do you think his father, the big man, disciplines him?

3. What does the **narrator** reveal about the wife's feelings towards the big man when she "[turns] her eyes away" (line 27) after he spits?

4. Why doesn't the big man look at the wife when he speaks to his son? (line 38)

5. Reread what the big man says in lines 39–40 and lines 49–52. What do you think he feels is the real and larger issue in this situation? What kind of people does he seem to think the wife and Morton are?

6. Why does the wife feel a "weakness in her knees" (line 41) as Morton becomes involved in the situation?

7. Why doesn't the wife leave the boys alone as they play since she says that she wants Larry "to fight his own battles"? (line 34)

8. What kind of person does the wife seem to be, based on her thoughts, words, and actions in this first part of the story? What kind of person does Morton seem to be?

B. Use these notes to help you write and perform the scene:

1. You will need six people (five characters and a narrator).

2. To set the stage, write a part for the narrator with introductory information about the characters, their relationships, and the setting.

3. Identify lines of dialogue from the story that you can use.

4. Write additional lines of dialogue to convey information that Kaufman leaves unsaid.

5. Be sure your scene makes these things clear: setting, main characters, their relationships, their characteristics and personalities, their feelings and attitudes.

6. Provide each person with a copy of the script.

7. After you write and revise the scene, allow time to rehearse it so that you can perform it smoothly, reading from your scripts.

C. Perform your scene for the class. Have fun!

Figurative Language

Irony

ACTIVITY 5

Writers often use **irony** to let readers know something that a character does not know. An ironic situation occurs when there is a clear difference between what we expect will happen and what actually happens. Here is an example of irony from "Sunday in the Park":

> The wife thinks "The whole thing was as silly as that, and not worth thinking about." (line 109) Yet, in contrast to what she asserts and to what readers would expect, she actually thinks a great deal about the incident. (lines 92–109)

In groups, discuss the following:

1. Look for another instance of irony in the story. Why is it ironic?

2. Besides the small examples of irony, there is a larger irony at work in "Sunday in the Park." Consider lines 115–116. What is ironic about the wife's last words, in view of the thoughts she has previously expressed? What does she reveal about herself and her expectations of her husband?

WRITING IN RESPONSE

Write briefly on these topics.

1. What would the effect be on the irony in this story if Kaufman had written it in the first person, from the wife's viewpoint, rather than the third person?

2. Describe an ironic situation you have been in or an ironic incident that you have heard about.

Exploring Further

Write or discuss the answers to these questions. Give evidence from the story to support your answers and include line numbers for each piece of evidence.

1. Morton does not finish the sentences he says to the big man. (lines 46–47, 58, and 66–67) Why do you think Morton leaves his sentences vague and incomplete? (Think about both his character and the situation.)

   Complete these sentences for Morton, saying what you think he has in mind.

   a. "but just because this is a public place _____." (lines 46–47)
   b. "you must realize _____." (line 58)
   c. "I must ask you _____." (line 67)

2. How does Morton feel about his wife? What helps you understand this?

3. How does Morton feel about himself? Look especially at line 90. Why is Morton the first to speak after the experience in the park?

4. What sort of father is Morton? What makes you think so?

5. How does Kaufman's choice of point of view affect our understanding of the characters and the events in this story? For example, is the description of the boy playing in the sandbox (lines 19–21) told objectively? Explain. Choose another characterization or event in the story and explain how it is affected by the use of third-person limited (the wife's) point of view.

6. Discuss the wife's attitude toward her son. What kind of boy does she want him to become? Does this relate in some way to her perception of her husband?

7. The wife thinks that the incident in the park has "something to do with her and Morton—something acutely personal, familiar and important." (lines 86–87) What does the incident have to do with the wife and husband?

WRITING IN RESPONSE

Write briefly on this topic.

If you were a family counselor, what advice would you give to Morton and his wife about their relationship?

ESSAY TOPICS

1. In the story, the wife has unspoken expectations of her husband, both in terms of his personality and in terms of the role he should play as a husband. Write an essay in which you explain the following:

   • What these expectations are
   • How the wife indirectly expresses her expectations to Morton
   • Whether her expectations are realistic
   • How readers know that Morton understands her expectations

   In your conclusion, discuss briefly your own view of how having expectations of a partner can affect a relationship.

2. Write an essay in which you discuss how Kaufman uses irony in "Sunday in the Park." Explain clearly what is ironic about the examples you cite from the story. Discuss how irony helps us understand the story's characters, events, and possible themes.

3. Explain how the author's choice of point of view affects our understanding of the story's characters and events. Describe how the story would be different if it were written in the third person (from Morton's or the big man's point of view). To illustrate your ideas, choose a passage from the story and rewrite it using the point of view you have chosen.

AUTHOR PROFILE

Bel Kaufman

Bel Kaufman was born in Berlin, Germany, was raised in Russia, and came to the United States at the age of twelve. Writing is a tradition in her family; her grandfather was the famous Yiddish humorist Sholom Aleichem.

Based on her twenty years of teaching in New York City schools, Kaufman wrote the novel for which she is most famous, *Up the Down Staircase,* which was adapted into a movie in 1967. Her second novel, *Love, Etc.,* is about a heroine whose shattering divorce twelve years before leads her on a journey to surprising truths about herself. Kaufman's other writing interests include plays and music lyrics. Kaufman has said that her best motivation for writing is guilt over deadlines, and she notes that she is still dedicated to teaching. She travels and lectures often on the topic of "Survival Through Humor."

The story "Sunday in the Park" was the National Education Association/P.E.N. short story contest winner in 1983.

CHAPTER 19

Black Boy

KAY BOYLE

PREPARATION

ACTIVITY 1

Atlantic City, New Jersey, was a popular beach resort in the late nineteenth and early twentieth centuries. Its famous Boardwalk was originally built to protect the carpets in the expensive hotels from sand brought in on the feet of guests. But the Boardwalk itself quickly became popular because it was a comfortable place to walk, shop, and look at the sea. It became famous for its rolling chairs (wide, high-backed, white rattan wheeled chairs for tourists to ride in along the Board-walk), its elaborate advertisements outlined in thousands of light bulbs, and its Million Dollar Pier of amusements. What have you heard about Atlantic City?

Discuss these questions with a partner or in small groups.

1. Describe any famous beach resorts that you have visited or heard about. How do the people who work at these places interact with the visitors?

2. Many beach resorts have boardwalks. Describe a boardwalk that you know. Do you or would you enjoy walking along a boardwalk? Why do you think some people like to spend time on the sand under a boardwalk?

WRITING IN RESPONSE

Answer this question in a few paragraphs. Compare your response with that of two or three classmates.

1. Think of a time when you misunderstood someone's reasons for a specific action, and, as a result, you said or did something inappropriate, wrong, or embarrassing. Describe what happened and why.

2. Think of a time when someone misinterpreted something that you did and then behaved inappropriately toward you. Explain what happened.

Black Boy

Kay Boyle

At that time, it was the forsaken part, it was the other end of the city, and on early spring mornings there was no one about. By soft words, you could woo the horse into the foam, and ride her with the sea knee-deep around her. The waves came in and out there, as indolent as ladies, gathered up their skirts in their hands and, with a murmur, came tiptoeing in across the velvet sand.

The wooden promenade° was high there, and when the wind was up the water came running under it like wild. On such days, you had to content yourself with riding the horse over the deep white drifts of dry sand on the other side of the walks; the horse's hoofs here made no sound and the sparks of sand
10   stung your face in fury. It had no body to it, like the mile or two of sand packed hard that you could open out on once the tide was down.

My little grandfather, Puss, was alive then, with his delicate gait and ankles, and his belly pouting in his dove-gray clothes. When he saw from the window that the tide was sidling out, he put on his pearl fedora° and came stepping down the street. For a minute, he put one foot on the sand, but he was not at ease there. On the boardwalk over our heads was some other kind of life in progress. If you looked up, you could see it in motion through the cracks in the timber: rolling chairs, and women in high heels proceeding, if the weather were fair.

20   "You know," my grandfather said, "I think I might like to have a look at a shop or two along the boardwalk." Or: "I suppose you don't feel like leaving the beach for a minute," or: "If you would go with me, we might take a chair together, and look at the hats and the dresses and roll along in the sun."

He was alive then, taking his pick of the broad easy chairs and the black boys.

"There's a nice skinny boy," he'd say. "He looks as though he might put some action into it. Here you are, sonny. Push me and the little girl down to the Million Dollar Pier and back."

The cushions were red velvet with a sheen of dew over them. And Puss settled back on them and took my hand in his. In his mind there was no hesitation
30   about whether he would look at the shops on one side, or out on the vacant side where there was nothing shining but the sea.

"What's your name, Charlie?" Puss would say without turning his head to the black boy pushing the chair behind our shoulders.

"Charlie's my name, sir," he'd answer with his face dripping down like tar in the sun.

"What's your name, sonny?" Puss would say another time, and the black boy answered:

"Sonny's my name, sir."

"What's your name, Big Boy?"
40   "Big Boy's my name."

°*promenade* a walkway for recreational walking in a scenic spot
°*fedora* a type of felt hat for men, popular in the first half of the twentieth century

He never wore a smile on his face, the black boy. He was thin as a shadow but darker, and he was pushing and sweating, getting the chair down to the Million Dollar Pier and back again, in and out through the people. If you turned toward the sea for a minute, you could see his face out of the corner of your eye, hanging black as a bat's wing, nodding and nodding like a dark heavy flower.

But in the early morning, he was the only one who came down onto the sand and sat under the beams of the boardwalk, sitting idle there with a languor fallen on every limb. He had long bones. He sat idle there, with his clothes shrunk up from his wrists and his ankles, with his legs drawn up, looking out at the sea.

"I might be a king if I wanted to be," was what he said to me.   50

Maybe I was twelve years old, or maybe I was ten when we used to sit eating dog biscuits together. Sometimes when you broke them in two, a worm fell out and the black boy lifted his sharp finger and flecked it carelessly from off his knee.

"I seen kings," he said, "with a kind of cloth over they heads, and kind of jewels-like around here and here. They weren't any blacker than me, if as black," he said. "I could be almost anything I made up my mind to be."

"King Nebuchadnezzar," I said. "He wasn't a white man."

The wind was off the ocean and was filled with alien smells. It was early in the day, and no human sign was given. Overhead were the green beams of the boardwalk and no wheel or step to sound it.   60

"If I was a king," said the black boy with his biscuit in his fingers, "I wouldn't put much stock in hanging around here."

Great crystal jelly beasts were quivering in a hundred different colors on the wastes of sand around us. The dogs came, jumping them, and when they saw me still sitting still, they wheeled like gulls and sped back to the sea.

"I'd be traveling around," he said, "here and there. Now here, now there. I'd change most of my habits."

His hair grew all over the top of his head in tight dry rosettes. His neck was longer and more shapely than a white man's neck, and his fingers ran in and out of the sand like the blue feet of a bird.   70

"I wouldn't have much to do with pushing chairs around under them circumstances," he said. "I might even give up sleeping out here on the sand."

Or if you came out when it was starlight, you could see him sitting there in the clear white darkness. I could go and come as I liked, for whenever I went out the door, I had the dogs shouldering behind me. At night, they shook the taste of the house out of their coats and came down across the sand. There he was, with his knees up, sitting idle.

"They used to be all kinds of animals come down here to drink in the dark," he said. "They was a kind of a mirage came along and gave that impression. I seen tigers, lions, lambs, deer; I seen ostriches drinking down there side by side   80 with each other. They's the Northern Lights gets crossed some way and switches the wrong picture down."

It may be that the coast has changed there, for even then it was changing. The lighthouse that had once stood far out on the white rocks near the outlet was standing then like a lighted torch in the heart of the town. And the deep currents of the sea may have altered so that the clearest water runs in another direction, and houses may have been built down as far as where the brink used to be. But the brink was so perilous then that every word the black boy spoke seemed to fall into a cavern of beauty.

90   "I seen camels; I seen zebras," he said. "I might have caught any one of them if I'd felt inclined."

The street was so still and wide then that when Puss stepped out of the house, I could hear him clearing his throat of the sharp salty air. He had no intention of soiling the soles of his boots, but he came down the street to find me.

"If you feel like going with me," he said. "we'll take a chair and see the fifty-seven varieties° changing on the electric sign."

And then he saw the black boy sitting quiet. His voice drew up short on his tongue and he touched his white mustache.

"I shouldn't think it a good idea," he said, and he put his arm through my arm.
100 "I saw another little oak not three inches high° in the Jap's° window yesterday. We might roll down the boardwalk and have a look at it. You know," said Puss, and he put his kid gloves carefully on his fingers, "that black boy might do you some kind of harm."

"What kind of harm could he do me?" I said.

"Well," said Puss with the garlands of lights hanging around him, "he might steal some money from you. He might knock you down and take your money away."

"How could he do that?" I said. "We just sit and talk there." Puss looked at me sharply.

110   "What do you find to sit and talk about?" he said.

"I don't know," I said. "I don't remember. It doesn't sound like much to tell it."

The burden of his words was lying there on my heart when I woke up in the morning. I went out by myself to the stable and led the horse to the door and put the saddle on her. If Puss were ill at ease for a day or two, he could look out the window in peace and see me riding high and mighty away. The day after tomorrow, I thought, or the next day, I'll sit down on the beach again and talk to the black boy. But when I rode out, I saw him seated idle there, under the boardwalk, heedless, looking away to the cool wide sea. He had been eating peanuts and the shells lay all around him. The dogs came running at the horse's heels,
120 nipping the foam that lay along the tide.

The horse was as shy as a bird that morning, and when I drew her up beside the black boy, she tossed her head on high. Her mane went back and forth, from one side to the other, and a flight of joy in her limbs sent her forelegs like rockets into the air. The black boy stood up from the cold smooth sand, unsmiling, but a spark of wonder shone in his marble eyes. He put out his arm in the short tight sleeve of his coat and stroked her shivering shoulder.

"I was going to be a jockey once," he said, "but I changed my mind."

°*fifty-seven varieties* a giant lighted billboard advertising products of the Heinz company
°*little oak not three inches high* reference to a *bonsai,* a miniature ornamental tree traditionally cultivated in a pot by the Japanese
°*Jap* a derogatory reference to a person of Japanese ancestry

I slid down on one side while he climbed up the other.

"I don't know as I can ride him right," he said as I held her head. "The kind of saddle you have, it gives you nothing to grip your heels around. I ride them with their bare skin." 130

The black boy settled himself on the leather and put his feet in the stirrups. He was quiet and quick with delight, but he had no thought of smiling as he took the reins in his hands.

I stood on the beach with the dogs beside me, looking after the horse as she ambled down to the water. The black boy rode easily and straight, letting the horse stretch out and sneeze and canter. When they reached the jetty, he turned her casually and brought her loping back.

"Some folks licks hell out of their horses," he said. "I'd never raise a hand to one, unless he was to bite me or do something I didn't care for." 140

He sat in the saddle at ease, as though in a rocker, stroking her shoulder with his hand spread open, and turning in the stirrups to smooth her shining flank.

"Jockeys make a pile of money," I said.

"I wouldn't care for the life they have," said the black boy. "They have to watch their diet so careful."

His fingers ran delicately through her hair and laid her mane back on her neck.

When I was up on the horse again, I turned her toward the boardwalk.

"I'm going to take her over the jetty," I said. "You'll see how she clears it. I'll take her up under the boardwalk to give her a good start." 150

I struck her shoulder with the end of my crop, and she started toward the tough black beams. She was under it, galloping, when the dogs came down the beach like mad. They had chased a cat out of cover and were after it, screaming as they ran, with a wing of sand blowing wide behind them, and when the horse saw them under her legs, she jumped sidewise in sprightliness and terror and flung herself against an iron arch.

For a long time I heard nothing at all in my head except the melody of some-one crying, whether it was my dead mother holding me in comfort, or the soft wind grieving over me where I had fallen. I lay on the sand asleep; I could feel it running with my tears through my fingers. I was rocked in a cradle of love, cra- 160 dled and rocked in sorrow.

"Oh, my little lamb, my little lamb pie!" Oh, sorrow, sorrow, wailed the wind, or the tide, or my own kin about me. "Oh, lamb, oh, lamb!"

I could feel the long swift fingers of love untying the terrible knot of pain that bound my head. And I put my arms around him and lay close to his heart in comfort.

Puss was alive then, and when he met the black boy carrying me up to the house, he struck him square across the mouth.

ANALYZING THE STORY

ACTIVITY 2

Answer the following questions. Give evidence from the story to support your answers, where appropriate, and include line numbers for each piece of evidence.

1. At what time of year and in what historical time period does the story take place?

2. What does the grandfather like to do at low tide? How does he feel about walking on the sand? What does this tell us about the grandfather?

3. Where are the girl's parents?

4. Why does the girl always go out with dogs? What advantage does this give her?

5. Why do the black boy and the girl eat dog biscuits? Who do you think provides them? What is the problem with eating them?

6. What is the grandfather's attitude toward the boy?

7. Where do you think the boy learned how to ride a horse?

8. Describe what happens to the girl when she tries to jump over the jetty.

9. The grandfather "put[s] his kid gloves carefully on his fingers" (line 102) as he warns the girl about the boy. How does this action **foreshadow** (see Appendix A for more information on terms in boldface type) the ending? What is the **irony** here? What do kid gloves traditionally represent? What kind of glove is associated with the action the grandfather takes at the end of the story?

10. Is the **narrator** a character in the story? How old is the narrator at the time the story takes place? How old do you think the narrator is at the time the story is told?

ACTIVITY 3

1. Fill in the following chart with information about the three main characters. Use words or phrases from the story and include line references.

	GIRL	BLACK BOY	GRANDFATHER
Approximate age			
Ethnicity and appearance			
Residence and economic status			
Distinguishing personality traits			

2. Compare your chart information with a partner as you answer these questions.

    a. What important information about the characters is missing in the story? Why do you think it was omitted?

    b. Which two characters have the most important similarities? Why are these similarities important?

    c. Which two characters have the most significant differences? Why are these differences important?

Elements of Literature

Characterization

ACTIVITY 4

Do the following in answering the questions below about **characterization.**

- In small groups, read each question, locate the part of the story being referred to, and make a quick decision about the answer.

- Your teacher will then assign one question for each group to discuss more fully. Return to the question that your teacher has assigned to your group and discuss the answer in detail.

- Prepare a well-supported and clearly explained answer to present to the class.

1. Why does the grandfather repeatedly ask the boy what his name is? (lines 32–40) What does this tell us about the grandfather? How does the boy always answer? Why?

2. The black boy says, "'They weren't any blacker than me, if as black.'" (line 55) Does his statement imply that he thinks being black is an advantage or a disadvantage? Explain.

3. What is the boy's great dream? How do you think this might differ from a white boy's dream at the time? Why?

4. "'I might even give up sleeping out here on the sand.'" (line 72) Does the black boy imply by this statement that sleeping on the sand is pleasant or unpleasant? Explain.

5. "The burden of his words was lying there on my heart when I woke up in the morning." (lines 112–113) What does the girl mean? How does she feel? Is she sure about her feelings?

6. Why does the phrase "was alive then" in reference to the grandfather appear three times in the story? (lines 12, 24, and 167) What is its significance? What does the phrase mean, and why does the narrator repeat it? Is there any special meaning to it the last time the narrator says it?

WRITING IN RESPONSE

Write briefly on these topics.

1. Describe the physical and emotional feelings a boy might have while pushing a rolling chair with two people in it.

2. The narrator lets the boy ride her horse despite her grandfather's warning. What differences does this decision reveal between the girl's relationship with her grandfather and with the boy?

CREATIVE WRITING

In 200 to 300 words, write a sequel to "Black Boy." What do you think happens next? Does the boy go away? Does he remain friends with the girl? Does the grandfather forbid the girl to have any contact with the boy? Do you think the girl will defend the boy to her grandfather? Try to answer some of these questions in your sequel. Follow Boyle's style as much as you can.

Figurative Language

ACTIVITY 5

A. "Black Boy" begins with a complex figure of speech, an extended **simile** that uses **personification** to describe the action of the ocean on the beach.

1. What associations do you have with the following words? Discuss in a group or with the class.

   ladies   skirts that can be gathered up   tiptoe
   skirts   murmur   velvet

2. Read the following excerpt in which the figures of speech are italicized. As you read, consider the associations that you discussed in item 1.

   "The waves came in and out there, *as indolent as ladies, gathered up their skirts in their hands* and, with a *murmur,* came *tiptoeing* in across the *velvet* sand." (lines 3–5)

3. Read the following partial analysis of the phrase "gathered up their skirts."

   The phrase "gathered up their skirts" calls to mind long skirts with white petticoats (long undergarments often made of lace) beneath them. The phrase suggests that the waves broke against the shore in white, bubbling foam.

How do the associations you made with *murmur, tiptoe,* and *velvet* in item 1 add to the scene?

4. Explain how the personification of the waves as ladies and the choice of velvet to describe the sand parallel the people on the boardwalk and their lifestyle.

B. Work alone to rewrite Boyle's sentence (lines 3–5) *without any figurative language* at all. Simply describe waves, water, and sand. Share your revised sentence with the class.

1. How do the revisions compare with Boyle's passage in "Black Boy"?

2. What advantage does Boyle's **figurative language** provide for readers?

ACTIVITY 6

1. Work in groups to discuss the following figures of speech (italicized). How do they add information about the characters or reveal what is actually happening in the story?
   a. The boy's face was "hanging black as a *bat's wing,* nodding and nodding like a *dark heavy flower.*" (lines 44–45)
   b. The boy never "*wore* a smile." (line 41)
   c. "I could feel the long *swift fingers* of love *untying the terrible knot* of pain that *bound* my head." (lines 164–165)

2. With your group, find another example of figurative language in the story. Write it on the board. If your choice has already been written on the board by another group, find a different example. Then explain to the class what your figure of speech adds to the event, character, or scene.

Setting

ACTIVITY 7

1. It's important to visualize the **setting** in "Black Boy." To help you do so, draw a simple sketch of the setting looking from above, like a map, and include the following:

   the Boardwalk and the shops   the lighthouse
   the girl's house   the ocean
   the Million Dollar Pier   the spot where the girl and the boy meet
   the jetty

2. Compare your sketch with your classmates' sketches. Which elements of the scene do you agree on? Which ones do you have questions about? Find answers to your questions in the story, where possible.

ACTIVITY 8

Even before we know that the story takes place in Atlantic City (when the Million Dollar Pier, lines 26–27, is mentioned), details about the setting tell us the story takes place at a seaside resort many years before the story is told.

1. Locate as many of these details as you can throughout the story. Write them under the appropriate category in the chart. Two examples have been done for you.

PHYSICAL ENVIRONMENT	STYLE OF DRESS	EXPRESSIONS OF TIME	ACTIVITIES
rolling chairs	fedora		

2. How do the following aspects of the setting in "Black Boy" help accommodate the friendship between the two children despite their different backgrounds?

an elevated boardwalk   a vacation resort
a beach   a "forsaken" (line 1) part of town

3. Find other details of the physical setting that help the relationship develop and the action take place.

4. In Activity 2, item 1, you decided when the story takes place. What aspects of the story, including the characters' attitudes and behavior, require this time period as a setting?

Exploring Further

Continue your analysis of "Black Boy" with these questions for discussion or writing.

1. What colors are mentioned in the story, and what does each color refer to? Which colors are mentioned more than once? Why? What is the significance of these repeated colors in relation to the plot, characters, and possible theme?

2. Examine the use of light and words related to light or reflection in the story. What colors are associated with these examples? How does the use of light and lights affect the mood of the story?

3. What is wrong with the lighthouse? How might this have happened? What could be the significance of such a lighthouse as a **symbol** in the story?

4. When the boy describes animals drinking together on the beach in the dark, why does he choose those particular animals? What is his point? What is the author trying to say?

5. After pointing out that he is as black as any king, the boy says, "'I could be almost anything I made up my mind to be,'" to which the girl responds, "'King Nebuchadnezzar . . . wasn't a white man.'" (lines 56–57) What does this brief exchange reveal about the gap between what the two children seem to understand about opportunities for black people? Find other evidence that reveals their consciousness of or confusion about race.

ESSAY TOPICS

1. Consider the fact that Boyle was a political activist and devoted advocate of civil rights. How does the setting of her story accommodate a social theme, and what is that theme?

2. The friendship in the story is between a white girl and a poor black boy—a friendship that many people, including the grandfather in the story, are uncomfortable with. What is Boyle trying to say about such relationships?

3. How does the use of color and figurative language throughout the story parallel the sociological theme about race relationships?

AUTHOR PROFILE

Kay Boyle

Born in St. Paul, Minnesota, in 1902, Kay Boyle spent her childhood in a variety of American cities, including Atlantic City. Her grandmother and her mother were independent, politically active women, while her father and grandfather (called Puss) were conservatives and disapproved of much of what the women did. Boyle followed in the women's footsteps, however, eventually breaking off completely with her father and grandfather and engaging in overtly political writing—about nationalism, expatriation, and women's rights. She believed that a writer must convey his or her strong beliefs to as many people as possible and that everyone's fate is determined by political and social struggles. Her stories are little personal dramas in the larger framework of history.

Her first collection of short stories appeared in 1929. Subsequently, she wrote more than thirty-five books: fourteen novels, including *The Crazy Hunter* (1940) and *Decision* (1948); eleven collections of short stories; five volumes of poetry; and two essay collections, as well as numerous articles and reviews. She won the O. Henry Award for Fiction twice, in 1935 and 1941. She has been called a brilliant stylist, describing landscapes with meticulous clarity, often using them as representations of inner states. She believed that love is essential for every individual, and the loss of a human connection is a tragedy.

CHAPTER 20

Gravity

David Leavitt

PREPARATION

ACTIVITY 1

With a partner or in small groups, discuss the following questions and do the activities.

1. Read the first sentence of "Gravity." Then write for five or ten minutes in response.

2. Discuss Theo's choice. What do you think is going to happen in the story?

3. What different meanings can you think of for the word *gravity*?

Gravity

DAVID LEAVITT

Theo had a choice between a drug that would save his sight and a drug that would keep him alive, so he chose not to go blind. He stopped the pills and started the injections—these required the implantation of an unpleasant and painful catheter just above this heart—and within a few days the clouds in his eyes started to clear up, he could see again. He remembered going into New York City to a show with his mother, when he was twelve and didn't want to admit he needed glasses. "Can you read that?" she'd shouted, pointing to a Broadway marquee,° and when he'd squinted, making out only one or two letters, she'd taken off her own glasses—harlequins° with tiny rhinestones in the corners—and shoved them onto his face. The world came into focus, and he gasped, astonished at the precision around the edges of things, the legibility, the hard, sharp, colorful landscape. Sylvia had to squint through *Fiddler on the Roof*° that day, but for Theo, his face masked by his mother's huge glasses, everything was as bright and vivid as a comic book. Even though people stared at him, and muttered things, Sylvia didn't care, he could *see*. 10

Because he was dying again, Theo moved back to his mother's house in New Jersey. The DHPG° injections she took in stride—she'd seen her own mother through *her* dying, after all. Four times a day, with the equanimity of a nurse, she cleaned out the plastic tube implanted in his chest, inserted a sterilized hypodermic and slowly dripped the bag of sight-giving liquid into his veins. They endured this procedure silently, Sylvia sitting on the side of the hospital bed she'd rented for the duration of Theo's stay—his life, he sometimes thought—watching reruns of *I Love Lucy*° or the news, while he tried not to think about the hard piece of pipe stuck into him, even though it was a constant reminder of how wide and unswimmable the gulf was becoming between him and the ever-receding shoreline of the well. And Sylvia was intricately cheerful. Each day she urged him to go out with her somewhere—to the library, or the little museum with the dinosaur replicas he'd been fond of as a child—and when his thinness and the cane drew stares, she'd maneuver him around the people who were staring, determined to shield him from whatever they might say or do. It had been 30 the same that afternoon so many years ago, when she'd pushed him through a lobbyful of curious and laughing faces, determined that nothing should interfere with the spectacle of his seeing. What a pair they must have made, a boy in ugly glasses and a mother daring the world to say a word about it! 20

°*Broadway marquee* the large projecting sign above a theater entrance (in this case, in New York's theater district), announcing the name of the current show

°*harlequins* large, almond-shaped women's glasses, popular in the 1950s; molded into the plastic is the diamond pattern of the harlequin, a commedia dell'arte character

°*Fiddler on the Roof* popular Broadway musical, which opened in New York in 1964

°*DHPG* the initials of the drug dihydroxypropoxymethylguanine, which is used to treat a viral eye disease in patients with HIV or other diseases that attack the immune system

°*I Love Lucy* a popular television situation comedy in the 1950s

This warm, breezy afternoon in May they were shopping for revenge. "Your cousin Howard's engagement party is next month," Sylvia explained in the car. "A very nice girl from Livingston. I met her a few weeks ago, and really, she's a superior person."

"I'm glad," Theo said. "Congratulate Howie for me."

40   "Do you think you'll be up to going to the party?"

"I'm not sure. Would it be okay for me just to give him a gift?"

"You already have. A lovely silver tray, if I say so myself. The thank-you note's in the living room."

"Mom," Theo said, "why do you always have to—"

Sylvia honked her horn at a truck making an illegal left turn. "Better they should get something than no present at all, is what I say," she said. "But now, the problem is, *I* have to give Howie something, to be from me, and it better be good. It better be very, very good."

"Why?"

50   "Don't you remember that cheap little nothing Bibi gave you for your graduation? It was disgusting."

"I can't remember what she gave me."

"Of course you can't. It was a tacky pen-and-pencil set. Not even a real leather box. So naturally, it stands to reason that I have to get something truly spectacular for Howard's engagement. Something that will make Bibi blanch. Anyway, I think I've found just the thing, but I need your advice."

"Advice? Well, when my old roommate Nick got married, I gave him a garlic press. It cost five dollars and reflected exactly how much I felt, at that moment, our friendship was worth."

60   Sylvia laughed. "Clever. But my idea is much more brilliant, because it makes it possible for me to get back at Bibi *and* give Howard the nice gift he and his girl deserve." She smiled, clearly pleased with herself. "Ah, you live and learn."

"You live," Theo said.

Sylvia blinked. "Well, look, here we are." She pulled the car into a handicapped-parking place on Morris Avenue and got out to help Theo, but he was already hoisting himself up out of his seat, using the door handle for leverage. "I can manage myself," he said with some irritation. Sylvia stepped back.

"Clearly one advantage to all this for you," Theo said, balancing on his cane, "is that it's suddenly so much easier to get a parking place."

70   "Oh Theo, please," Sylvia said. "Look, here's where we're going."

She leaned him into a gift shop filled with porcelain statuettes of Snow White and all seven of the dwarves, music boxes which, when you opened them, played "The Shadow of Your Smile," complicated-smelling potpourris in purple wallpapered boxes, and stuffed snakes you were supposed to push up against drafty windows and doors.

"Mrs. Greenman," said an expansive, gray-haired man in a cream-colored cardigan sweater. "Look who's here, Archie, it's Mrs. Greenman."

Another man, this one thinner and balding, but dressed in an identical cardigan, peered out from the back of the shop. "Hello there!" he said, smiling. He

80   looked at Theo, and his expression changed.

"Mr. Sherman, Mr. Baker. This is my son, Theo."

"Hello," Mr. Sherman and Mr. Baker said. They didn't offer to shake hands.

"Are you here for that item we discussed last week?" Mr. Sherman asked.

"Yes," Sylvia said. "I want advice from my son here." She walked over to a large ridged crystal bowl, a very fifties sort of bowl, stalwart and square-jawed. "What do you think? Beautiful, isn't it?"

"Mom, to tell you the truth, I think it's kind of ugly."

"Four hundred and twenty-five dollars," Sylvia said admiringly. "You have to feel it."

Then she picked up the big bowl and tossed it to Theo, like a football.   90

The gentlemen in the cardigan sweaters gasped and did not exhale. When Theo caught it, it sank his hands. His cane rattled as it hit the floor.

"That's heavy," Sylvia said, observing with satisfaction how the bowl had weighted Theo's arms down. "And where crystal is concerned, heavy is impressive."

She took the bowl back from him and carried it to the counter. Mr. Sherman was mopping his brow. Theo looked at the floor, still surprised not to see shards of glass around his feet.

Since no one else seemed to be volunteering, he bent over and picked up the cane.

"Four hundred and fifty-nine, with tax," Mr. Sherman said, his voice still a bit   100
shaky, and a look of relish came over Sylvia's face as she pulled out her check-book to pay. Behind the counter, Theo could see Mr. Baker put his hand on his forehead and cast his eyes to the ceiling.

It seemed Sylvia had been looking a long time for something like this, some-thing heavy enough to leave an impression, yet so fragile it could make you sorry.

They headed back out to the car.

"Where can we go now?" Sylvia asked, as she got in. "There must be some-place else to go."

"Home," Theo said. "It's almost time for my medicine."

"Really? Oh. All right." She pulled on her seat belt, inserted the car key in the   110
ignition and sat there.

For just a moment, but perceptibly, her face broke. She squeezed her eyes shut so tight the blue eye shadow on the lids cracked.

Almost as quickly she was back to normal again, and they were driving. "It's getting hotter," Sylvia said. "Shall I put on the air?"

"Sure," Theo said. He was thinking about the bowl, or more specifically, about how surprising its weight had been, pulling his hands down. For a while now he'd been worried about his mother, worried about what damage his illness might se-cretly be doing to her that of course she would never admit. On the surface things seemed all right. She still broiled herself a skinned chicken breast for dinner every   120
night, still swam a mile and a half a day, still kept used teabags wrapped in foil in the refrigerator. Yet she had also, at about three o'clock one morning, woken him up to tell him she was going to the twenty-four-hour supermarket, and was there anything he wanted. Then there was the gift shop: She had literally pitched that bowl toward him, pitched it like a ball, and as that great gleam of flight and

potential regret came sailing his direction, it had occurred to him that she was trusting his two feeble hands, out of the whole world, to keep it from shattering. What was she trying to test? Was it his newly regained vision? Was it the assurance that he was there, alive, that he hadn't yet slipped past all her caring, a little lost

130   boy in rhinestone-studded glasses? There are certain things you've already done before you even think how to do them—a child pulled from in front of a car, for instance, or the bowl, which Theo was holding before he could even begin to calculate its brief trajectory. It had pulled his arms down, and from that apish posture he'd looked at his mother, who smiled broadly, as if, in the war between heaviness and shattering, he'd just helped her win some small but sustaining victory.

ANALYZING THE STORY

ACTIVITY 2

Answer the following questions. Where appropriate, give evidence to support your answers and line numbers for each piece of evidence.

1. Who are Theo and Sylvia? How old do you think Theo is?

2. What, in your own words, does Sylvia mean by "shopping for revenge"? (line 35)

3. Who are Bibi, Howard (Howie), and the "very nice girl from Livingston," (line 37) and how are they related to one another and to Sylvia and Theo?

4. Finish Theo's response to his mother: "'Mom . . . why do you always have to—'" (line 44)

5. In the gift shop, one of the salesclerks smiles at Theo's mother but changes his expression after seeing Theo. (lines 79–80) How do you think his expression changes, and why?

6. Sketch a picture of a "ridged crystal bowl . . . stalwart and square-jawed." (line 85) How much do you think such a bowl would weigh?

7. Sylvia tells Theo that she needs his advice about a gift for Howie. (line 56) In the store, does she seem to care about Theo's opinion of the bowl? Explain.

8. At the beginning of the story, we learn that Theo chose not to take a drug that "would keep him alive . . . ." (line 2) Left unsaid is whether this drug would have kept Theo alive for a short time or for a long time. Why do you think the author doesn't make this clear?

9. Why do you think Theo made the choice he made about medication?

Elements of Literature

Characterization

ACTIVITY 3

1. In groups, study the lines, which are said by or about Theo or Sylvia, in the chart and then complete it. Determine what each quotation shows about the character and explain why you think so. The first one has been done for you.

QUOTATION	WHAT IT SHOWS ABOUT THE CHARACTER	EXPLANATION
a. "[W]hen he'd squinted . . . she'd taken off her own glasses—harlequins with tiny rhinestones in the corners—and shoved them onto his face." (lines 8–10)	Sylvia is a flamboyant character who observes her son carefully and takes action without asking first.	The author describes Sylvia's bold and flashy glasses in detail. Though Theo has said nothing, Sylvia realizes that he needs glasses when she sees him squinting. The verb shove, which describes the way she puts the glasses on Theo, suggests that she is bold in her actions as well as in her appearance.
b. "Even though people stared at him, and muttered things, Sylvia didn't care, he could see." (lines 14–15)		
c. "The DHPG injections she took in stride—" (line 17)		
d. "'[A]nd really, she's a superior person.'" (lines 37–38)		
e. "'Mom . . . why do you always have to—'" (line 44)		
f. "'[T]hat cheap little nothing Bibi gave you for your graduation?'" (lines 50–51)		
g. "'I can't remember what she gave me.'" (line 52)		
h. "'I can manage myself,' he said with some irritation." (lines 66–67)		
i. "'Home,' Theo said. 'It's almost time for my medicine.'" (line 109)		
j. "For just a moment, but perceptibly, her face broke . . . . Almost as quickly she was back to normal again . . . ." (lines 112–114)		

2. After your group discusses each line separately, summarize your conclusions about Theo and his mother. What kind of person is Theo? What kind of person is his mother? What additional evidence from the story can you find to support your characterizations? Share your answers with classmates.

ACTIVITY 4

Answer these questions about the effect of Theo's illness on him and on his mother.

1. How has Theo's life changed because of his illness?

2. How has Sylvia's life been affected because of Theo's illness? What do we know about her character that seems to make it possible for her to deal with her son's illness as she does?

3. How is being ill with AIDS different from being ill with other life-threatening diseases?

WRITING IN RESPONSE

Write briefly on these topics. Compare your responses with those of two or three classmates.

1. Describe the relationship between Theo and his mother. How do you feel about the way in which Sylvia handles her son's choice of medication?

2. How would this story be different if Theo and his mother were poor?

3. Has your life ever been changed by a serious illness or by caring for someone who is ill or dying? If so, explain in as much detail as you can.

Tone

ACTIVITY 5

Tonal irony is achieved when a writer uses words and expressions that are unexpected or surprising in a given situation or context. (See Appendix A for more information about terms in boldface type.)

Explore the effect that tonal irony in "Gravity" has on the reader by discussing the following questions.

1. Reread the first sentence in the first three paragraphs of the story. What specific words or combinations of words in these sentences are unusual or unexpected?

2. What is unusual about the way words are combined in the following phrases:
   - "the ever-receding shoreline of the well"? (lines 25–26)
   - "intricately cheerful" (line 26)
   - "the spectacle of his seeing" (line 33)

3. How are the following ironic: Theo's choice; the throwing of the bowl; a mother's taking care of a dying son?

Figurative Language

Symbolism

ACTIVITY 6

Divide the class into two groups. Each group takes one of the following topics and answers the questions about **symbolism.** Then the groups report their conclusions to the class.

The Pair of Glasses at the Broadway Musical

1. Brainstorm all associations you have with *eyeglasses.*
   a. Reread the lines in which the narrator makes a comparison between these two situations:

      Sylvia's actions when people stare at her son because he is thin and walks with a cane (lines 28–30)

      People's staring at Theo, at the age of twelve, because he was wearing his mother's glasses at the theater (lines 30–34)

   b. Which of your associations with *eyeglasses* are related to the story "Gravity"?

2. How is the much earlier incident with the glasses at the theater symbolic of Theo's and Sylvia's current situation? Highlight sections of the story where the earlier incident is described or mentioned and then complete the chart. Write specific references about the two different situations in item 1a that you feel are related and then explain how they are connected. Consider Theo's actions, the mother's actions, and the actions of people around them. An example is done for you.

AT THE THEATER	NOW	HOW THE SITUATIONS ARE RELATED
"a boy in ugly glasses" (lines 33–34)	"his thinness and the cane" (lines 28–29)	Theo's appearance attracts attention

3. Highlight all words in the story associated with *seeing*. Brainstorm all associations you have with *seeing* and explain which of these are related to the story.

The Crystal Bowl

1. Brainstorm all associations you have with a *crystal bowl* and then explain which of these associations are related to the story.

2. Highlight all references to the bowl in the story.

3. In the final sentence of "Gravity," Theo reflects on the incident with the bowl and its connection to "the war between heaviness and shattering." (lines 134–135) Discuss various meanings for *heaviness* and *shattering*. Which of these meanings could relate to the story? Explain.

4. Write the following words and phrases under one of the two headings in the chart that follows. Your group may create more than one chart. For each chart, explain how words in each category are related.

glass	weight	gravity
stalwart	pulled arms down	alive
square-jawed	football	newly regained vision
great gleam of flight	potential regret	slipped past all her caring
fragile		

HEAVINESS	SHATTERING

5. How is the bowl symbolic of Sylvia's character? Of her situation? Of Theo's situation?

Exploring Further

Continue your analysis of "Gravity" with these questions for writing or discussion.

1. In the first paragraph of the story, the **narrator** jumps abruptly from Theo's current situation to something he remembers in the past: "[H]e could see again. He remembered going into New York City . . . ." (line 5) What is the effect of such a sudden change of time and place within a single paragraph?

2. In explaining her idea for a gift for Howard and his bride, Sylvia remarks that "'you live and learn,'" (line 62) and Theo responds by saying "'You live . . . .'" (line 63) What do you think he means, and what does his answer imply about his situation?

3. What does "this" refer to in line 104? Consider all possibilities. Explain what is meant by "leave an impression" and "so fragile it could make you sorry" in relationship to your understanding of "this." (line 105)

4. Reflecting on the bowl incident, Theo realizes that "[t]here are certain things you've already done before you even think how to do them—a child pulled from in front of a car . . . or the bowl, which Theo was holding before he could even begin to calculate its brief trajectory." (lines 130–133) Give other examples from your experience or observations that illustrate such moments. Explain Theo's point in your own words. How does catching the bowl exemplify this idea?

5. What is the "small but sustaining victory" that Theo has helped his mother win? (line 135) Consider the following questions as you answer:

   a. What is "the war between heaviness and shattering"? (lines 134–135)
   b. Has anything been lost or anyone been defeated in this "war"?
   c. Who or what is "sustained" by the victory?

ESSAY TOPICS

1. Write an essay in which you analyze the symbolism of the bowl. Examine closely the physical object itself, explaining how associations we have with the bowl—and the way it is used in the story—represent the mother's character, her situation, and/or Theo's choice.

2. In an essay, illustrate how Leavitt uses irony to highlight the central action of the story. This action includes but is not limited to Theo's choice and Sylvia's taking care of her dying son.

3. Explain why you think this story is entitled "Gravity." Make sure to consider various definitions of the word *gravity*.

AUTHOR PROFILE

David Leavitt

Born in 1961 in Pittsburgh, Pennsylvania, David Leavitt grew up in Palo Alto, California, and attended Yale. He published his first collection of short stories, *Family Dancing,* at the age of twenty-three. His 1986 novel, *The Lost Language of Cranes,* was made into a film in 1991. The story "Gravity" appears in the collection *A Place I've Never Been* (1990). Leavitt often writes about issues specific to the lives of homosexuals and their families, but his themes are universal. His plots often center around family relationships: loyalty and betrayal, the telling of secrets, and death and dealing with the dying.

Leavitt has been praised for his character development and his ability to use a character's physical actions and gestures to give meaning to an entire piece. Leavitt often writes, as he does in "Gravity," about mothers who are vulnerable and sensitive, and who, in an attempt to be supportive, are sometimes smothering. As one critic noted, he seems to achieve "his moments of clearest perception when he faces a character who is completely different from himself."

CHAPTER 21

The Confounding

STEVE SANFIELD

PREPARATION

ACTIVITY 1

With a partner or in small groups, discuss the following questions.

1. What do you associate with the word *grace*? Brainstorm possibilities.

2. Discuss what you know about the wildlife and vegetation of the desert of western North America. Describe plants, animals, and the land.

3. What does it mean to confound something or somebody? Give examples. The title of the piece you are about to read is "The Confounding." Discuss the possible significance of the title, especially considering the use of *the*.

4. What is the difference between hearing a story that someone retells aloud and silently reading a story?

ACTIVITY 2

What do you know about the four literary forms in the left-hand column of the following chart?

1. Draw lines to connect them with their features in the column on the right. Some features will connect with more than one form.

FORMS	FEATURES
Poem	Explains an event in nature Heroic human characters Rhythm
Fable	Nonhistorical but accepted as historical Has animal characters Imaginative language
Legend	Traditional tale Represents a belief of a culture Fictitious story
Myth	Verse Teaches a lesson Concerns gods or godlike heroes

2. What similarities and differences do you find among the forms?

3. What distinguishes a *tale* from the four forms in the preceding chart? How does the retelling of a tale cause it to change?

4. Where do storytellers get their information? Read the "Author Profile" (page 284) on Steve Sanfield, the author of "The Confounding." Where did Sanfield get the information for this tale? How does Sanfield's retelling serve as a link in the oral tradition of the story?

WRITING IN RESPONSE

Respond briefly to this question in writing.

Imagine what it would be like if all living things could speak the same language. How would our world of today be different?

The Confounding
A Paiute Tale to Be Told Aloud
Steve Sanfield

This tale is told by the Paiute Indians who live in the
Great Basin of Utah, Nevada, & California. It has been
told for hundreds of years—long before there was any
written language. Some say it is a tale of coyote,° that

5   it explains why he lives as a vagabond and an outlaw.
Others say it is a tale about language. Still others say it
is about ourselves. The Narro-gwe-nap, or keepers of
the legends, say nothing except that it changes each time
it is shared. After you read it, tell it to someone else and

10   see if the Narro-gwe-nap speak the truth.

When the earth was made
the gods went to all the living things and asked:
What do you want to be?　What do you want to be?
What do you want to be?

15   Some said:
We want to fly with grace in the blueness of the sky.
Okay, said the gods, we will make you into birds
all kinds of birds
big birds　little birds

20   all kinds of birds.
The sky shall be your home
and you shall fly in it forever.

And some said:
We want to swim with grace in the coolness of the water.

25   Okay, said the gods, we will make you into fish
all kinds of fish
big fish　little fish
all kinds of fish.
The lakes and rivers and seas shall be your home

30   and you shall swim in them forever.

Others said:
We want to move with grace upon the land.
We want to climb mountains and run through the valleys.
We want to lie down and sleep in the forest.

35   Okay, said the gods, we will make you into animals
all kinds of animals
big animals　small animals

°*coyote* wolflike mammal, smaller than most wolves and known for its loud and prolonged howl-
ing at night

all kinds of animals.
The mountains and valleys and forests shall be your home
    and you shall move through them forever.   40

    Still others said:
We want to live with the grace of gods in the world.
We want to live in harmony with all living things.
Okay, said the gods, we will make you into human beings
        all kinds of human beings   45
        some big   some small
      all kinds of human beings.
    The world shall be your home
    and you shall live in it forever.

    Thus all of the living things   50
    chose the form they would take
    and the kind of life they would lead.
    At that time all the creatures
    spoke in the same tongue.
    They were all friends.   55
    They danced and sang together.
    Each day they gathered
    at the Great Council of Living Things.
    They all drank sweet water
    and ate grasses and berries   60
    and leaves and fruit that grew
    out of vast Mother Earth.

    One day coyote did not go to the Council.
    He stayed away and hid himself in the brush.

        I am tired of company.   65
        I am tired of roots and grasses.
        They are tasteless.
        I hunger for something else.

    Coyote lay there thinking these thoughts
    and in the quiet of the afternoon   70
    sleep fell upon him.
    And while he slept in the warm sunshine
    Unupit° came and put fresh red flesh by his nose.

Unupit whispered: It is good.
                It is good.   75
                Taste it.
                It is good.

°*Unupit* a god in Paiute culture

Coyote woke slowly: The meat.
                      The meat.
80   It smells good.

                      It is good.
                      It is very good.
                      Taste it.   urged Unupit.

        And when coyote had tasted it, he said:
85   I will never eat grass again.

    A brown cottontail bounding across a field
                a leap   a tear
            teeth sinking into flesh
    and coyote had made the first kill.
90 No longer did he go to the Great Council.
    He stayed in the brush
    among the manzanita thickets.
    The small animals, when they met him,
    greeted coyote in brotherhood
95 as has always been the way.
    But lust and greed were alive in the world
    and coyote would pounce upon them
    and kill them and eat them.

    'The tortoise leaves a trail in the dust
100 when he drags his tail.'

    Now all the small animals and birds
    would not speak with coyote.
    They would not go near him.
    It had never been like this before.
105 Now there was fear in the hearts of living things
    and the fear was of other living things.
    Mice, rabbits, quail did not go to the Great Council.
    They stayed in their nests and burrows and dens.
    The sparrows and juncos stayed high in the pines and oaks.
110 The smaller creatures became ever more fearful
    as each day passed.
    No longer was there singing and dancing
    among all the living things.

    The large animals sat alone at the Council
115 and wondered what had happened in the world.
        Coyote was our friend.
        Now he kills his brothers.
        He is without friends
        among those weaker than himself.
120   It could happen to all of us.

We can trust only ourselves.
Let us change our ways and customs
and we will be safe.
Let us change our signs and language
and keep to ourselves.   125

So it was that skunks
spoke only to other skunks
and squirrels only to other squirrels
and my clans only to other my clans.
The Great Council of Living Things met no more.   130
No more meetings in brotherhood
as was the way from the beginning.
A few seasons passed
and the tongue that all the creatures
had shared and understood   135
was forgotten.
      And so it is today
that we find it so difficult to speak
with our brothers and sisters.

                                      The End   140

ANALYZING THE STORY

ACTIVITY 3

Answer the following questions. Give evidence from the story to support your answers, where appropriate, and include line numbers for each piece of evidence.

1. Who is telling the story? Who is the story being told to?

2. What kind of story is it? Explain which terms apply: poem, fable, legend, or myth.

3. Describe how Earth was made, according to the Paiute Indians. (lines 11–62) What is common in the requests that each group of living things makes?

4. In your own words, describe the "Great Council of Living Things." (line 58) How do the living things communicate? What do they eat? What are their activities? What is their relationship to one another?

5. Why does coyote decide to stay away from the Council? (lines 63–68)

6. What does Unupit do while coyote is asleep? (line 73) Why does Unupit "whisper" (line 74) and "urge"? (line 83) What is the result of the encounter between coyote and Unupit?

7. What kinds of animals does coyote attack? How do these animals respond? How do the large animals respond? (lines 86–125)

8. How do coyote's actions affect all the living things? What do they do in an attempt to be safe?

9. What is the final result for the Great Council of Living Things? What happens to the *grace* in the world?

10. Who are "our brothers and sisters"? (line 139)

ACTIVITY 4

For each quotation that follows, you will find questions to discuss. Divide into four groups, one quotation for each group, and answer the questions. Then report your ideas to the class. Note the **figurative language** in item 1. (See Appendix A for more information about terms in boldface type.)

1. "But lust and greed were alive in the world/and coyote would pounce upon [the small animals]/and kill them and eat them." (lines 96–98)

   a. Why does the story refer to lust and greed as being "alive in the world"?
   b. According to this tale, what causes the lust and greed?
   c. Using the example of coyote and the meat, explain the meanings of the words *lust* and *greed*. What is the difference between them?

2. "'The tortoise leaves a trail in the dust/when he drags his tail.'" (lines 99–100)

   a. Why do you think this line has quotation marks around it?
   b. What are the possible meanings of this saying?
   c. Why is this "trail in the dust" important?
   d. How does this quotation refer to and represent the actions of coyote?

3. "The large animals sat alone at the Council/and wondered what had happened in the world." (lines 114–115)

   a. How has the world been before coyote decides to eat flesh?
   b. What has the relationship between all living things been?
   c. What negative emotions and forces are created in the world by coyote's actions?

4. "The Confounding"

   a. What does *confounding* mean? According to the tale, what causes "the confounding"?
   b. What causes the animals to change their "ways and customs" (line 122) and "signs and language"? (line 124)
   c. How does fear affect this change of customs and language? What causes the fear?
   d. According to the tale, how does this fear affect us today?

Elements of Literature

Characterization

ACTIVITY 5

Answer these questions about the two main characters in "The Confounding."

Unupit

- Unupit, the character who introduces coyote to the taste of meat, is a god in Paiute culture. What do you think Unupit represents?

- Can you think of characters similar to Unupit in other tales or myths with which you are familiar? Discuss the similarities between Unupit and other characters you may know.

Coyote

- Coyote is a legendary animal figure in the cultures of Native American peoples of the American West. Coyote usually tries to trick other animals or people, often to better his position or situation. What or who do you think coyote represents?

- In many tales of Native American peoples, coyote is the fool and mischief maker, one who playfully makes trouble. The problem for coyote is that he is usually tricked as well. In this story, coyote is more destructive than playful, and he ends up living as "a vagabond and an outlaw." (line 5) How does coyote trick himself in this story? What can we learn from his actions?

Language and Style

ACTIVITY 6

As a storyteller, Sanfield took a tale that he heard and wrote it down for others to read and enjoy, to retell aloud. What do you notice about the language and style of this tale?

Write or discuss the answers to these questions. Give evidence from the story to support your answers.

1. Using "The Confounding" as an example, describe the form of the written tale. How does the written form relate to the tale as it would be told aloud?

2. Find examples of repetition in "The Confounding." Why does the storyteller use repetition? What effect does the repetition have?

3. "The Confounding" contains a mixture of both formal and informal language. Add examples of each to the following chart. Two have been done for you. Why do you think both types of language appear in the tale? What is the effect?

FORMAL LANGUAGE	INFORMAL LANGUAGE
"The sky shall be your home" (use of the formal shall) (line 21)	*"Okay, said the gods" (use of the informal expression okay) (line 17)*

4. "The Confounding" also contains special language that is common to many tales. For example, rather than saying that all the animals and humans spoke the same language, the storyteller says "all the creatures/spoke in the same tongue." (lines 53–54) Instead of saying that coyote fell asleep, the storyteller says "sleep fell upon him." (line 71) Find other examples of special language in "The Confounding" and explain their effect. Why does the storyteller use this type of language? Where does it come from?

5. How is the language and style of a tale different from the language and style of a story? Explain.

Exploring Further

Work in small groups to create a visual representation of the events in "The Confounding." You may want to create a sketch, a diagram, a flowchart, a collage—anything that appeals to you and helps to show the connections between the actions, events, and outcomes of the tale.

Follow these steps:

1. As a class, brainstorm a list of the events and factors that contribute to "The Confounding." Include events such as "the first kill" and emotions such as "greed." You should be able to think of ten or twelve items.

2. In your group, create a visual representation of the tale. Show the connections between the actions, events, and outcomes as graphically as possible and be prepared to display and explain it to the class.

3. As a class, compare all the visual representations. What do you notice about the similarities and differences? What factors did different groups choose to focus on?

WRITING IN RESPONSE

Write briefly on one or more of these topics.

1. What have you learned from "The Confounding" about the values of the Paiutes? Are their values important today? Why or why not?

2. How is another myth, legend, or fable with which you are familiar similar to or different from "The Confounding"?

3. Based on what you know from studying the story and reading about the author, do you consider "The Confounding" to be an authentic retelling of the tale? As you respond to this question, consider who you think has the authority to retell stories from a culture and carry on the oral tradition of a tale.

CREATIVE WRITING

Using language and a style similar to "The Confounding," retell a tale with which you're familiar. Consider the following aspects of Sanfield's storytelling as you prepare your tale: repetition, **rhythm,** poetry, and the mixture of formal and informal language. After you write your story, read it aloud to the class.

ESSAY TOPICS

1. Why do you think the Paiute people tell the story of "The Confounding"? In your essay, consider what you think the "keepers of the legends" are trying to teach all those who hear it.

2. Since "The Confounding" is a story of the behavior of living things, it has many parallels with the characters or themes of other stories. Choose a character from a story or a poem you have read for this course and discuss how he or she illustrates a message from "The Confounding."

3. How is the language and style of "The Confounding" important in delivering its message?

4. Do you think it is possible for a society or culture to exist without a "coyote"? Why or why not?

AUTHOR PROFILE
Steve Sanfield

Steve Sanfield (1937–   ), author, poet, and professional storyteller, is the author of more than twenty-four volumes of poetry, illustrated children's books, and folklore representing numerous cultures, including Jewish, Japanese, and African American. About "The Confounding," Sanfield writes: "It was at an Indian Rodeo in Reno [Nevada] that I first heard a fragment of this tale. I was so intrigued that for the next two years I kept poking and prodding and inquiring, picking up bits and pieces of the story at various gatherings and 'big times' until I was finally able to put it all together. Only then did I dare to present it to some of the tribal elders who were pleased to see it made whole again."

Sanfield became the first full-time Storyteller-in-Residence in the United States in 1977 under the sponsorship of the California Arts Council. Since then he has continued to perform, lecture, and conduct workshops at festivals, conferences, schools, and community centers throughout North America. Sanfield is the founder and Artistic Director of the Sierra Storytelling Festival and the Sierra Storytelling Institute, held each July. His awards include Notable Book of the Year by the American Library Association, The Children's Book Council, and the National Council for Social Studies. He was also the first recipient of the Pacific Region Leadership Award from the National Storytelling Association.

Glossary

Chapter 1 *Gaston*

nap short rest
funny strange
kilo kilogram
stem stick that grows out of the top of a piece of fruit, attaching it to the tree branch
cavity hole
feeler antenna
poke out come out slightly
grip hold firmly
hoist lift with effort
dweller animal or person who lives in a place
creature animal
harvest collect from a field or orchard when ready to eat
squash crush, smash
holler yell, shout
porch outside, roofed extension of a home, where people can sit

Chapter 2 *At Home in the World*

husk remove the hard shell
whitewash cover with a white paint
douse cover or immerse suddenly in liquid

Chapter 3 *Raymond's Run*

hustle work quickly, cleverly
mind take care of, look after
track meet series of track and field events at schools and camps
dash short foot race
relay foot race in which several runners are a team, each one running after the other has finished
put out the tale tell people a lie about someone else in the hope that the lie will travel
freckle small spot of color on the skin, especially on children's faces
subject to fits of fantasy often experiencing strong, distracting experiences of the imagination

gutter lowered side section of street, next to curb, carrying rain and other waste water into corner drains

slosh make splashing sound with feet in water

cuff folded bottom of pant leg

let on admit

high-prance run with knees raised high

rodeo pony small horse used in cowboy competitions

uptight nervous, embarrassed, and/or angry

spelling bee spelling competition

clutch grab, hold onto quickly and hard

ole well-loved person or thing (from "good old")

prodigy child who is unusually talented or intelligent in a special area

trot slow run, jog

liable to apt to, probably going to

allowance money received periodically by children from their parents

sidekick person who stands by a superior

throw stones criticize

chicken afraid

chit-chat informal conversation

a lotta a lot of

salty sarcastically challenging

whup hit, spank

ventriloquist person who can throw his or her voice to a doll to make it seem as if the doll (dummy) is speaking

mule team pair or group of mules working together

Fatso insulting term to describe an overweight person

organdy thin, silky fabric

sash wide belt made of fabric

Hansel and Gretel popular children's story about two children who get lost in the forest and discover a witch's house made of candy and cookies made of baked children

pageant play with little or no speaking or action, but with many costumes, characters, and scenery

jam-packed crowded

corsage small flower or bunch of flowers worn on clothing

parkee park worker

rowdy wild, undisciplined

swirl make circular movements, spin

glockenspiel portable xylophone-like musical instrument with bell-like sound

stilts long poles with footholds, used for walking and for the purpose of making a person much taller

a run for your money challenging competition

periscope viewing instrument, used in submarines, that projects out of the water and uses two angled mirrors for seeing at a right angle from the viewer

stomp pound the feet on the floor

run smack into crash into, hit hard and suddenly

holler scream, yell

static interference noise on radio

choo-choo train word for train used with children to imitate the sound of a steam engine

chug make the throbbing sound of a steam engine

crouch bend low with arms and legs close to the body
get on your mark prepare to start a race
zoom move very quickly
blurred impossible to see clearly
jut out stick out, project
tuck place under something
walk tall be proud
whine long, high-pitched sound, as a sad dog or complaining child
huff and puff breathe noisily
yank pull quickly and hard
shush tell or motion someone to be quiet
smiling to beat the band showing great happiness
phony artificial, fake
bug ask again and again, bother repeatedly, nag
rep reputation
baddest dialect for "best"

Chapter 4 *Bluebirdbluebirdthrumywindow*

fundamental basic
procreate produce, have children
ulcerated with open sores
harridan old woman
polkadot decorated with a pattern of dots or circles
shroud cloth used to cover dead bodies
leper person with a rare infectious disease that causes open sores and loss of body parts
baptized used water in a sacrament as in the Christian ritual for entry into the church
goddess female god
Siamese a person from Siam, the former name of Thailand; a reference to a faraway, exotic land; a breed of cat
scramble on move quickly and in a disorderly way
sinister dark, troubling, threatening

Chapter 5 *Two Kinds*

prodigy child who is unusually talented or intelligent in a special area
to lop off to cut off carelessly
soggy very wet
clump small bunch of hair stuck together
listlessly without energy or interest
prop up support
bellow loud, deep sound
frenzied very excited and fast paced
mesmerize demand full attention; hypnotize
sauciness slightly impolite, almost overconfident behavior
curtsy bow performed by a female
bad-mouth speak critically of someone or something
pick on criticize
encore additional performance in response to the applause of the audience
Grieg Norwegian composer Edvard Grieg (1843–1907)
ear-splitting having a loud and unpleasant tone
discordant inharmonious, unmatched in tone and pitch

squabble argue
snotty acting in a superior and unfriendly manner
Chinatown a neighborhood in San Francisco
Schumann German composer Robert Schumann (1810–1856)
dawdle waste time by moving slowly or doing unrelated activities
debut first public appearance
squawk make an unpleasant, screeching sound
tutu short ballet dress for a dancer
stricken miserable, shocked
Madama Butterfly an opera by Giacomo Puccini, which debuted in 1904
devastate to completely hurt or shock
gawker person who stares out of curiosity, often after an unfortunate event
fiasco complete failure
budge move
nonchalantly in an easy-going, nonserious manner
Alakazam word used in magic when someone or something appears, disappears, or
    changes form
brittle easily damaged or destroyed as a result of excessive stiffness
plead beg

Chapter 6 *The Waltz*

a peach of a world a wonderful world
corker something delightful or wonderful (often used sarcastically)
a stitch any
sue ask politely, as a gentleman to a lady
bewilderment confusion
futility hopelessness
degradation disgrace, humiliation
brooding serious thinking, worrying
scrape very low bow as a result of excessive, often false, politeness
may-I-have-this-one request to dance
struck right down dead killed for lying (people often jokingly call upon lightning to
    strike and kill them if they are lying)
a day in the country an easy, happy time
labor pain pain associated with giving birth
scaredy-cat person who is too easily frightened (used among children)
beri-beri paralyzing disease caused by vitamin deficiency
won the toss at the beginning of many games, a coin is thrown (tossed) into the air to
    decide who starts
thrilled very happy, excited (often used sarcastically)
tonsils lumps of tissue at the back of the throat, on each side, which frequently
    become infected and are often removed by surgery during childhood
get under way start
grasp understanding
hold out not give in; insist gently
sitting it out not dancing one dance
acclimate become used to the situation or environment
down time period in a football game
shin front part of the leg below the knee which is very sensitive to being hit
traces where he is at the moment

lie low wait and do nothing

cloister protect from the outside world, as in a convent or monastery

outraged indignant; very angry because of insult or injustice

maliciously purposely mean or cruel

high spirits very good mood, state of being full of energy (often used to to describe young horses)

captious too critical or fault finding

sinew tissue connecting muscles to the bones of the body (used for animals)

hurl throw, move very quickly

scrimmage struggle, especially fighting over the ball in football

plaster cast cloth covered with fine white clay that is put over a broken bone and allowed to harden in order to protect the break by preventing it from moving

dreary dull, boring

effete overrefined; excessively and falsely sophisticated and cultured

instep inside part of the arch of the foot

hulking big, heavy, and clumsy

gangplank board used for walking between a boat and land or a dock; board used for a condemned sailor or criminal on board ship to walk off into the sea and die

swaddle wrap cloth around

"The Fall of the House of Usher" horror story by Edgar Allen Poe

fearful toll terrible destruction, damage

degenerate cunning crazy and cruel cleverness

stumble false step, near fall

twenty-yard dash short, fast foot race

leer look at threateningly, lustfully, or with cruel triumph

bestial like a wild beast

noxious bad for the health

obscene immoral, disgustingly terrible

travesty ridiculous, poor imitation

gyration circular movement

splinter break into pieces

capsize turn upside down in water (refers to boats)

Chapter 7 *Silent Snow, Secret Snow*

trinket small, unimportant object, often decorative

link connecting piece; cuff link (jewelry used in place of a button to hold sleeve cuff closed)

trod walk upon

carnelian red or reddish brown quartz (a kind of stone)

seclusion state of being hidden away or separated from other people

Big Dipper the constellation Ursa Major: seven stars shaped like a large dipper

minnow very small fish (one to two inches long) commonly found near lakeshores and traveling in groups of twenty or more

sash long, narrow piece of fabric used as a belt

swamp wetlands

headrail wooden or metal railing at the head of a bed frame, behind the pillow

cobbled paved with large, rounded stones (cobblestones)

clumsy not graceful, awkward; not in complete physical control

muffle soften, make less loud as a result of some kind of covering or barrier

remoteness state of being far away

inaudible too soft to be heard

ragged irregular, uneven; not smooth or straight

hush produce quiet, silence

seethe move as if boiling, often associated with anger

thump make a dull, indistinct, heavy knocking or pounding sound

sheathed covered or enclosed in something that fits closely and has the same shape as what it is covering

obliterate hide from view or destroy

delusion false, dreamlike thought or impression

flicker alternate in brightness—first bright, then dim, and so on

dimple shallow indentation or wrinkle in the skin, usually on the cheeks

interval period of time between events when nothing related to the events is happening

disingenuous with intended deception; dishonest

Northwest Passage hypothetical water route from the East to West Coast of North America

distressing upsetting

mute silent

utterly completely

extract pull out from some larger or more general element, often with difficulty

obscure hard to see or identify

palpable capable of being felt or touched; real, not abstract

soothing relaxing; reducing pain or discomfort

perfunctory mechanical; done quickly without thinking

inherent naturally contained inside someone or something

varnish cover with a hard, clear, smooth paint

mirthful happy

twig very small branch, usually leafless

dessicate dry out

starling small, brown bird

weather vane metal device usually placed on top of house or barn to show wind direction

gutter canal-like depression in a street carrying waste water into drainage system under the street

delta point where river spreads out and breaks up into smaller streams as it enters an ocean or a bay (in shape of Greek letter "delta")

eczema skin rash caused by allergic reaction

runneled covered with little canals

burr rough, thorny, soft outer shell of horse chestnut (large, silky-brown inedible nut)

congeal stick together in lumps

inlay small picture or lettering set permanently into same material of different color, or different material altogether, usually for artistic effect

hollow indentation, depression

cunningly very cleverly

mortar cement, attach

gnawing result of slow eating or biting

tether tie to something stable to prevent escape

persevere continue trying

severance cutting off, disconnecting

resolute firmly decided

wren bird with dark, silky feathers

grazingly slightly

dalliance playful pause or break in normal activity

enhancement increase in positive qualities

laden heavily, thickly covered

mirage illusion

encroach slowly move in on another's property or territory

defraud trick out of, rob

menace danger

inquisition serious questioning for purpose of finding fault; originally interrogation by the Roman Catholic Church to find nonbelievers

hearth fireplace

evasiveness attempt to avoid answering questions directly or honestly

steed horse

brine salt water

scrutiny close examination

prestidigitation skillful movement of fingers and hands to perform magic

sooty blackened from fire

flutter small, rapid, up-and-down or side-to-side movement

banish send away to a foreign land

deference respect

hiss make a sound like an "s"

farce silly comedy making fun of events and behavior; unreal event

grotesque ugly; strangely, horribly shaped

parody humorous imitation

gross big and ugly

humdrum ordinary, common, boring

abundant in large supply

formidable scary, threatening

imminent coming soon

appallingly horrifyingly, disgustingly, shockingly

disconcerted confused, unsure about what to think or what to do next

resonant sounding deep, loud, and full

inevitably unavoidably, definitely

sibilance the sound of "s" or "sh"

smother cover completely to stop sound or breathing

exult show extreme happiness or triumph

gash large, ugly cut or wound

brutally cruelly and violently

clutch grab

loathing hatred

exorcise pull out all the bad or evil

seamless perfectly smooth, with no break in evenness

waver move back and forth or up and down

counterpoint accompanying sound or movement that is different from or in opposition to the main sound or movement, but is in harmony with it

paling pointed, vertical board used in a fence

Chapter 8 *A Blessing*

bound move with a leap or series of leaps

willow tree with long, slender, light green leaves and drooping branches

barbed wire wire fencing with sharp points to discourage escape

pasture field were animals eat grass

graze eat wild grass or plants (refers to animals only)

ripple move with small waves or with an up-and-down motion (describes the horse's skin in the poem)

munch eat slowly and calmly

tuft bunch of soft, lightweight material growing together

slenderer thinner

nuzzle rub gently and affectionately with the nose

caress touch or stroke lovingly or gently

Chapter 9 *Aunt Moon's Young Man*

omen sign that something bad will happen in the future

in tarnation (idiom) used to express annoyance; similar to damning

cutting edge tone capable of hurting feelings

lukewarm close to being right

sullen gloomy, silent, resentful

wistful full of wishing for something that may not be satisfied or of thoughts of the past

hypnotist person who produces a sleeplike state in another person and who, as a result, can control the actions or thoughts of that person

charge fill with excitement and emotion

reckon think (informal)

rodeo show in which performers ride horses and rope cattle

crew cut very short hair cut

furtively quietly, secretly

pious showing a conspicuous—and often false—respect for God and religion

revival a public religious meeting, often with music and impassioned speaking, intended to awaken religious faith

unruffled undisturbed

mirage the effect of hot-air conditions, which creates the illusion of water or the distortion of distant objects

ailment illness

card sharp expert in cheating at card games

fallow characterized by inactivity; (land) plowed but left unseeded

slumberous sleepy; quiet; calm

smug showing too much self-satisfaction

butt strike [the tree] with the head

rabies disease of the nervous system, passed on by the bite of an infected animal and causing madness and death

sage an herb

burro donkey

lost her pallor lost her smug attitude; *pallor* refers to an unnatural paleness of the complexion

Chapter 10 *D.P.*

Rhine a river in Germany

ration predetermined amount of something restricted—in this case, food

numbly without feeling

artillery larger, stationary guns (as opposed to handguns)

sergeant noncommissioned officer in the army/marines, ranking just above a private

maneuvers planned movements of troops or warships
lieutenant an officer in the army/marines, ranking above sergeant
sinew a tendon in the body

Chapter 11 *Mass of the Moon Eclipse*

frayed worn out in places
stately dignified
resurrection renewal; the rising from the grave of the dead
allurement a thing that attracts us
husk the outer covering of a vegetable, fruit or seed; something worthless; something
    that serves as support
unquenchable impossible to satisfy
firefly a beetle which, at night when it is active, produces a flash of light
implacable incapable of being altered
trivial unimportant or insignificant
increment process of regular increases in size

Chapter 13 *On the Road*

freight freight train (carrying material goods, not passengers)
seep slowly drip through or along something
sopping completely wet to the point of dripping
flaky in small, light delicate pieces
reverend minister of a church
hunch over bend forward with the back arched
pillar column that supports a building
crucifix cross with the body of Christ on it; symbol of the Roman Catholic Church
lacy window window with a decorative pattern in concrete, stone, or metal
ramrod metal rod used to load ammunition into a gun
grunt heavy throaty noise
screaking screaming + cracking = screaking
ferociously with intense fierceness, strength
lunge sudden forward movement (of the body)
rafter wooden beam (board) that supports the roof
debris broken remains
bum unemployed homeless person
hobo unemployed homeless person, often traveling from place to place
hobo jungle temporary living place that hobos build from scraps of wood and metal
barren bare, without leaves
embankment raised area of dirt next to railroad tracks
makeshift temporary, not well made
side-tracking leaving, getting off the road
rapped hit hard
night stick wooden club (a thick stick) used by police to control people
wham banging, hitting sound
holler yell loudly
corridor hall
sloppy messy, dirty looking
nursing taking care of something that has been hurt
undue excessive

Chapter 14 *The Local Production of Cinderella*

battered beaten by a spouse
schizophrenic mentally ill
weary deeply tired because of prolonged fatiguing circumstances
pluck pull out quickly, deliberately
butterflies nervousness
aloha shirt brightly colored Hawaiian shirt
crater giant circular hole, as in a volcano
bond paper high-quality white 8½ × 11-inch paper for business letters
queasy nauseated, sick to the stomach
cuckoo crazy
scoot move a very short distance quickly and smoothly
swivel chair chair that turns 360 degrees, as an office chair or bar stool
gnat small flying insect that bites
slug small, elongated, crawling animal resembling a snail without a shell
succulent dry-climate plant with thick leaves that retain moisture
luau Hawaiian feast
ukulele small Hawaiian guitar
romp run playfully
javelin spear used in throwing competitions
catamaran recreational boat with two parallel hulls
swish make a hissing or rustling sound
zing make a buzzing or ringing sound
bolt eat very quickly
muumuu loose Hawaiian dress
lei Hawaiian necklace made of flowers
garland chain of flowers
ace perform extremely well on a test
flop fail
flawless perfect
snivelling wimpering, crying lightly
lurch move a very short distance quickly and uncontrollably
wayward traveling in an unknown direction
loom threaten, look threatening
prance run in a jumping fashion, like a horse
willowy with long arms and legs and moving gracefully
nudge touch with a strong movement to get someone's attention
clop make a soft knocking sound
shrug raise shoulders to gesture "I don't know"
verve enthusiasm, energy
extension ballet: raising and straightening of the leg
shabby sloppy; badly done
shrink psychiatrist
scum lazy or dishonest people

Chapter 15 *One Human Hand*

scroll long, straight piece of paper with a roller attached at the top and bottom
crane bird with long legs and neck, which lives near water
blight-struck diseased or spoiled

shrike songbird with a high voice and hooked beak, colored gray, black, or white
gizzard second stomach of a bird
rice paper paper made out of rice
flee hurry away from something or someplace
nigh near

Chapter 16 *The Magic Barrel*

meager containing little; poor
repose rest
menagerie collection of animals
ascetic thin; leading a life of denial
curriculum vitae academic résumé
dowry money or goods paid by the family of the bride to the husband
imperceptible not noticeable
tactless inconsiderate; impolite
guffaw laugh loudly
upbraid scold
dismiss send away
melancholy sad
cupid angel of love
conscience-stricken feeling guilty
avow swear; claim
entangle himself catch himself in his own argument
fedora felt hat with a brim
trepidation fear
strew throw
calling profession
Highest God
wince make a pained facial expression
mystical having a connection with the spiritual
wilt become limp
profusion of many
machination devious plan
revelation realization
waylay pull aside
abjectly in a begging manner
sanctified holy
refrain stop oneself
chide scold
wanly weakly
by-product side effect
relentless persistent
shudder tremble with fear or dread
discard item thrown aside
tenement poor apartment building in need of repair
asthmatic breathing with great effort
ghastly gray or white, like a ghost
vestibule entrance way
frenziedly hysterically
haggard worn out

mock make fun of

chant recite in a songlike monotone

Chapter 17 *Romero's Shirt*

bolt fasten with metal construction material

pecan type of nut

den room used for family activities

burr rough, roundish seed pod

graded leveled

one-by tongue and groove overhang wooden construction material that is one inch thick

amputation removal of a limb

juniper evergreen bush or shrub with prickly vegetation

baptism Christian sacrament or rite of initiation into the church

mass Roman Catholic service

run-off overflow of water

conspicuously in plain sight

crust hardened wax

pliers tool used for bending wires

prune cut or trim

shears large scissorslike tool used for cutting

brusque abrupt or rough in manner

virtuous morally pure, upright

ruse a trick

cynicism state of distrust or disbelief

mulberry type of tree that bears an edible berry

Chapter 18 *Sunday in the Park*

sandbox an area filled with sand, where children play

stolid unemotional

insolent insulting

menace threaten

suffuse fill

impotent powerless

rapt attentive

chant song

acutely extremely

Chapter 19 *Black Boy*

forsaken deserted, empty

woo try to attract by showing affection or kindness

foam thick white bubbles

indolent lazy, slow moving, relaxed

murmur talk softly

tiptoe walk on toes in order to be quiet

drift hill-like pile of sand created by wind

spark tiny flash of fire

tide periodic rising and falling movement of the oceans caused by the pull of the Moon

gait speed of walking

pout stick out in a round shape

sidle step sideways

boardwalk raised wooden walkway along a beach

timber wood

sheen soft shine

dew early morning drops of water on grass and other plants outside

vacant empty, unoccupied

tar black, sticky substance used for paving roads

beam long piece of cut wood, like a board

idle lazy, inactive

languor laziness, a state of inactivity and deep relaxation

limb arm or leg

fleck knock off with a quick movement of the finger

quiver shake quickly, briefly, slightly

wheel turn or move around in a semicircular pattern

gull kind of bird usually living by the sea

rosette small rose shape

mirage illusion, something that a person thinks she or he sees but is not really there, as water in a desert

Northern Lights colorful moving streaks of light seen in northern nighttime skies

outlet place where water from inland, like a river, pours into the sea

torch large, thick stick with fire burning at one end, usually for light

brink edge of something

perilous dangerous

cavern large cave

sole bottom of a shoe

kid gloves leather gloves made of baby goat skin, usually very expensive; the expression "to treat with kid gloves" means to treat someone very carefully as if he or she is very delicate or sensitive

garland chain of flowers or other decorative item hung in a wavelike pattern from balconies, ceilings, or walls

stable place where horses are kept

saddle leather seat on a horse for rider to sit on

ill at ease uncomfortable

high and mighty proud

heedless inattentive, uncaring

nip take small bites out of something

draw up approach

forelegs front legs of a horse

jockey horse-race rider

canter move at a moderately fast speed; used for horses

jetty small pier, often made of rocks, projecting into water to reduce currents

flank side of a horse

crop riding stick or small whip

gallop running speed, used for horses

sprightliness high energy, liveliness

fling throw quickly

arch rounded overhead part of a door or window

grieve feel great sadness because of a death

cradle rocking bed for a baby

wail make a loud, sad noise like crying
kin relatives

Chapter 20 *Gravity*

catheter a thin tube surgically inserted into the body in order to inject or remove fluids
take in stride do without difficulty
equanimity calmness
tacky cheap and in poor taste
blanch become pale because of embarrassment or disgust
leverage mechanical advantage; help
potpourri dried and scented flower petals and leaves; used for adding fragrance
mop wipe off sweat
shard broken piece
relish feeling of pleasure
trajectory path of an object thrown into the air
apish like an ape

Chapter 21 *The Confounding*

vagabond someone without a home and who travels from place to place
cottontail rabbit
brush bushes
manzanita low-growing thick bush with small tough leaves and berries
thicket bushes growing together in a cluster
pounce jump upon swiftly and suddenly
tortoise a reptile that lives in desert areas and is similar in appearance to a turtle
quail small bird
burrow home that animals dig for themselves underground
sparrow small bird
junco small bird
clan group of families or tribes who share common ancestry

Author Profile Bibliography

Chapter 1 *Gaston*

Balakian, Nona. *The World of William Saroyan: A Literary Interpretation*. Lewisburg, PA: Bucknell UP, 1997.

Gifford, Barry and Lawrence Lee. *Saroyan: A Biography*. University of California Press, 1998.

Chapter 2 *At Home in the World*

Milligan, Bryce, Mary Guerrero Milligan, and Angela de Hoyos. *Floricanto Si!* New York: Penguin, 1998.

Catacalos, Rosemary, "David Talamantéz on the Last Day of Second Grade." *The Arts: National Endowment for the Arts*. <http://www.arts.endow.gov/explor/Writers/catacalos.html>.

Rosemary Catacalos, "1999–2000 Affiliated Scholars," *The Institute for Research on Women & Gender*, Stanford University. <http://www.standford.edu/group/IRWG>.

Chapter 3 *Raymond's Run*

Byerman, Keith. *Fingering the Jagged Grain: Tradition and Form in Recent Black Fiction*. Athens: U of Georgia P, 1985. 101; 114–115.

———.*The Oxford Companion to Women's Writing in the United States*. Ed. Cathy N. Davidson and Linda Wagner-Martin. New York: Oxford UP, 1995. Byerman, Keith. "Bambara, Toni Cade."

Deck, Alice A. *Black Women in America: An Historical Encyclopedia*. Ed. Darlene Clark Hine, Elsa Barkley Brown, and Rosalyn Terbog-Penn. Vol. 1. Bloomington and Indianapolis: Indiana UP, 1993. Deck, Alice A. "Bambara, Toni Cade."

Morrison, Toni. *Literature and the Urban Experience: Essays on the City and Literature*. Ed. Michael C. Jaye and Ann Chalmer Watts. New Brunswick: Rutgers UP, 1981. 40–41. Morrison, Toni. "City Limits, Village Values: Concepts of the Neighborhood in Black Fiction."

Serafin, Steven R., comp. and ed. *A Library of Literary Criticism: Modern Black Writers Supplement*. Vol. 2. New York: A Frederick Ungar Book, Continuum, 1995.

Taylor, Eleanor W. *Black Women Writers (1950–1980): A Critical Evaluation*. Ed. Mari Evans. New York: Doubleday, 1984. 65–66. Taylor, Eleanor W. "Music as Theme: The Jazz Mode in the Work of Toni Cade Bambara."

Vertreace, Martha M. *American Women Writing Fiction: Memory, Identity, Family Space.* Ed. Mickey Pearlman. Lexington: UP of Kentucky, 1989. 155–56; 165–66.

Chapter 4 *Bluebirdbluebirdthrumywindow*

Gates, Henry Louis, and Nellie Y. McKay, eds. *African American Literature.* New York: Norton, 1997. 1251–54.

Sanchez, Sonia. Interview. *The Morning Show.* KPFA, Berkeley, CA. 11 Mar. 1999.

———. *Shake Loose My Skin.* Boston: Beacon, 1999.

Chapter 5 *Two Kinds*

Huntley, E. D. *Amy Tan: A Critical Companion.* Westport, CT: Greenwood, 1998.

Schell, Orville. "Your Mother Is In Your Bones." *New York Times Book Review*, 19 Mar. 1989: 3, 28.

Chapter 6 *The Waltz*

Calhoun, Randall. *Dorothy Parker: A BioBibliography.* Westport, CT: Greenwood, 1993.

Kinney, Arthur F. *Dorothy Parker, Revised.* New York: Twayne, 1998.

Chapter 7 *Silent Snow, Secret Snow*

Martin, Harry. *The Art of Knowing: The Poetry and Prose of Conrad Aiken.* Columbia: U of Michigan P, 1988.

Spivey, Ted R. *Time's Stop in Savannah: Conrad Aiken's Inner Journey.* Macon, GA: Mercer UP, 1997.

Spivey, Ted, and Arthur Waterman. *Conrad Aiken: A Priest of Consciousness.* New York: AMS Press, 1989.

Chapter 8 *A Blessing*

Smith, D. *The Pure Clear Word: Essays on the Poetry of James Wright.* Urbana: U of Illinois P, 1982.

Chapter 9 *Aunt Moon's Young Man*

Allen, Paula Gunn. "This Wilderness in My Blood: Spiritual Foundations of the Poetry of Five American Indian Women." In *The Sacred Hoop: Recovering the Feminine in American Indian Traditions.* Boston: Beacon, 1986. 165–84.

Votteler, Thomas, ed. *Contemporary Literary Criticism.* Vol. 73. Detroit: Gale, 1993. 147–165.

Chapter 10 *D.P.*

Boon, Kevin A. *Chaos Theory and the Interpretation of Literary Texts: The Case of Kurt Vonnegut.* Tuscaloosa, AL: U of Alabama P, 1994.

Chernuchin, Michael, ed. *Vonnegut Talks!* Forest Hills, NY: Pylon, 1997.

Chapter 11 *Mass of the Moon Eclipse*

Dear, P., ed. *Contemporary Authors: New Revisions Series.* Vol. 50. Detroit: Gale, 1996.

Matuz, R., ed. *Contemporary Literary Criticism.* Vol. 66. Detroit: Gale, 1991.

Peacock, S., ed. *Contemporary Authors.* Vol. 163. Detroit: Gale, 1998.

Chapter 12 *Hills Like White Elephants*

Baker, Carlos. *Ernest Hemingway: A Life Story.* New York: Scribner, 1968.
Mellow, James R. *A Life without Consequences: Hemingway.* Boston: Houghton Mifflin, 1992.
Meyers, Jeffrey. *Hemingway: A Biography.* New York: Harper and Row, 1985.

Chapter 13 *On the Road*

Emanuel, James A., and Theodore Gross, eds. *Dark Symphony: Negro Literature in America.* New York: Free Press, 1968. 191–213.
Gates, Henry Louis, and Nellie Y. McKay, eds. *African American Literature.* New York: Norton, 1997. 1251–54.

Chapter 14 *The Local Production of Cinderella*

Dickstein, Morris. "Ghost Stories: The New Wave of Jewish Writing." Literary Symposium *Tikkun* Nov.–Dec. 1997.
Lambert, Miriam V. "Other People's Autobiographer." *Harvard Magazine* March/April 1997. <http://www.harvard-magazine.com/ma97/alum-other.html>.
"Allegra Goodman: A Community Apart." *PublishersWeekly*.com 27 Jul. 1998 <http://www.publishersweekly./articles/19980727_70225.asp>

Chapter 15 *One Human Hand*

Lee, Li-Young. *Rose.* Brockport, NY: BOA Editions. 1986.
———. *The City in Which I Love You.* Brockport, NY: BOA Editions, 1990.
———. *The Winged Seed, A Remembrance.* New York: Simon and Schuster, 1995.

Chapter 16 *The Magic Barrel*

Abramson, Edward. *Bernard Malamud Revisited.* New York: Twayne, 1993.
Malamud, Bernard. *The Stories of Bernard Malamud.* New York: Farrar, Straus and Giroux, 1983. vii–xii.
Salzberg, Joel. *Critical Essays on Bernard Malamud.* Boston: Hall, 1987.

Chapter 17 *Romero's Shirt*

Gilb, Dagoberto. *The Magic of Blood.* New York: Grove, 1994.
———. "Notes on Lit from the Americas." *ANQ* 10. 2 (1997): 40–43.
Reid, Jan. "Dagoberto Gilb." *The Texas Monthly* 23.9 (1995): 130–31, 170.

Chapter 18 *Sunday in the Park*

Mitgang, Herbert, *New York Times Book Review,* 14 Feb. 1965.
Washington Post Book World 11 Nov. 1979.
Kaufman, Bel. *Up the Down Staircase.* Englewood Cliffs, NJ: Prentice-Hall, 1965.

Chapter 19 *Black Boy*

Davidson, Cathy N., and Linda Wagner-Martin, eds. *Oxford Companion to Women's Writing in the United States.* New York: Oxford UP, 1995.
Boyle, Kay. *Life Being the Best & Other Short Stories.* Ed. and introd. by Sandra Spanier. New York: New Directions, 1988.
———. *Nothing Ever Breaks Except the Heart.* Garden City, NY: Doubleday, 1966.

Chapter 20 *Gravity*

Hall, S., ed. *Contemporary Literary Criticism. Yearbook 1984.* Detroit: Gale, 1985.
Jones, D., and J. D. Jorgenson, eds. *Contemporary Authors: New Revision Series.* Vol. 62. Detroit: Gale, 1998.

Chapter 21 *The Confounding*

Feineman, Carol. "Steve Sanfield: Writer." *Union* [Grass Valley–Nevada City, CA] 12 June 1998.
Sanfield, Steve. Personal interview. 30 Aug. 1999.
———. Letter to the author. 7 Oct. 1999.

Literary Terms

CHARACTERIZATION

Development of a character; the deliberate and careful accumulation of details that create a complete person or character in a work of literature. Readers understand a character because of these details, such as background, attitudes, conversations, thoughts, behavior, and information from and interaction with other characters.

> In the story "Gravity," details about the mother's behavior appear from the beginning of the story to develop a complete character. For example, in a flashback in which she notices that her twelve-year-old son is having trouble seeing a Broadway marquee, she gives him her own glasses to wear so that he can see the show from his seat. Then she behaves as if to defy anyone to look at or comment about the glasses. Such details concerning the mother's actions toward her son accumulate through the story to define her character.
>
> Often a single detail can develop a characterization very rapidly. In "The Magic Barrel," the main character, Leo Finkle, a young man living in New York City in the mid-twentieth century, considers taking a walking stick with him on a blind date. The fact that he can contemplate doing something so out-of-fashion tells us that he has extremely limited contact with the world around him.

FIGURATIVE LANGUAGE

Language that makes connections and causes the reader to make associations that are not always automatically made.

> In "Aunt Moon's Young Man," the writer describes tornadoes as "taking away the saints and leaving behind the devils." There are neither saints nor devils in the story, but the reader's associations with saints and devils add saintly qualities to the victims of a disaster and evil qualities to those who escape unharmed.
>
> In "Gravity," the author compares illness to a body of water. The main character's illness is ". . . a constant reminder of how wide and unswimmable the gulf [is] becoming between [the young man] and the ever receding shoreline of the well . . . ." Here, the author uses the image of an ever-widening body of water, with all its implications of danger and drowning, to emphasize how, when a person is dying, hope becomes weaker and weaker, and the dying person feels less and less connection with others.

Metaphor

A comparison of two seemingly unrelated things that, upon analysis, have common qualities. Metaphors are different from similes in that the writer does not use *like* or *as*.

> In "Aunt Moon's Young Man," one character is described as follows: "His eyes were broken windows." The author equates the eyes of the character with broken windows. The reader, by recalling associations with broken windows—such as glass, fragility, uselessness, vulnerability, sharpness, and impaired visibility—learns something about the character.
>
> In "Raymond's Run," the narrator, a girl called Squeaky, refers to two other girls her age as "ventriloquist" and "dummy." This simple comparison makes the relationship between those two children clear.

Simile

A comparison of two seemingly unrelated things that, upon analysis, have common qualities. The comparison in a simile is signaled by *like*, *as*, or *as if*.

> In "Bluebirdbluebirdthrumywindow," the homeless woman's "cape surrounded her like a shroud." In this simile, the author equates the cape to a shroud. The reader recalls the meaning of shroud, a cloth used to cover a body when it is being buried, and understands that the homeless woman lives in a deathlike state.
>
> In "Raymond's Run," the author equates grass with sidewalk when she says the grass is "as hard as sidewalk" for the young narrator. The reader knows that sidewalks are made of cement and understands that the city grass is unnaturally hard.

Personification

Giving human qualities to animals, inanimate objects, or abstract concepts.

> The 100-year-old Chinese scrolls in "One Human Hand" are moved about by breezes that "send their bones all knocking against the walls." Bones knocking on walls gives a human quality to the scrolls, a quality associated with the old, even the dead, thus giving both life and age to the scrolls simultaneously.
>
> In "Gaston," the father refers to the bug in the peach as a *grand boulevardier* who is "out of house and home." By giving the creature human qualities, the father tries to allay the child's fears. At the same time, the author implies that the plight of a bug in a peach may have similarities with human problems.

Symbolism

A concrete physical object, person, or situation used to represent an abstract concept. Symbols often are clues to larger issues, wider implications, or themes.

> In "Aunt Moon's Young Man," Aunt Moon's silver jewelry symbolizes Indian culture as distinct from the gold that the Europeans came searching for in their conquest of the new world.
>
> The stranded lighthouse in "Black Boy" may be a symbol of something that we're looking for in the distance but that is in fact all around us.

The symbol of the white elephant in "Hills Like White Elephants" gives the reader clues about the characters and theme because of what it represents: something useless, unwanted, or burdensome to the person who possesses it.

FORESHADOWING

Clues about what will happen later in the story.

The grandfather's kid gloves in "Black Boy" are mentioned very early in the story. They ironically foreshadow the purpose for which those hands will be used at the end of the story—a purpose associated with a very different kind of glove.

In "D.P.," an incongruity appears near the beginning of the story that foreshadows a potential source for trouble later in the story. As a small boy is out walking with his peers from an orphanage in Germany, some German people watching the children refer to the boy as obviously "an American"; an instant later, the same boy greets these onlookers "in German, the only language he knew."

Sometimes a sentence early in a story foreshadows later conflict by the addition of a single key word, as in the opening sentence of "Two Kinds": "My mother believed you could be anything you wanted to be in America." The use of *believed* here suggests that the statement, because it is only a belief, may be proven incorrect.

IMAGERY

Language used to appeal to the five senses: smell, touch, taste, sight, and hearing.

The snow creeping down the man's neck in "On the Road" is described as "seeping down his neck, cold, wet, sopping in his shoes . . . ." This helps the reader to feel the unpleasant dampness and cold. Later, the man experiences a "cold stone wall" and wet clothing, "clammy cold wet and shoes sloppy with snow water." Again, the reader senses mentally the physical discomfort of the coldness and wetness.

In "Aunt Moon's Young Man," the description of Bessie's environment appeals to the reader's sense of hearing: "But Bessie was unruffled. She walked on in the empty mirage of heat, the sound of her cane blending in with horses' hooves and the rhythmic pumping of oil wells out east." The blended sounds of Bessie's cane, the horses, and the oil wells help the reader hear the combined sounds and think about the aspects of life they represent.

IRONY

An incongruity between expectation and reality or between appearance and truth, often shown by the author's pairing of words and events that do not normally belong together. Irony is used to highlight a difficult truth by pointing out a contradiction within it.

Situational irony

A contrast between what is expected or intended and what actually happens, between appearance and truth, between what a character intends to communicate and what is perceived as the message, or between what a character believes and a reader knows.

In "On the Road," the door of a church, a traditional refuge of the poor, is slammed in the face of a cold, hungry, penniless wanderer.

Tonal irony

An unexpected or surprising word or phrase in a sentence.

> An unexpected final item in a series in "Bluebirdbluebirdthrumywindow" adds a twist
> to the tone: ". . . she sits through winter, spring, summer, fall, and law students . . . ."

Verbal irony

Intentional contradiction that is conveyed through language and that shows deliberate contrast between appearance and truth or between expectation and reality; sarcasm.

> In "On the Road," after the church door is slammed on the poor man, the man who
> slammed it is referred to as "the holy man." He is clearly not "holy" after what he has
> done.
>   In "Bluebirdbluebirdthrumywindow," the homeless black woman is called the
> "old black goddess of our American civilization at its peak." Any civilization at its
> "peak" would not produce a starving, homeless "goddess."

MOOD

The overall atmosphere or feeling of a work of literature created by tone, setting, and/or
figurative language.

> In keeping with the mood suggested by the title, a strong mood of peace and content-
> ment opens "Sunday in the Park": "It was still warm in the late afternoon sun, and the
> city noises came muffled through the trees in the park. She put her book down on the
> bench, removed her sunglasses, and sighed contentedly."
>   Setting combines with imagery to create the mood of "D.P.," which is set partly in
> a "large estate overlooking the Rhine" in the American zone of occupied Germany
> after World War II. Into this area of beautiful isolation in severe postwar conditions,
> orphaned children—abandoned children who "might have wandered off the face of
> the earth, searching for parents who had long ago stopped searching for them"—are
> introduced. Yet, these children were also "81 sparks of human life." The image of
> "sparks" to describe these abandoned children in this picturesque but lonely setting
> adds a subordinate mood of hope to a larger atmosphere of hopelessness.

NARRATOR

The teller of the story; the narrator can be a character in the story.

> In "Silent Snow, Secret Snow," the narrator takes the point of view of the boy so that
> he seems to be telling the story, but in fact the mature style and insight of the narration
> reveal the author's voice.

PARADOX

Something that seems contradictory or impossible but upon further analysis is possible.

> A reference is made to the narrator's "dying again" in "Gravity." A person cannot die
> again. By examining this paradox, the reader understands that this is not the first time
> the character has thought he was dying; thus, the immediacy and urgency of this death

are weakened, while the lack of certainty about when death will occur adds a different kind of tension.

PLOT

The actions of a story, carefully chosen and sequenced, traditionally structured around a conflict, reaching a climax, and concluding with a resolution of the conflict. The resolution may be implied or ambiguous.

In "Gaston," the story begins with a father and his six-year-old daughter spending a few days together for the first time since she was much younger. The confusion of the child about her mother and father comprise the conflict. The climax is a telephone conversation between the mother and daughter, and the resolution is the final decision of the daughter about her parents.

POINT OF VIEW

The perspective through which the story is told as revealed through the narrator. The point of view may change within a single story.

First-person

The narrator is a character in the story and the story is told in that character's actual words.

The child Squeaky is the first-person narrator of "Raymond's Run." Everything that happens and all the characters presented are described and judged through the eyes of this young girl.

Second-person

The narrator, who is not a character in the story, addresses the reader directly.

At different times in "Bluebirdbluebirdthrumywindow" the narrator asks the reader direct questions and addresses the reader with the words, "You've seen her. You know you have."

Third-person omniscient

The narrator, who is not a character in the story, tells the story from the perspective of more than one character.

Although the narration of "The Magic Barrel" is primarily third person from the perspective of Leo Finkle, this omniscient narrator occasionally comments from the perspective of the other main character, Salzman, in order to give information about Leo that could not be given from the character himself.

Third-person objective-observer

The narrator is an outside observer who tells what is seen and heard without revealing the thoughts and feelings of the characters or judging them or their actions in any way. In

"Hills Like White Elephants," the narrator gives minimal background, primarily telling only the actions, gestures, and dialogue of the two characters without presenting the thoughts and feelings of either one.

Third-person limited

The narrator assumes the perspective of a character in the story.

> Like "Raymond's Run," the story "Silent Snow, Secret Snow" is told from the perspective of a child. However, it is told in the third person. Even though the story is limited therefore to one character's perspective, the author uses third person rather than first person for various reasons, among them to create some distance from the character and to allow more mature observations from the narrator than a child could actually make.

PROSE POEM

A poem without line breaks.

> "Bluebirdbluebirdthrumywindow" and "One Human Hand" are prose poems.

RHYME

A rhyme is created when a vowel sound and all the sounds that follow it in one word are repeated in another word. When two lines of poetry end with this duplication of sounds, they rhyme. A half rhyme occurs when sounds in adjacent words are closely related but not identical; for example, the vowel sounds in two words might be the same, but the consonant sounds that follow might be different.

> Both rhyme and half rhyme occur in one line of "One Human Hand": "The second scroll was mostly white except for the blight-struck pine, and one bird perched at the tip: a shrike, surviving, last carrier of seed and stones in his little gizzard." (lines 7–9) In this example, *white* and *blight* rhyme. *Pine, shrike,* and *surviving* are half rhymes of the first two words.

RHYTHM

In language, a pattern of sound created by a combination of elements including stress, pitch, repetition, and/or rhyme. In poetry, when the rhythm occurs at regular intervals, it creates a formal pattern.

> "At Home in the World" has rhythm as follows:
> "The dréam is of sómething cóming. Grówing/as the héart does in lóve, inevitably bént on its ówn mótion, a súnflower túrning/a rípe fáce toward its sóurce." (lines 1–4)
> A rhythm is created in these lines by the repetition of the "-ing" ending, the half rhymes in *own* and *motion,* and the stresses on important words such as *dream, something, coming,* and *growing.*

SATIRE

A literary piece or elements of a literary piece written to be amusing, using humor as a weapon to make fun of contemporary society or behavior.

"The Waltz" is a satire that makes fun of men and women in social situations in which they must be polite and gracious even though they may dislike each other.

SETTING

The physical surroundings and time period in which the action takes place. The setting suggests atmosphere and mood, provides an appropriate background, and, most important, allows the specific events to take place and the characters to develop.

"Black Boy" is set in Atlantic City, New Jersey, in the early twentieth century, when this seaside town was flourishing as a summer beach resort. People of various economic and social levels came there, while local people, especially African Americans, worked in service jobs that catered to the visitors. This relaxed vacation setting allows the two main characters, a vacationing young white girl and a poor, working black boy, to become friends on the frequently deserted beach under the Boardwalk.

STYLE

The writer's individual, characteristic use of language, including the choice of words; the use of figurative language, imagery, and prose rhythm; the repetition of words, phrases, and other syntactical patterns; the structuring of paragraphs and sections of a story; and the pace.

"Raymond's Run" is written in an informal, childlike, conversational style. Nearly every sentence is introduced with a coordinate conjunction that connects it to the previous sentence and keeps it flowing naturally, informally. Colloquialisms add to the informality, and present tense narrative helps create immediacy. Colorful figures of speech, part of the street language, and childish metaphors like *beanstalk* and *big mouth* complete the youthful conversational style.

THEME

The central idea or ideas of a literary work regarding universal human behavior or the human condition. Authors reveal themes through the actions of the characters as they respond to situations.

"Hills Like White Elephants," like many of Hemingway's stories, presents a version of his theme about how people act during times of crisis.

"Sunday in the Park" reveals how expectations affect a relationship, in this case that of a married couple.

"Gravity" shows how parents may cope with their dying child.

TONE

The author's attitude (disdainful, amused, sympathetic) toward the events and characters, in combination with the mood or atmosphere of a literary work.

"Bluebirdbluebirdthrumywindow" opens with "And the Supreme Court said housing and welfare are not fundamental human rights." The blatant incongruity between what the government recognizes as basic human rights and what people's basic needs really are reveals the author's attitude of disdain for the law and sympathy for people in unfortunate situations. Later, "Isn't it lovely," used to describe the tragic condition of homelessness, clarifies the tone of bitter irony.

"Two Kinds," in an informal and understated tone, minimizes the seriousness of the events: "Soon after my mother got this idea about Shirley Temple, she took me to a beauty training school . . . . I emerged with an uneven mass of crinkly black fuzz. My mother dragged me off to the bathroom and tried to wet down my hair." The mother's disappointment and wasted money are turned into a comic memory of a mother's sincere but hopeless attempts to transform her daughter into something the daughter is not.

The humorously insulting sarcasm of "The Waltz" reveals an attitude of contempt toward life's absurd yet inescapable situations—and the people who create them.

Writing about Literature: A Guide for Students

THE READING WRITING CONNECTION
Interpreting a Story or Poem

The activities in *Inside Out/Outside In* are designed to help you understand and write about literature. When you read a story or poem for the first time, you form a general impression about the piece. Each time you reread the story or poem, analyzing specific parts of the text and reflecting on how they contribute to an overall understanding of the piece, you will need to adjust your earlier impressions. This process of uncovering new and significant elements of a story or poem sharpens your reading skills and helps you generate ideas for writing. The process can also be part of the pleasure of reading fiction.

Keep an open mind as you read. In the collection of stories and poems in *Inside Out/Outside In*, you will read about people, places, or experiences that are familiar to you and that confirm your feelings or beliefs. At other times, however, you will come across people, places, or experiences that are foreign to you and that challenge your views and understanding of the world. People's backgrounds, beliefs, and attitudes affect the way they understand a piece of literature; keep this in mind as you consider possible interpretations. Moving beyond your own vision and experiences as you read fiction helps you become a better reader and a better writer.

Working through the *Inside Out/Outside In* activities helps you not only to understand a particular story or poem but also to appreciate and write about how a writer creates a piece of literature. As preparation for both informal and formal writing assignments, many of the activities guide you through the process of analyzing how a writer's use of one or more literary elements contributes to your understanding of the whole piece.

Annotating a Story or Poem

Annotating, or writing questions and notes in the margins, helps you read actively and interact personally with the story or poem. As you reread a story or poem in order to analyze the writer's use of a particular literary element, you might also find it helpful to mark words or passages with symbols or abbreviations. This makes it easier to refer to the literary piece when writing or in class discussion. The following is an example of an annotated passage from the story "Gaston."

Why no names?   They were to eat peaches, as planned, after her nap, and now she sat across

Why stranger?   from the man who would have been a total stranger except that he was in

child's POV   fact her father. They had been together again (although she couldn't quite

remember when they had been together before) for almost a hundred years

now, or was it only since the day before yesterday? Anyhow, they were to-

funny how?   gether again, and he was kind of funny. First, he had the biggest mustache

she had ever seen on anybody, although to her it was not a mustache at all;

it was a lot of red and brown hair under his nose and around the ends of

his mouth. Second, he wore a blue-and-white striped jersey instead of a shirt

is this what she's used to?   and tie, and no coat. His arms were covered with the same hair, only it was

a little lighter and thinner. He wore blue slacks, but no shoes and socks. He

was barefoot, and so was she, of course.

negative: girl's POV   He was at home. She was with him in his home in Paris, if you could

call it a home. He was very old, especially for a young man—thirty-six, he

had told her; and she was just six, just up from sleep on a very hot after-

noon in August.

Dealing with Unfamiliar Words

The first time you read a story or poem, you may want to circle or highlight words you
stumble over so you can come back to them. Stop to look up only those unfamiliar words
that interfere with your ability to comprehend something that seems important to understanding the whole piece.

In this textbook, you will discuss important geographic, cultural, and historical terms
in the prereading activities or find them defined in footnotes to the story or poem. Other
words are defined in the glossary at the back of the book.

When you search for a definition in a dictionary, try to find the meaning that seems
the most appropriate for the context in which the word appears.

WRITING ABOUT LITERATURE
Understanding the Writing Process

Some writers write first and organize later. Others write detailed outlines and follow them
closely as they write. Some writers revise many times. Others barely revise once. Some
use one, or a combination, of the approaches outlined here.

A NONLINEAR APPROACH	A LINEAR APPROACH
• Freewrite for ideas • Develop a point or choose a topic • Use text to find evidence • Write a draft of essay • Write a working thesis statement • Categorize ideas • Reorganize paragraphs • Revise thesis statement • Write conclusion • Freewrite again • Revise essay • Edit and proofread	• Freewrite for ideas • Develop a point or choose a topic • Write a working thesis • Use text to find evidence • Use an outline to organize ideas • Write a draft of essay • Revise thesis statement • Revise essay • Edit and proofread

As you write about literature, you may modify your process to fit the task.

Clarifying an Assignment

Your instructor may ask you to choose from "Essay Topics" in *Inside Out/Outside In* or give you a different writing assignment. Before you start writing, make sure you understand the assignment. Ask yourself:

- What are the parts of the assignment?

- What does this assignment ask me to do?

- How much textual analysis is required?

- Is personal response required?

- Which textbook activities are related to the assignment?

- How much background is required to orient the reader?

- If the assignment focuses on literary elements, do I have a clear understanding of these elements in relation to this story or poem?

- Are there examples of this kind of writing to refer to?

Prewriting

Generating Ideas

As you do the activities in *Inside Out/Outside In* and participate in class discussions, you can begin to generate ideas for writing by asking yourself some general questions about the story or poem:

- What are the themes?

- Which literary elements stand out in this piece?

- What stands out about the writer's style in comparison to other stories or poems I've read?

- What interests me most in this piece?

- What would interest my readers?

- Which of my ideas could be effectively developed with specific evidence?

As you look over your answers, highlight ideas that work together and discard those that don't. Begin to focus your writing by categorizing your ideas.

Generating and Focusing Your Point

Your instructor may ask you to develop a point you want to make, giving you some general guidelines, including an approximate essay length. Use the following to guide you in finding a point that works:

- Focus on an aspect of the story or poem that requires interpretation, not summary.

  Example:
  Not effective: What happens to the father in "Gaston"?
  Effective: What is the relationship between Gaston and the father?

- Narrow your topic so you can focus your discussion.

  Example:
  Not effective: How do the characters in "Aunt Moon's Young Man" change?
  Effective: How do the narrator and her mother change in "Aunt Moon's Young Man"?

- Choose a point that you can effectively develop with specific support from the story. Go back to the story, your notes, and the activities in *Inside Out/Outside In* and highlight possible supporting ideas and textual evidence. You may need either to narrow or broaden your point, based on the evidence you find and on the length of the essay assigned by your instructor.

Getting Started

In addition to reviewing your class notes, the textbook activities you've completed, and the "Writing in Response" sections you've done, you may want to freewrite or loop to help you find a point and gather ideas. While these techniques will not help you find specific evidence from the text to support your ideas, they can be a good way to find what you are interested in and develop ideas.

- *Freewrite:* Write a question about the story or poem and answer it by writing rapidly for several minutes without stopping to reread.

- *Loop:* Using a previous freewrite, underline a word or phrase you'd like to write more about. Write that word or phrase on a different sheet of paper and freewrite again. Repeating this process often results in very detailed, specific questions and answers that may be developed into a thesis.

Considering Your Audience

Before you write, consider your audience. Follow guidelines discussed in your course and/or answer the following questions about your audience:

- Have they read the story or poem?
- If they have read the piece, when did they read it and in what context (for pleasure; in a class)?
- How might their background, beliefs, or attitudes affect the way they understand the story or poem?
- How much evidence and explanation will be needed to convince this audience of your interpretation?

Establishing a Purpose

Before you write, it's important to know what your purpose is. You may be

- Analyzing one or more literary elements of the story or poem.
- Analyzing the writer's style.
- Comparing literary elements and/or writers' styles in two or more pieces.
- Giving a personal response to some aspect of the piece.
- Writing creatively in response to the poem or story.

Essay topics frequently require some combination of these. Here are some examples of topics and purposes:

Purpose: Analysis of one or more literary elements of the story or poem
Write an essay in which you illustrate how David Leavitt, in his story "Gravity," uses irony to highlight the central action of the story, including but not limited to Theo's choice and his mother's taking care of her dying son.

Purpose: Analysis of the style
Ernest Hemingway said the following about his style of writing: "I always try to write on the principle of the iceberg. There is 7/8 of it below the water for every eighth that shows." How does Hemingway use the "iceberg principle" in his story "Hills Like White Elephants"?

Purpose: Analysis and personal response
Drawing on all the stories and poems we have read this semester, choose one character whom you would most like to meet. In an essay, discuss what interests or bothers you about him or her. Use specific evidence from the story or poem to explain your choice.

Purpose: Creative writing and analysis
What do you think will happen next in the story or poem? That is, what might have happened after the "official" end of the piece? Support your ideas with evidence from the story or poem.

Purpose: Creative writing
Using Dorothy Parker's satirical story "The Waltz" to inspire you, write a satire of a social ritual in society.

Writing a Working Thesis

A working, or preliminary, thesis states the point you intend to develop in your essay. It presents your interpretation or answers the question raised in an assignment. It should also reflect your purpose in writing. You will refine your working thesis in a later stage of your writing process.

- Use your working thesis to guide a close analysis of the text and to help you gather appropriate evidence.
- Discuss your working thesis with other students and/or your instructor: Is it clear? Is it specific enough? Does it address the assignment?

Gathering Evidence

You will need to find support for your working thesis and the main points you will be making. To do this, read the text carefully several times to find specific evidence to include in the body of your essay.

- Highlight, underline, or write down evidence from the text related to the points you are making.
- Make a note of why or how the evidence supports your thesis or main point.
- Consider how the use of a word or phrase affects your understanding of a particular character or situation and your overall interpretation of the piece.

Example (about "Gaston"):
Working thesis: Because the father and the girl are so different from each other, they cannot remain together for long.

They were to eat peaches, as planned, after her nap, and now she sat across

from the man who would have been a total stranger except that he was in

fact her father. They had been together again (although she couldn't quite

very young—no
sense of time
remember when they had been together before) for almost a hundred years

now, or was it only since the day before yesterday? Anyhow, they were to-

she's not used to
seeing BIG
mustaches
gether again, and he was kind of funny. First, he had the biggest mustache

she had ever seen on anybody, although to her it was not a mustache at all;

it was a lot of red and brown hair under his nose and around the ends of

she's used to some-
thing more formal
his mouth. Second, he wore a blue-and-white striped jersey instead of a shirt

and tie, and no coat. His arms were covered with the same hair, only it was

a little lighter and thinner. He wore blue slacks, but no shoes and socks. He

was barefoot, and so was she, of course.

3 times mentions
home—
He . . . home
his home
a home, but not
her home
He was at home. She was with him in his home in Paris, if you could call

it a home. He was very old, especially for a young man—thirty six, he had

told her; and she was just six, just up from sleep on a very hot afternoon in

August.

Writing

When you write your essay, you will not necessarily write in the order presented here. Be sure to write in an order that is appropriate for your topic and your individual writing process.

The Introduction

When you write about literature, your introduction should do some or all of the following:

- Engage your readers and make them want to read your essay.
- Provide background information on the characters and situation to orient readers and establish a context for the thesis.
- Provide a focus for the essay in the form of a thesis statement.

To engage your readers, you may, for example:

- Ask and/or answer a question.
- Give a short personal example.
- Relate an aspect of the story or poem to the present.
- Open with a relevant quotation from the story, poem, or other piece of writing.

Avoid beginning with obvious generalizations or by telling readers something they already know.

Referring to the Text

To convince the readers that your interpretation of a story or poem is reasonable, you'll want to include evidence from the story or poem that supports your ideas. Evidence can be in the form of paraphrase or quotations. The following are guidelines and examples for appropriate paraphrasing and quoting, using the story "Gaston."

a. Cite the line reference in parentheses immediately following the paraphrase or quotation. When you incorporate a short quotation, your goal is to blend it smoothly into your writing. Your sentence controls the punctuation and grammar. Note how the following sentences incorporate words from "Gaston."

   Example:
   In Paris, the little girl spends her time with her father "not being excited or anything—[with] no plans, that is." (line 26) In New York, on the other hand, where "'there's *always* a lot of [birthday parties],'" (line 173) her life seems to be filled with social events.

b. If you quote an entire sentence, you may introduce it with a colon or a period at the end of the preceding sentence and avoid the words *for example* or *such as*.

   Example:
   As with most children, the daughter wants to imitate her father's actions: "[The father] was barefoot, and so was she, of course." (line 11)

c. A line number by itself is not a sufficient reference to support your ideas. You must always include either a quotation or paraphrase of the text.

Example:

Incorrect: We can see from the beginning that the father is eager to please his daughter. (lines 23–24)

Correct: By giving his daughter the "biggest and best-looking peach" and saving the "flawed" one for himself, the father shows that he is anxious to please his daughter. (lines 23–24)

d. At times, you will need to change a quotation to make it fit smoothly and grammatically into your sentence. If you add a word or change the form of a word, place the change in brackets. You may use three dots (ellipses) to remove part of a quotation, but your sentence must remain grammatical and logical. When the ellipsis is at the end of your sentence, add a period (four dots in all).

Example:

The little girl's pain is most apparent after her mother calls. As she watches Gaston on the plate, she "crie[s] a little, but only inside . . . because [she thinks] if you ever [start] to cry it seem[s] as if there [is] so much to cry about you almost [can't] stop . . . ." (lines 161–163)

e. You may want to quote a line from the story or poem that includes direct speech or words in quotation marks. In these cases, the text that's in quotation marks in the story or poem must be placed within single quotation marks when you use it as quoted material in your essay.

Example:

When the mother asks the daughter if the father is "crazy," (line 150) the daughter responds: "'Yes. I mean, no.'" (line 151)

f. If you're quoting a longer passage from a story (more than three lines), indent the entire passage and single space it. Don't include quotation marks around the passage, but do use any quotation marks that are used in the original story or poem.

Example:

Early in the phone conversation, the daughter quickly comes to the defense of "'Gaston the grand something.'" (line 135) However, after her mother's comments about all of the "foolishness," (line 137) the little girl's attitude changes. Whereas only a few minutes before she told her father that she didn't want a "perfect peach" but "a peach with people," (line 102) she now sees Gaston as

> ". . . just a bug, isn't it, *really?*"
> "That's all it is."
> "And we'll *have* to squash it?"
> "That's right" . . . "Good-bye."
> The girl watched Gaston on the plate, and she actually didn't like him. He was *ugh,* as he had been in the first place. He didn't have a home anymore and he was wandering around the white plate and he was silly and wrong and ridiculous and useless and all sorts of other things. (lines 152–161)

The girl's attitude about Gaston sadly mirrors her own feelings about her father, who also seems "silly and wrong and ridiculous." (lines 160–161)

Organizing the Body of Your Essay

Some writers like to organize before they begin. Others write first and organize as they revise. Following are some methods that may help you organize either during prewriting or during the writing stage:

- List your points and evidence.

- Categorize your ideas. Use formal or informal outlines or any other graphic technique that helps you see how ideas are related.

- Make notes of the evidence you are planning to use to support each main idea.

- Write a descriptive outline after you have written a first draft: For each body paragraph, paraphrase the main point, list the evidence, and then note whether that paragraph raises a new idea related to your thesis or extends a main idea made in the previous paragraph.

As you plan or write your essay, you will become aware of different possible organizational patterns. If you are writing about characterization, for example, you could organize the essay according to specific character traits. You could also organize the essay by focusing on the various literary elements that help readers understand the characters. In the process of writing, you may find that one pattern is more workable than another.

Developing Individual Paragraphs

Each body paragraph sets forth and develops a main point related to the thesis or extends and develops a main idea from a previous paragraph. Often, one or more topic sentences express the main idea of the paragraph. As you introduce evidence to support an idea, make sure to clearly explain how the evidence supports the point you are making.

Ordering Body Paragraphs

Avoid the temptation to order the paragraphs in your essay based on the order that the evidence appears in the story or poem. Instead, consider how the order will affect your reader. For instance, you might do one or more of the following:

- Begin the body of your essay with an idea that you find easy to discuss and support, that your readers will easily understand, and/or that is less important than your other ideas. In this case, your essay will become stronger as you develop ideas that are more difficult to support, that your reader may find difficult to understand, and/or that you consider particularly original or important.

- Reverse the above order. Engage your reader with a compelling idea in the first paragraph of the body of the essay and move toward more generally understood ideas, ones that—for example—were discussed in class. In this case, you may need to write a stronger conclusion.

Use language that helps your reader understand the connection between ideas within and between paragraphs so that your main ideas flow together smoothly and logically.

Using Explanation and Evidence

It isn't enough to state your thesis, present your main ideas, and provide evidence in the form of paraphrase and quotation. You must also explain the connection between your ideas and the evidence. Don't assume that the reader will understand the evidence you have chosen and fill in the necessary connections because he or she has read the story or poem. Your reader may in fact have a different understanding of how a piece of evidence reflects the situation and action of the story or poem. You will need to convince him or her that your interpretation is valid.

In these two examples from the story "Gaston," notice how the writers use some of the same pieces of evidence to support two different points:

- The similarity between Gaston and the father is made clear by the daughter's similar response to the two. When the girl and father are "together again" (line 3) for the first time in a long time, she describes him as "kind of funny." (line 6) He has "the biggest mustache she had ever seen" (line 6) and "a blue-and-white striped jersey instead of a shirt and tie." (lines 8–9) She responds in a similar way to Gaston, the worm, having "never seen anything like it" before—"a whole big thing made out of brown color, a knob-head, feelers, and a great many legs." (lines 38–39) Both her father and Gaston are strange and different for her.

- The difference between the girl's and the father's lifestyles becomes clear in her response to him. When the girl and father are "together again" (line 3) for the first time in a long time, she describes him as "kind of funny." (line 6) Her father's "funny" appearance, his "blue-and-white striped jersey instead of a shirt and tie" (lines 8–9) and behavior, going "barefoot" (line 11), are clearly foreign to a little girl who goes to lots of parties and who is picked up by a "chauffeur." (line 122)

The Conclusion

A conclusion should flow smoothly and logically from the body of the essay, providing a sense of closure. You may conclude by using some of the following techniques:

- Briefly summarize your main points.
- Refer to something you wrote in the introduction.
- Make connections. If, for example, you're focusing on a literary element, explain how it relates to the theme of the story or poem.
- Raise a question for further analysis that is closely tied to your discussion in the body of your essay.
- Relate the theme to your life and/or to your observations of others in a way that closely connects to your essay.

In your conclusion, avoid

- Introducing new ideas that need further development.
- Summarizing at length.
- Directly addressing your reader.
- Ending abruptly.

Revising

Allow some time to pass between writing and revising your essay and/or ask another student or your instructor to read it and give you feedback. Ask yourself the following questions as you revise:

- Does the essay have a clear main point?
- Do I need to rewrite the thesis to better reflect the content of the essay?

- Does the essay move logically and smoothly from beginning to end?
- Does each body paragraph introduce or extend an idea related to the thesis?
- Do I provide enough (or too much) evidence?
- Do I provide enough explanation of the evidence?
- Is my introduction effective? Does it engage and orient the reader?
- Is my conclusion effective? Does it provide closure and end in a memorable way?
- Will the essay interest my readers?

Depending on your individual writing process, your experience writing about literature, and your skill as a writer, you may need to revise several times.

Finishing Up

It's important to spend time editing your sentences for logic and clarity and proofreading for grammar and spelling errors. Some of the following tips may help you polish your essay.

- Don't rely only on the spell-check programs on a word processor for correcting spelling errors. Words that have the same spelling but different meanings will not appear as errors. Use a dictionary.
- Rely on your own knowledge of grammar rules rather than on the grammar-check programs on a word processor.
- Proofread for grammar errors by reading through the essay, focusing on one type of error at a time.
- Proofread for punctuation and typographical errors.
- Proofread at least once by reading the last sentence of the essay first, working backward to the beginning of the essay. This technique keeps you focused on language rather than content.
- Use reference materials. For nonnative speakers of English, use a learner's dictionary to look for common word combinations and idiomatic expressions.

Creative Writing:
Writing a Story or Poem

OVERVIEW

The process of writing a story or poem will take you through several steps. Some of these steps may have a direct connection to what you write, and others may be connected only indirectly. Still others might have no connection at all to what you finally write. By trying all of them, however, you will discover what works for you.

Here are the major steps in writing fiction:

1. *Reviewing what you've read*   You will make connections between what you've read and what you might write.

2. *Brainstorming ideas*   As you brainstorm, you may find inspiration from what you have read this semester and what you have experienced.

3. *Reading the assignment and preparing to write*   You will read the assignment and work at getting ready to write.

4. *Finding inspiration and writing the first draft*   Several activities may help you find ideas and begin to write.

5. *Revising*   You will use feedback from your classmates and your instructor to help you revise.

REVIEWING WHAT YOU HAVE READ

Reviewing what you have read may give you ideas concerning what you'd like to write about and how you'd like to write it.

ACTIVITY 1

In groups, fill out the information in the following chart about one story or poem you have read in *Inside Out/Outside In*. Then discuss and be prepared to explain to the class what you think is most interesting about each of the following: character, plot, setting, point of view, figurative language, and theme.

TITLE:					
CHARACTER	PLOT	SETTING	POINT OF VIEW	FIGURATIVE LANGUAGE	THEME

Writing in Response

Write briefly on this topic: Of all the stories and poems you've read in *Inside Out/Outside In,* which ones would you most like to have written yourself? Why?

BRAINSTORMING IDEAS

As you brainstorm ideas in the following activities, let your intuition take over. Write whatever comes to your mind, even though you may not know why you are writing it.

ACTIVITY 2

Begin with character, setting, and plot. Work alone or with classmates.

- *Character*   Make a list of people you might like to write about. Your list could include types of people (a business executive, a person who is blind, a talking cat, a ten-year-old boy, a lonely woman) or specific people whom you know or have heard about.

- *Setting*   Make a list of settings you'd like to write about. These should be places you've been or are familiar with.

- *Plot*   Make a list of experiences you feel are interesting and important. Include your own and/or those of others. Your list should include both positive and negative experiences. Write whatever comes to mind.

ACTIVITY 3

Choose one of the characters and one of the settings from the lists you brainstormed in Activity 2 and complete the following information. Be as creative as you want in making up details for your fictional story or poem.

WHAT IS YOUR CHARACTER'S . . .	
1. Name?	
2. Age?	
3. Ethnicity and native language?	

4. Gender and physical appearance?	
5. Educational level?	
6. Favorite color? Food? Drink?	
7. Favorite thing to do with friends?	
8. Worst habit? Most positive trait?	
9. Major success and failure?	
10. Biggest dream for the future?	
• What interests you most about your character?	
• What would you like to discover about your character by writing about him or her?	

WHAT IS YOUR SETTING'S . . .	
1. Location?	
2. Description? (include the season, year, and century)	
3. Strongest or most noticeable smell?	
4 Typical noise?	
5. Population?	
6. Best characteristic? Worst characteristic?	
7. Best time of day?	
• What interests you most about your setting?	
• What symbolic meaning might your setting have?	

ACTIVITY 4

One way to begin developing a plot is to turn your experience into fiction.

• Choose two personal experiences from the list you brainstormed in Activity 2 that you might want to write about. You should feel comfortable sharing these experiences with your classmates.

- In groups, share your experiences. Tell what they were and how they changed you.

- Discuss how you would turn your "true" experience into a piece of fiction. What should stay the same about the character, setting, and plot? What should change?

- What might make the experiences worth writing about? How could your experiences relate to a universal theme?

Writing in Response

Freewrite about one of your experiences, but write in the third person. Before you begin, choose a different name for the character in the experience.

READING THE ASSIGNMENT

ACTIVITY 5

Read the following assignment and discuss in groups any questions that you have.

Write a story or poem and develop the following:

- Plot

- Character: Include main character(s) and minor character(s).

- Setting: Set the *time*—both historical time and time that passes in the story or poem, and *place*—both geographical and physical.

- Figurative language: Use figurative language that helps the reader understand character, setting, and theme. (See Appendix A for kinds of figurative language.)

- Point of view: Choose first person (I) or third person (she or he).

- Theme: What do you want the reader to understand? Choose a theme with depth.

A fiction-writing caution: Writing a story or poem is different from writing nonfiction such as the analytical essays you've been writing about literature. Instead of explaining and giving evidence, in fiction you create settings, conversations, and actions for the reader to interpret. When you revise a fictional piece, instead of making explanations more thorough, as you do with essays, you may discover sections of explanation to cross out and replace with action, dialogue, symbolism, or narrative.

A note about poetry: Depending on what kind of poem you write, you may not develop plot, character, or some other element of fiction. If you prefer to write very short poems, write several of them.

PREPARING TO WRITE

You will need to make several decisions as you prepare to write and then write. Will you write a poem or a short story? Will you use a lot of dialogue? Will you focus on only one character or on several? Who will narrate your piece?

You may make some of these decisions completely intuitively—that is, you may write in the form or style that feels "right" or "natural." Other decisions may be more practical as you choose the style or form that you think is best.

Remember that you'll revise and change things after you've written your first draft. It's not important to get the story or poem right the first time. Most fiction writers rewrite countless times before they finally submit their work for publication.

ACTIVITY 6

As you are deciding whether to write a poem or a story, discuss the following questions in groups.

1. What are the differences between writing a story or poem and writing an essay? Consider both the process (how to write it) and the product (the finished piece) as you fill in the chart. Examples have been done for you. Be prepared to share your ideas with the class.

ESSAY	STORY OR POEM
Makes a point directly	*Makes points indirectly*

2. What are the differences between writing poems and writing short stories? Write your ideas in the chart. Examples have been done for you. Be prepared to present your ideas to the class.

STORY	POEM
Narrates events	*Presents ideas through images*

3. Which would you prefer to write, a story or a poem? Why?

4. Why do you think people write fiction (stories, poems, novels, plays)? Make a list of reasons and be prepared to share them. Why would you like to write a piece of fiction?

5. What are some fears you have about writing fiction?

FINDING INSPIRATION AND WRITING THE FIRST DRAFT

Writing the first draft can be the hardest work.

ACTIVITY 7

Do some or all of the following things to help you generate ideas and details for your story or poem. This activity will help you fulfill the assignment and may also make your story or poem more exciting to read.

1. Freewrite about the story or poem you plan to write.

2. Make a list of symbols and colors you would like to include. Write yourself a brief note about the possible significance of each item on your list.

3. Share what you've written with a partner. Take turns asking questions about what you're planning. Then freewrite again for a few minutes about your latest ideas or list them.

4. If your story or poem has two or more characters, write a letter or e-mail message from your main character to another character.

5. Look through magazines or catalogs and choose clothes and products that your main character might own or like to own. Cut them out and make a collage with these pictures.

6. Choose the first sentence (or any other sentence) from a story or poem you've read. Then write your own story or poem to follow it.

7. Take a character from a story or poem that you've read in *Inside Out/Outside In*. Write another story or poem around that person. Give him or her a different ethnic background and a different setting.

8. What is your all-time favorite story or poem? Write a continuation of it.

9. Write a conversation between any two fictional characters that you know. They don't have to be from the same story or poem.

10. Do you know of any other strategies that can help generate ideas and details for writing a story or poem? If so, share them with your classmates.

Unlikely Tips to Help You Write a First Draft

1. Throw away all the preliminary work you've done and start fresh OR read through everything you've written five times, put it around you as you write, and refer to it frequently.

2. Start writing at midnight and plan to write until dawn OR write at the library in short breaks between classes.

3. Do not continue until you have a perfect first line OR start in the middle of your story or poem and write furiously. Plan to revise everything five times.

REVISING

Giving Feedback

Read the story or poem that one of your classmates wrote. The following are tips on giving feedback.

- *Start positive.*   The first thing you say should be about something you liked.

- *Focus on the writing.*   Work with what the writer has written, not with what you think the writer should have written.

- *If the content is sensitive, acknowledge this.*   Say, for example, "This must have been difficult to write about."

- *Be specific.* Give feedback about specific elements of the story or poem; pinpoint which areas you feel need improvement; give suggestions for ways to improve.
- *Notice reactions.* If the facial expression or body language of the writer changes as you are giving feedback, modify what you are saying and how you are saying it.
- *Put yourself into the writer's shoes.* What kind of feedback would you like, and how would you like to hear it?

ACTIVITY 8

Answer the following questions in writing, either on separate paper or on your classmate's draft.

1. What are three things you like about the story or poem?
2. What are five things you want to know more about?
3. What are possible themes you see in the piece?

Read your classmate's story or poem again with the following questions in mind. Answer in writing, either on separate paper or on your classmate's draft. Some of the questions may not apply to a poem.

Organization

Does the order of paragraphs or stanzas make sense? Are there places where you get lost and can't follow the story or poem?

Development

1. What is the time and place of the setting? Include all the settings. On the draft, mark places where you think the setting could be more vividly described.
2. Who are the characters (main and minor)? Mark places where you want to know more about the characters. Write your questions in the margin.
3. What point of view (first person, third person) is the writer using? Does it work? Why or why not?
4. Where does the story or poem need more imagery? Ask for more details in the margins.
5. Are there any places where you think the writer explains too much (goes into essay-writing mode)? Put a box around these sections to help the writer decide whether to delete or revise them.
6. What do you think the writer needs to do to make this story or poem better? Give specific suggestions.

ACTIVITY 9

Give your feedback to the writer and spend at least ten minutes discussing your comments and questions. *Note to the writer:* After you discuss your peer reviewer's comments, how will you revise your story or poem? Make a few notes to yourself now.

Second Draft and Beyond

ACTIVITY 10

After you discuss the feedback from your classmate, go to work revising your story or poem. You'll probably find things you want to change, add to, or get rid of. As you revise, work with your peer reviewer on some of these activities.

1. With your peer reviewer, talk about what makes a poem or short story strong. Discuss examples of what you feel is especially strong in your own and your partner's fiction. Use the following list of elements as topics. In your discussion, bring up examples from the stories and poems you've read in *Inside Out/Outside In*. This review may help you think of something you need to add to or change in your story or poem.

   action and plot
   character (include dialogue)
   setting (include time sequence and any flashbacks)
   figurative language
   point of view
   theme

2. Prepare brief examples to present to the class. Choose an example of one element from the preceding list. The example may come from your draft, from your partner's draft, or from a story or poem in *Inside Out/Outside In*. Be prepared to explain why you think the example is effective or where it needs work. Talk about what you can learn from this example as you write and revise.

3. With your partner, review the writing ideas in Finding Inspiration and Writing the First Draft, page 326. Discuss which of these might be helpful to do—or do again—at this point in your writing process.

4. Make some notes to yourself about what you would like to change, add to, or delete as you write your next draft.

5. After you write your next draft, show it to your partner or to another peer reviewer. Go through Activities 8 and 9 again with this draft. Write as many drafts as necessary to get your story or poem right.

6. Be sure to proofread your final draft.

Meeting with Your Instructor in Conference

To prepare for a conference with your instructor, make a list of questions and concerns about your story or poem that you would like to discuss. Be sure to bring the list with you to the conference. Ask your instructor to give you specific feedback on the questions and concerns you raise, in addition to any ideas he or she wants to bring up.

Credits